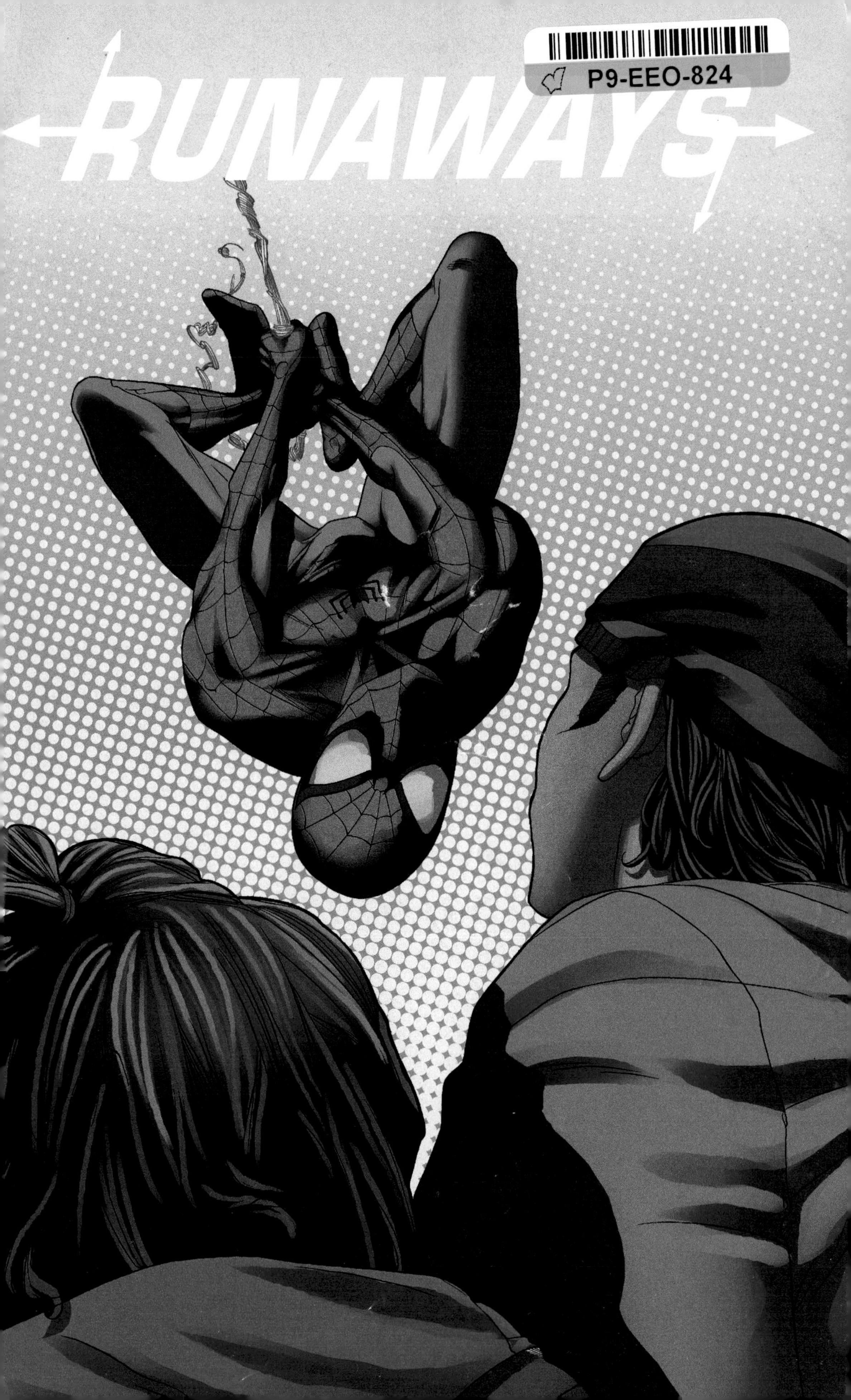
RUNAWAYS

RUNAWAYS

WRITER: **BRIAN K. VAUGHAN**
PENCILS: **TAKESHI MIYAZAWA** (#7-8), **ADRIAN ALPHONA** (#9-12)
INKS: **CRAIG YEUNG**
COLORS: **CHRISTINA STRAIN**
LETTERS: **VC's RANDY GENTILE**
COVER ART: **CHRIS BACHALO** & **TIM TOWNSEND** (#7-8),
　　　　JO CHEN (#9-10) AND **JAMES JEAN** (#11-12)

FREE COMIC BOOK DAY 2006
WRITER: **BRIAN K. VAUGHAN**
ARTIST: **SKOTTIE YOUNG**
LETTERER: **VC'S RANDY GENTILE**
COVER ART: **JO CHEN**

RUNAWAYS VOL. 5: ESCAPE TO NEW YORK. Contains material originally published in magazine form as RUNAWAYS #7-12 and FREE COMIC BOOK DAY 2006: Second edition. First printing 2017. ISBN# 978-1-302-90870-6. Published by MARVEL WORLDWIDE, INC., a subsidiary of MARVEL ENTERTAINMENT, LLC. OFFICE OF PUBLICATION: 135 West 50th Street, New York, NY 10020. Copyright © 2017 MARVEL No similarity between any of the names, characters, persons, and/or institutions in this magazine with those of any living or dead person or institution is intended, and any such similarity which may exist is purely coincidental. **Printed in the U.S.A.** DAN BUCKLEY, President, Marvel Entertainment; JOE QUESADA, Chief Creative Officer; TOM BREVOORT, SVP of Publishing; DAVID BOGART, SVP of Business Affairs & Operations, Publishing & Partnership; C.B. CEBULSKI, VP of Brand Management & Development, Asia; DAVID GABRIEL, SVP of Sales & Marketing, Publishing; JEFF YOUNGQUIST, VP of Production & Special Projects; DAN CARR, Executive Director of Publishing Technology; ALEX MORALES, Director of Publishing Operations; SUSAN CRESPI, Production Manager; STAN LEE, Chairman Emeritus. For information regarding advertising in Marvel Comics or on Marvel.com, please contact Vit DeBellis, Integrated Sales Manager, at vdebellis@marvel.com. For Marvel subscription inquiries, please call 888-511-5480. **Manufactured between 6/2/2017 and 7/3/2017 by QUAD/GRAPHICS WASECA, WASECA, MN, USA.**

10 9 8 7 6 5 4 3 2 1

ASSISTANT EDITOR: **NATHAN COSBY**
EDITOR: **MACKENZIE CADENHEAD**
SPECIAL THANKS TO C.B. CEBULSKI

RUNAWAYS CREATED BY
BRIAN K. VAUGHAN & **ADRIAN ALPHONA**

COLLECTION EDITOR: JENNIFER GRÜNWALD
ASSISTANT EDITOR: CAITLIN O'CONNELL
ASSOCIATE MANAGING EDITOR: KATERI WOODY
EDITOR, SPECIAL PROJECTS: MARK D. BEAZLEY
VP PRODUCTION & SPECIAL PROJECTS: JEFF YOUNGQUIST
SVP PRINT, SALES & MARKETING: DAVID GABRIEL

EDITOR IN CHIEF: AXEL ALONSO
CHIEF CREATIVE OFFICER: JOE QUESADA
PRESIDENT: DAN BUCKLEY
EXECUTIVE PRODUCER: ALAN FINE

PREVIOUSLY:

AT SOME POINT IN THEIR LIVES, ALL KIDS THINK THAT THEY HAVE THE MOST EVIL PARENTS IN THE WORLD, BUT KAROLINA DEAN AND HER FRIENDS REALLY DID.

DISCOVERING THAT THEY WERE THE CHILDREN OF A GROUP OF SUPER VILLAINS KNOWN AS THE PRIDE, THE TEENAGERS STOLE WEAPONS AND RESOURCES FROM THESE CRIMINALS BEFORE RUNNING AWAY FROM HOME AND EVENTUALLY DEFEATING THEIR PARENTS. BUT THAT WAS JUST THE BEGINNING.

THE YOUNG GROUP'S NEWEST RECRUIT IS VICTOR MANCHA, THE HALF-ROBOT/HALF-HUMAN SON OF AN EVIL KILLING MACHINE CALLED ULTRON. TOGETHER, VICTOR AND HIS FELLOW RUNAWAYS NOW HOPE TO ATONE FOR THEIR PARENTS' CRIMES BY TAKING ON THE NEW THREATS TRYING TO FILL THE PRIDE'S VOID.

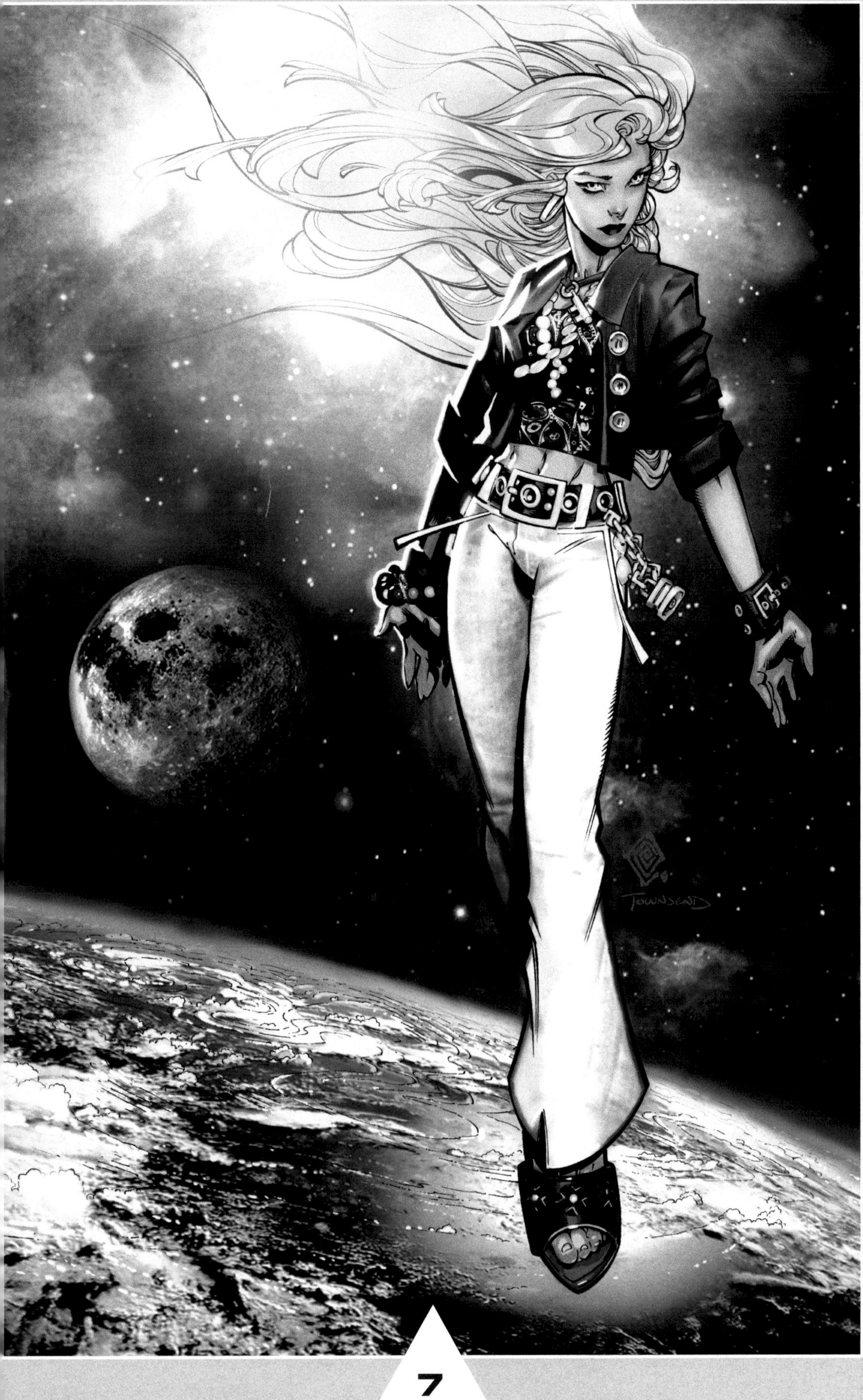
TOWNSEND

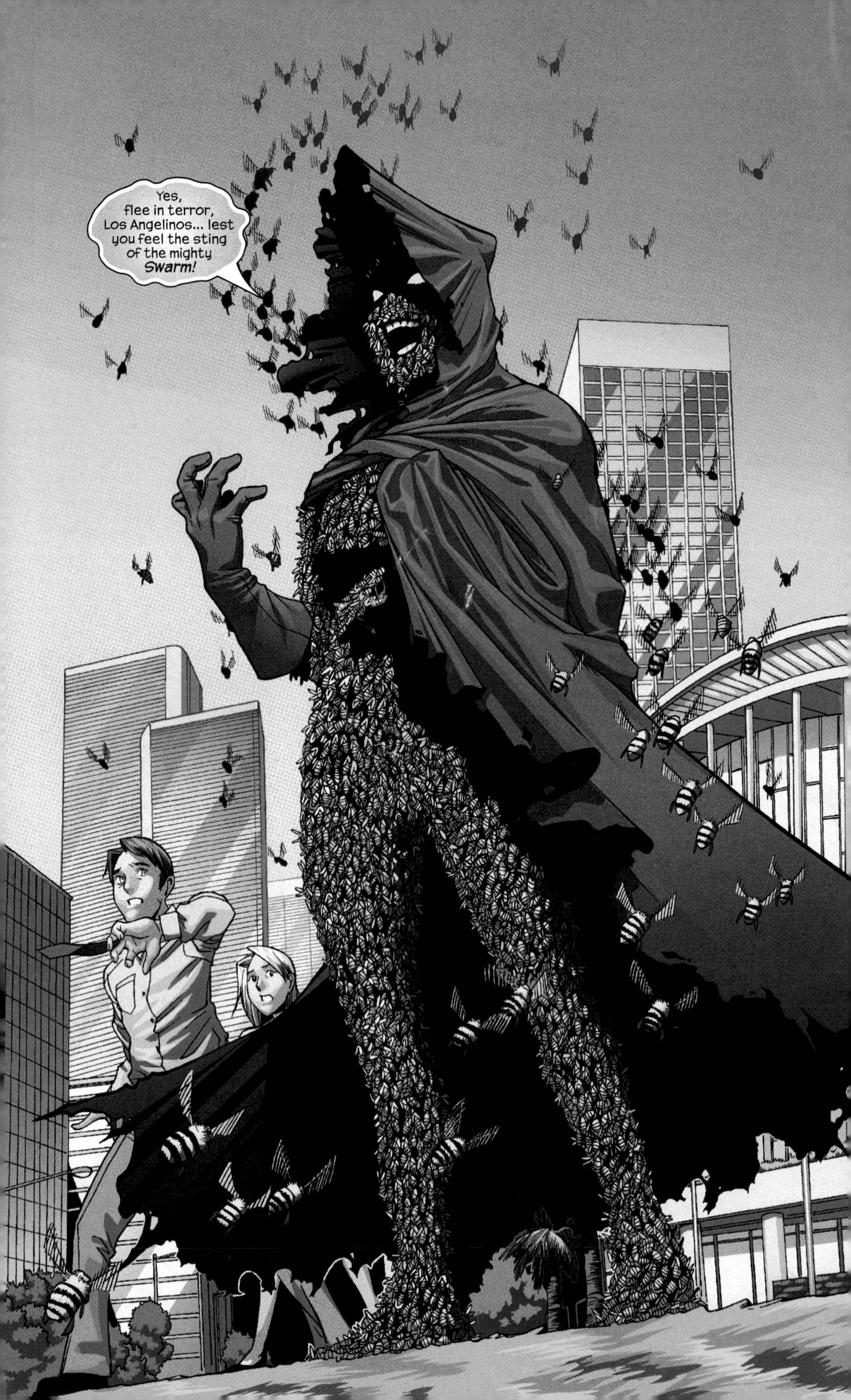
Yes, flee in terror, Los Angelinos... lest you feel the sting of the mighty *Swarm!*

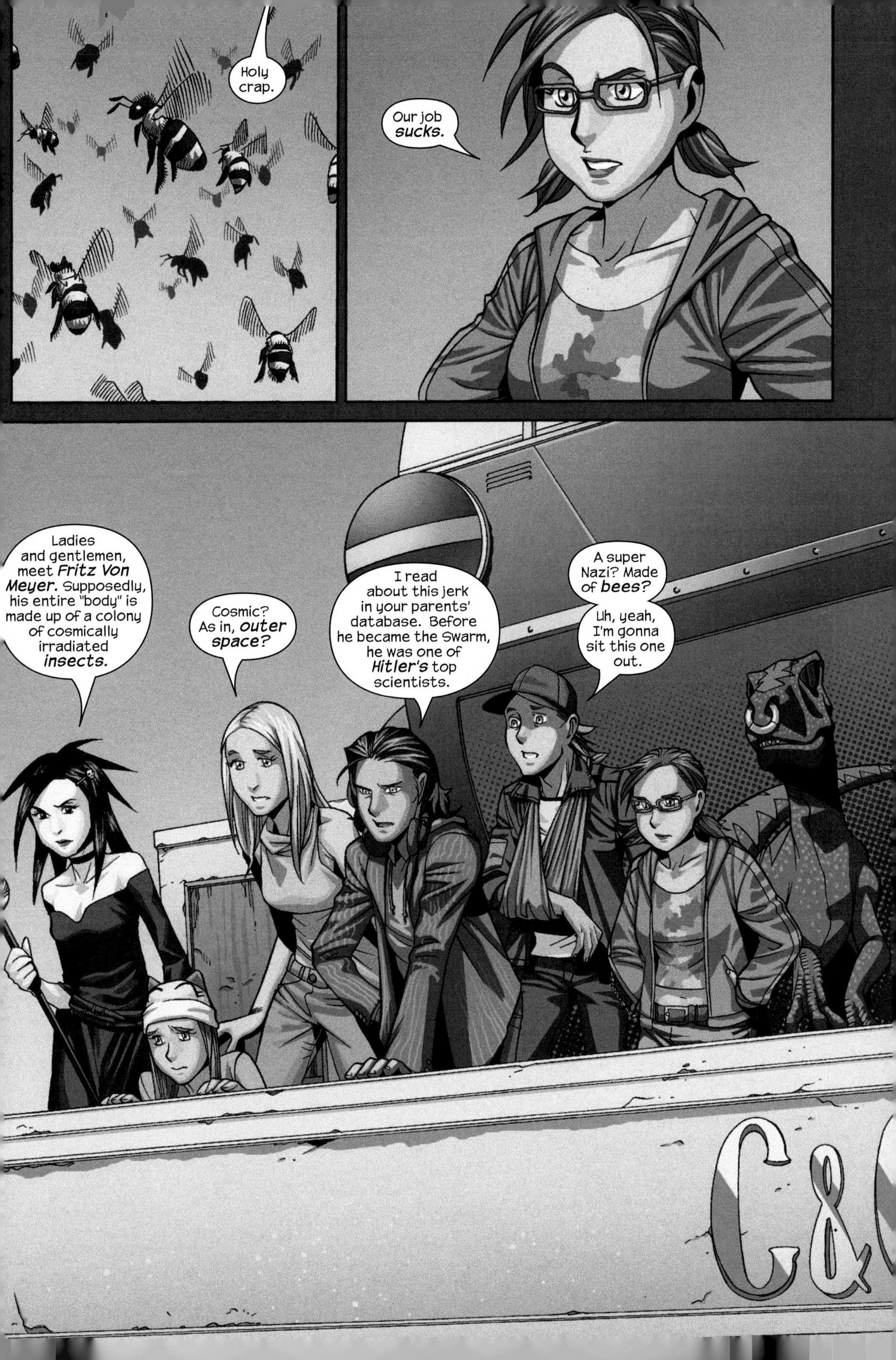
Holy crap.
Our job *sucks.*
Ladies and gentlemen, meet *Fritz Von Meyer.* Supposedly, his entire "body" is made up of a colony of cosmically irradiated *insects.*
Cosmic? As in, *outer space?*
I read about this jerk in your parents' database. Before he became the Swarm, he was one of *Hitler's* top scientists.
A super Nazi? Made of *bees?*
Uh, yeah, I'm gonna sit this one out.
C&

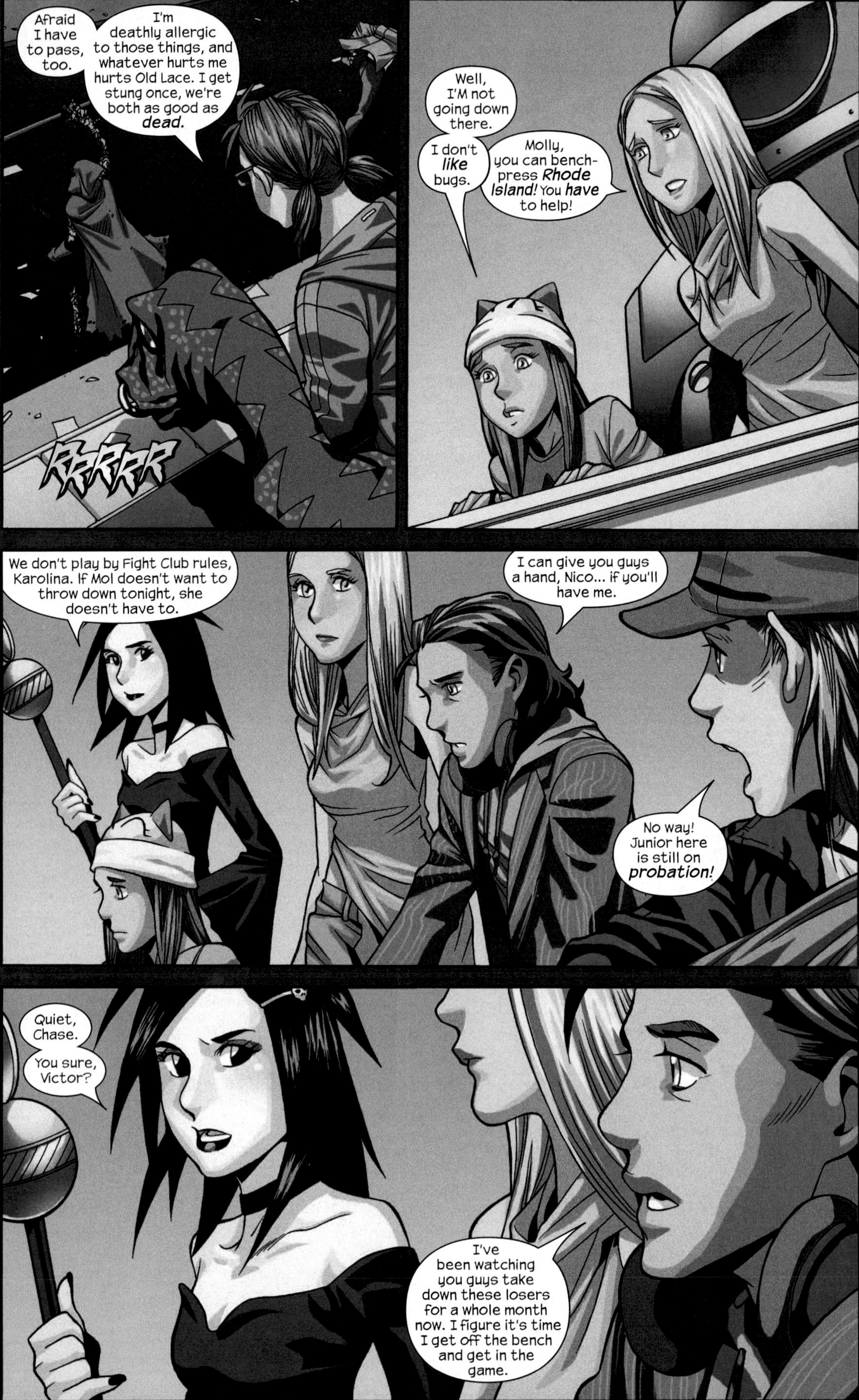
Afraid I have to pass, too.
I'm deathly allergic to those things, and whatever hurts me hurts Old Lace. I get stung once, we're both as good as *dead.*
RRRRR
Well, I'M not going down there.
I don't *like* bugs.
Molly, you can bench-press *Rhode Island!* You *have* to help!
We don't play by Fight Club rules, Karolina. If Mol doesn't want to throw down tonight, she doesn't have to.
I can give you guys a hand, Nico... if you'll have me.
No way! Junior here is still on *probation!*
Quiet, Chase.
You sure, Victor?
I've been watching you guys take down these losers for a whole month now. I figure it's time I get off the bench and get in the game.

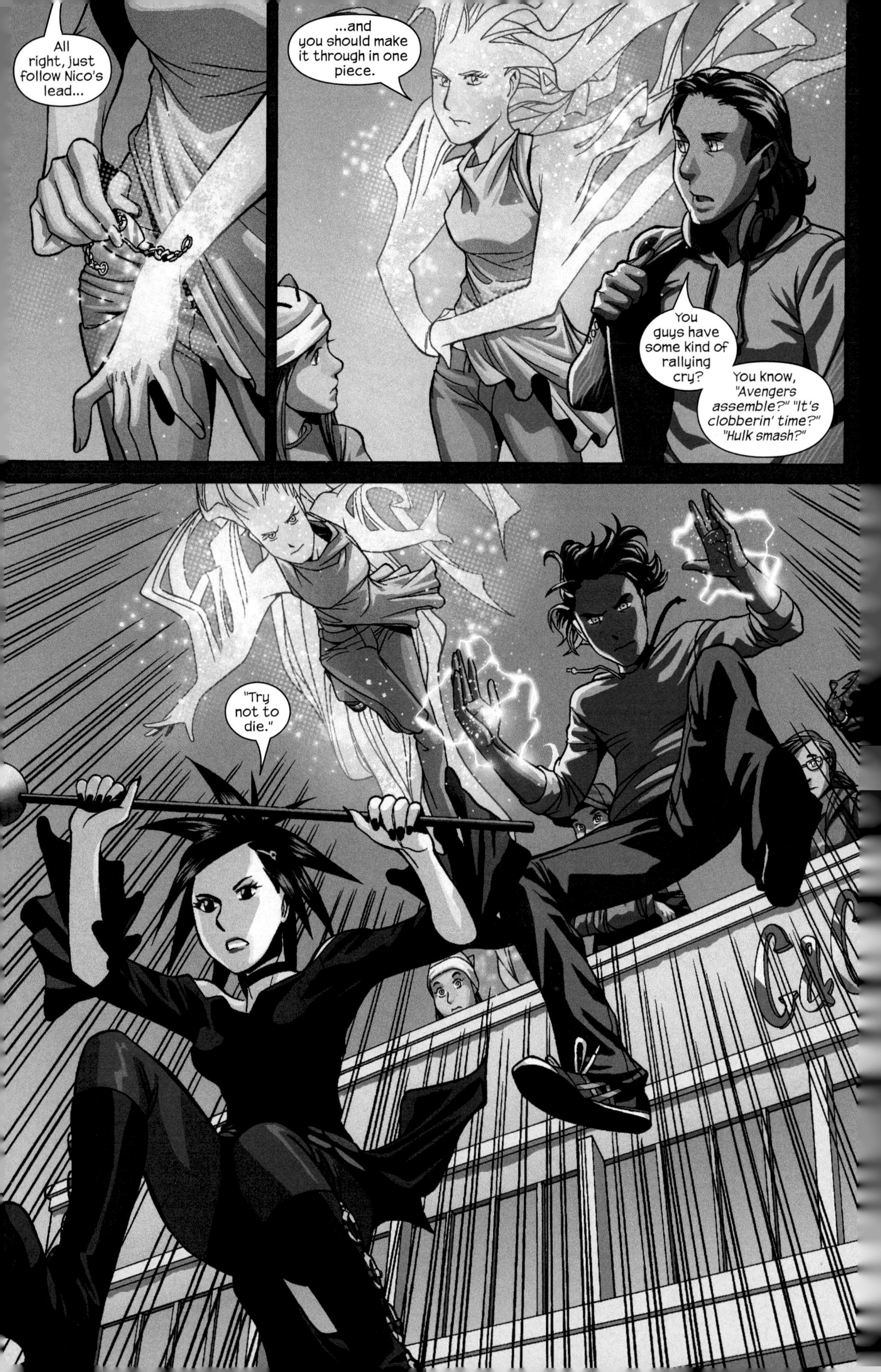
All right, just follow Nico's lead...
...and you should make it through in one piece.
You guys have some kind of rallying cry?
You know, "Avengers assemble?" "It's clobberin' time?" "Hulk smash?"
"Try not to die."

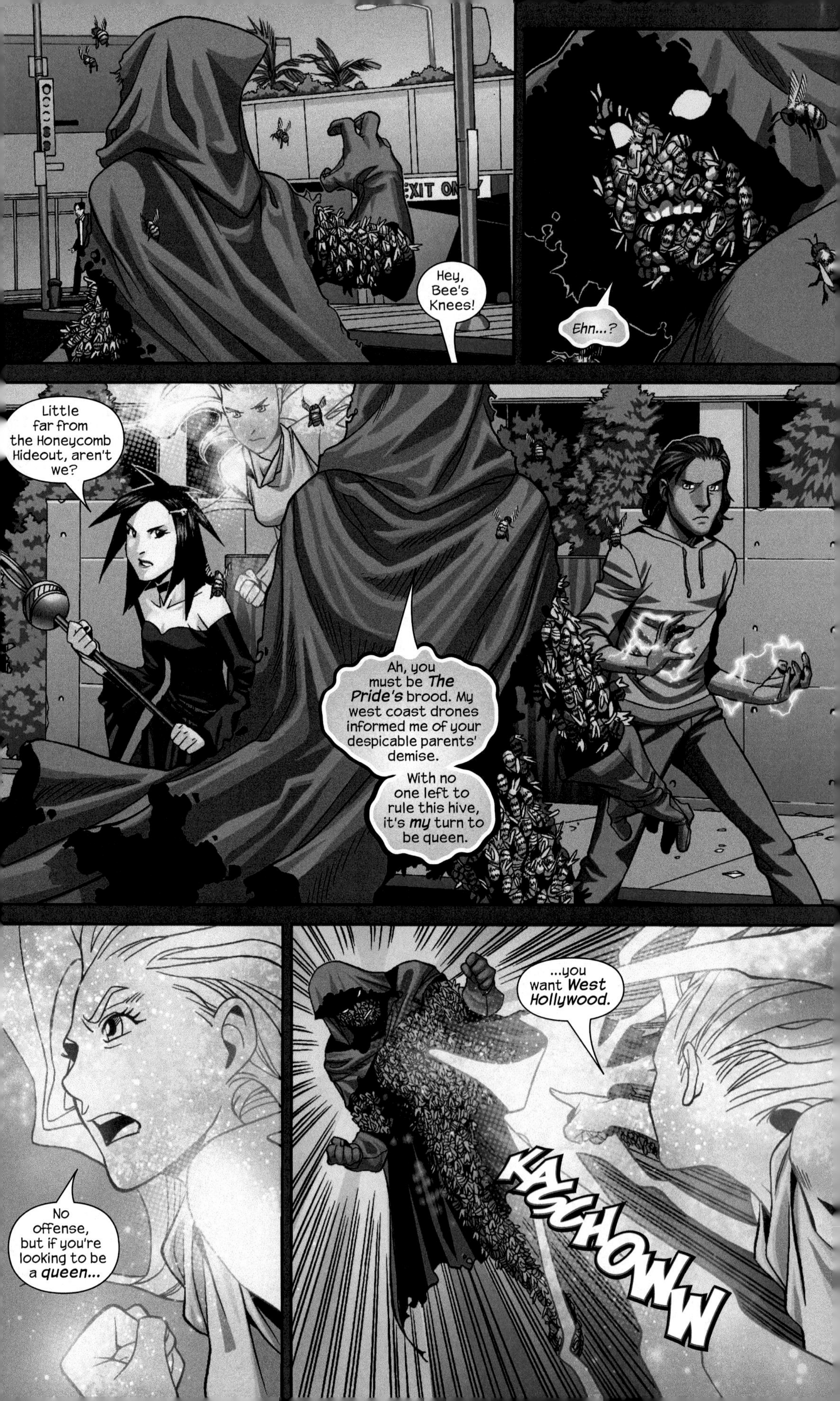
EXIT ONLY
Hey, Bee's Knees!
Ehn...?
Little far from the Honeycomb Hideout, aren't we?
Ah, you must be The Pride's brood. My west coast drones informed me of your despicable parents' demise.
With no one left to rule this hive, it's my turn to be queen.
No offense, but if you're looking to be a queen...
...you want West Hollywood.
KACHOWW

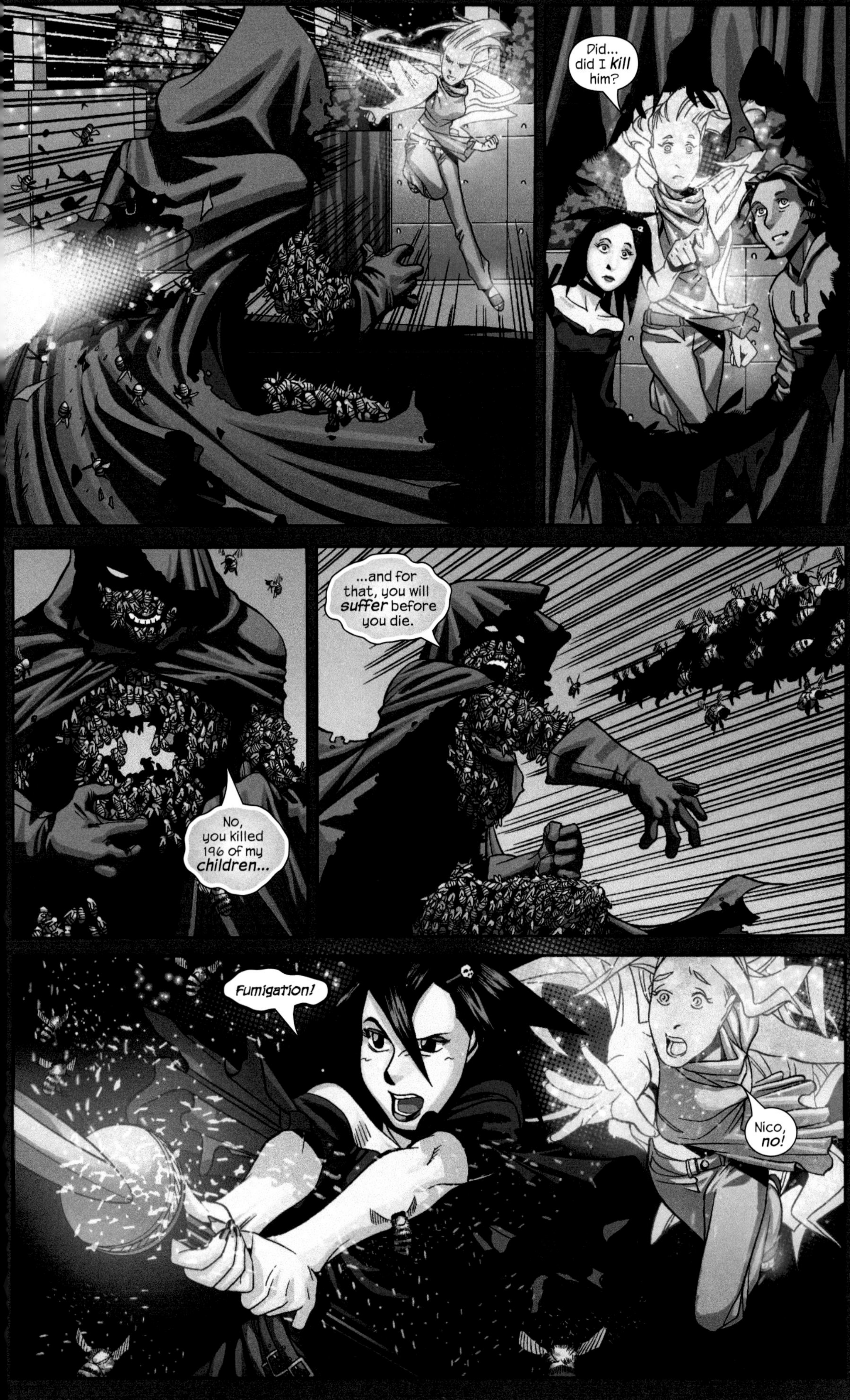

Did... did I kill him?
No, you killed 196 of my children...
...and for that, you will suffer before you die.
Fumigation!
Nico, no!

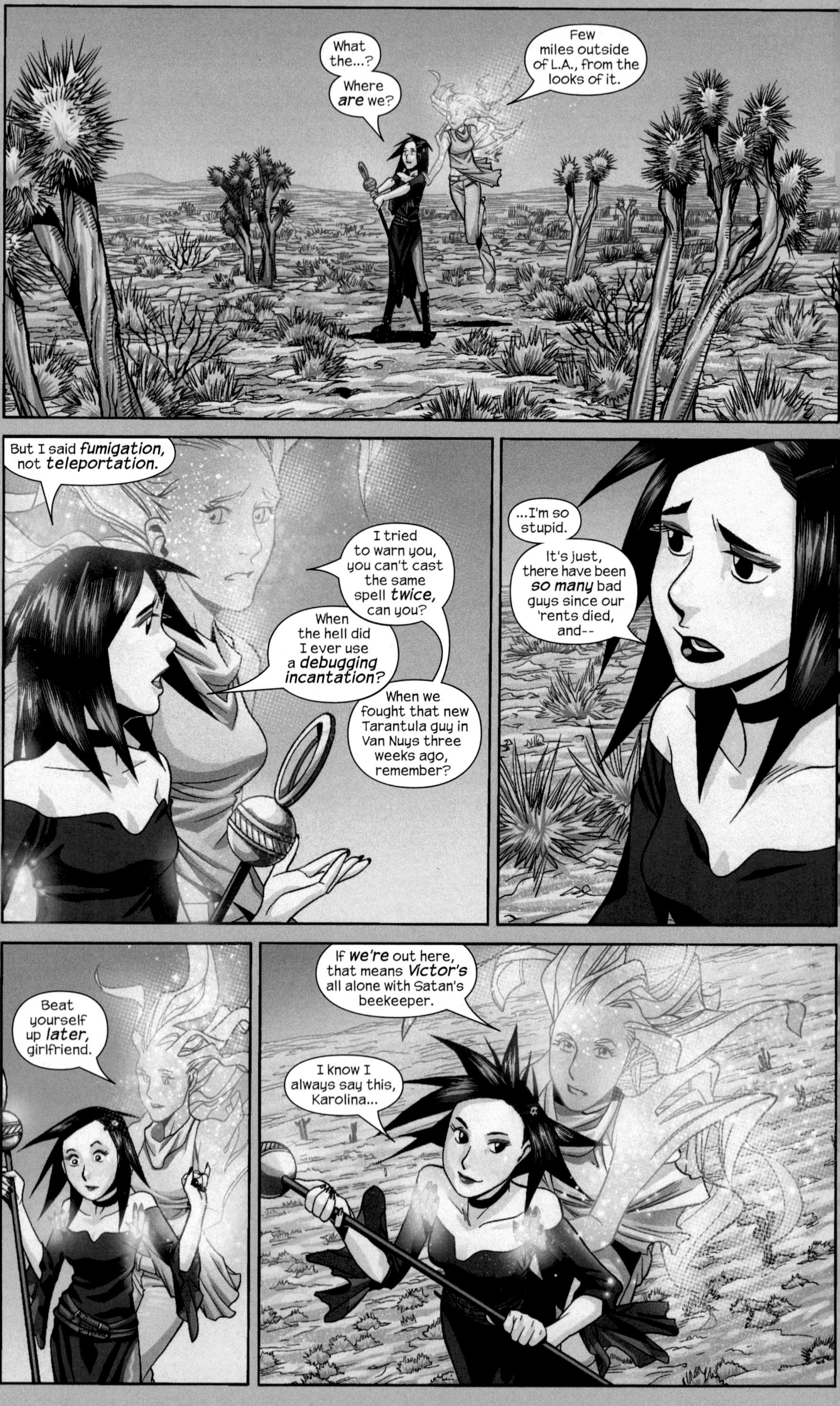
What the...?
Where are we?
Few miles outside of L.A., from the looks of it.
But I said fumigation, not teleportation.
I tried to warn you, you can't cast the same spell twice, can you?
When the hell did I ever use a debugging incantation?
When we fought that new Tarantula guy in Van Nuys three weeks ago, remember?
...I'm so stupid.
It's just, there have been so many bad guys since our 'rents died, and--
Beat yourself up later, girlfriend.
If we're out here, that means Victor's all alone with Satan's beekeeper.
I know I always say this, Karolina...

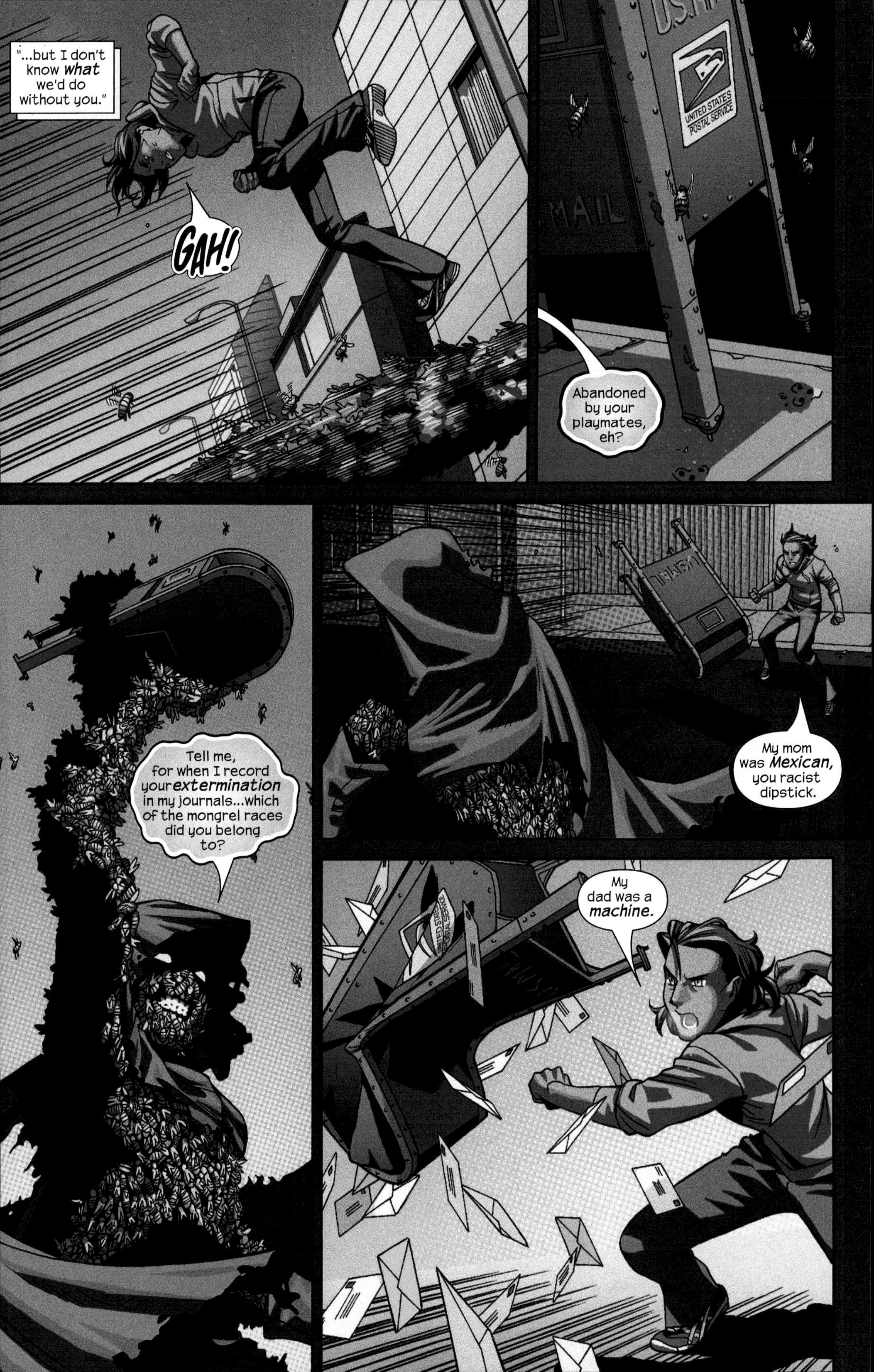
"...but I don't know *what* we'd do without you."
GAH!
U.S. MAIL
UNITED STATES POSTAL SERVICE
MAIL
Abandoned by your playmates, eh?
Tell me, for when I record your *extermination* in my journals...which of the mongrel races did you belong to?
My mom was *Mexican*, you racist dipstick.
My dad was a *machine*.

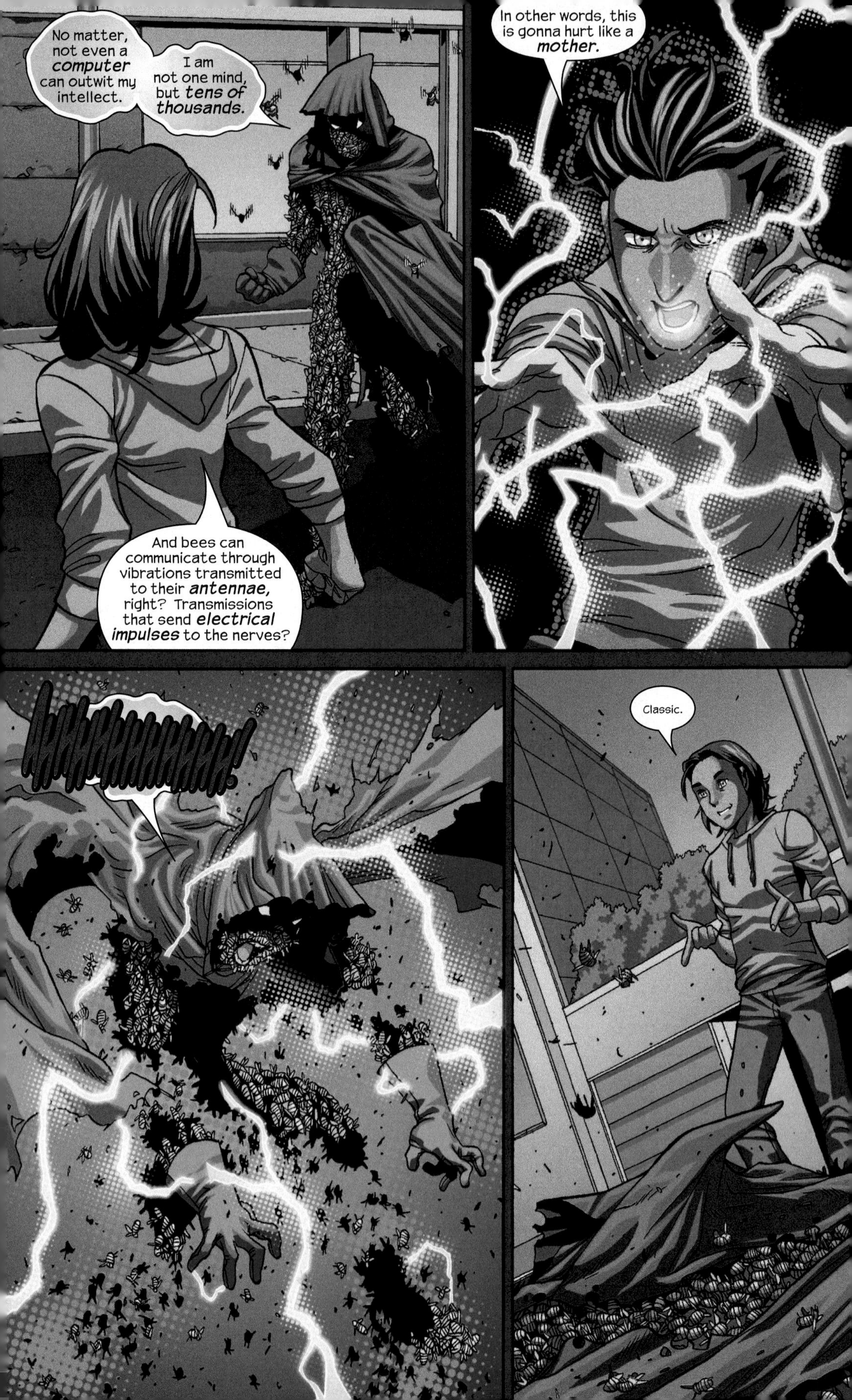
No matter, not even a *computer* can outwit my intellect.
I am not one mind, but *tens of thousands.*
And bees can communicate through vibrations transmitted to their *antennae,* right? Transmissions that send *electrical impulses* to the nerves?
In other words, this is gonna hurt like a *mother.*
Classic.

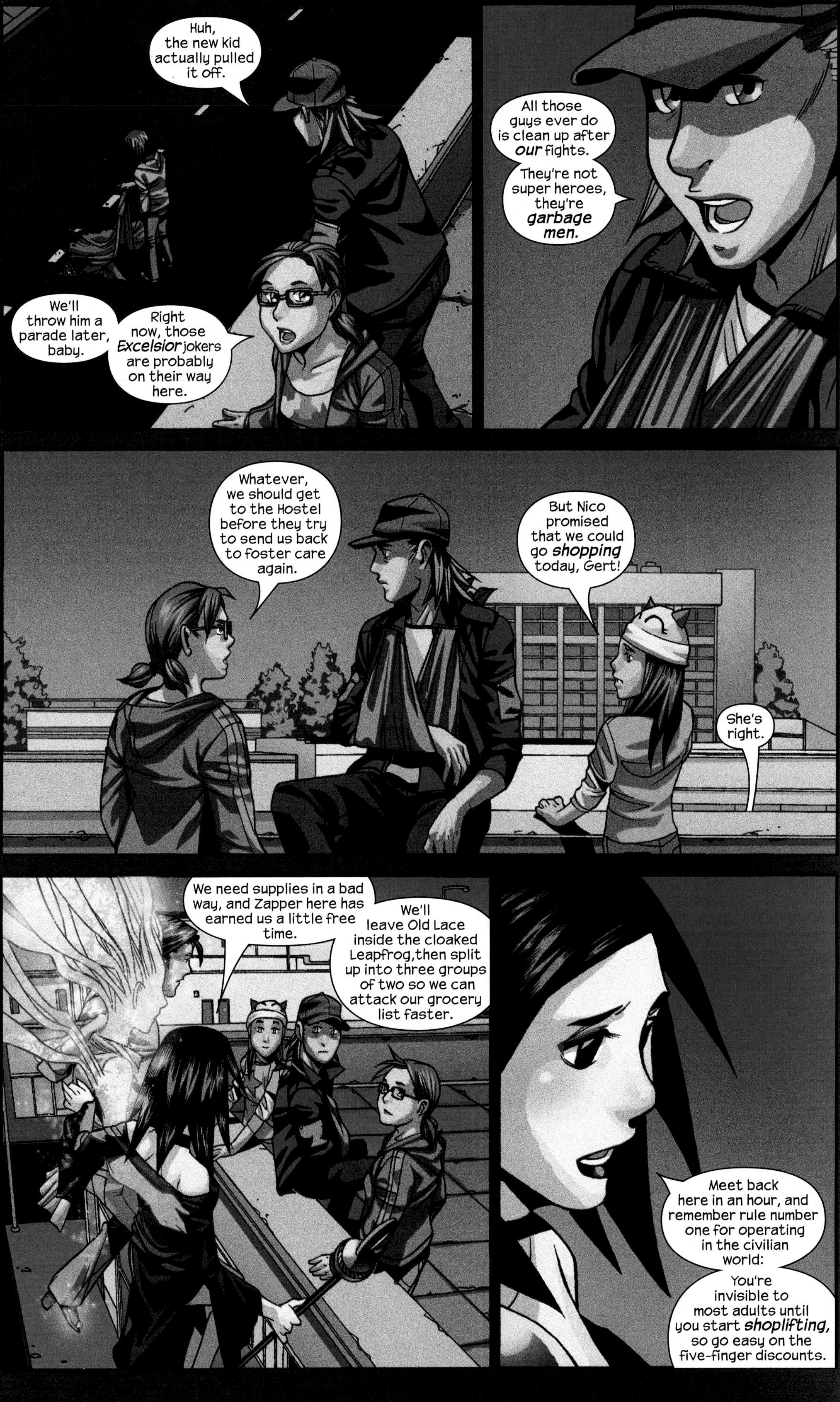
Huh, the new kid actually pulled it off.
We'll throw him a parade later, baby.
Right now, those Excelsior jokers are probably on their way here.
All those guys ever do is clean up after our fights.
They're not super heroes, they're garbage men.
Whatever, we should get to the Hostel before they try to send us back to foster care again.
But Nico promised that we could go shopping today, Gert!
She's right.
We need supplies in a bad way, and Zapper here has earned us a little free time.
We'll leave Old Lace inside the cloaked Leapfrog, then split up into three groups of two so we can attack our grocery list faster.
Meet back here in an hour, and remember rule number one for operating in the civilian world:
You're invisible to most adults until you start shoplifting, so go easy on the five-finger discounts.

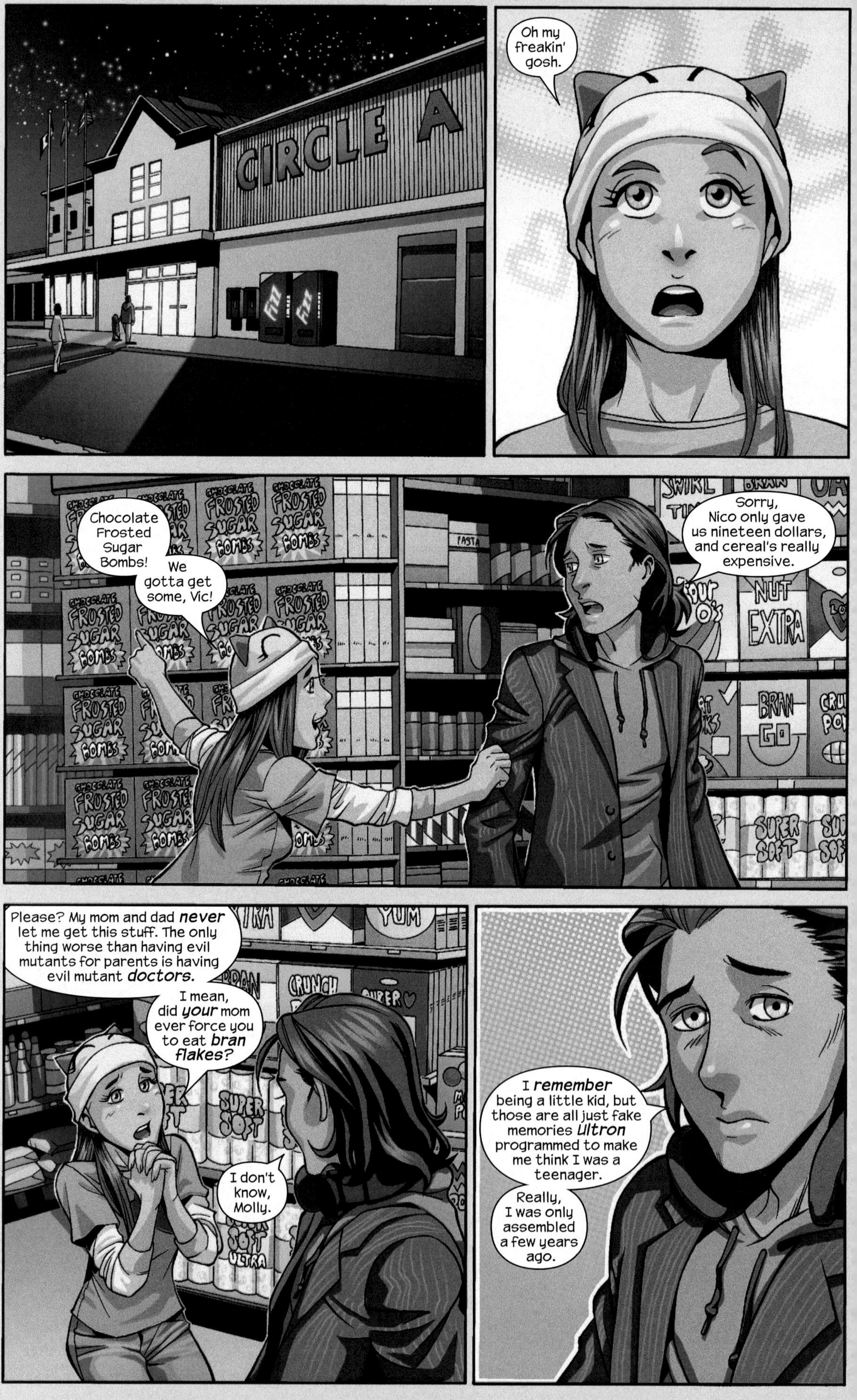

CIRCLE A
FIZZ
Oh my freakin' gosh.
Chocolate Frosted Sugar Bombs!
We gotta get some, Vic!
Sorry, Nico only gave us nineteen dollars, and cereal's really expensive.
Please? My mom and dad *never* let me get this stuff. The only thing worse than having evil mutants for parents is having evil mutant *doctors.*
I mean, did *your* mom ever force you to eat *bran flakes?*
I don't know, Molly.
I *remember* being a little kid, but those are all just fake memories *Ultron* programmed to make me think I was a teenager.
Really, I was only assembled a few years ago.

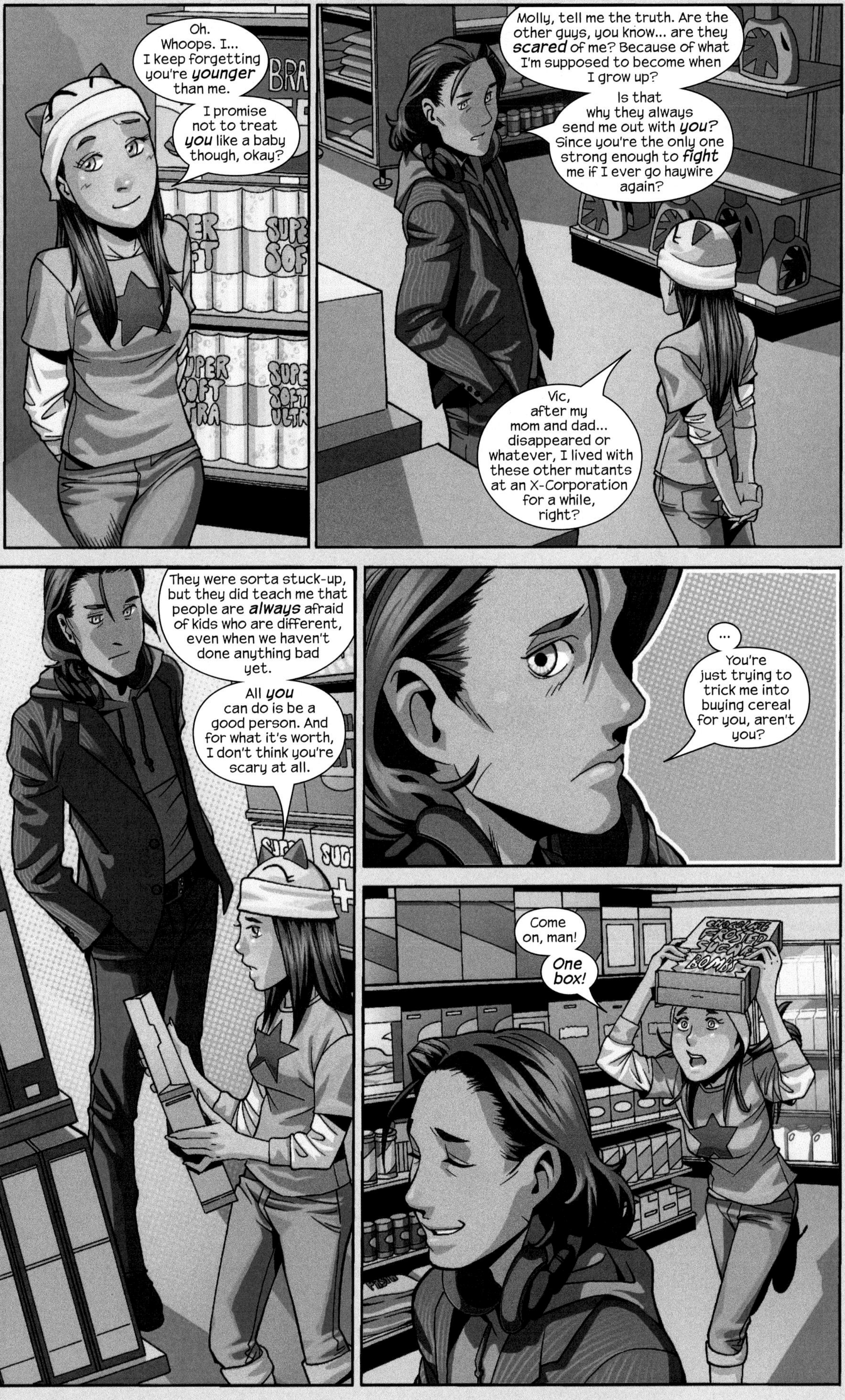
Oh. Whoops. I... I keep forgetting you're younger than me.
I promise not to treat you like a baby though, okay?
BRA
SUPER SOFT
SUPER SOFT ULTRA
Molly, tell me the truth. Are the other guys, you know... are they scared of me? Because of what I'm supposed to become when I grow up?
Is that why they always send me out with you? Since you're the only one strong enough to fight me if I ever go haywire again?
Vic, after my mom and dad... disappeared or whatever, I lived with these other mutants at an X-Corporation for a while, right?
They were sorta stuck-up, but they did teach me that people are always afraid of kids who are different, even when we haven't done anything bad yet.
All you can do is be a good person. And for what it's worth, I don't think you're scary at all.
...
You're just trying to trick me into buying cereal for you, aren't you?
Come on, man!
One box!
CHOCOLATE FROSTED SUGAR BOMBS

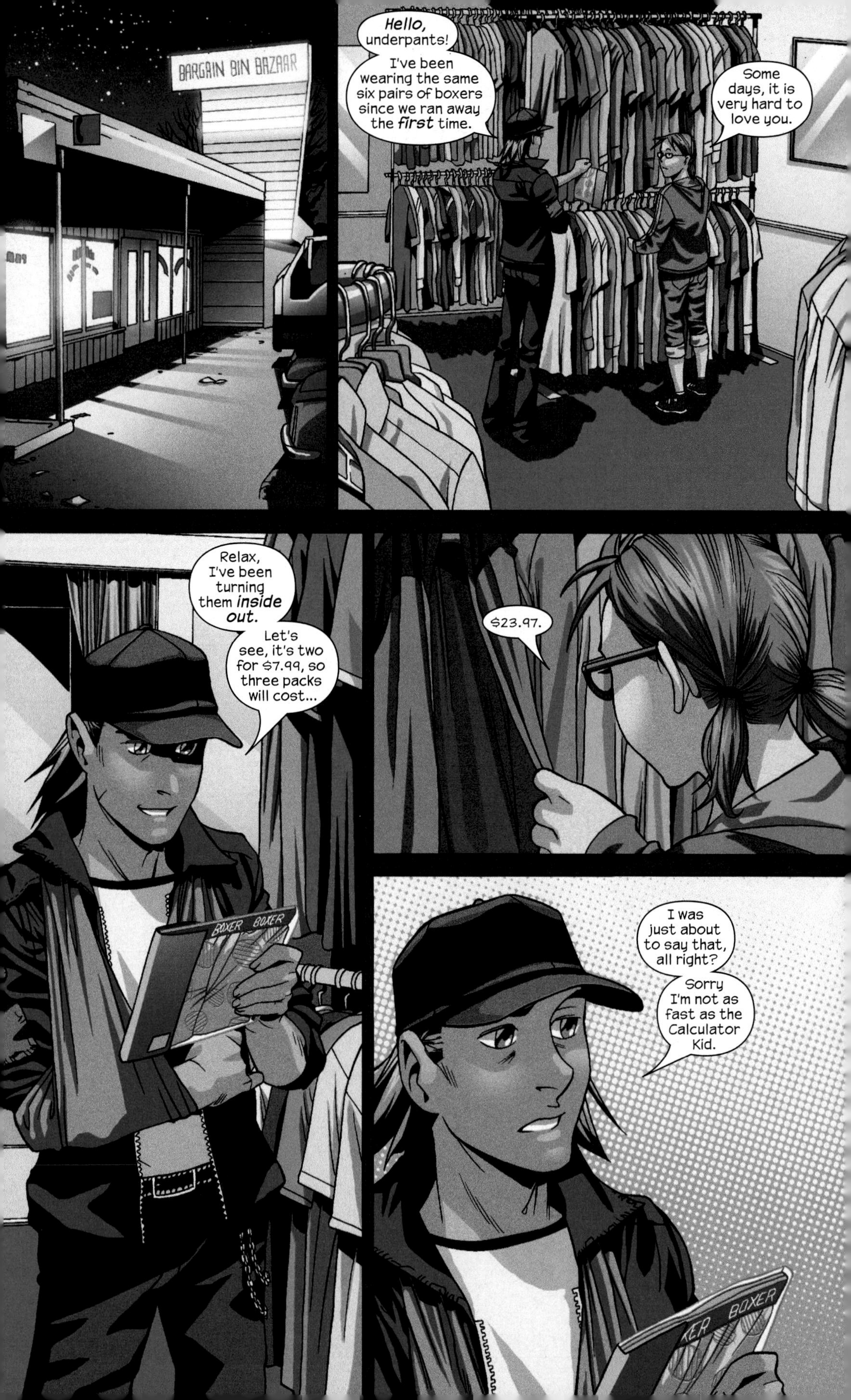
BARGAIN BIN BAZAAR
Hello, underpants!
I've been wearing the same six pairs of boxers since we ran away the *first* time.
Some days, it is very hard to love you.
Relax, I've been turning them *inside out.*
Let's see, it's two for $7.99, so three packs will cost...
BOXER BOXER
$23.97.
I was just about to say that, all right?
Sorry I'm not as fast as the Calculator Kid.
BOXER

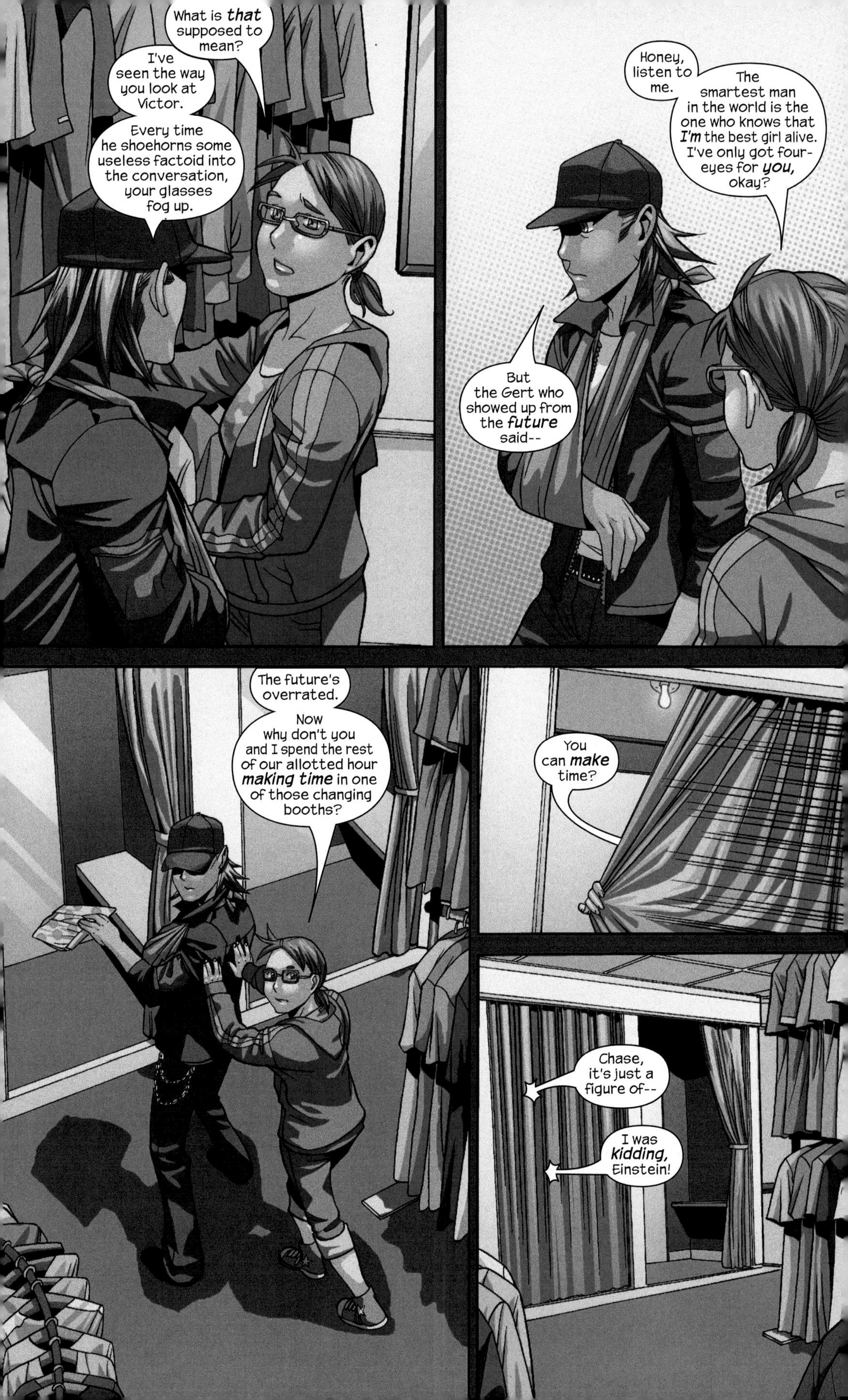
What is *that* supposed to mean?
I've seen the way you look at Victor.
Every time he shoehorns some useless factoid into the conversation, your glasses fog up.
Honey, listen to me.
The smartest man in the world is the one who knows that *I'm* the best girl alive. I've only got four-eyes for *you,* okay?
But the Gert who showed up from the *future* said--
The future's overrated.
Now why don't you and I spend the rest of our allotted hour *making time* in one of those changing booths?
You can *make* time?
Chase, it's just a figure of--
I was *kidding,* Einstein!

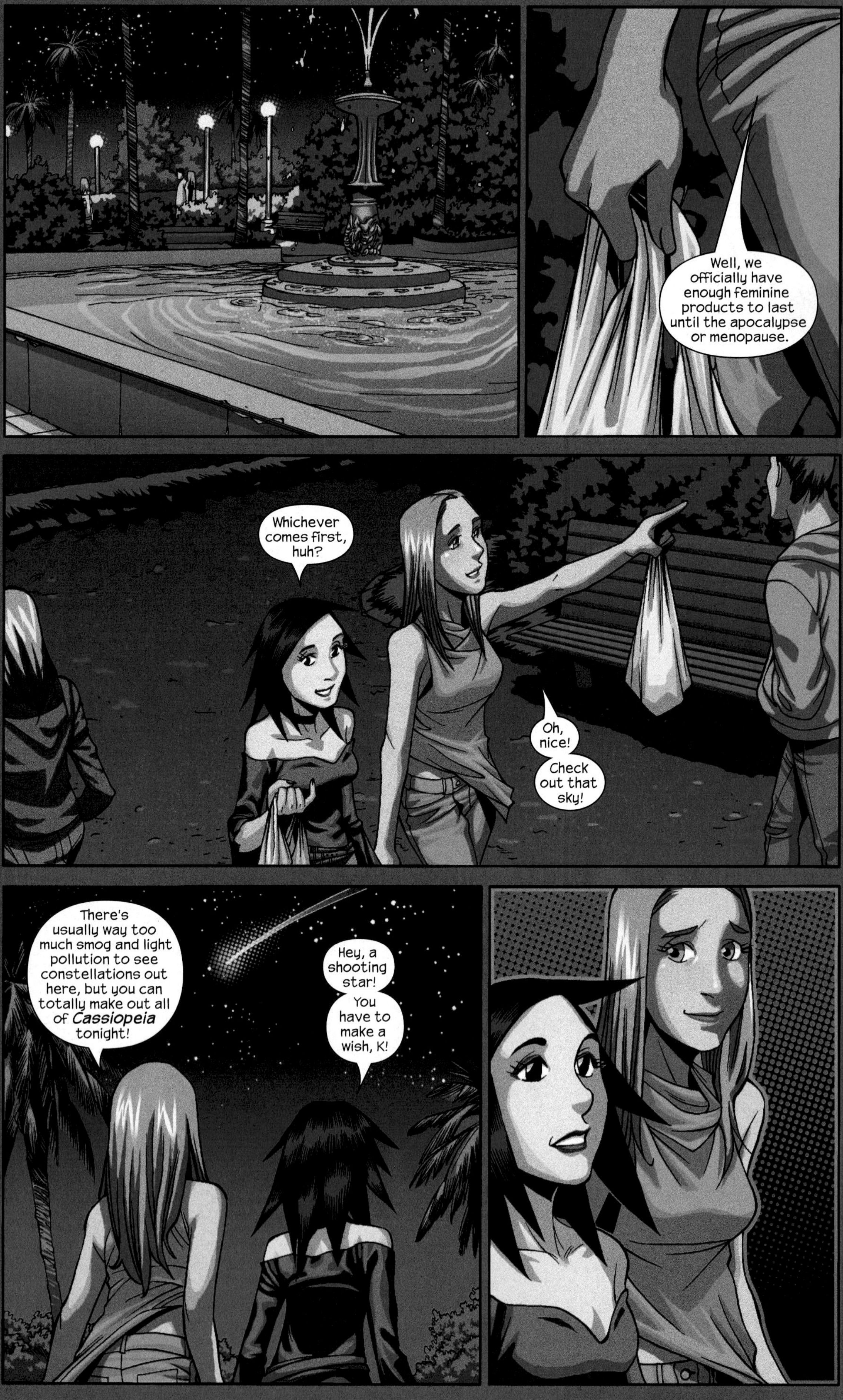
Well, we officially have enough feminine products to last until the apocalypse or menopause.
Whichever comes first, huh?
Oh, nice!
Check out that sky!
There's usually way too much smog and light pollution to see constellations out here, but you can totally make out all of *Cassiopeia* tonight!
Hey, a shooting star!
You have to make a wish, K!

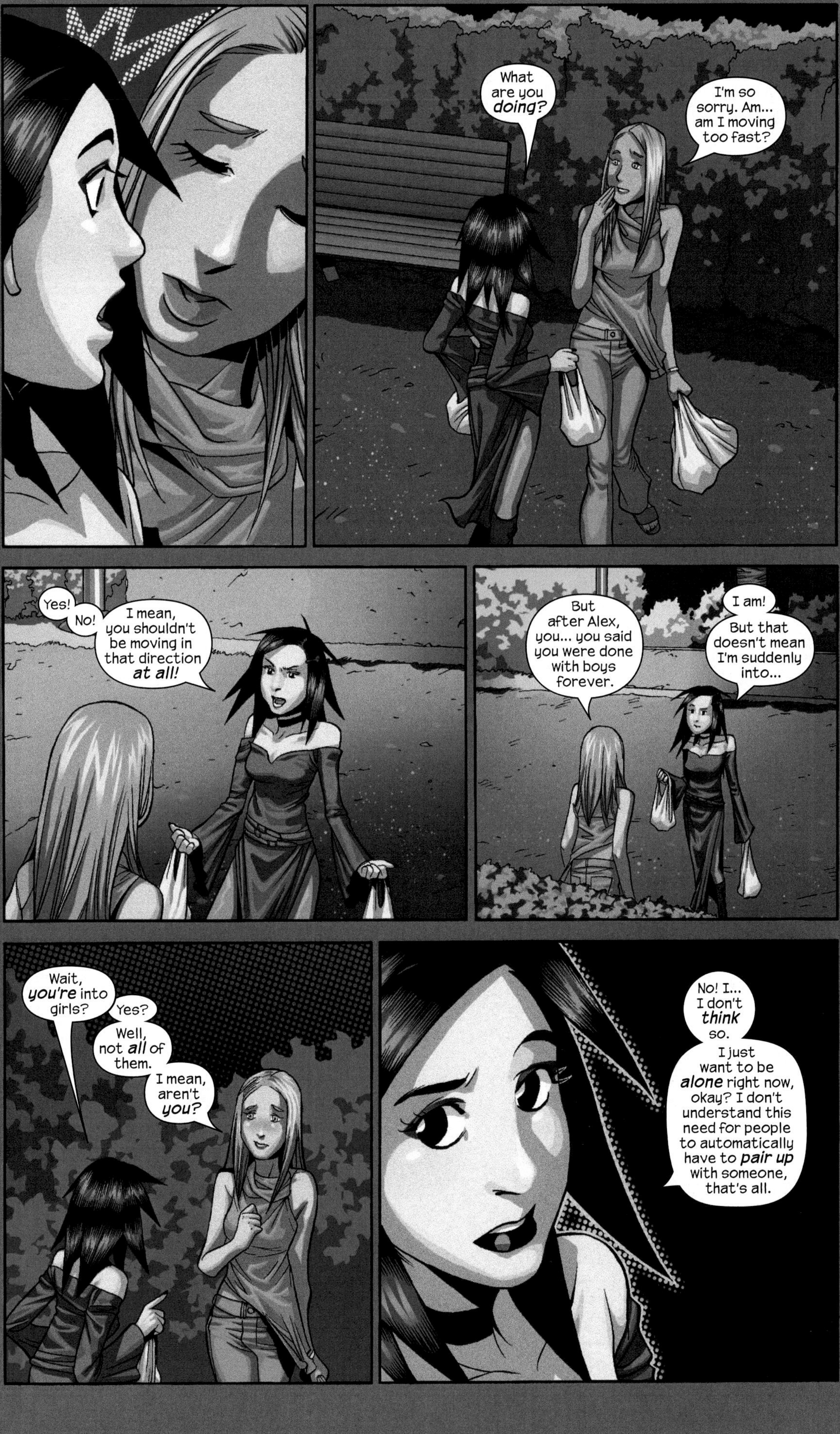
What are you doing?
I'm so sorry. Am... am I moving too fast?
Yes!
No!
I mean, you shouldn't be moving in that direction at all!
But after Alex, you... you said you were done with boys forever.
I am!
But that doesn't mean I'm suddenly into...
Wait, you're into girls?
Yes?
Well, not all of them.
I mean, aren't you?
No! I... I don't think so.
I just want to be alone right now, okay? I don't understand this need for people to automatically have to pair up with someone, that's all.

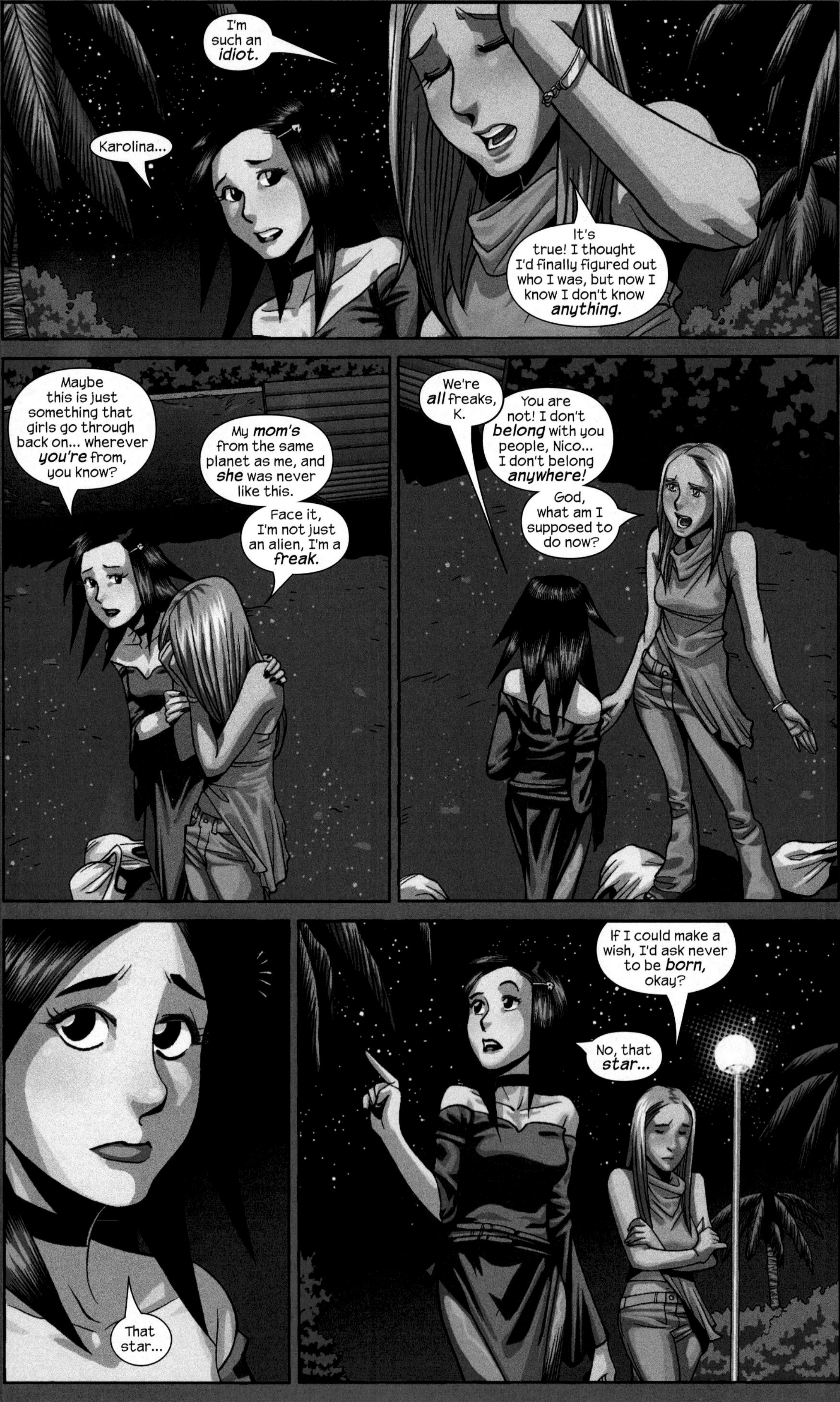
I'm such an idiot.
Karolina...
It's true! I thought I'd finally figured out who I was, but now I know I don't know anything.
Maybe this is just something that girls go through back on... wherever you're from, you know?
My mom's from the same planet as me, and she was never like this.
Face it, I'm not just an alien, I'm a freak.
We're all freaks, K.
You are not! I don't belong with you people, Nico... I don't belong anywhere!
God, what am I supposed to do now?
That star...
If I could make a wish, I'd ask never to be born, okay?
No, that star...

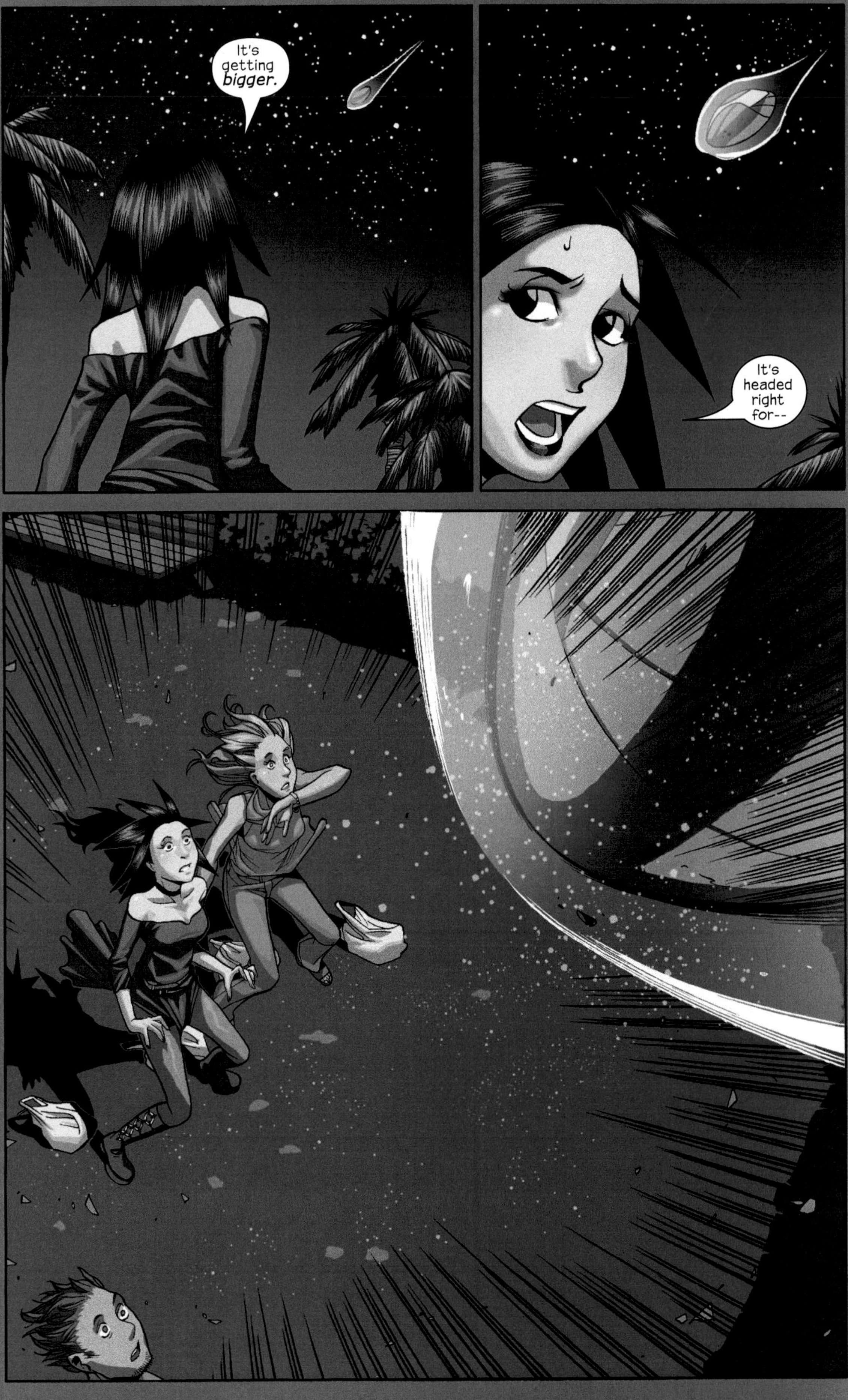
It's getting *bigger.*
It's headed right for--

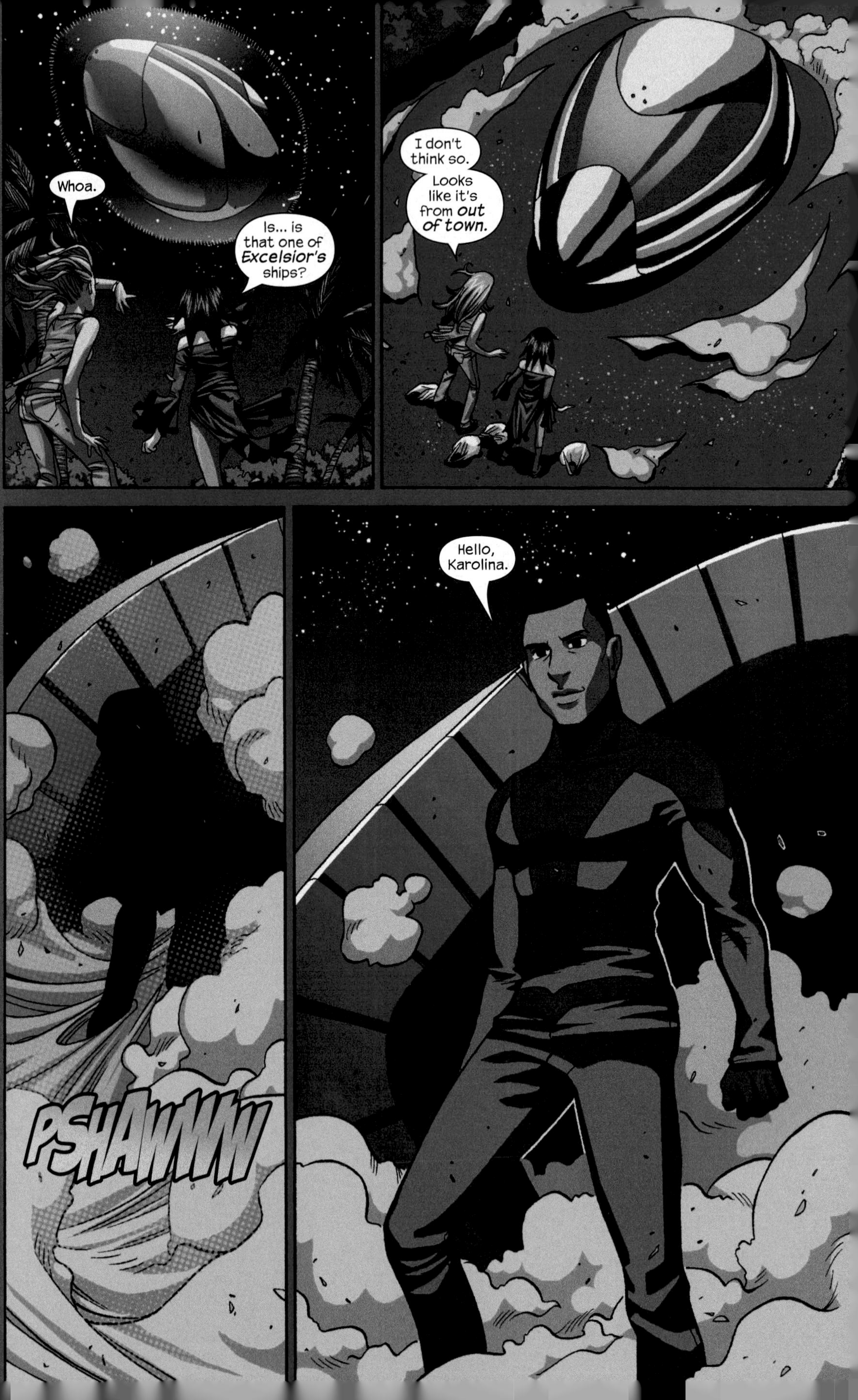
Whoa.
Is... is that one of *Excelsior's* ships?
I don't think so.
Looks like it's from *out of town.*
PSHAWWW
Hello, Karolina.

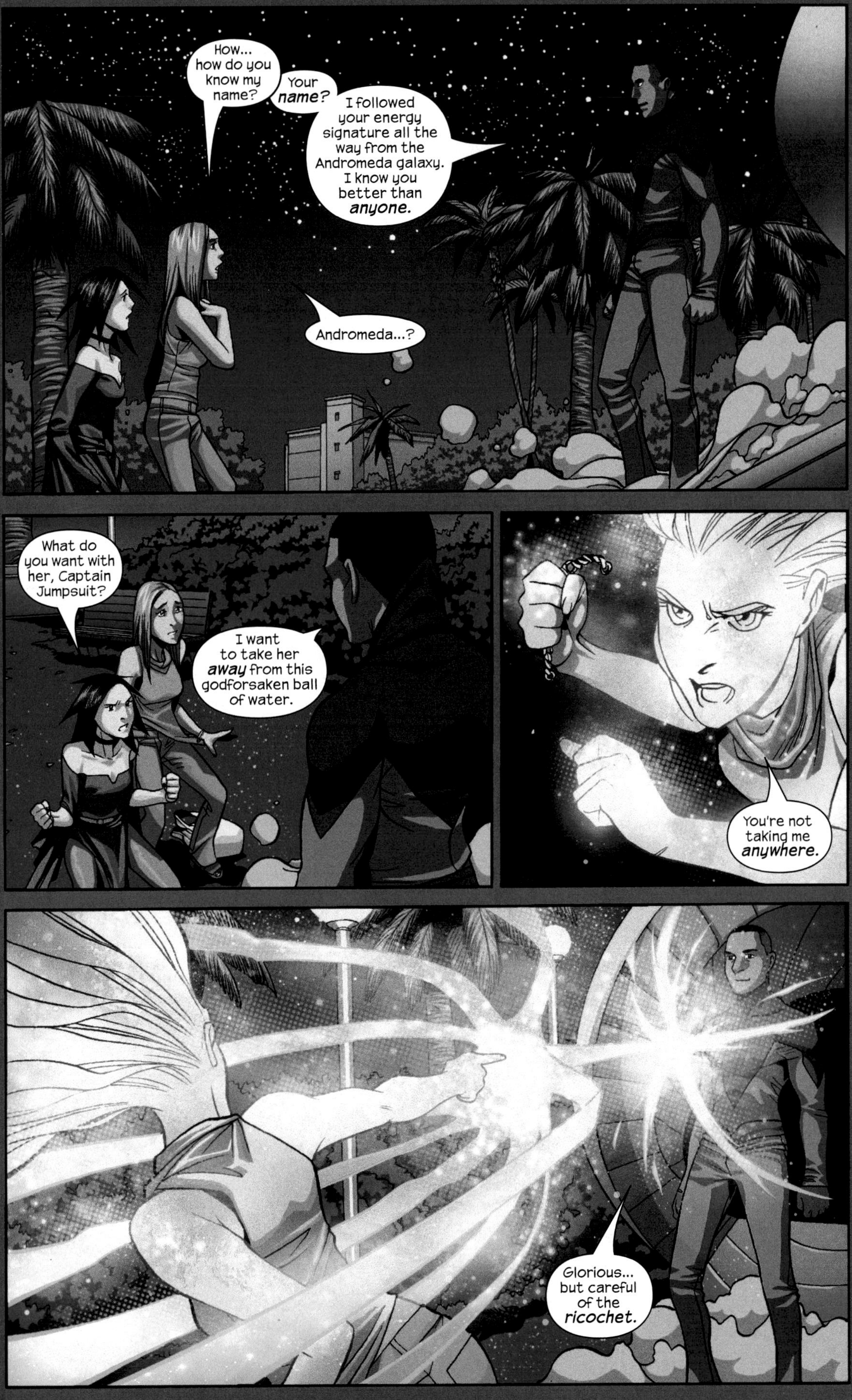
How... how do you know my name?
Your name?
I followed your energy signature all the way from the Andromeda galaxy. I know you better than anyone.
Andromeda...?
What do you want with her, Captain Jumpsuit?
I want to take her away from this godforsaken ball of water.
You're not taking me anywhere.
Glorious... but careful of the ricochet.

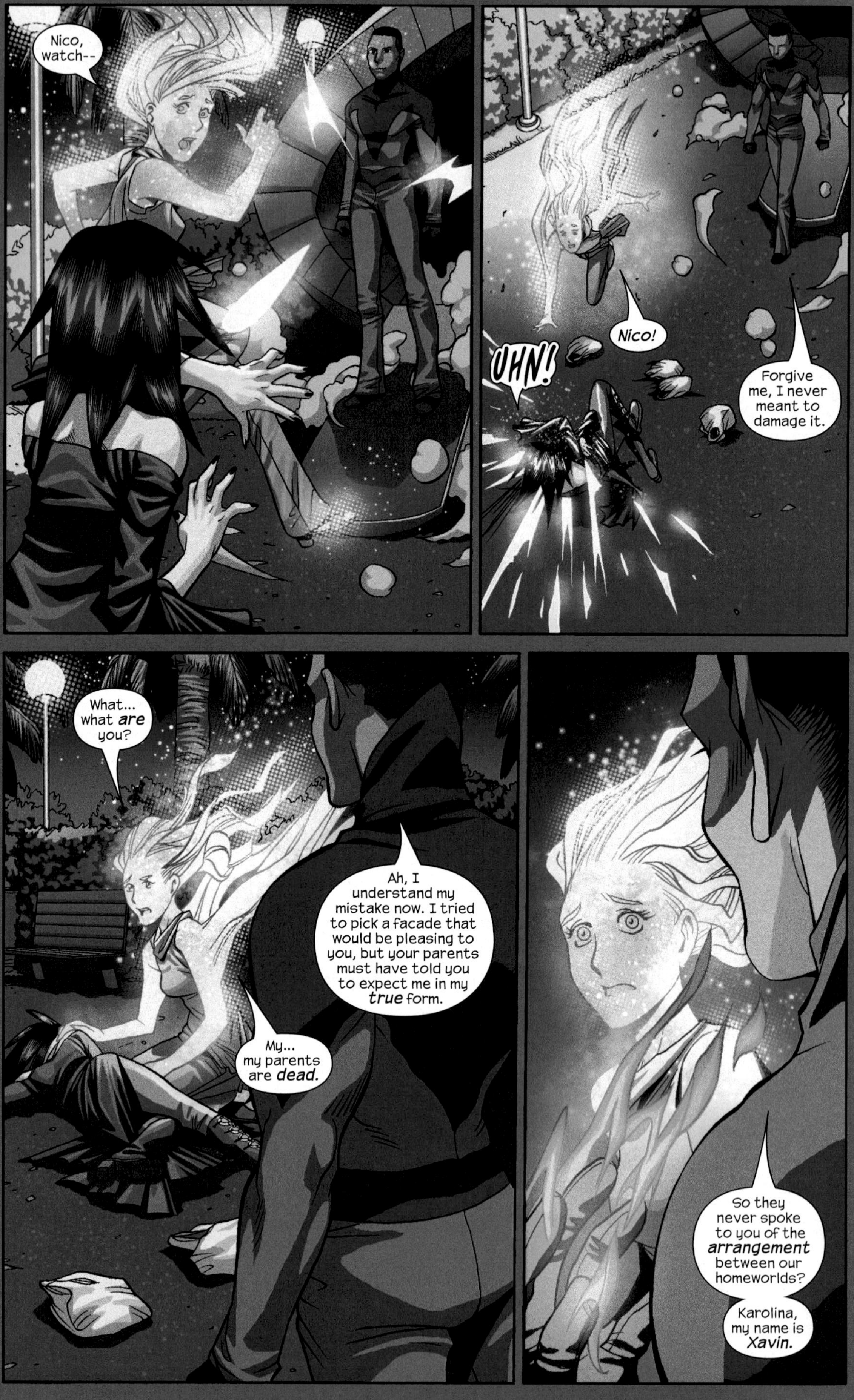

Nico, watch--
Nico!
UHN!
Forgive me, I never meant to damage it.
What... what *are* you?
Ah, I understand my mistake now. I tried to pick a facade that would be pleasing to you, but your parents must have told you to expect me in my *true* form.
My... my parents are *dead.*
So they never spoke to you of the *arrangement* between our homeworlds?
Karolina, my name is *Xavin.*

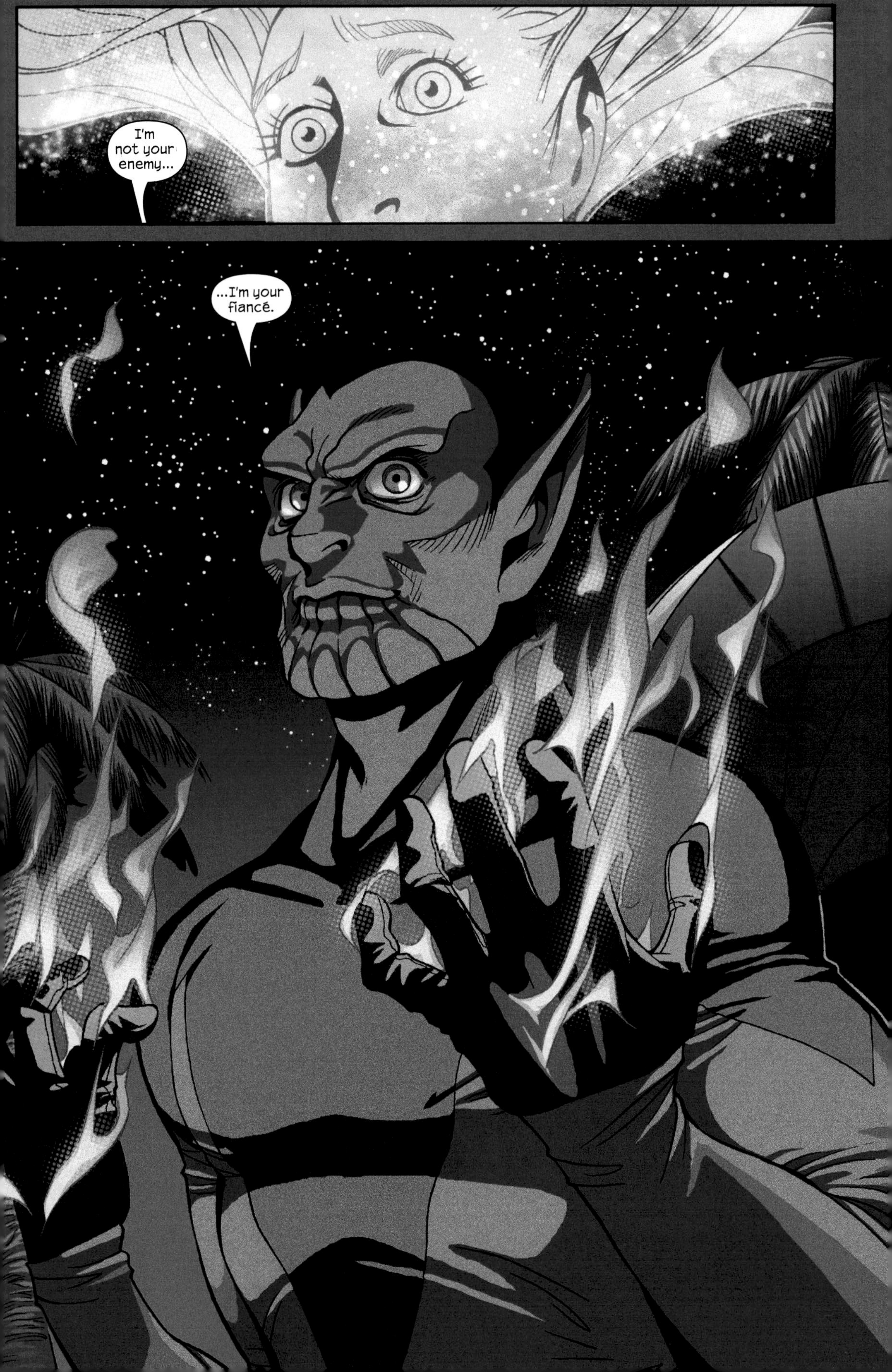
I'm not your enemy...
...I'm your fiancé.

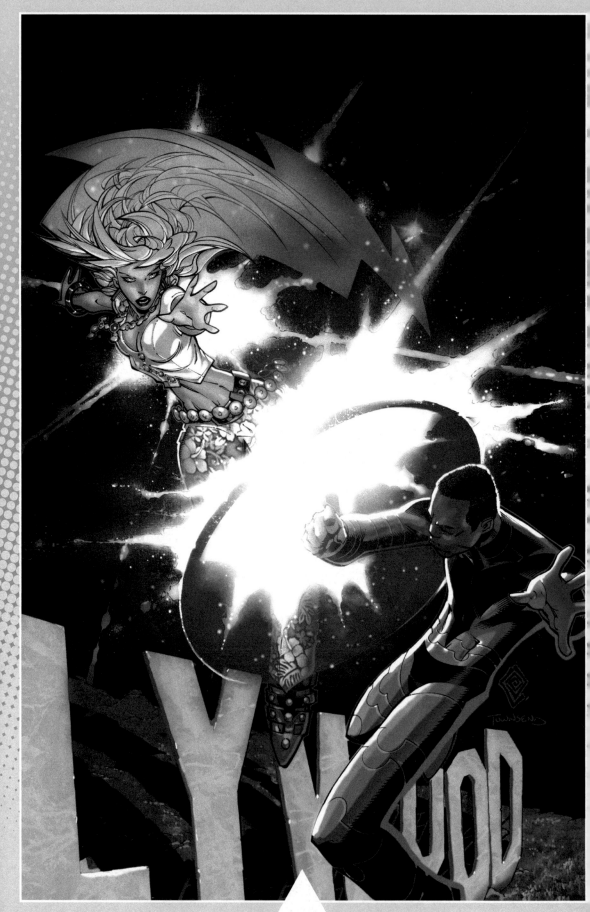

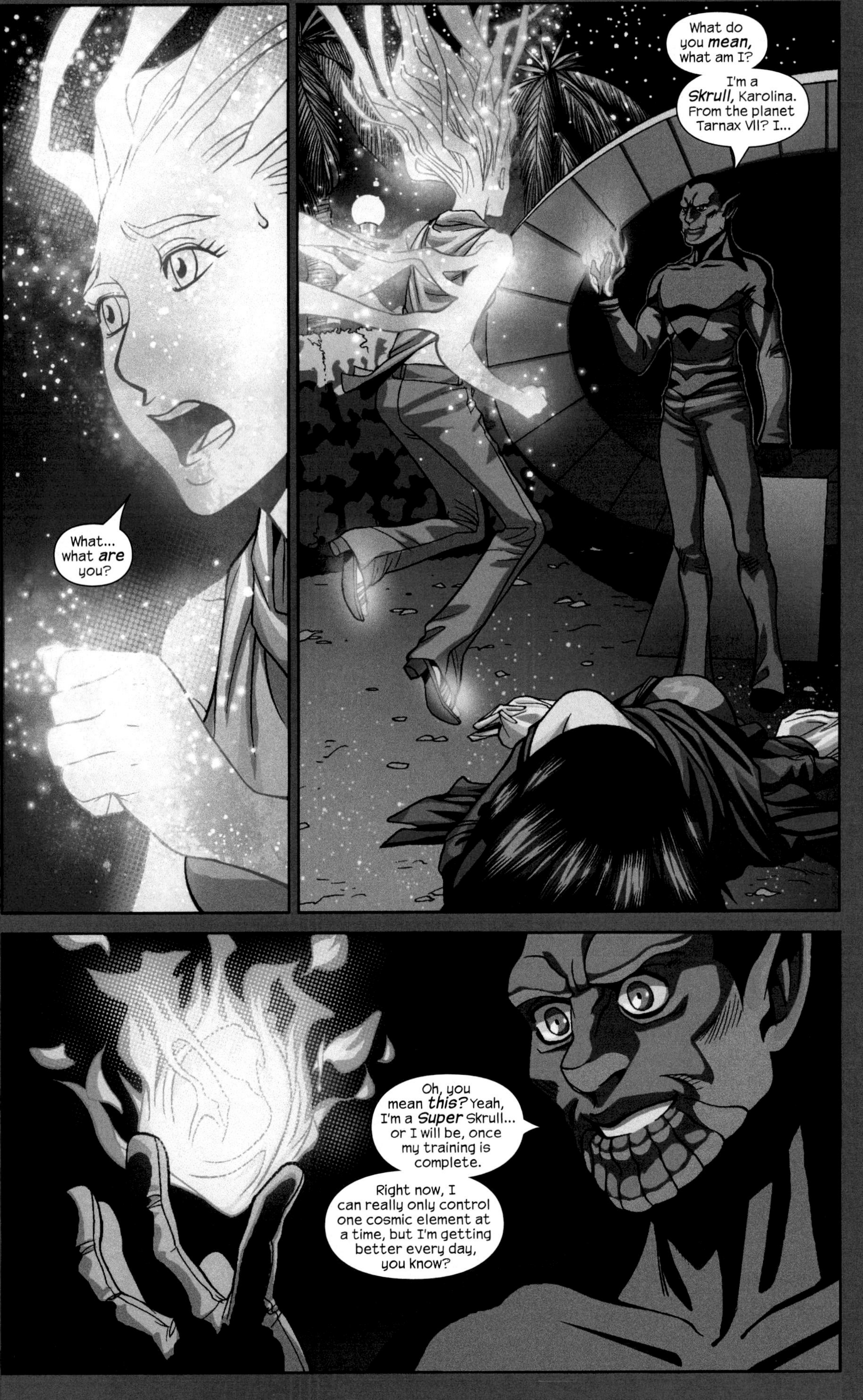

What... what *are* you?
What do you *mean,* what am I?
I'm a *Skrull,* Karolina. From the planet Tarnax VII? I...
Oh, you mean *this?* Yeah, I'm a *Super* Skrull... or I will be, once my training is complete.
Right now, I can really only control one cosmic element at a time, but I'm getting better every day, you know?

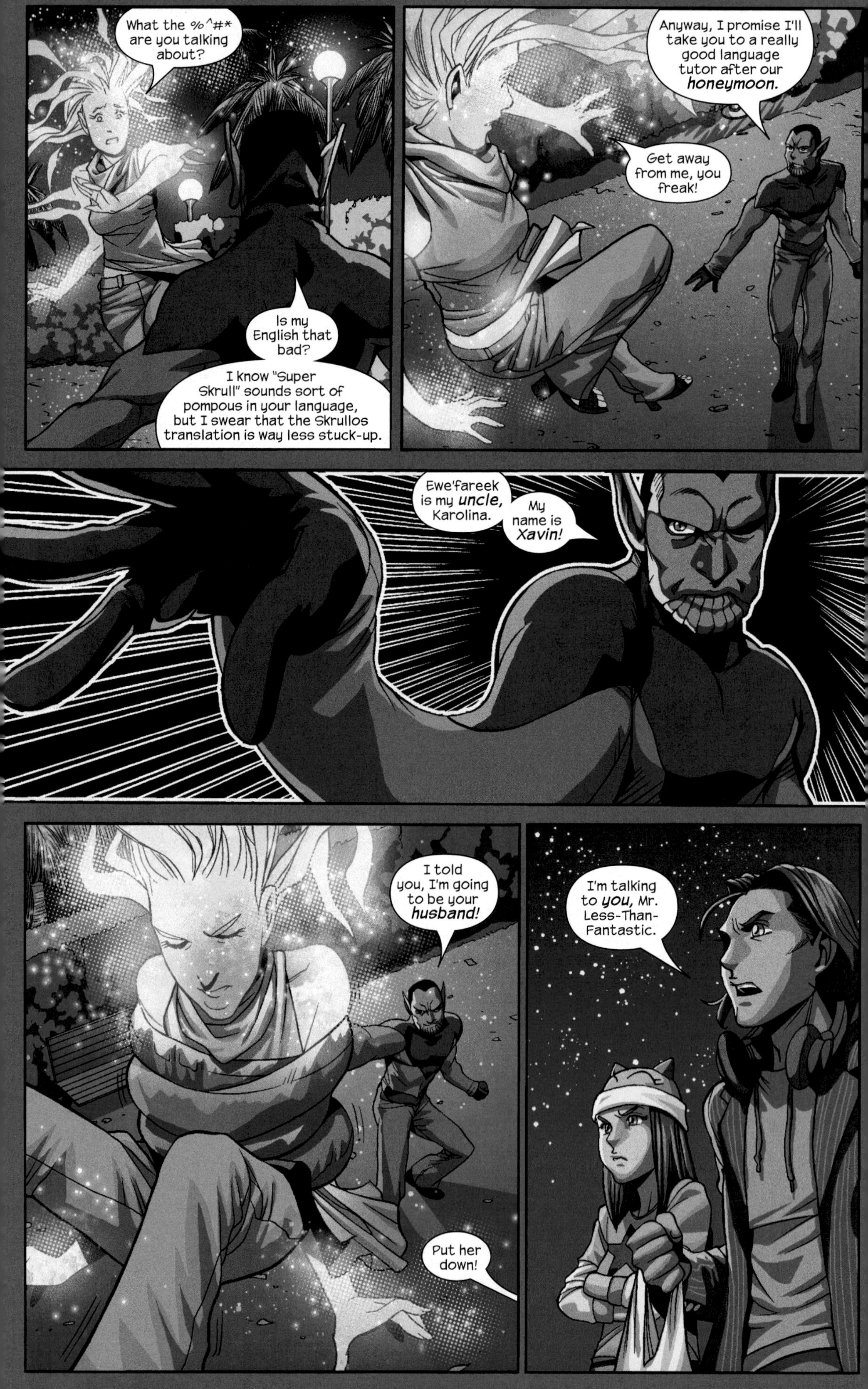

What the %^#* are you talking about?
Is my English that bad?
I know "Super Skrull" sounds sort of pompous in your language, but I swear that the Skrullos translation is way less stuck-up.
Anyway, I promise I'll take you to a really good language tutor after our honeymoon.
Get away from me, you freak!
Ewe'fareek is my uncle, Karolina.
My name is Xavin!
I told you, I'm going to be your husband!
Put her down!
I'm talking to you, Mr. Less-Than-Fantastic.

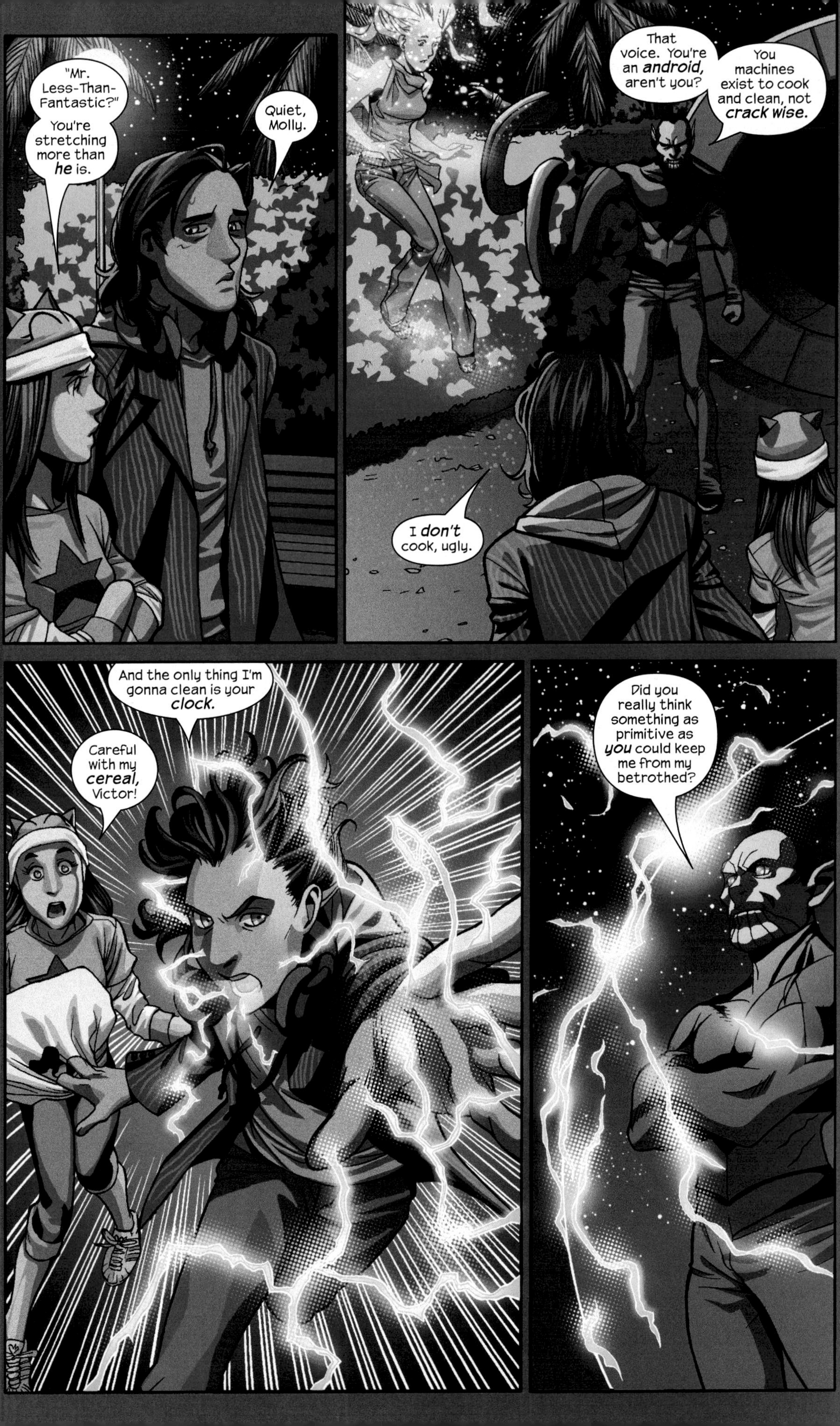
"Mr. Less-Than-Fantastic?"
You're stretching more than **he** is.
Quiet, Molly.
That voice. You're an **android,** aren't you?
You machines exist to cook and clean, not **crack wise.**
I **don't** cook, ugly.
And the only thing I'm gonna clean is your **clock.**
Careful with my **cereal,** Victor!
Did you really think something as primitive as **you** could keep me from my betrothed?

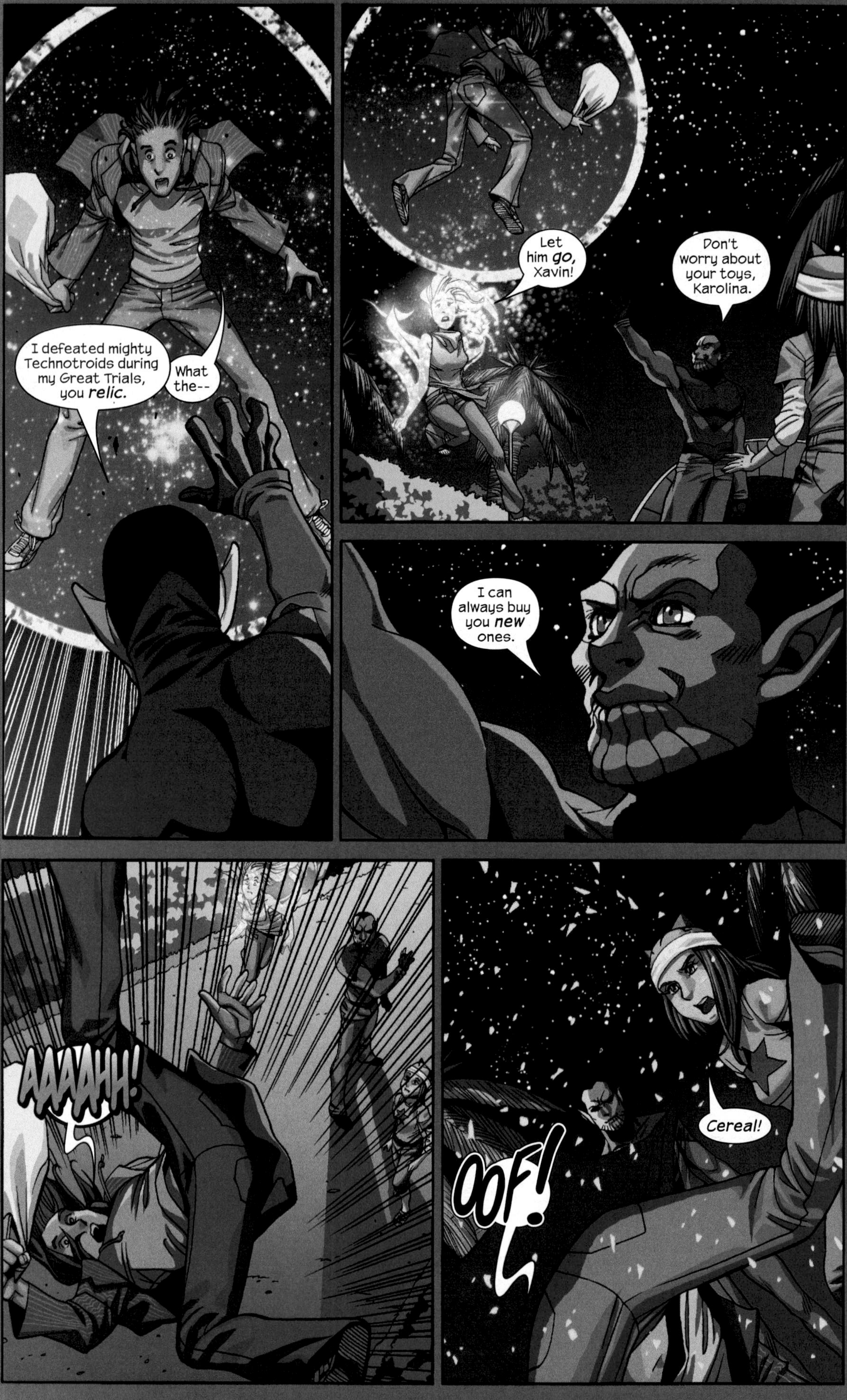
I defeated mighty Technotroids during my Great Trials, you *relic.*
What the--
Let him *go,* Xavin!
Don't worry about your toys, Karolina.
I can always buy you *new* ones.
AAAAHH!
Cereal!
OOF!

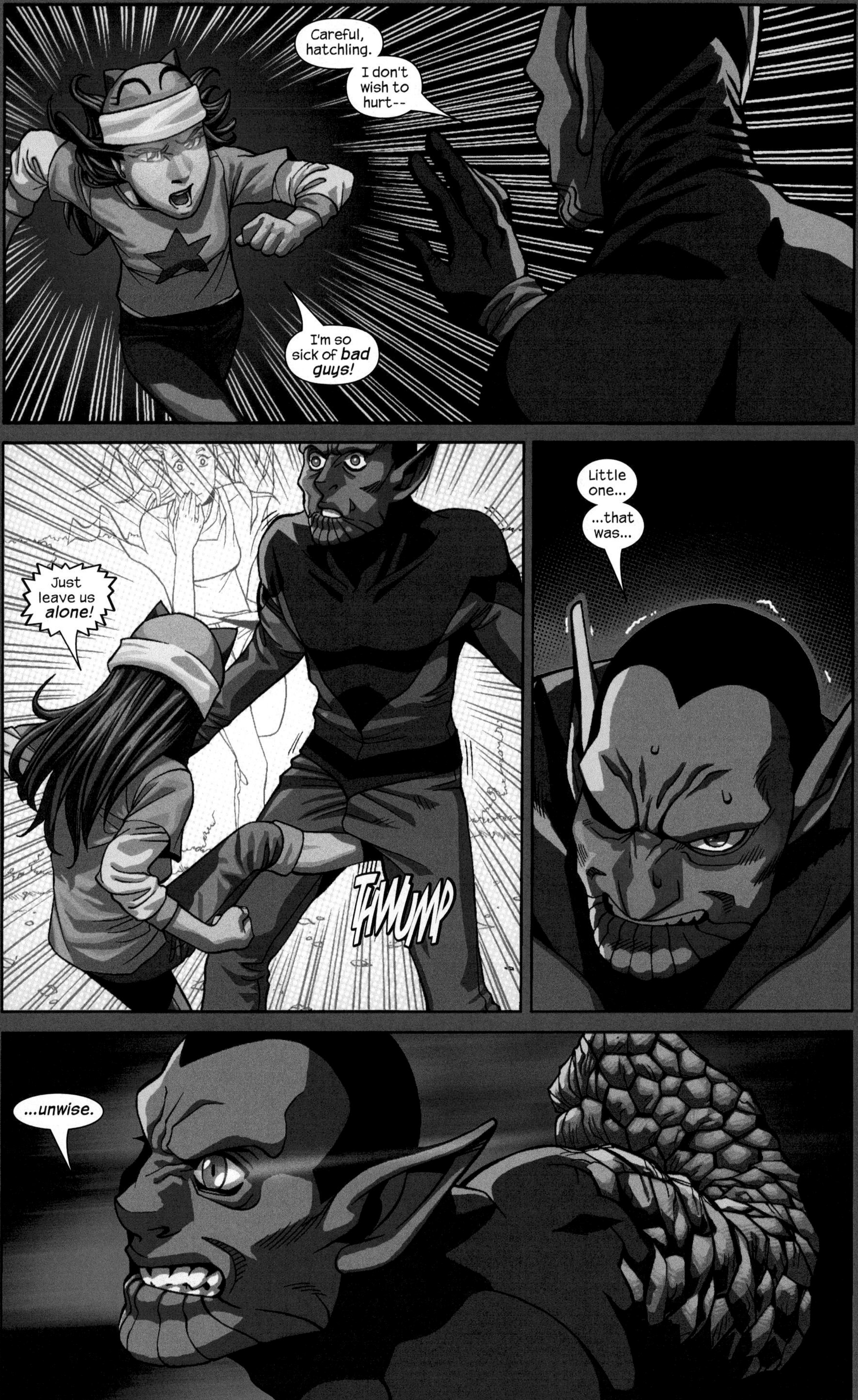
Careful, hatchling.
I don't wish to hurt--
I'm so sick of *bad guys!*
Just leave us *alone!*
THWUMP
Little one...
...that was...
...unwise.

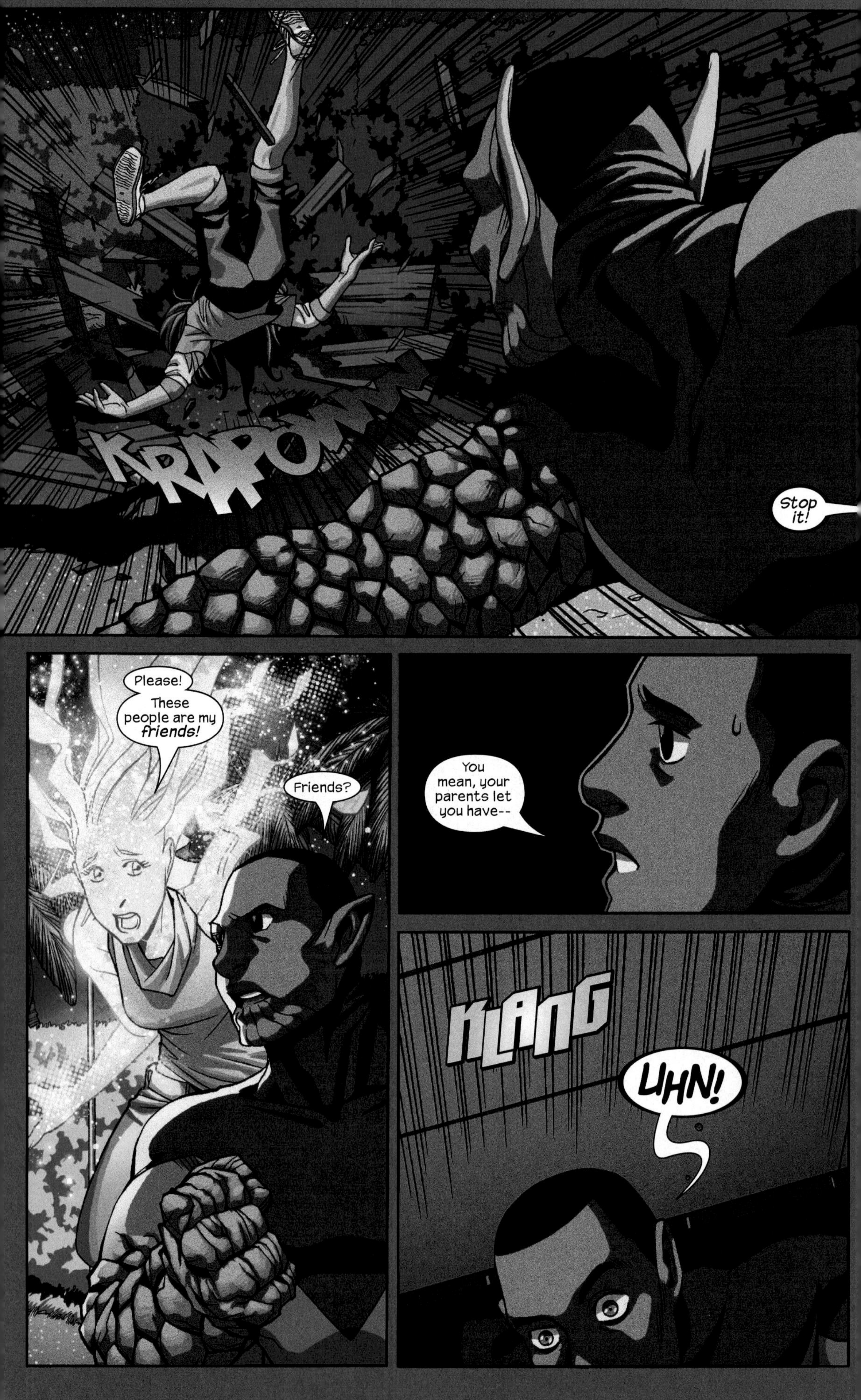
KRAPOW
Stop it!
Please! These people are my friends!
Friends?
You mean, your parents let you have--
KLANG
UHN!

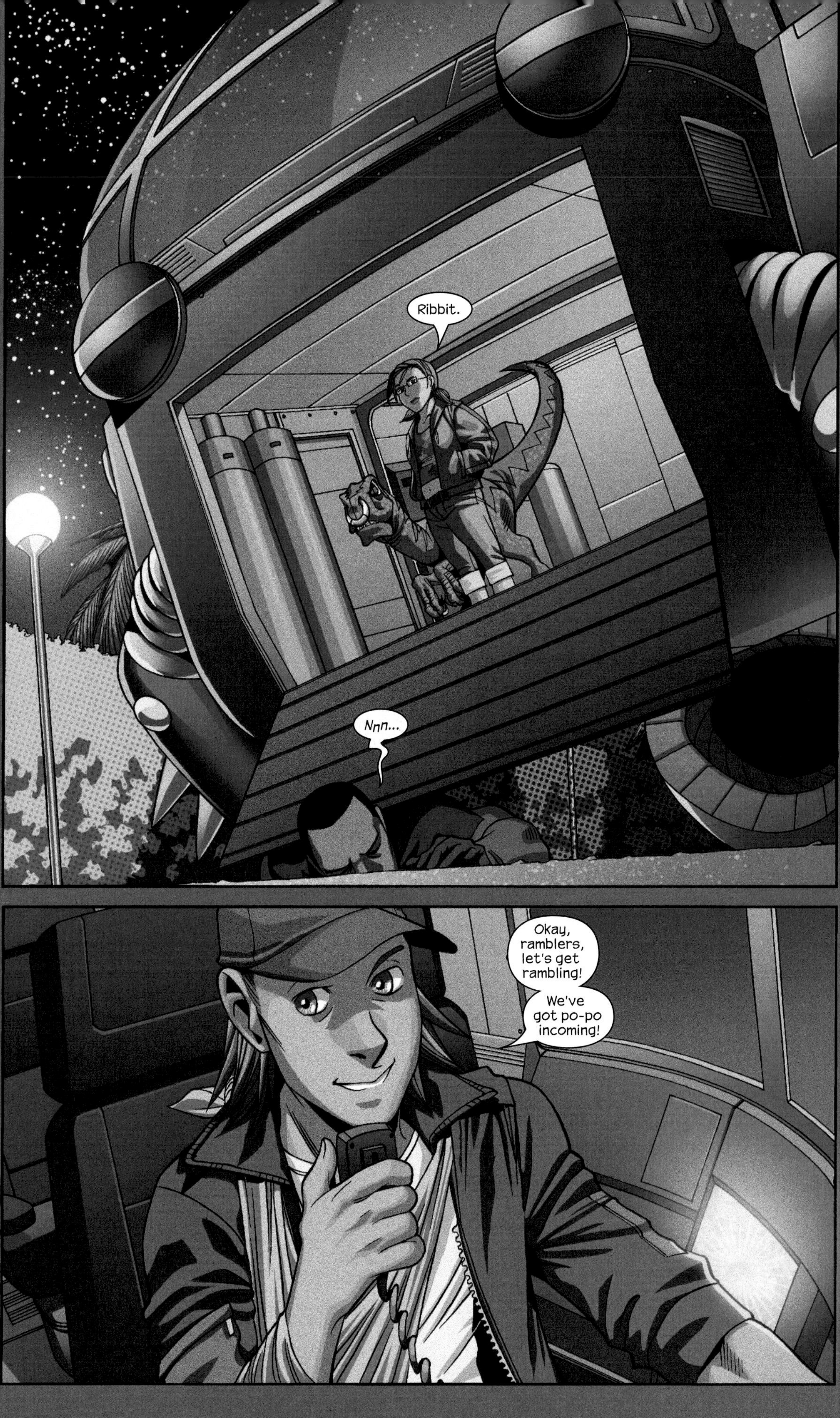
Ribbit.
Nnn...
Okay, ramblers, let's get rambling!
We've got po-po incoming!

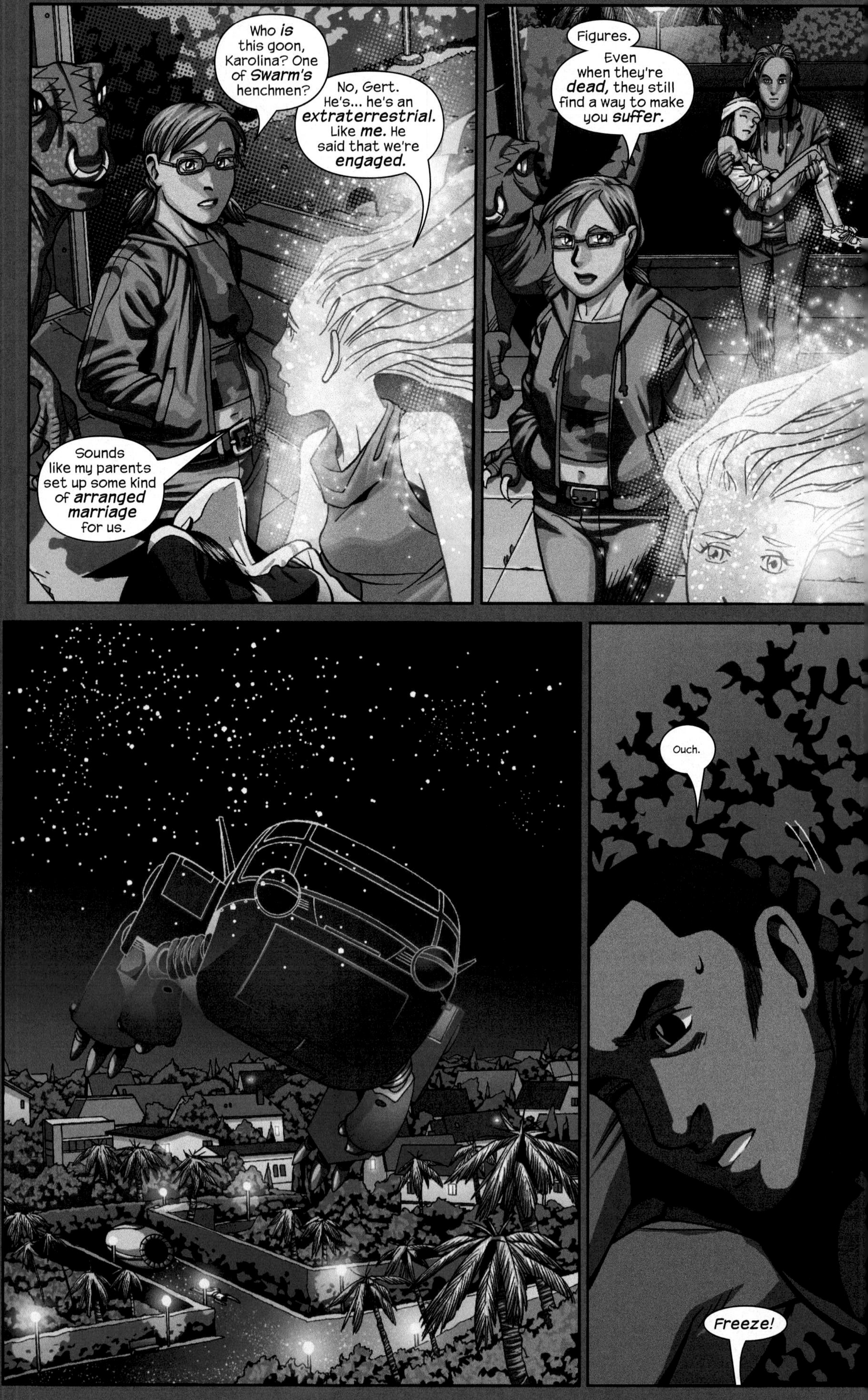
Who is this goon, Karolina? One of Swarm's henchmen?
No, Gert. He's... he's an extraterrestrial. Like me. He said that we're engaged.
Sounds like my parents set up some kind of arranged marriage for us.
Figures. Even when they're dead, they still find a way to make you suffer.
Ouch.
Freeze!

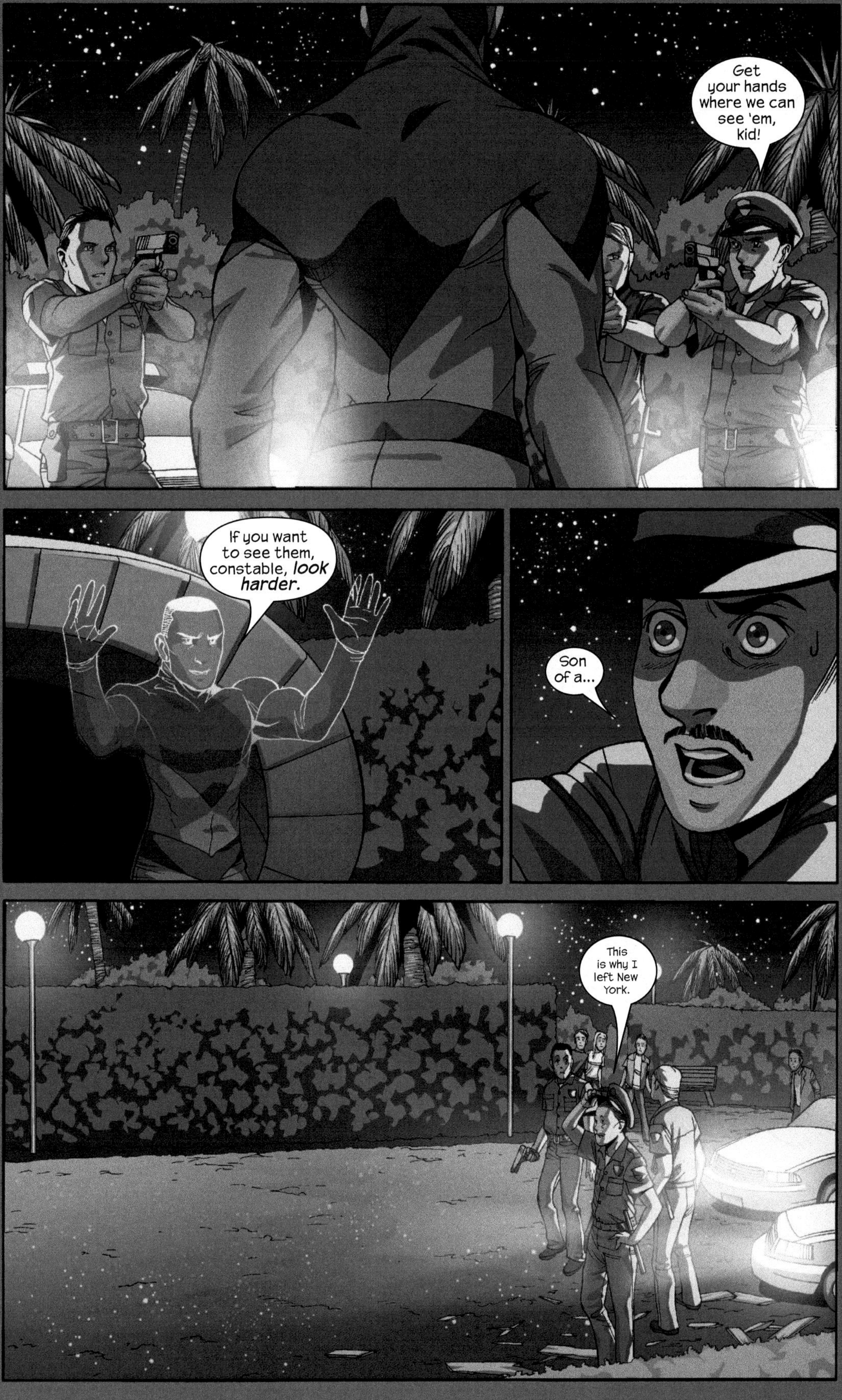
Get your hands where we can see 'em, kid!
If you want to see them, constable, *look harder*.
Son of a...
This is why I left New York.

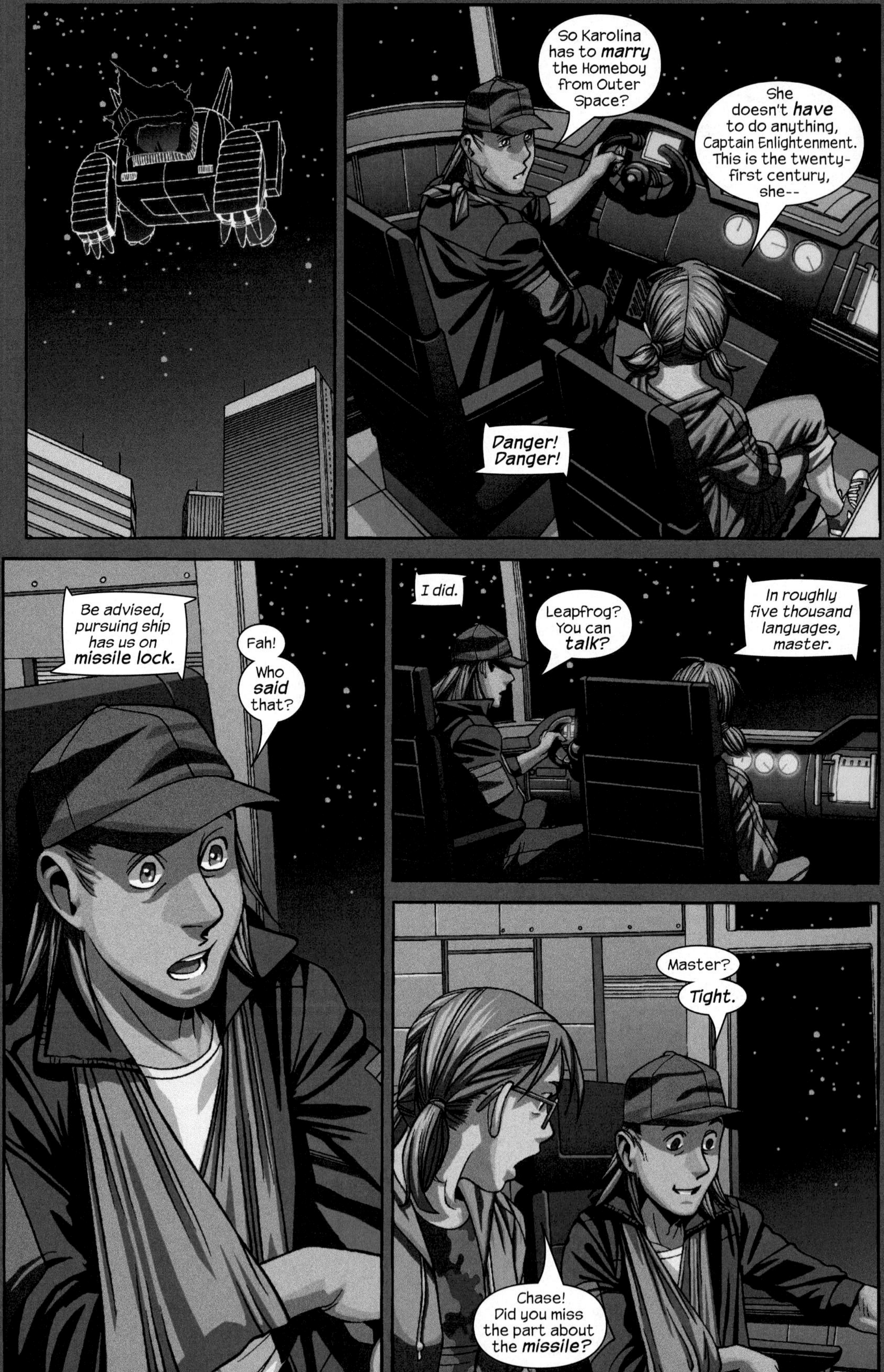
So Karolina has to *marry* the Homeboy from Outer Space?
She doesn't ***have*** to do anything, Captain Enlightenment. This is the twenty-first century, she--
Danger! Danger!
*Be advised, pursuing ship has us on **missile lock.***
Fah!
Who *said* that?
I did.
Leapfrog? You can *talk?*
In roughly five thousand languages, master.
Master?
Tight.
Chase! Did you miss the part about the *missile?*

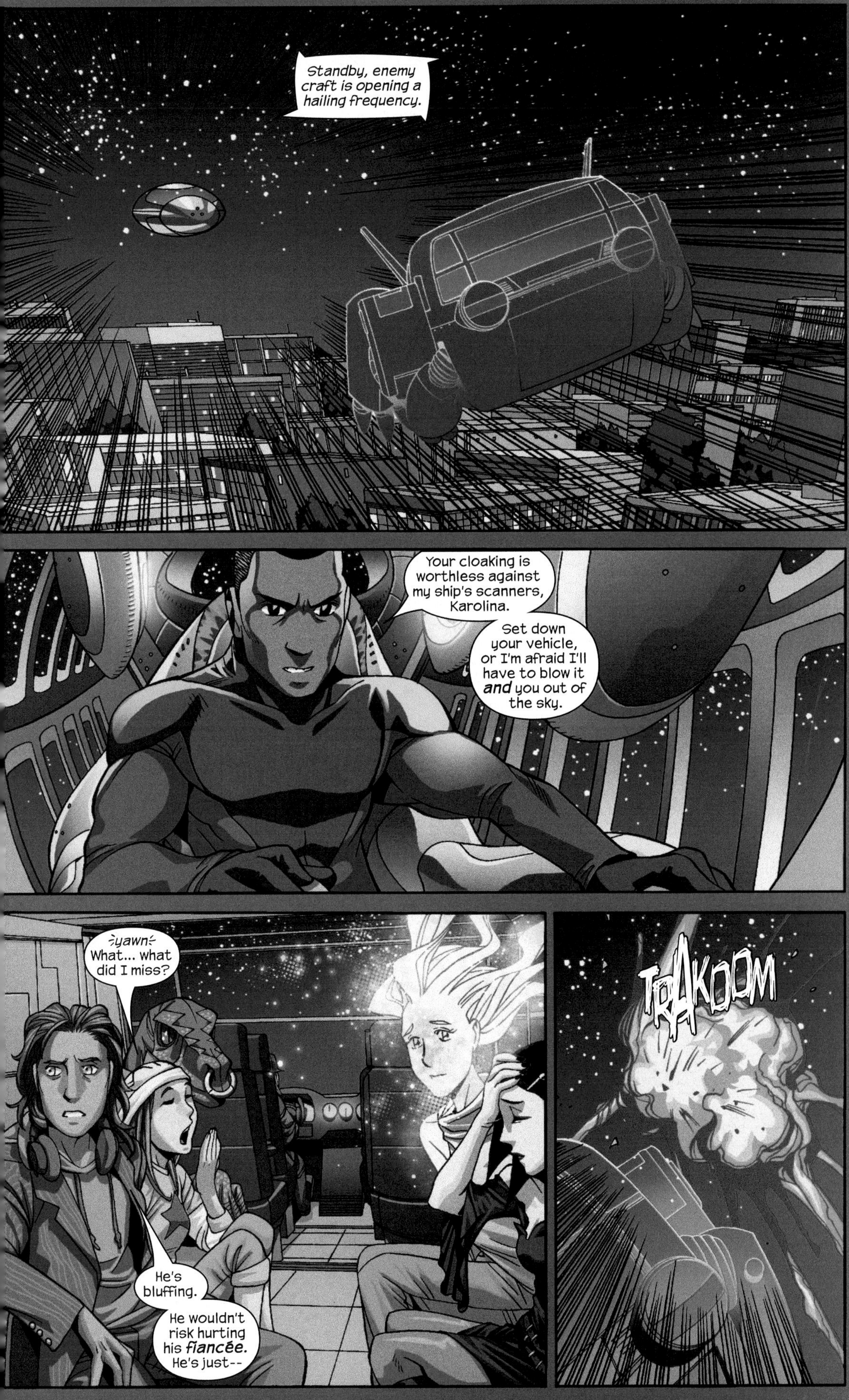

Standby, enemy craft is opening a hailing frequency.
Your cloaking is worthless against my ship's scanners, Karolina.
Set down your vehicle, or I'm afraid I'll have to blow it *and* you out of the sky.
-yawn-
What... what did I miss?
He's bluffing.
He wouldn't risk hurting his *fiancée*. He's just--
TRAKOOM

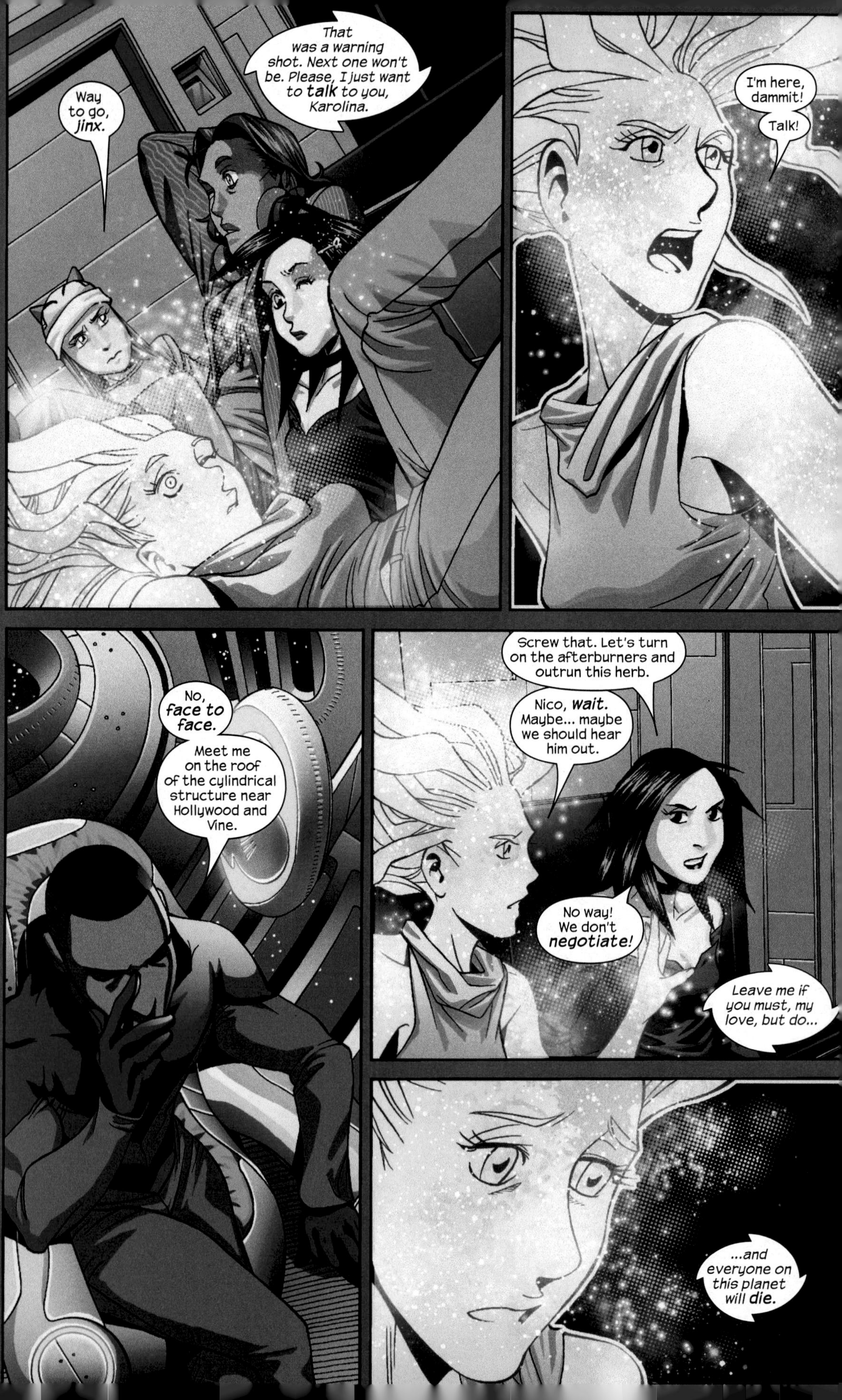
Way to go, *jinx.*
That was a warning shot. Next one won't be. Please, I just want to **talk** to you, Karolina.
I'm here, dammit!
Talk!
No, **face to face.**
Meet me on the roof of the cylindrical structure near Hollywood and Vine.
Screw that. Let's turn on the afterburners and outrun this herb.
Nico, **wait.** Maybe... maybe we should hear him out.
No way! We don't **negotiate!**
Leave me if you must, my love, but do...
...and everyone on this planet will **die.**

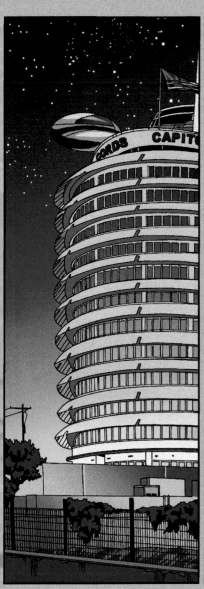

Karolina, can't... can't we have a moment *alone*?

Whatever you have to say to me, you can say it in front of them.

And feel free to turn all green and scaly, but I'm warning you right now, that routine doesn't exactly *scare* us.

RRRRRRR

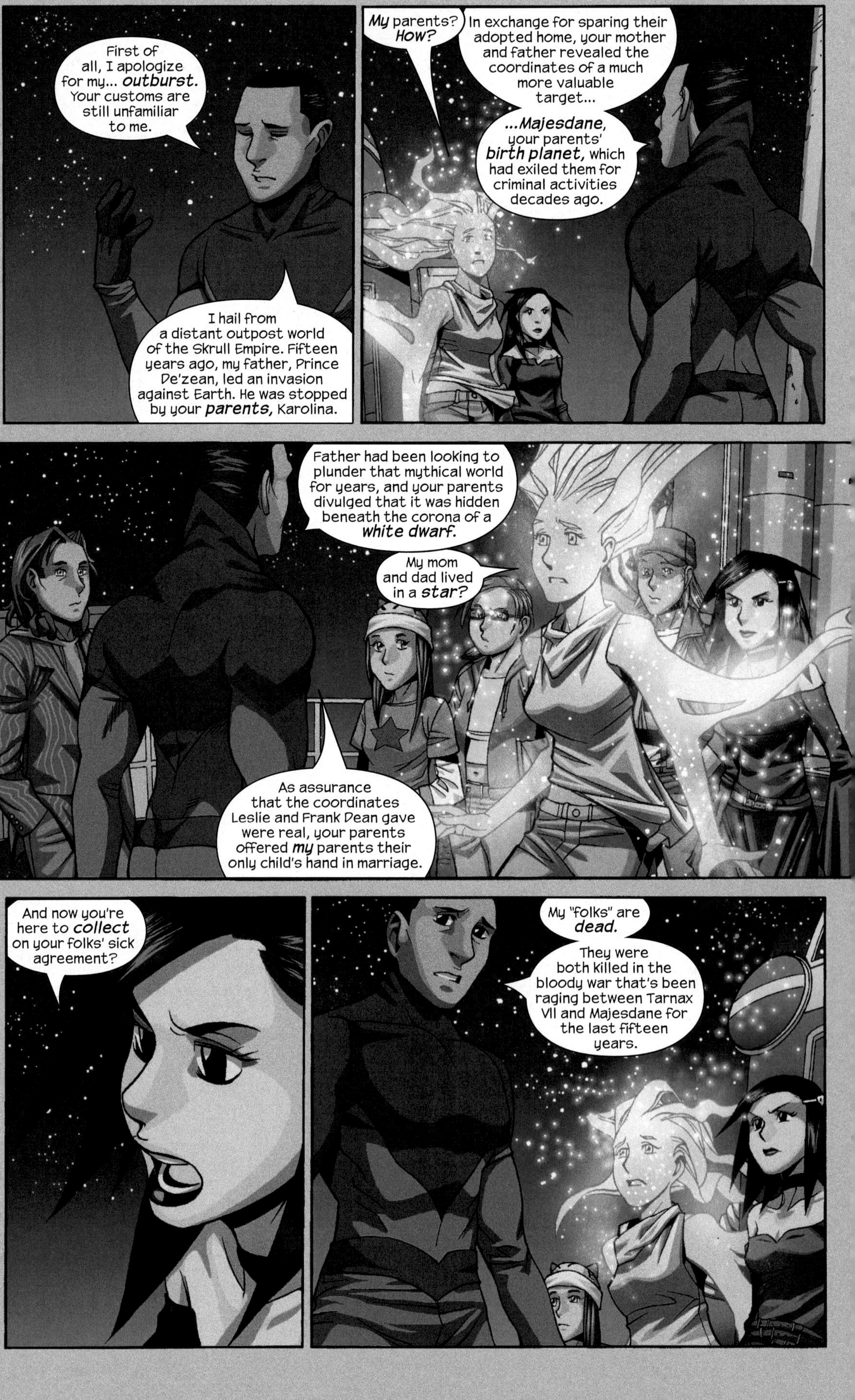
First of all, I apologize for my... outburst. Your customs are still unfamiliar to me.
I hail from a distant outpost world of the Skrull Empire. Fifteen years ago, my father, Prince De'zean, led an invasion against Earth. He was stopped by your parents, Karolina.
My parents? How?
In exchange for sparing their adopted home, your mother and father revealed the coordinates of a much more valuable target...
...Majesdane, your parents' birth planet, which had exiled them for criminal activities decades ago.
Father had been looking to plunder that mythical world for years, and your parents divulged that it was hidden beneath the corona of a white dwarf.
My mom and dad lived in a star?
As assurance that the coordinates Leslie and Frank Dean gave were real, your parents offered my parents their only child's hand in marriage.
And now you're here to collect on your folks' sick agreement?
My "folks" are dead.
They were both killed in the bloody war that's been raging between Tarnax VII and Majesdane for the last fifteen years.

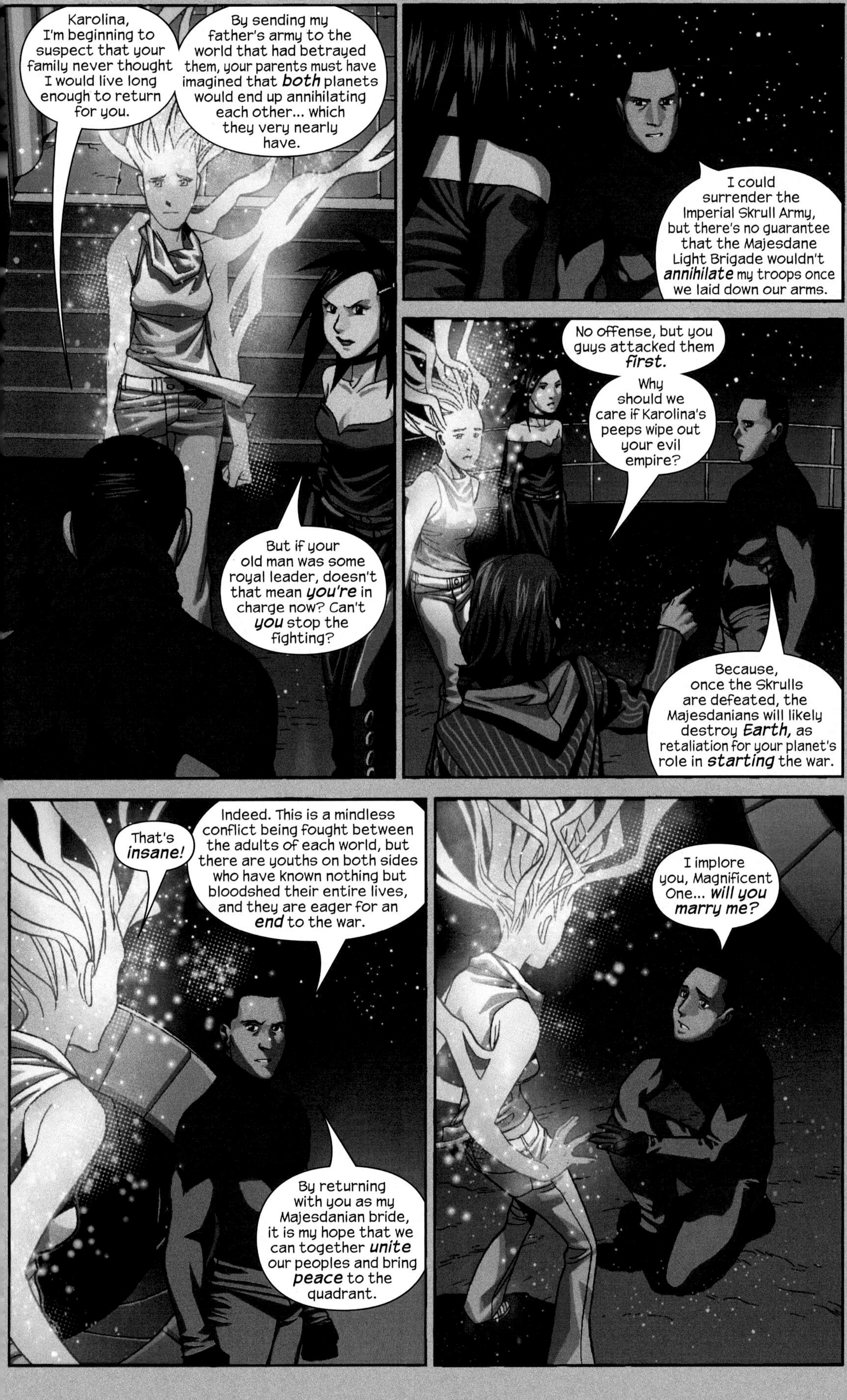

Karolina, I'm beginning to suspect that your family never thought I would live long enough to return for you.
By sending my father's army to the world that had betrayed them, your parents must have imagined that *both* planets would end up annihilating each other... which they very nearly have.
But if your old man was some royal leader, doesn't that mean *you're* in charge now? Can't *you* stop the fighting?
I could surrender the Imperial Skrull Army, but there's no guarantee that the Majesdane Light Brigade wouldn't *annihilate* my troops once we laid down our arms.
No offense, but you guys attacked them *first.*
Why should we care if Karolina's peeps wipe out your evil empire?
Because, once the Skrulls are defeated, the Majesdanians will likely destroy *Earth,* as retaliation for your planet's role in *starting* the war.
That's *insane!*
Indeed. This is a mindless conflict being fought between the adults of each world, but there are youths on both sides who have known nothing but bloodshed their entire lives, and they are eager for an *end* to the war.
By returning with you as my Majesdanian bride, it is my hope that we can together *unite* our peoples and bring *peace* to the quadrant.
I implore you, Magnificent One... *will you marry me?*

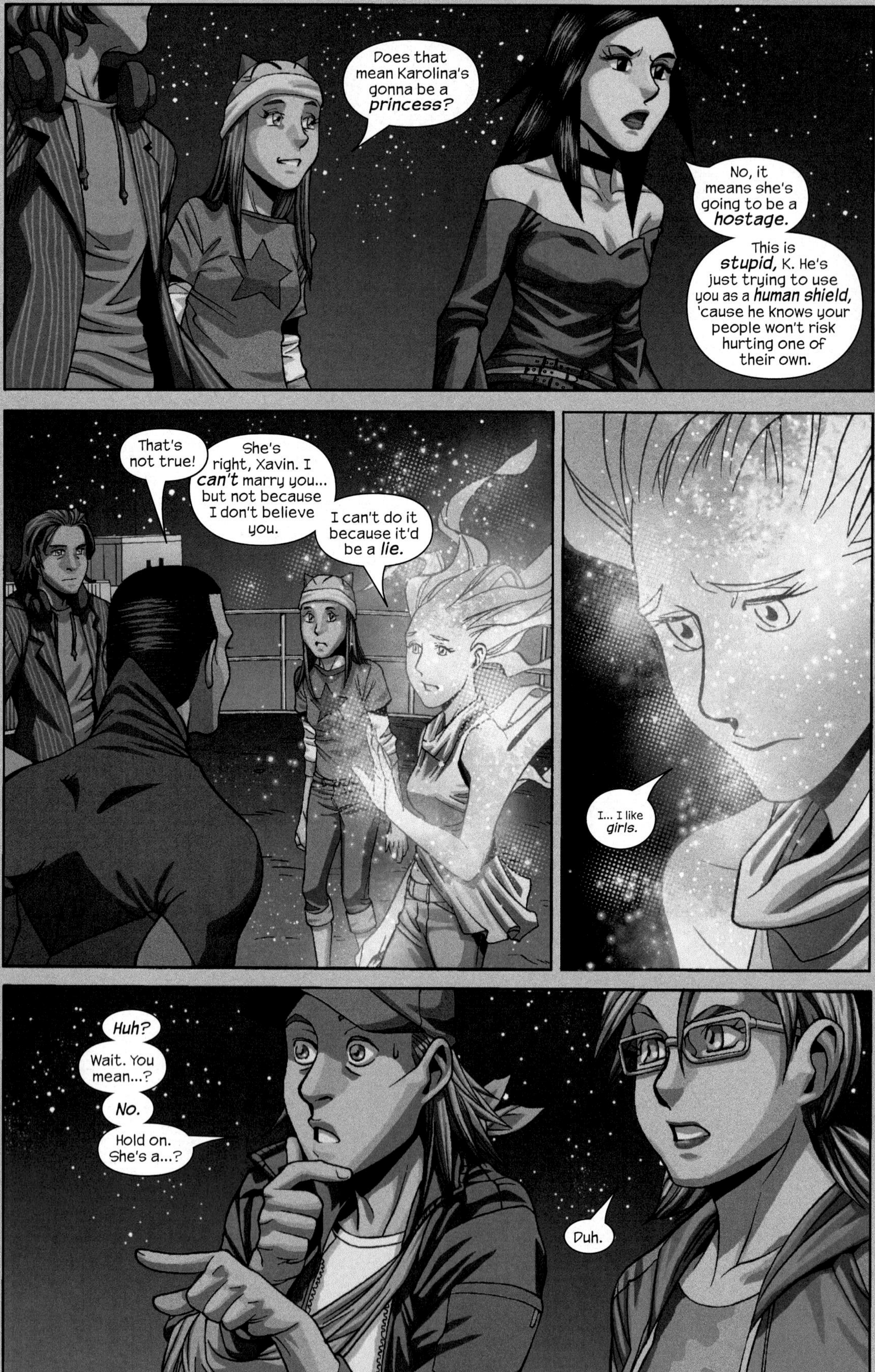
Does that mean Karolina's gonna be a *princess?*
No, it means she's going to be a **hostage.**
This is **stupid,** K. He's just trying to use you as a **human shield,** 'cause he knows your people won't risk hurting one of their own.
That's not true!
She's right, Xavin. I **can't** marry you... but not because I don't believe you.
I can't do it because it'd be a *lie.*
I... I like *girls.*
Huh?
Wait. You mean...?
No.
Hold on. She's a...?
Duh.

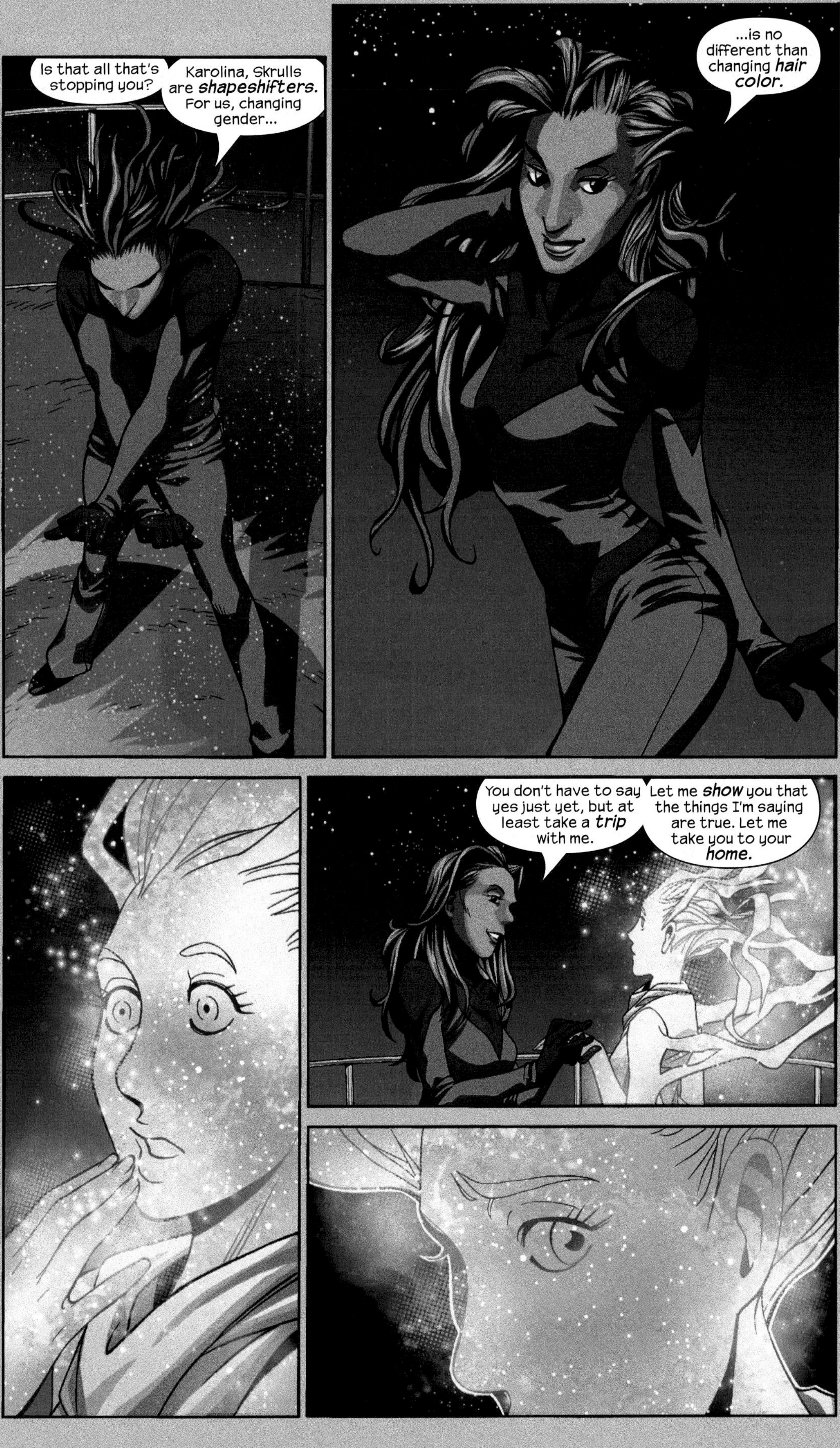
Is that all that's stopping you?
Karolina, Skrulls are shapeshifters. For us, changing gender...
...is no different than changing hair color.
You don't have to say yes just yet, but at least take a trip with me.
Let me show you that the things I'm saying are true. Let me take you to your home.

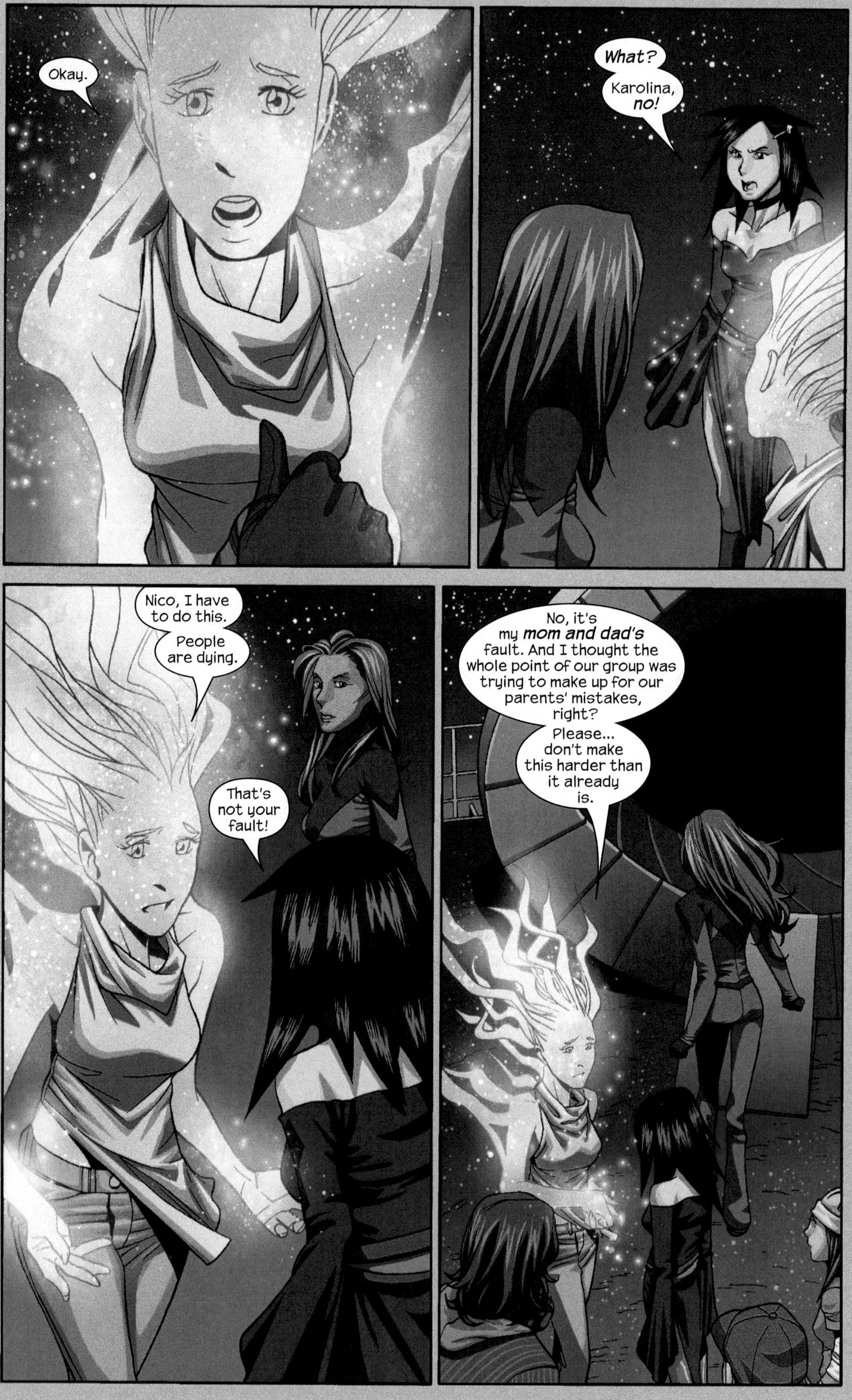
Okay.
What?
Karolina, no!
Nico, I have to do this.
People are dying.
That's not your fault!
No, it's my mom and dad's fault. And I thought the whole point of our group was trying to make up for our parents' mistakes, right?
Please... don't make this harder than it already is.

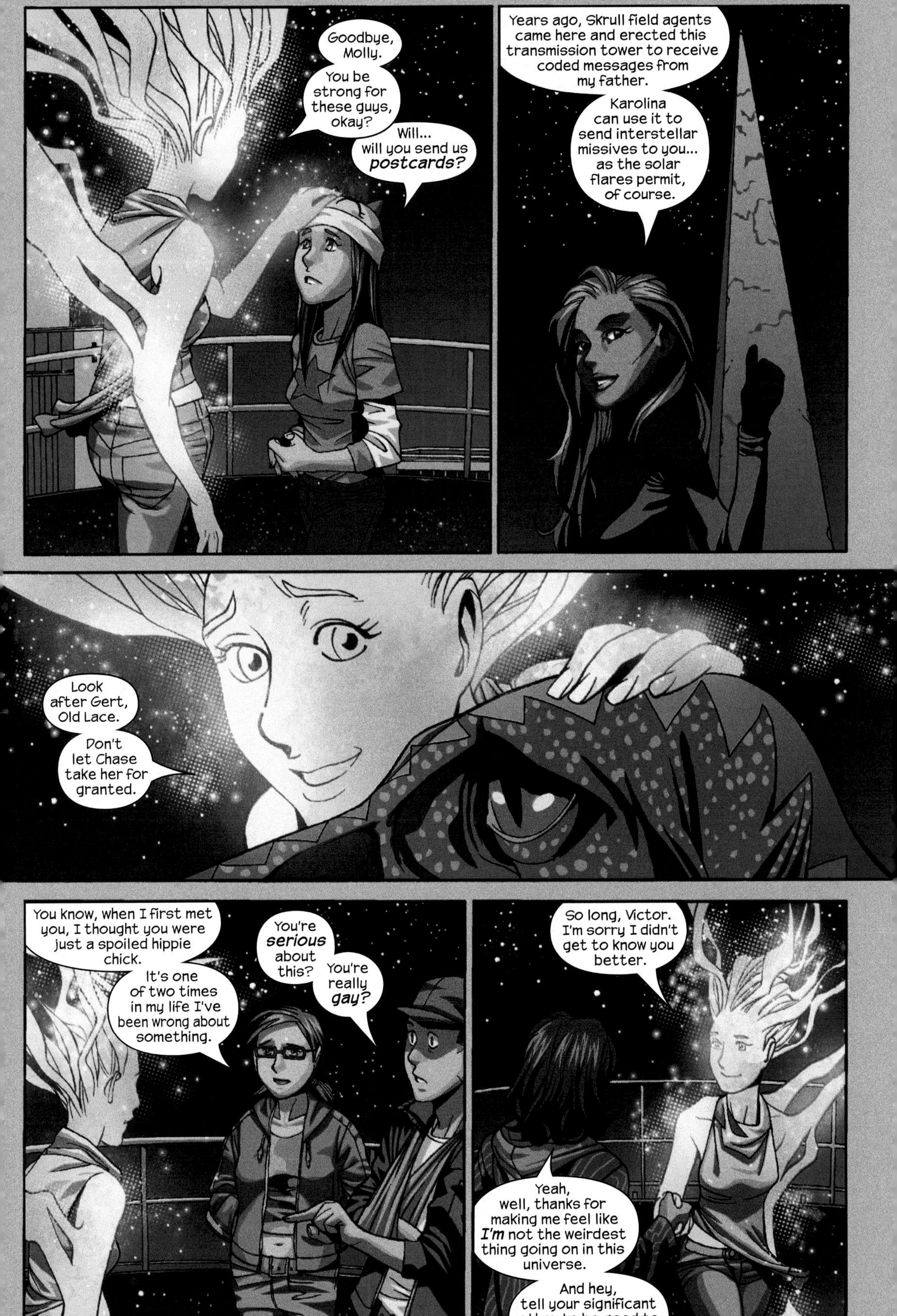
Goodbye, Molly.
You be strong for these guys, okay?
Will... will you send us postcards?
Years ago, Skrull field agents came here and erected this transmission tower to receive coded messages from my father.
Karolina can use it to send interstellar missives to you... as the solar flares permit, of course.
Look after Gert, Old Lace.
Don't let Chase take her for granted.
You know, when I first met you, I thought you were just a spoiled hippie chick.
It's one of two times in my life I've been wrong about something.
You're serious about this?
You're really gay?
So long, Victor. I'm sorry I didn't get to know you better.
Yeah, well, thanks for making me feel like I'm not the weirdest thing going on in this universe.
And hey, tell your significant other to be good to his/her 'bots, cool?

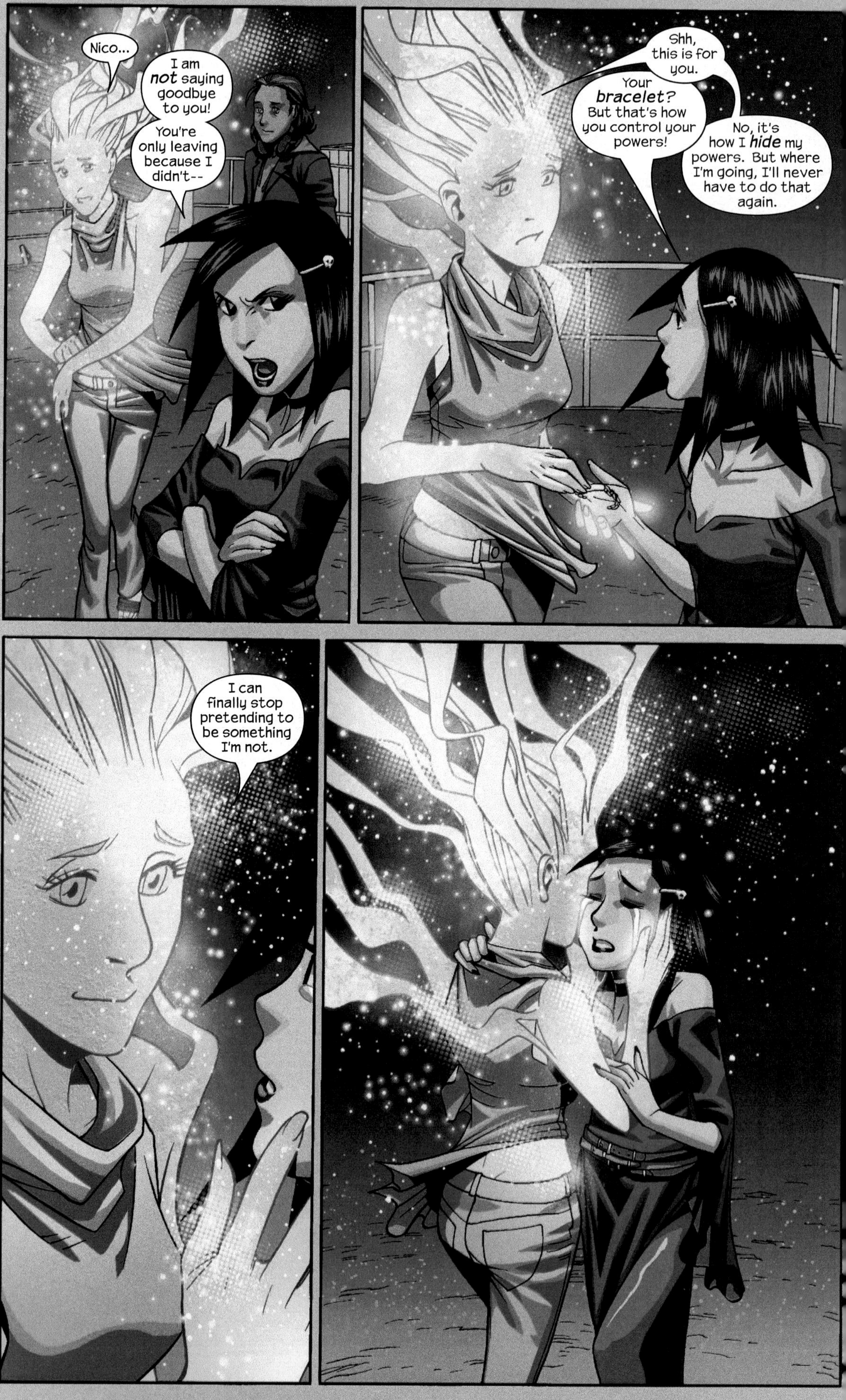

Nico...
I am not saying goodbye to you!
You're only leaving because I didn't--
Shh, this is for you.
Your bracelet? But that's how you control your powers!
No, it's how I hide my powers. But where I'm going, I'll never have to do that again.
I can finally stop pretending to be something I'm not.

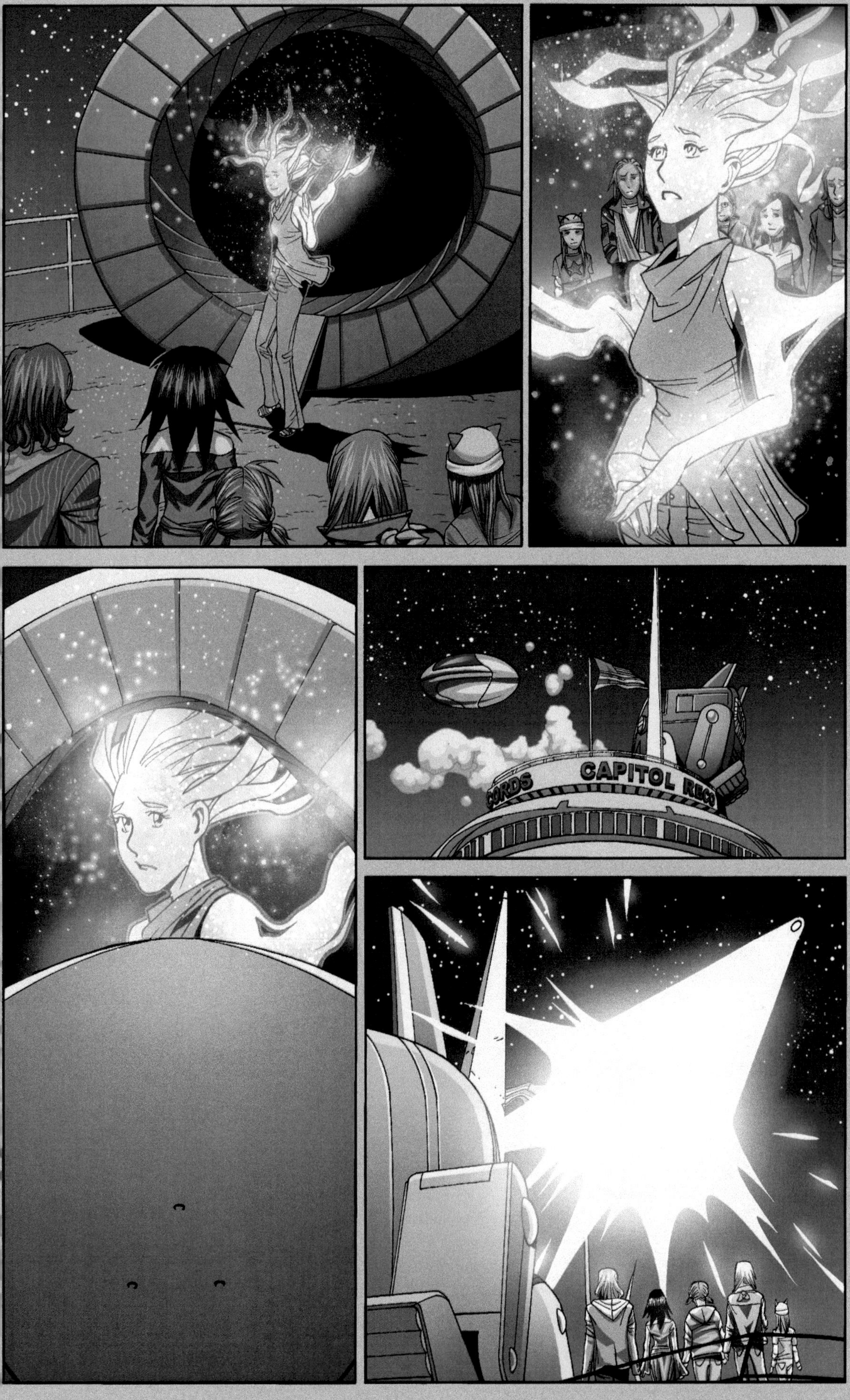
CORDS
CAPITOL RECO

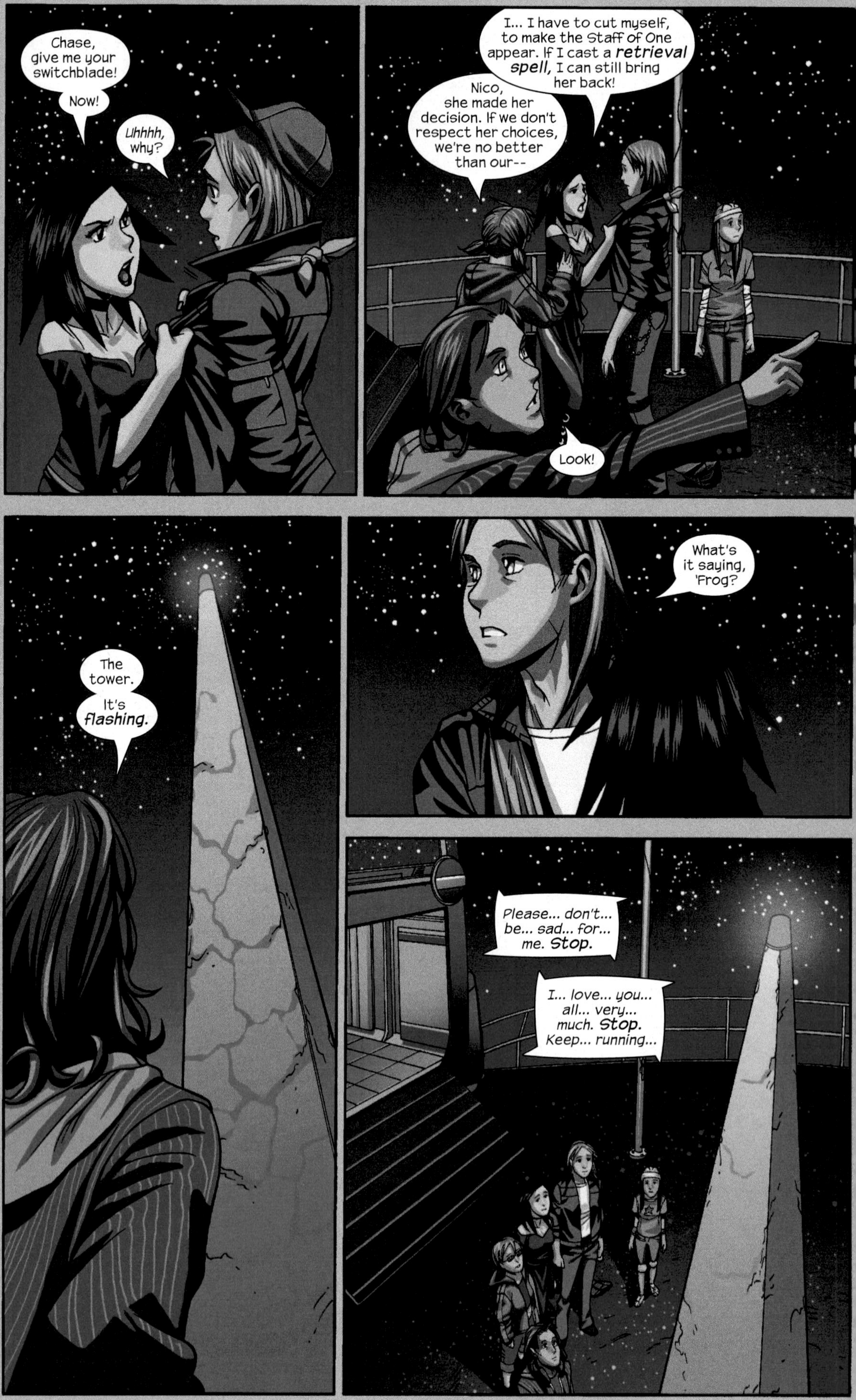

Chase, give me your switchblade!
Now!
Uhhhh, why?
I... I have to cut myself, to make the Staff of One appear. If I cast a ***retrieval spell,*** I can still bring her back!
Nico, she made her decision. If we don't respect her choices, we're no better than our--
Look!
The tower. It's *flashing.*
What's it saying, 'Frog?
Please... don't... be... sad... for... me. ***Stop.***
I... love... you... all... very... much. ***Stop.*** *Keep... running...*

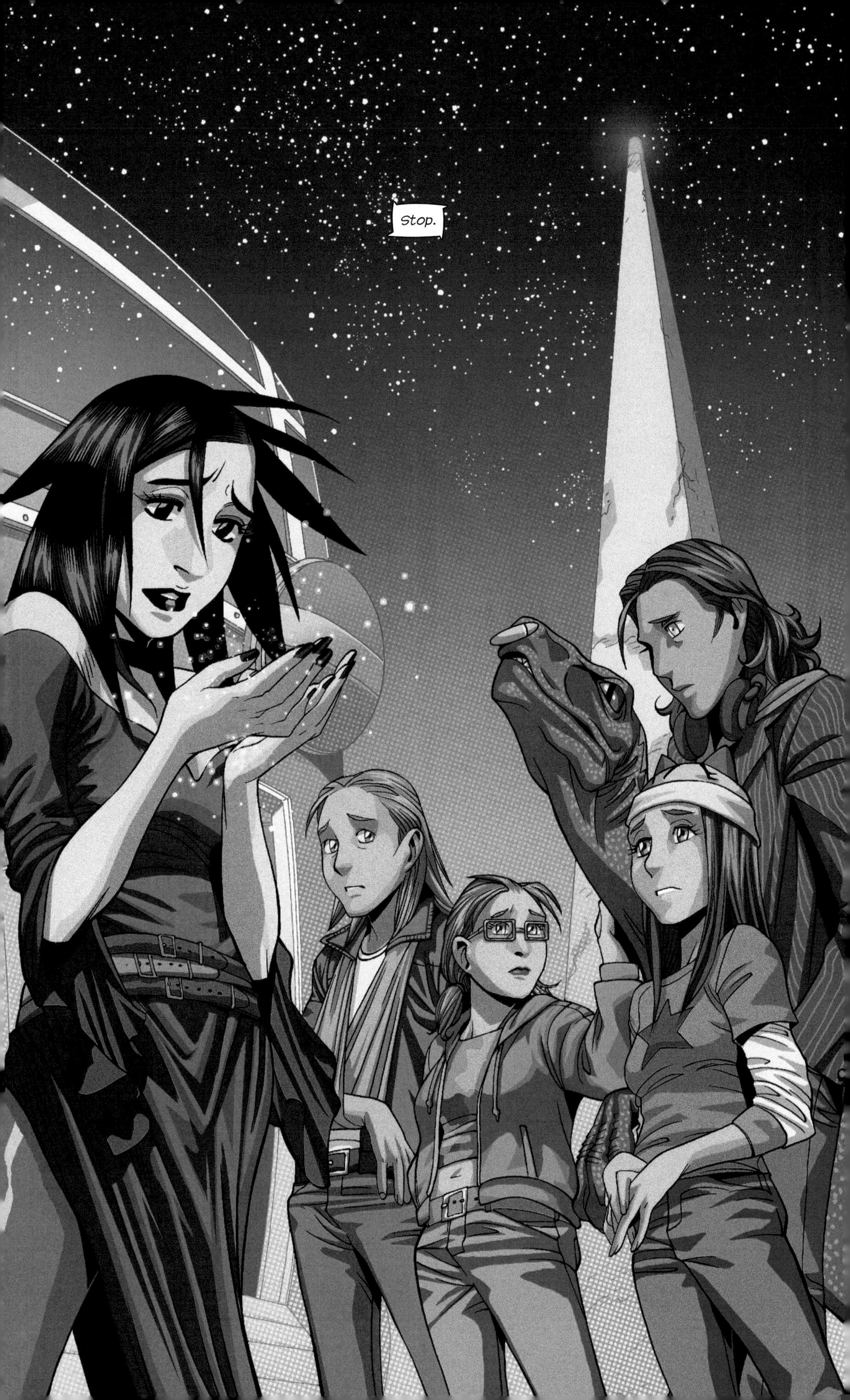
Stop.

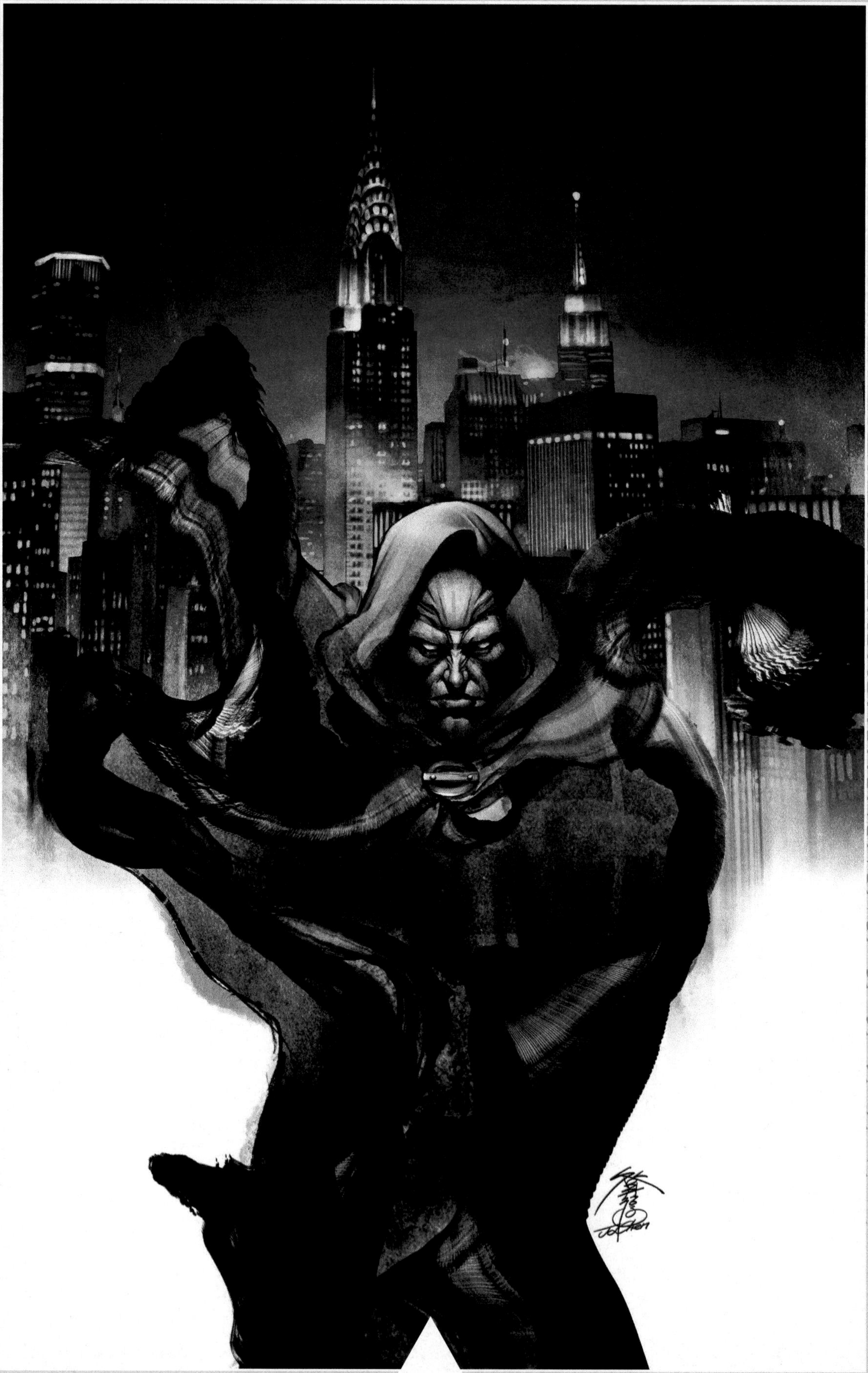

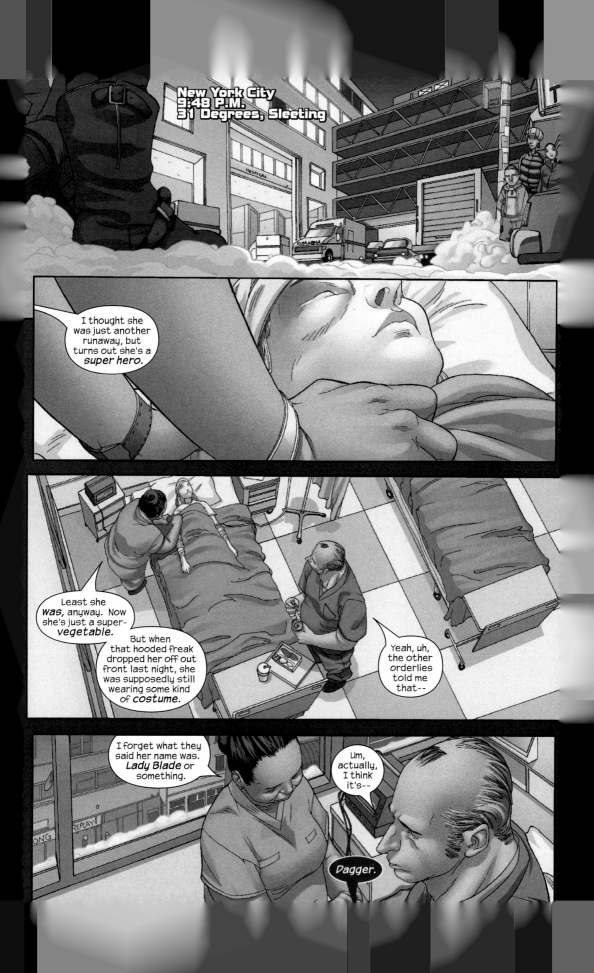

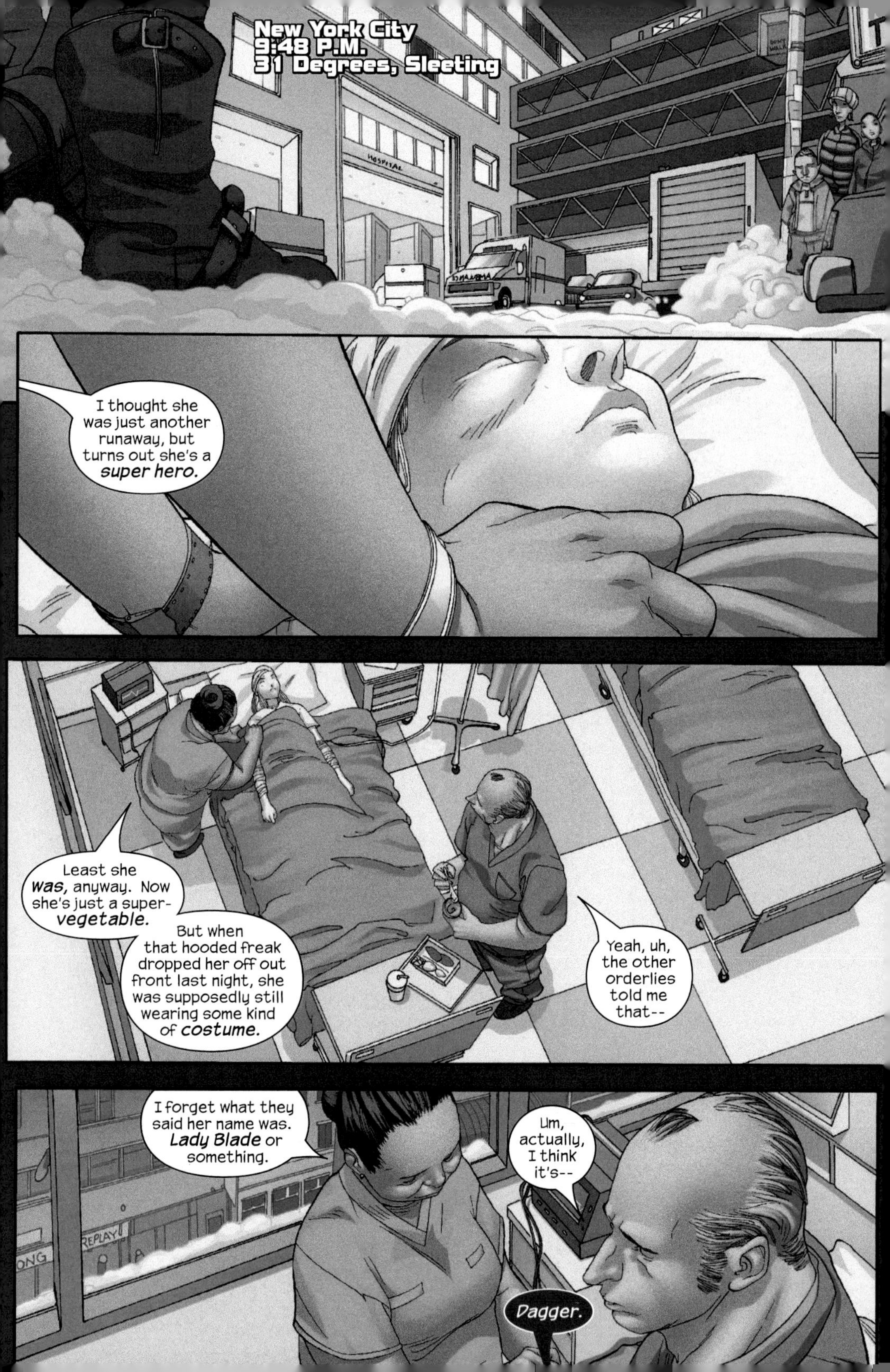
New York City
9:48 P.M.
31 Degrees, Sleeting
I thought she was just another runaway, but turns out she's a super hero.
Least she was, anyway. Now she's just a super-vegetable.
But when that hooded freak dropped her off out front last night, she was supposedly still wearing some kind of costume.
Yeah, uh, the other orderlies told me that--
I forget what they said her name was. Lady Blade or something.
Um, actually, I think it's--
Dagger.
REPLAY

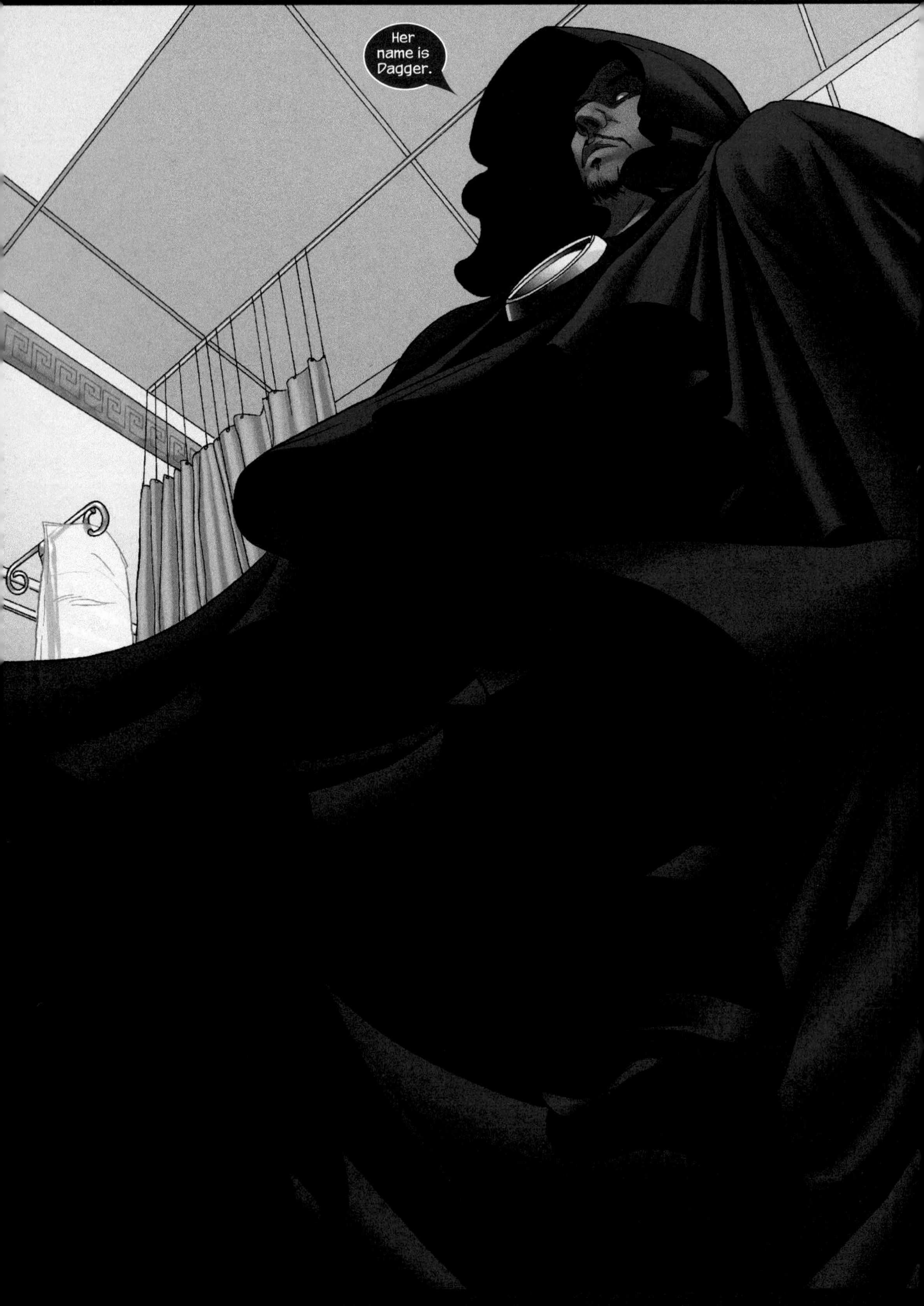
Her name is Dagger.

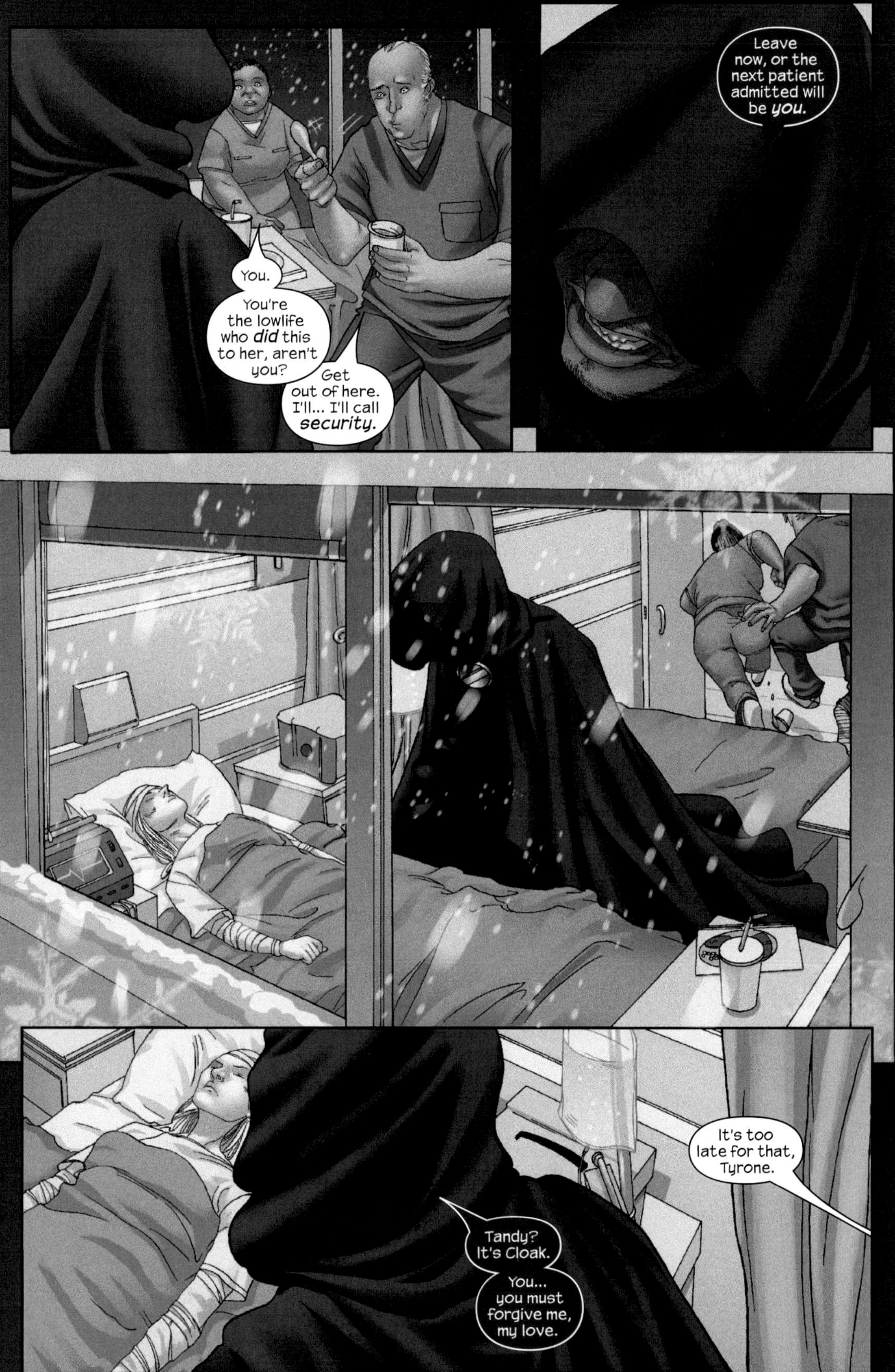
You.
You're the lowlife who *did* this to her, aren't you?
Get out of here. I'll... I'll call *security.*
Leave now, or the next patient admitted will be *you.*
Tandy? It's Cloak.
You... you must forgive me, my love.
It's too late for that, Tyrone.

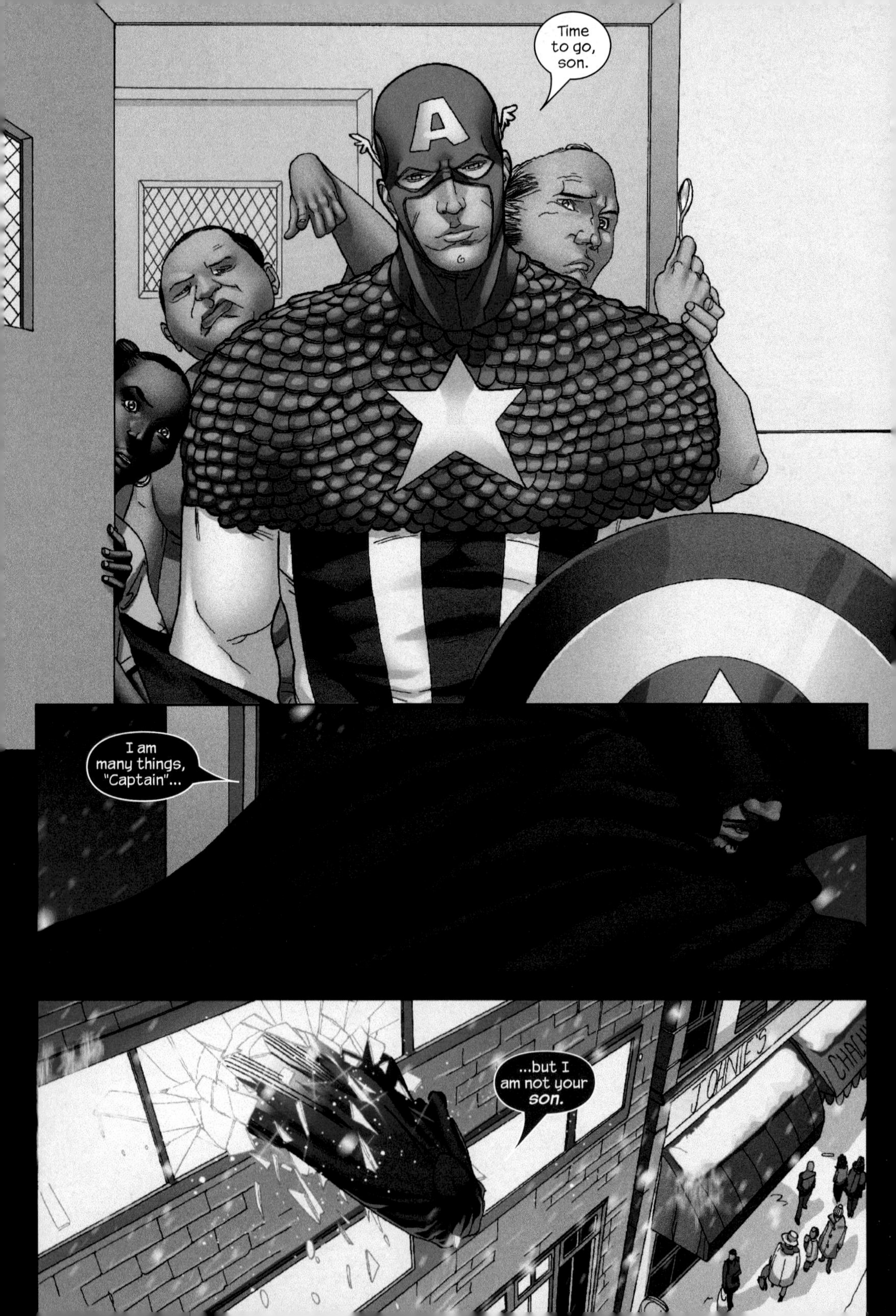
Time to go, son.
I am many things, "Captain"...
...but I am not your *son.*
JOHNIE'S

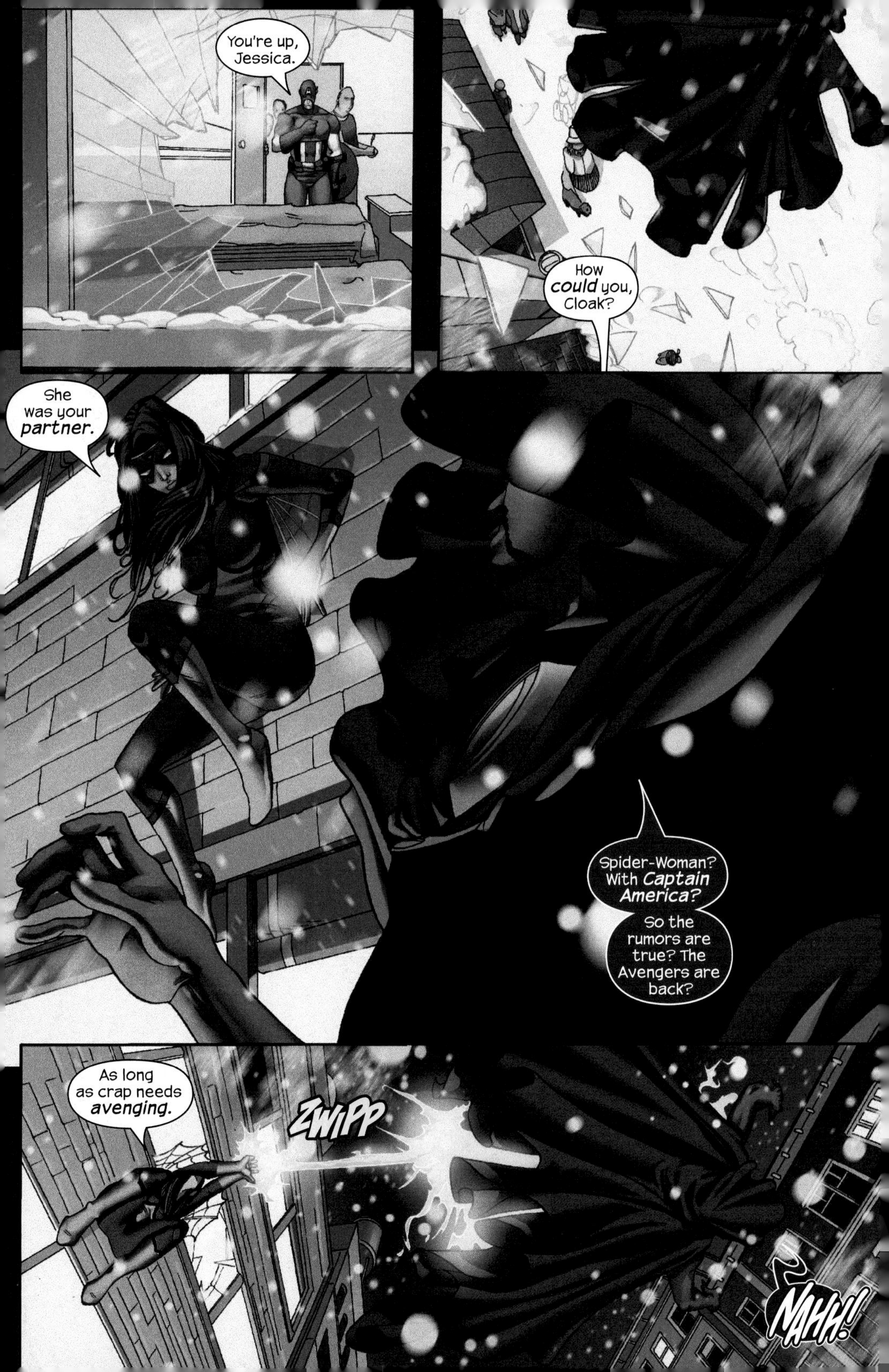
You're up, Jessica.
How could you, Cloak?
She was your partner.
Spider-Woman? With Captain America?
So the rumors are true? The Avengers are back?
As long as crap needs avenging.
ZWIPP
NAHH!

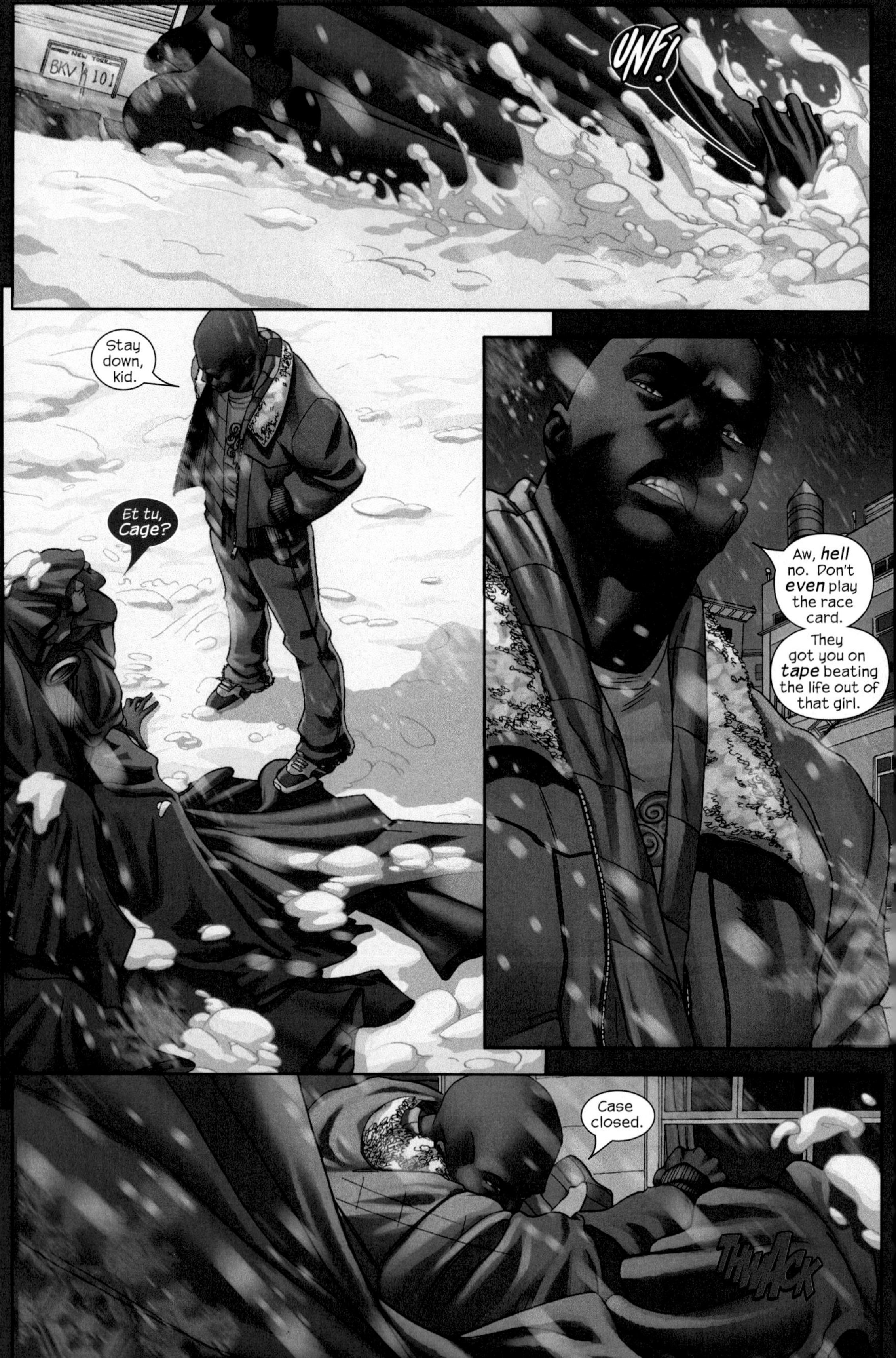
NEW YORK
BKV 101
UNF!
Stay down, kid.
Et tu, Cage?
Aw, hell no. Don't even play the race card.
They got you on tape beating the life out of that girl.
Case closed.
THWACK

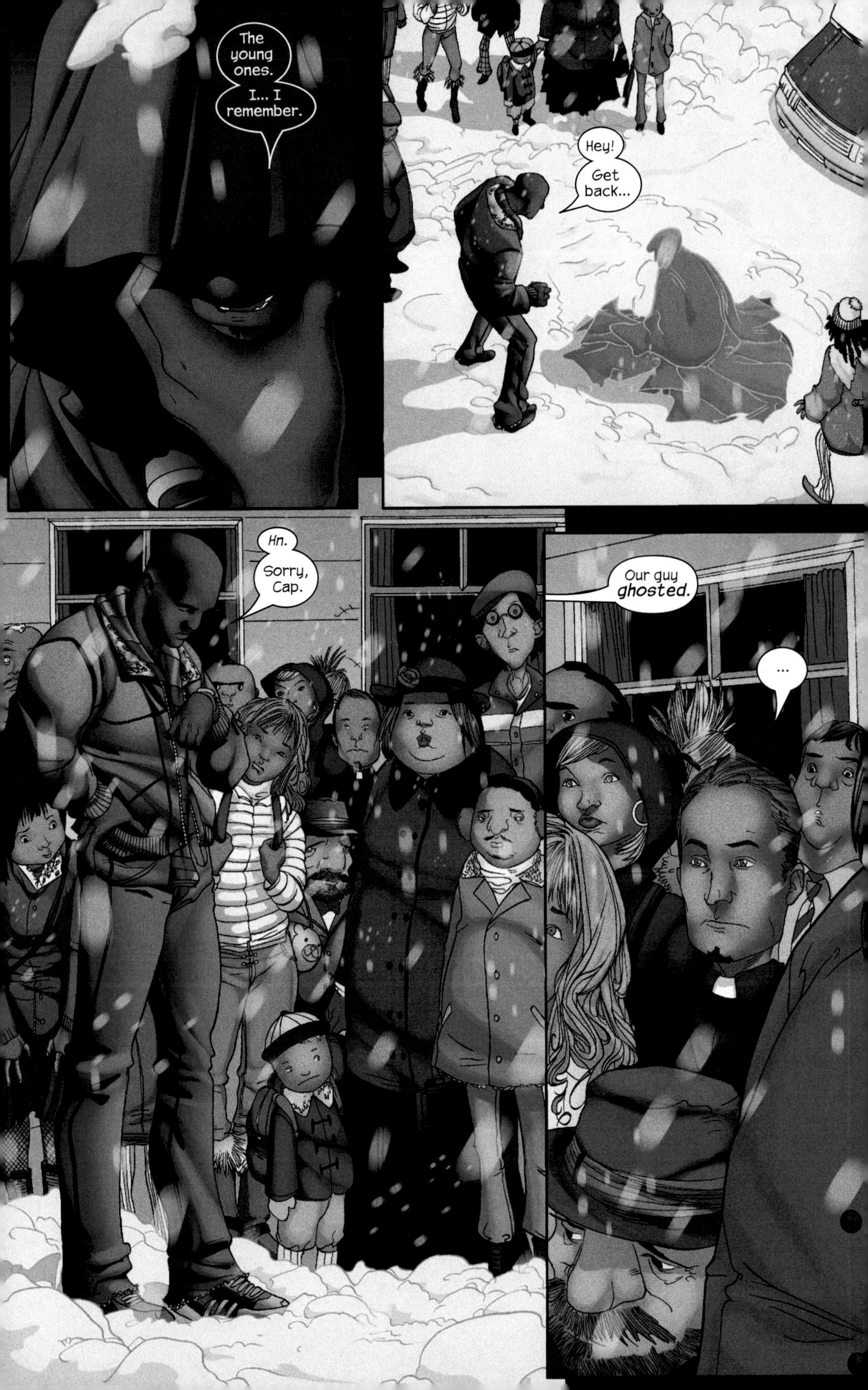
The young ones.
I... I remember.
Hey!
Get back...
Hn.
Sorry, Cap.
Our guy *ghosted*.
...

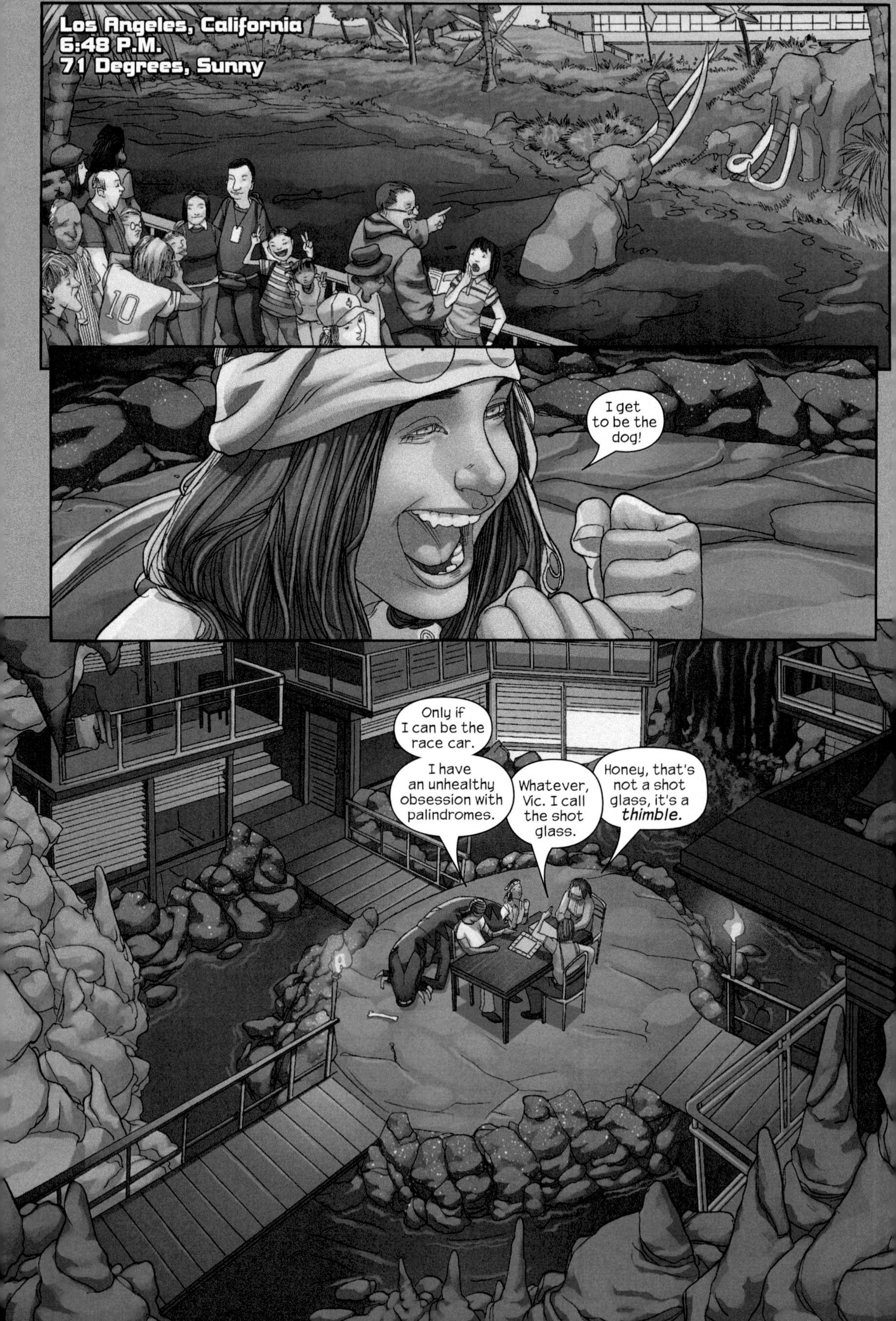
Los Angeles, California
6:48 P.M.
71 Degrees, Sunny
I get to be the dog!
Only if I can be the race car.
I have an unhealthy obsession with palindromes.
Whatever, Vic. I call the shot glass.
Honey, that's not a shot glass, it's a *thimble.*

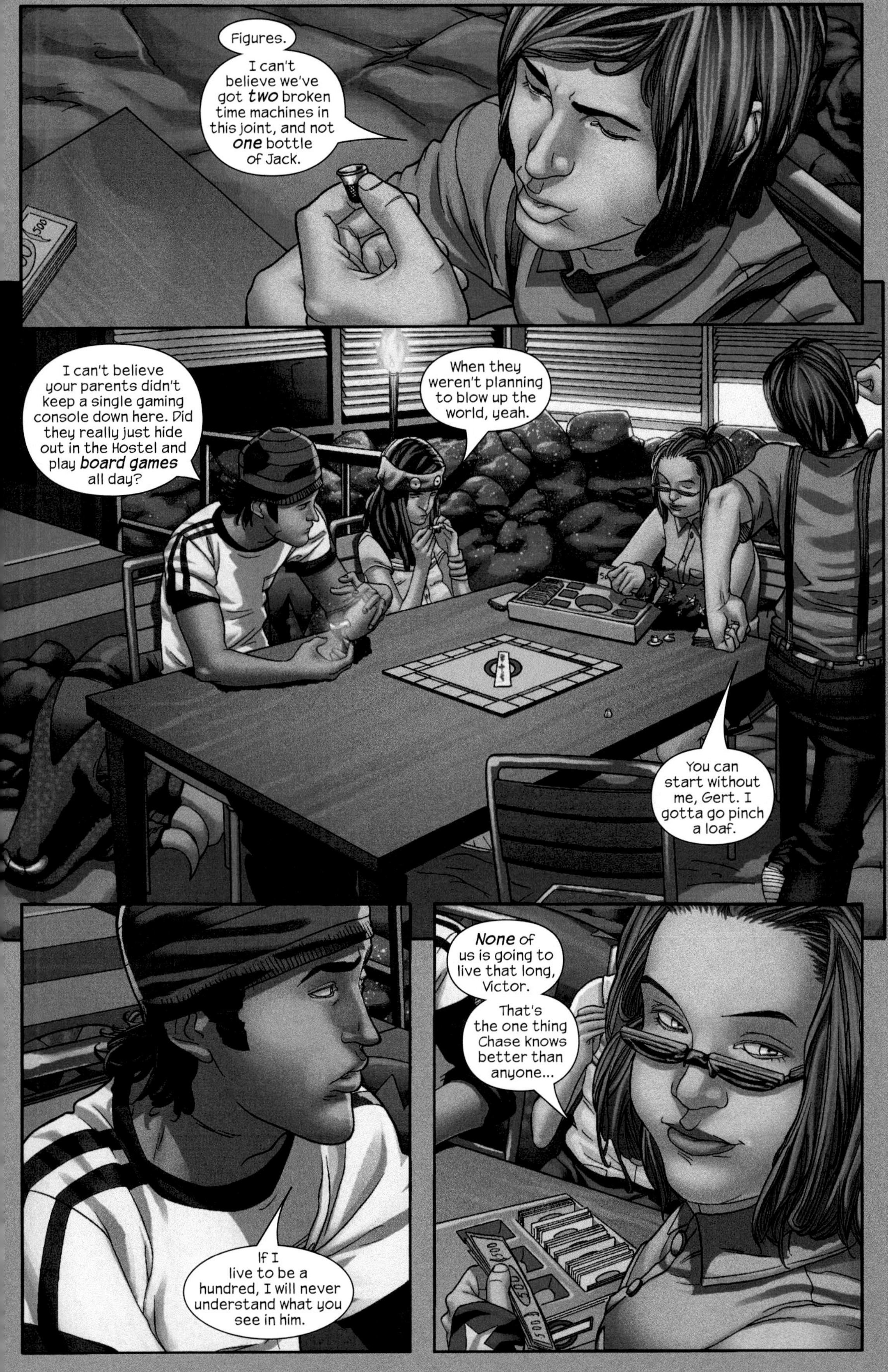
Figures.
I can't believe we've got *two* broken time machines in this joint, and not *one* bottle of Jack.
I can't believe your parents didn't keep a single gaming console down here. Did they really just hide out in the Hostel and play *board games* all day?
When they weren't planning to blow up the world, yeah.
You can start without me, Gert. I gotta go pinch a loaf.
If I live to be a hundred, I will never understand what you see in him.
None of us is going to live that long, Victor.
That's the one thing Chase knows better than anyone...

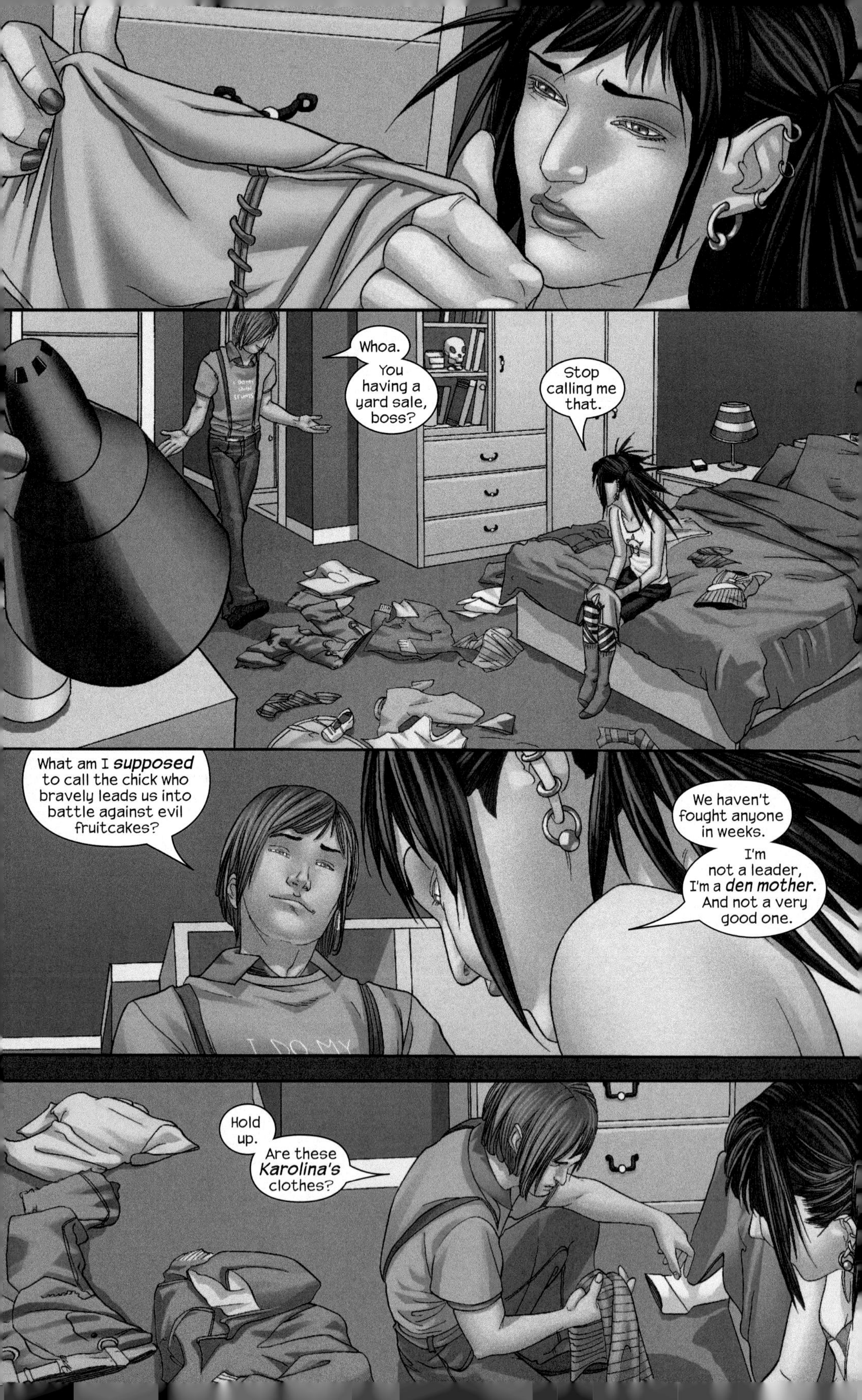
Whoa.
You having a yard sale, boss?
Stop calling me that.
What am I *supposed* to call the chick who bravely leads us into battle against evil fruitcakes?
We haven't fought anyone in weeks.
I'm not a leader, I'm a *den mother.* And not a very good one.
Hold up.
Are these *Karolina's* clothes?

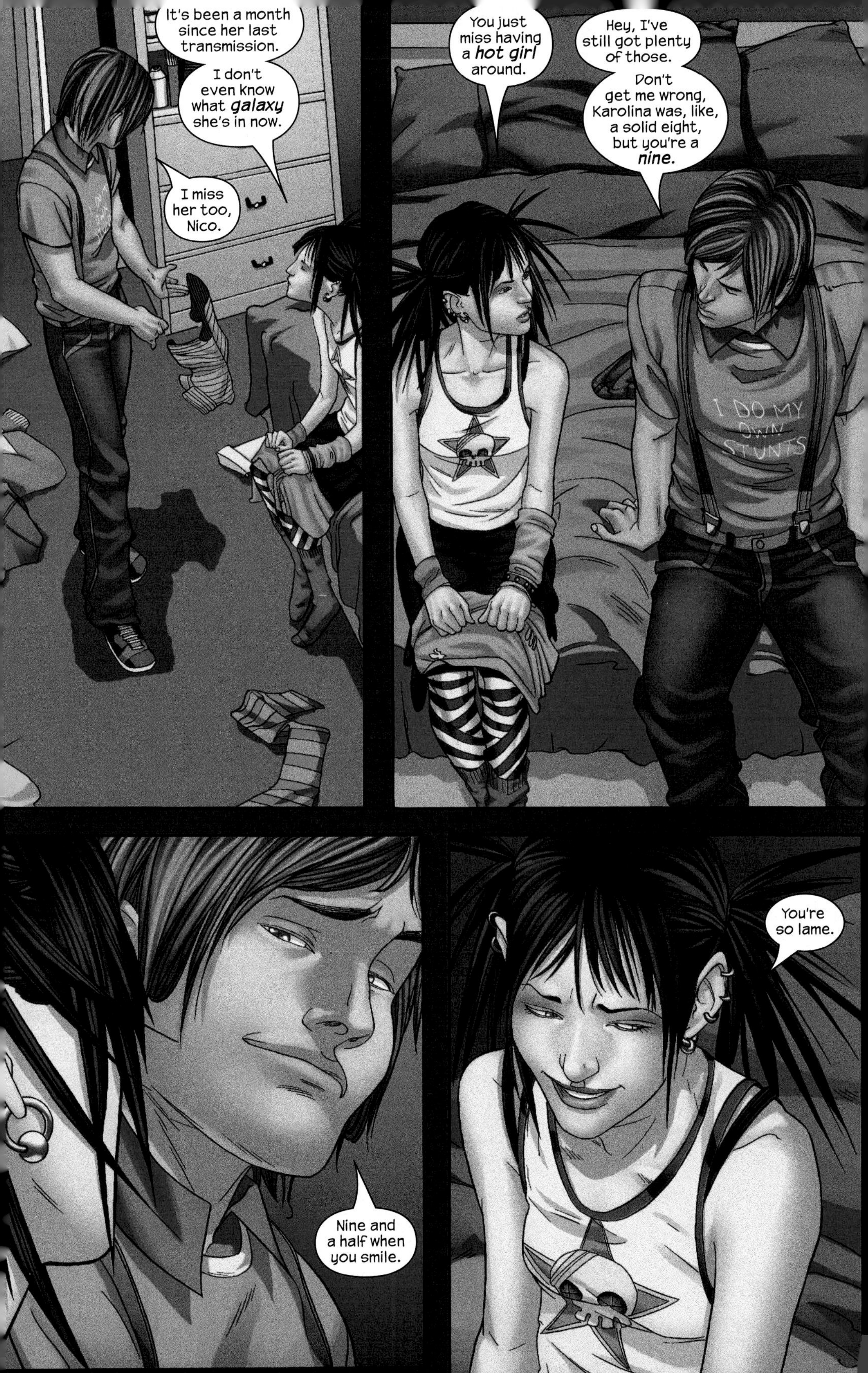
It's been a month since her last transmission.
I don't even know what *galaxy* she's in now.
I miss her too, Nico.
You just miss having a *hot girl* around.
Hey, I've still got plenty of those.
Don't get me wrong, Karolina was, like, a solid eight, but you're a *nine.*
I DO MY OWN STUNTS
Nine and a half when you smile.
You're so lame.

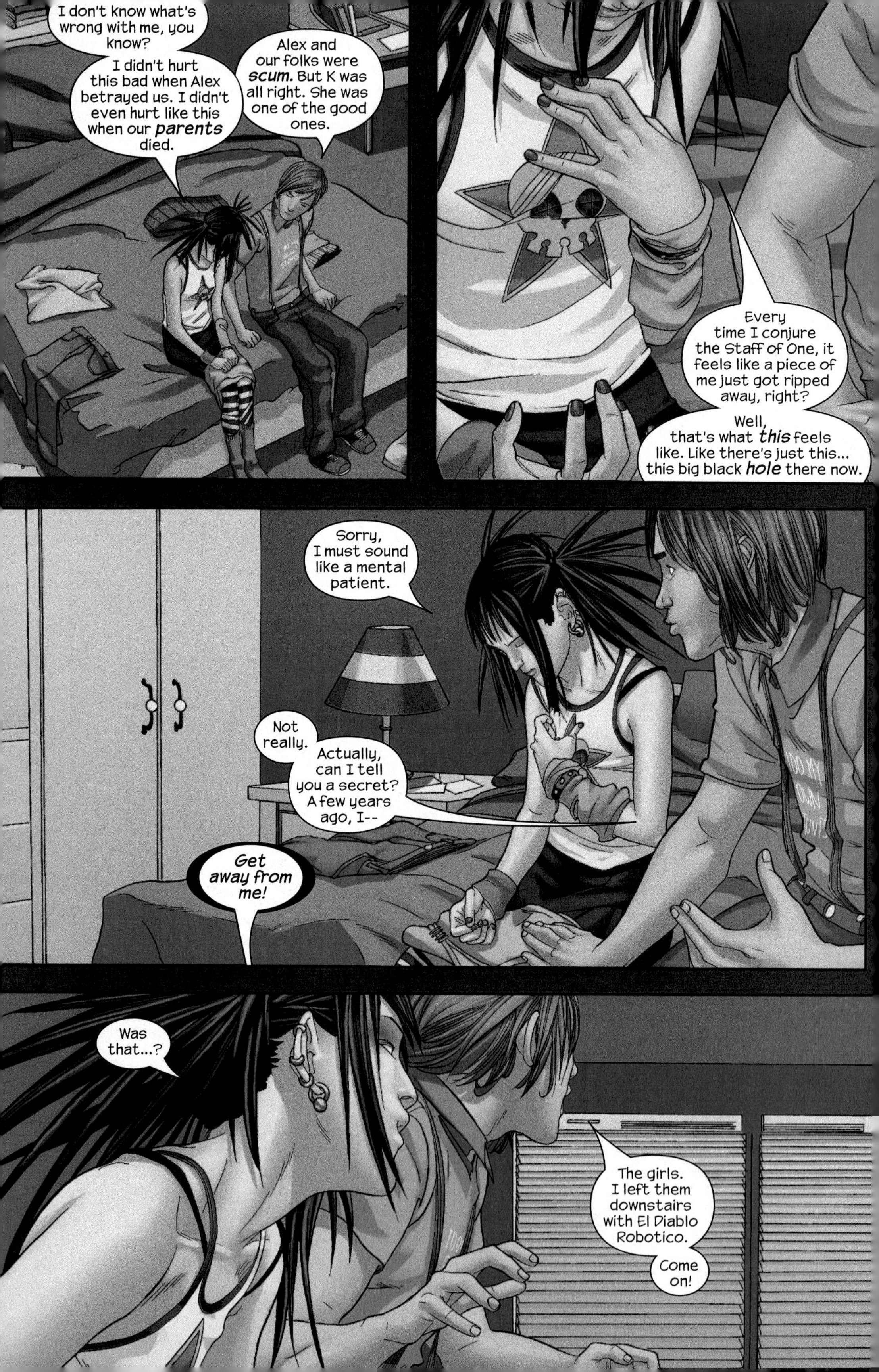
I don't know what's wrong with me, you know?
I didn't hurt this bad when Alex betrayed us. I didn't even hurt like this when our *parents* died.
Alex and our folks were *scum.* But K was all right. She was one of the good ones.
Every time I conjure the Staff of One, it feels like a piece of me just got ripped away, right?
Well, that's what *this* feels like. Like there's just this... this big black *hole* there now.
Sorry, I must sound like a mental patient.
Not really.
Actually, can I tell you a secret? A few years ago, I--
Get away from me!
Was that...?
The girls. I left them downstairs with El Diablo Robotico.
Come on!

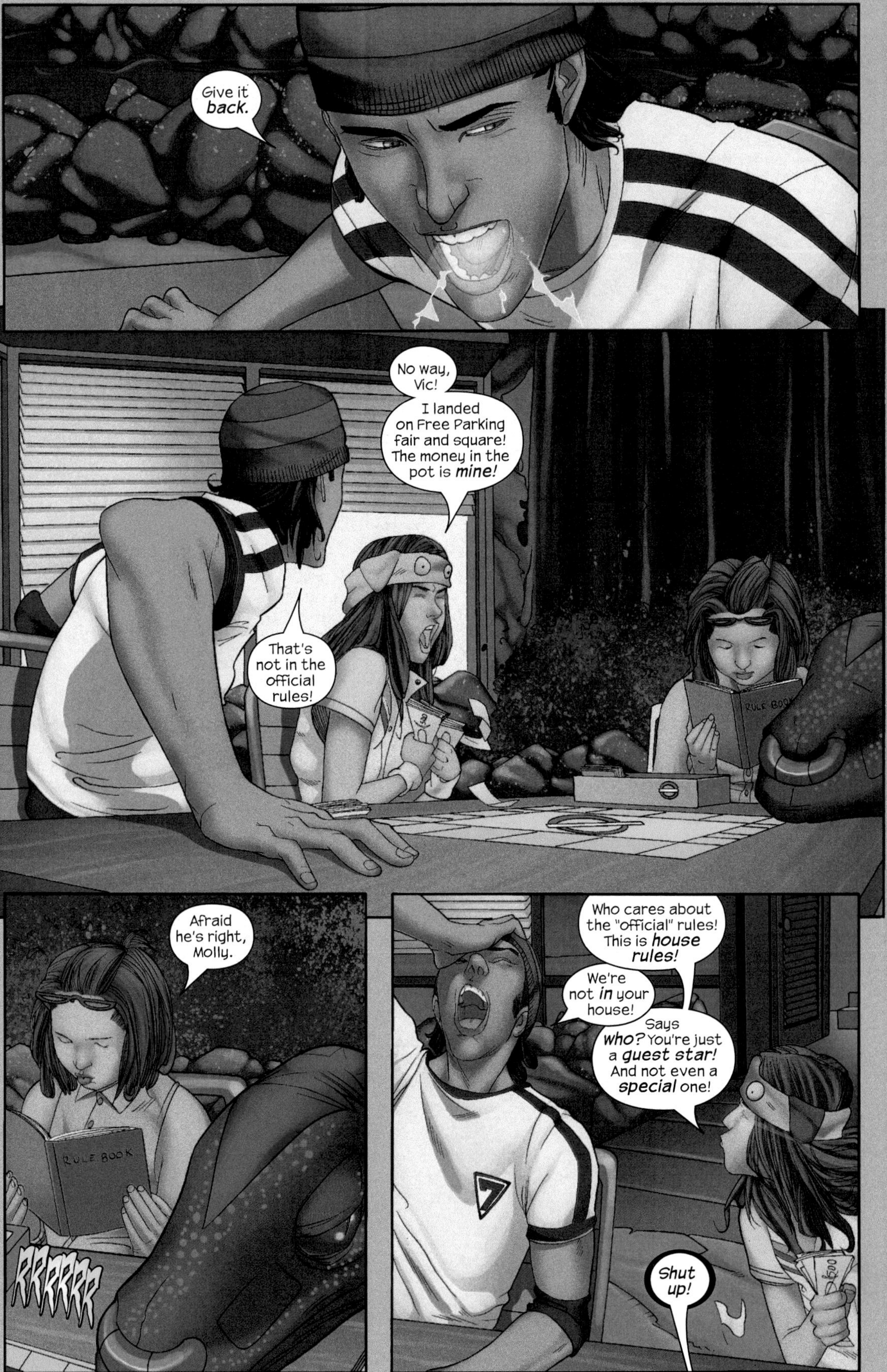

Give it *back.*
No way, Vic!
I landed on Free Parking fair and square! The money in the pot is *mine!*
That's not in the official rules!
RULE BOOK
Afraid he's right, Molly.
RULE BOOK
RRRRRR
Who cares about the "official" rules! This is *house rules!*
We're not *in* your house!
Says *who?* You're just a *guest star!* And not even a *special* one!
Shut up!

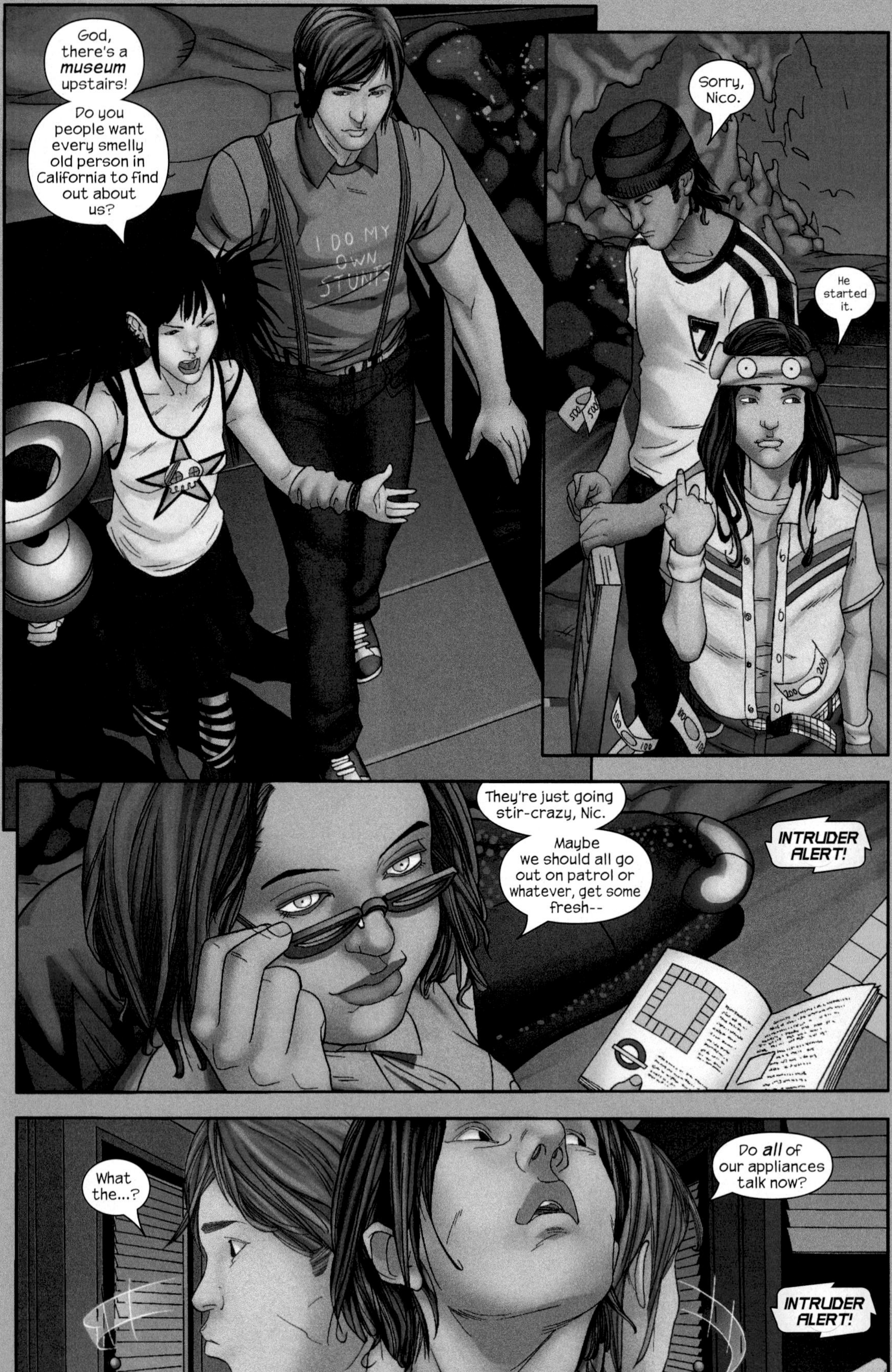

God, there's a *museum* upstairs!
Do you people want every smelly old person in California to find out about us?
I DO MY OWN STUNTS
Sorry, Nico.
He started it.
They're just going stir-crazy, Nic.
Maybe we should all go out on patrol or whatever, get some fresh--
INTRUDER ALERT!
What the...?
Do *all* of our appliances talk now?
INTRUDER ALERT!

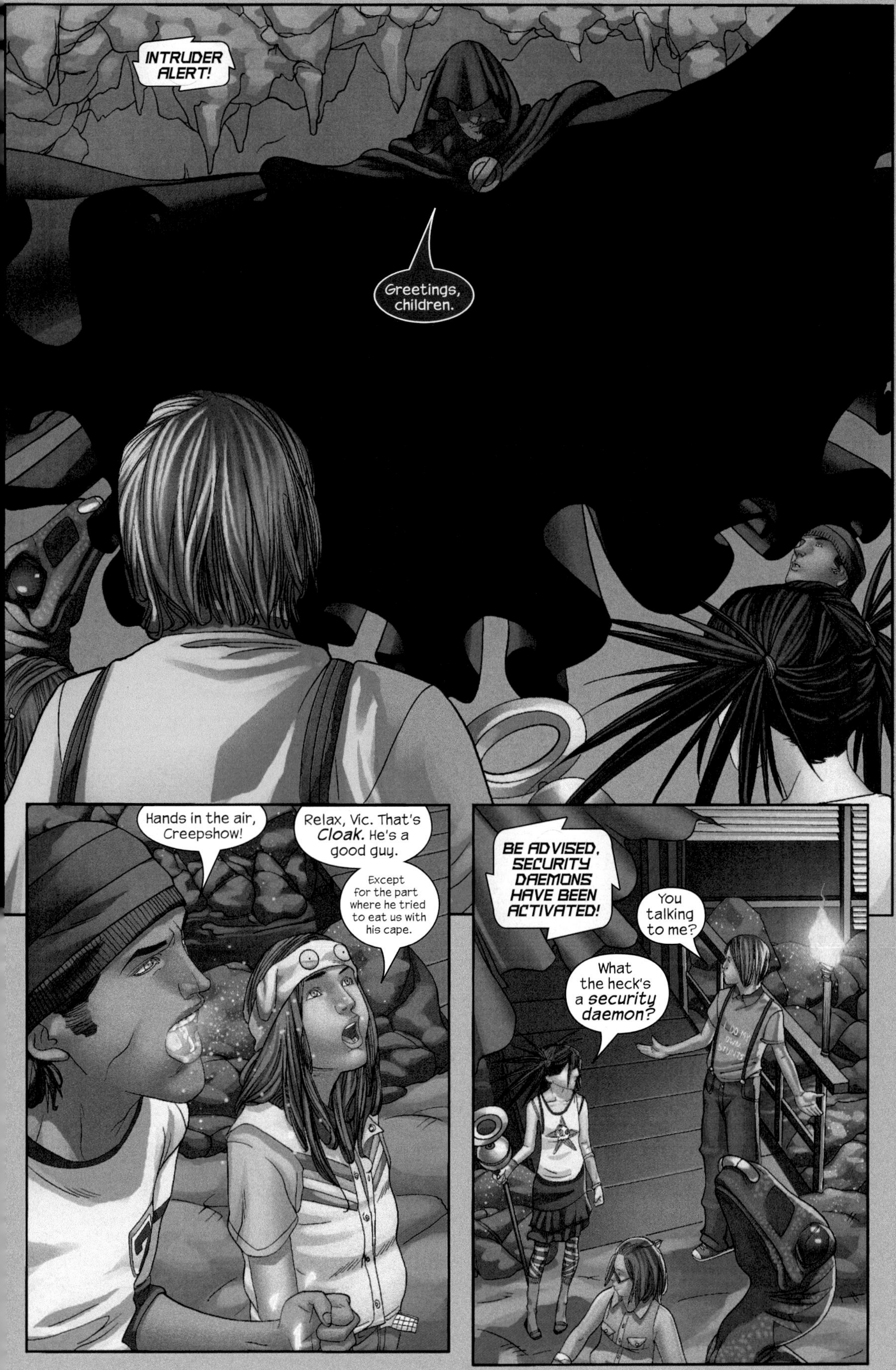
INTRUDER ALERT!
Greetings, children.
Hands in the air, Creepshow!
Relax, Vic. That's *Cloak.* He's a good guy.
Except for the part where he tried to eat us with his cape.
BE ADVISED, SECURITY DAEMONS HAVE BEEN ACTIVATED!
You talking to me?
What the heck's a *security daemon?*

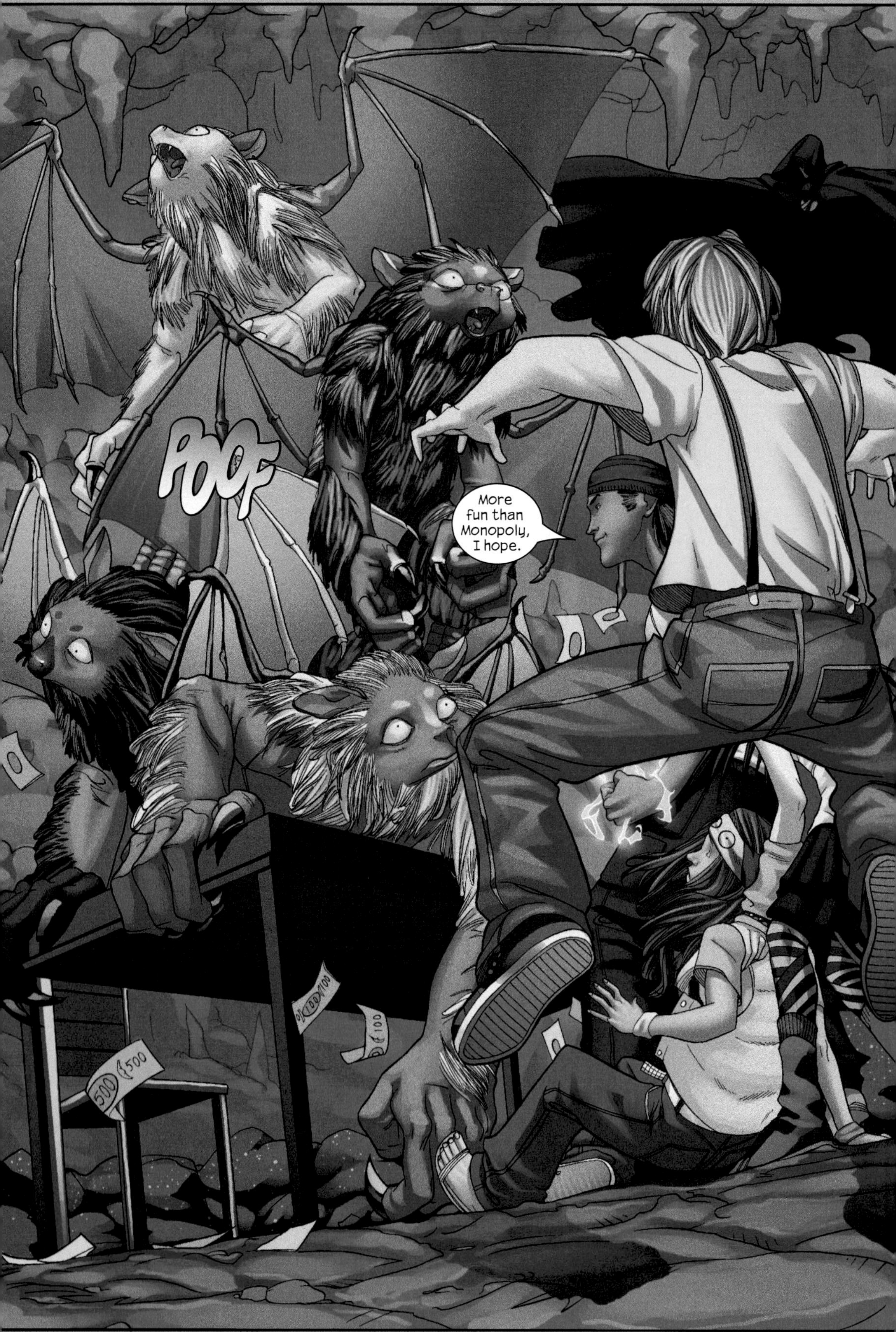
POOF
More fun than Monopoly, I hope.

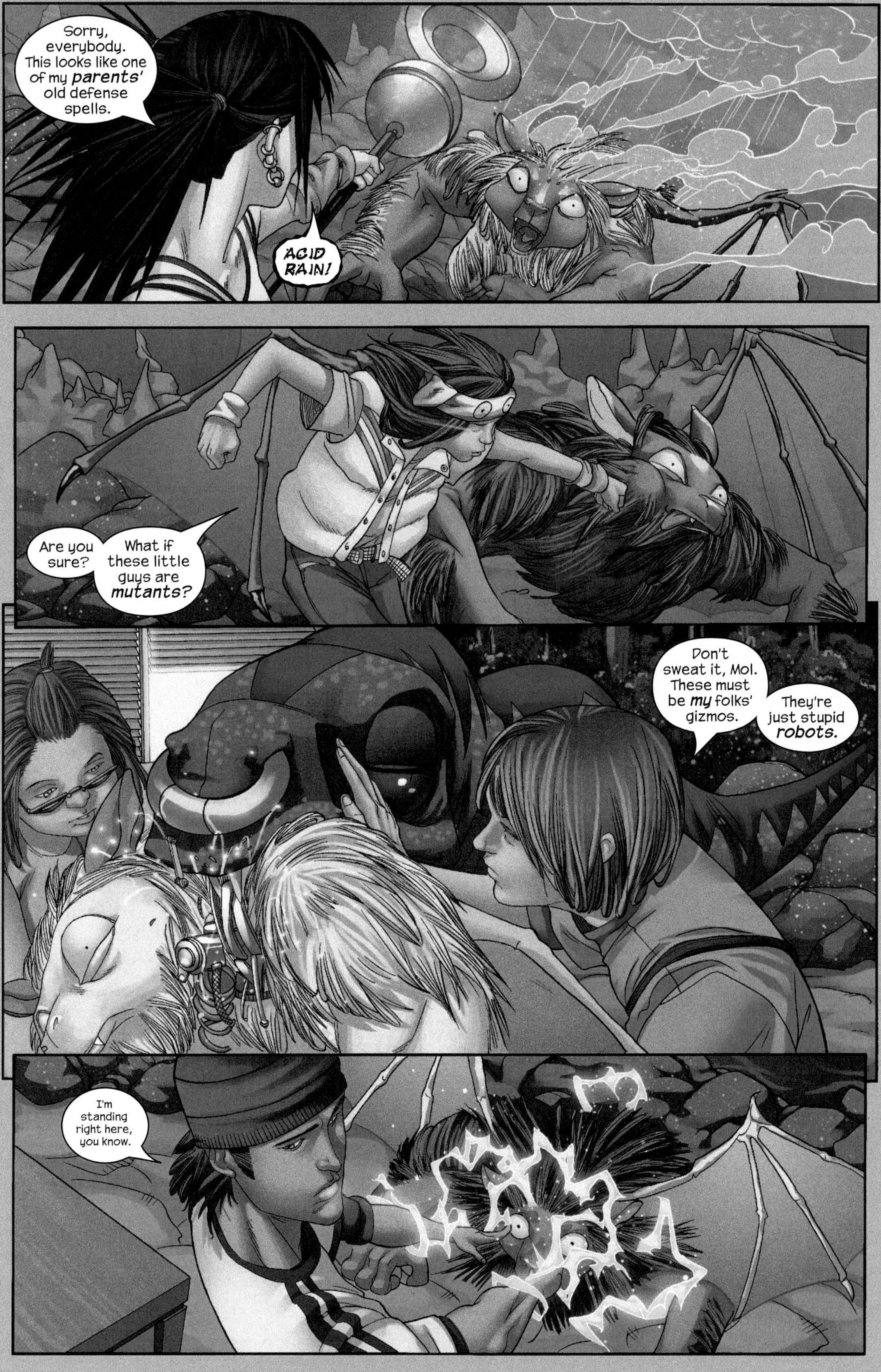
Sorry, everybody. This looks like one of my parents' old defense spells.
ACID RAIN!
Are you sure?
What if these little guys are mutants?
Don't sweat it, Mol. These must be my folks' gizmos.
They're just stupid robots.
I'm standing right here, you know.

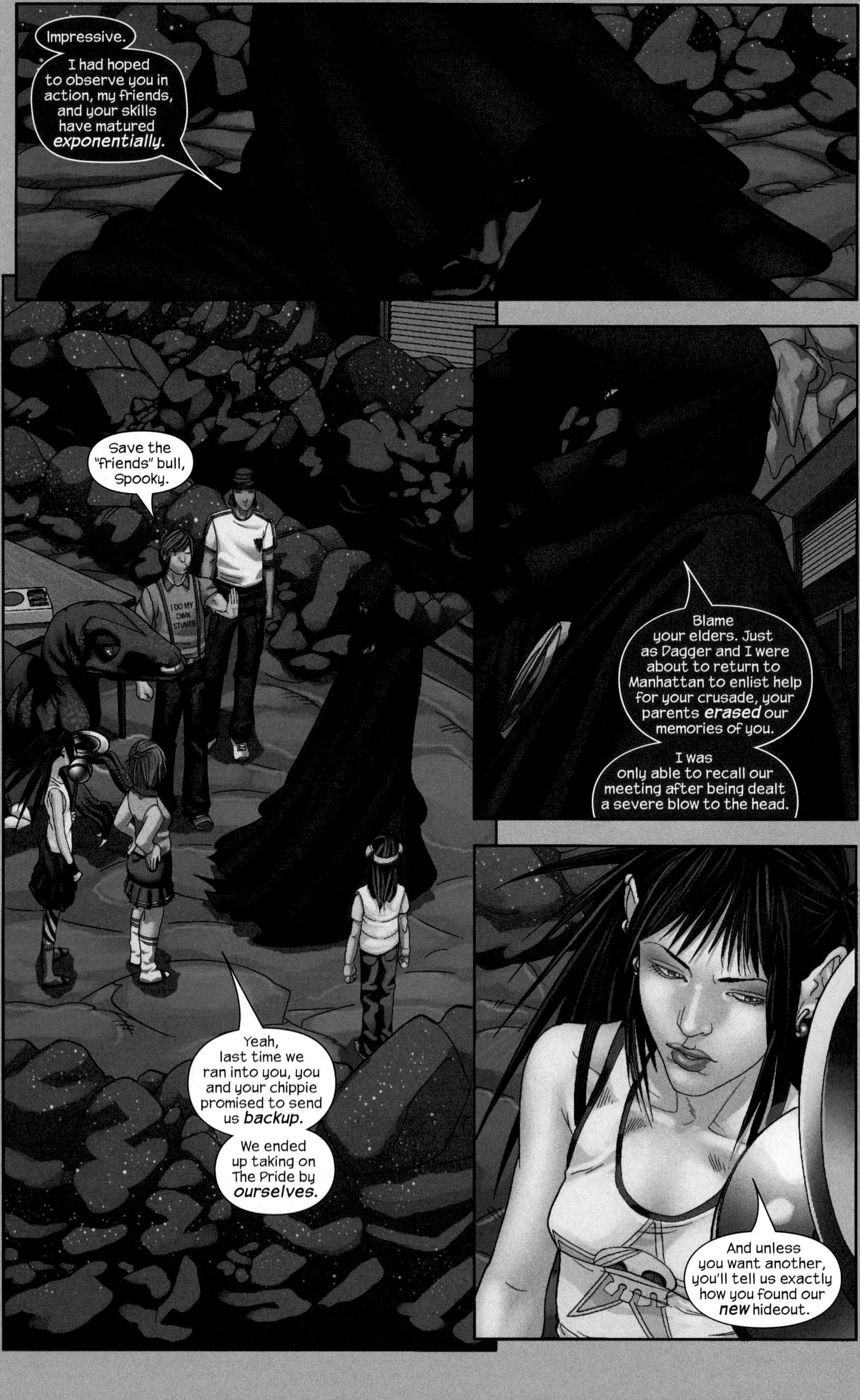
Impressive.
I had hoped to observe you in action, my friends, and your skills have matured *exponentially.*
Save the "friends" bull, Spooky.
Yeah, last time we ran into you, you and your chippie promised to send us *backup.*
We ended up taking on The Pride by *ourselves.*
I DO MY OWN STUNTS
Blame your elders. Just as Dagger and I were about to return to Manhattan to enlist help for your crusade, your parents *erased* our memories of you.
I was only able to recall our meeting after being dealt a severe blow to the head.
And unless you want another, you'll tell us exactly how you found our *new* hideout.

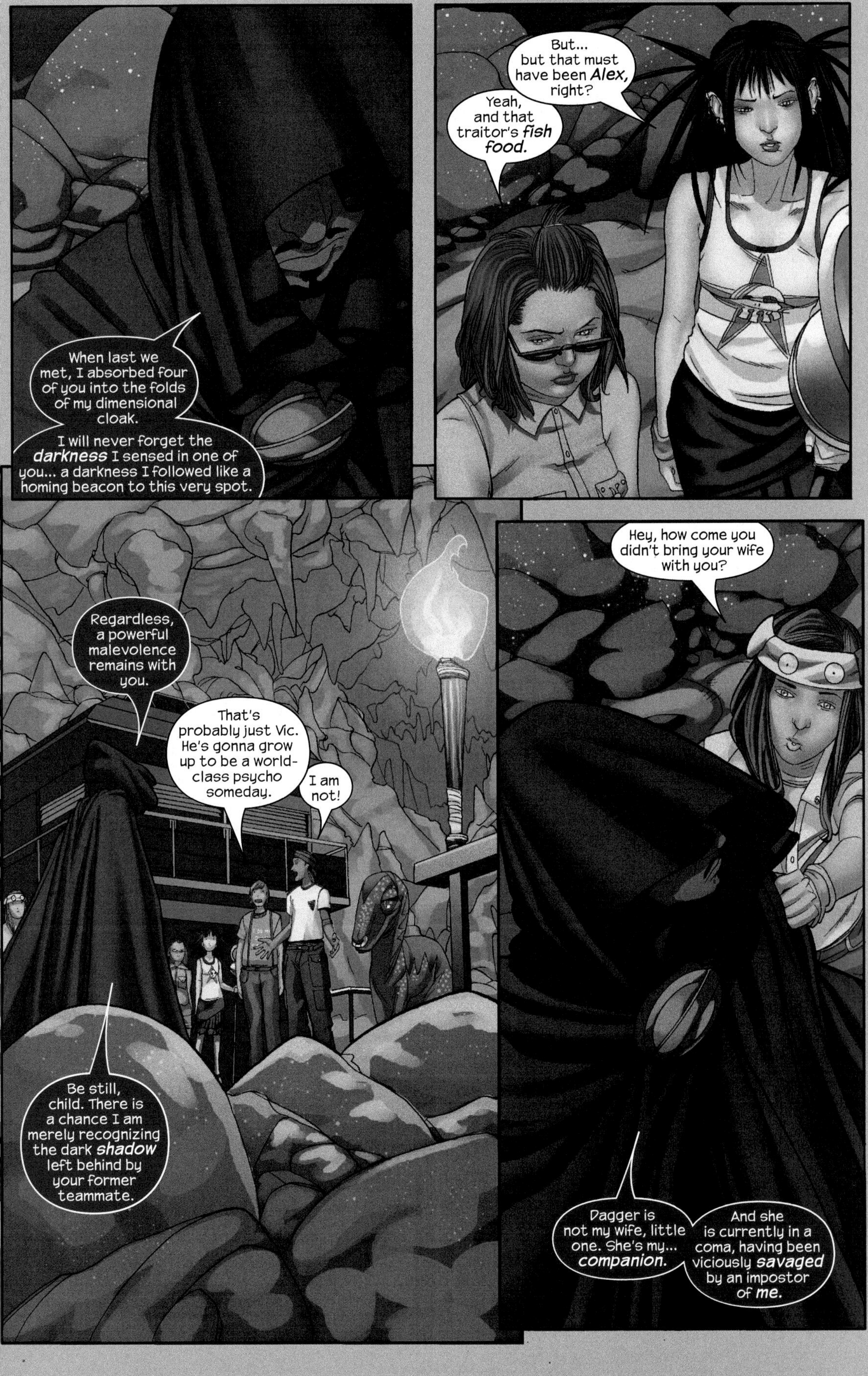

When last we met, I absorbed four of you into the folds of my dimensional cloak.
I will never forget the *darkness* I sensed in one of you... a darkness I followed like a homing beacon to this very spot.
But... but that must have been *Alex,* right?
Yeah, and that traitor's *fish food.*
Regardless, a powerful malevolence remains with you.
That's probably just Vic. He's gonna grow up to be a world-class psycho someday.
I am not!
Be still, child. There is a chance I am merely recognizing the dark *shadow* left behind by your former teammate.
Hey, how come you didn't bring your wife with you?
Dagger is not my wife, little one. She's my... *companion.*
And she is currently in a coma, having been viciously *savaged* by an impostor of *me.*

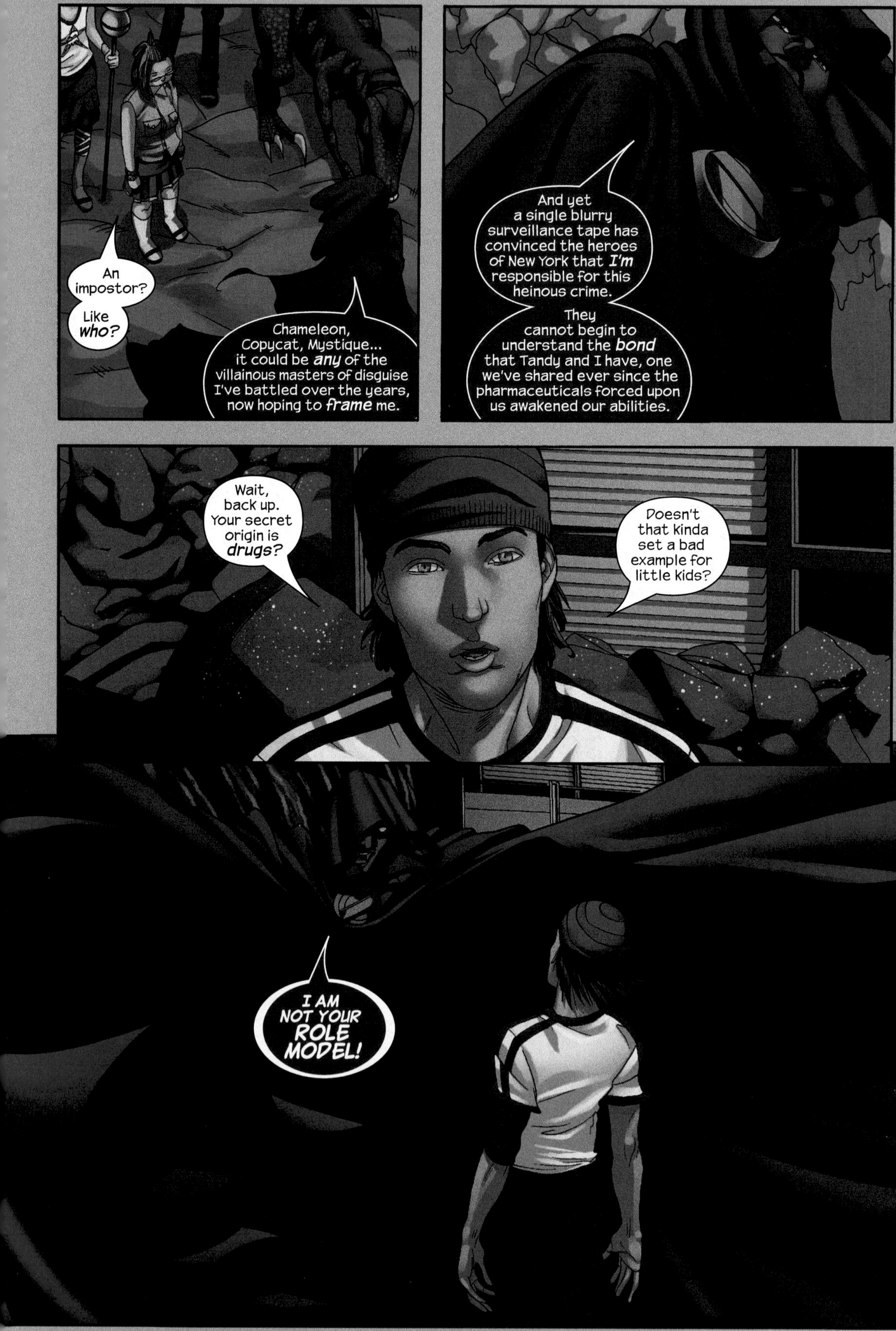

An impostor?
Like who?
Chameleon, Copycat, Mystique... it could be any of the villainous masters of disguise I've battled over the years, now hoping to frame me.
And yet a single blurry surveillance tape has convinced the heroes of New York that I'm responsible for this heinous crime.
They cannot begin to understand the bond that Tandy and I have, one we've shared ever since the pharmaceuticals forced upon us awakened our abilities.
Wait, back up. Your secret origin is drugs?
Doesn't that kinda set a bad example for little kids?
I AM NOT YOUR ROLE MODEL!

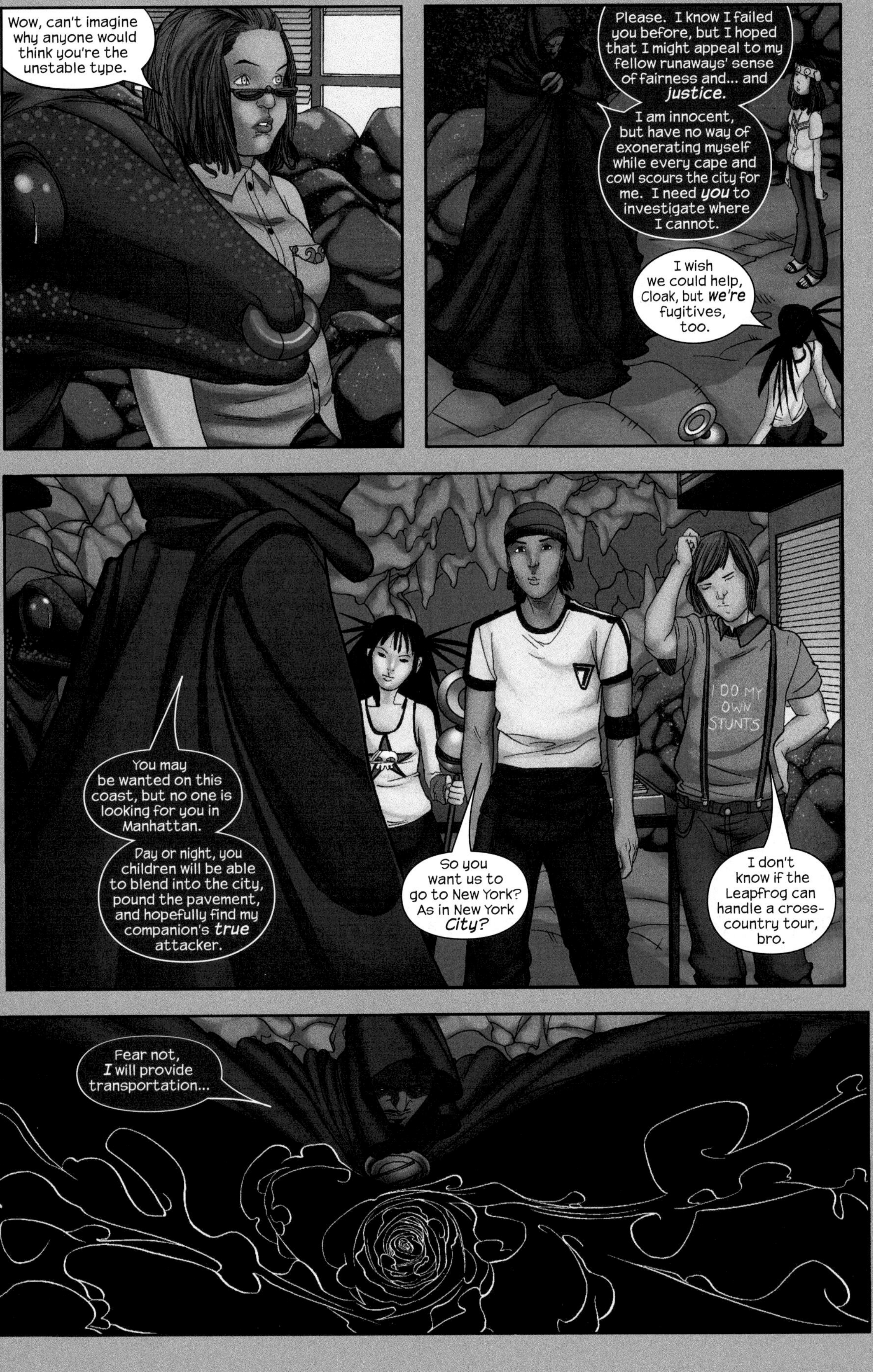
Wow, can't imagine why anyone would think you're the unstable type.
Please. I know I failed you before, but I hoped that I might appeal to my fellow runaways' sense of fairness and... and justice.
I am innocent, but have no way of exonerating myself while every cape and cowl scours the city for me. I need you to investigate where I cannot.
I wish we could help, Cloak, but we're fugitives, too.
I DO MY OWN STUNTS
You may be wanted on this coast, but no one is looking for you in Manhattan.
Day or night, you children will be able to blend into the city, pound the pavement, and hopefully find my companion's true attacker.
So you want us to go to New York? As in New York City?
I don't know if the Leapfrog can handle a cross-country tour, bro.
Fear not, I will provide transportation...

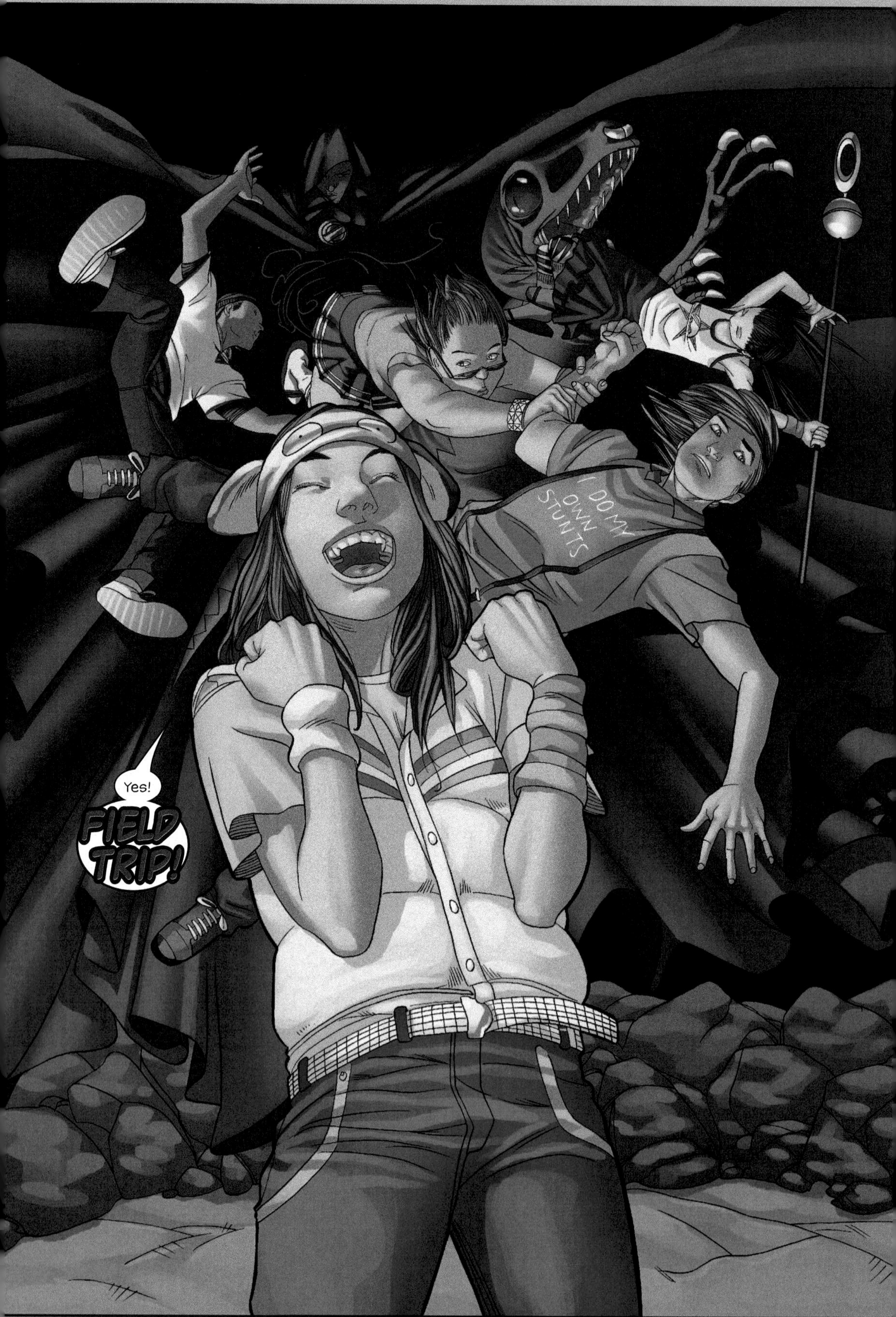
I DO MY OWN STUNTS
Yes!
FIELD TRIP!

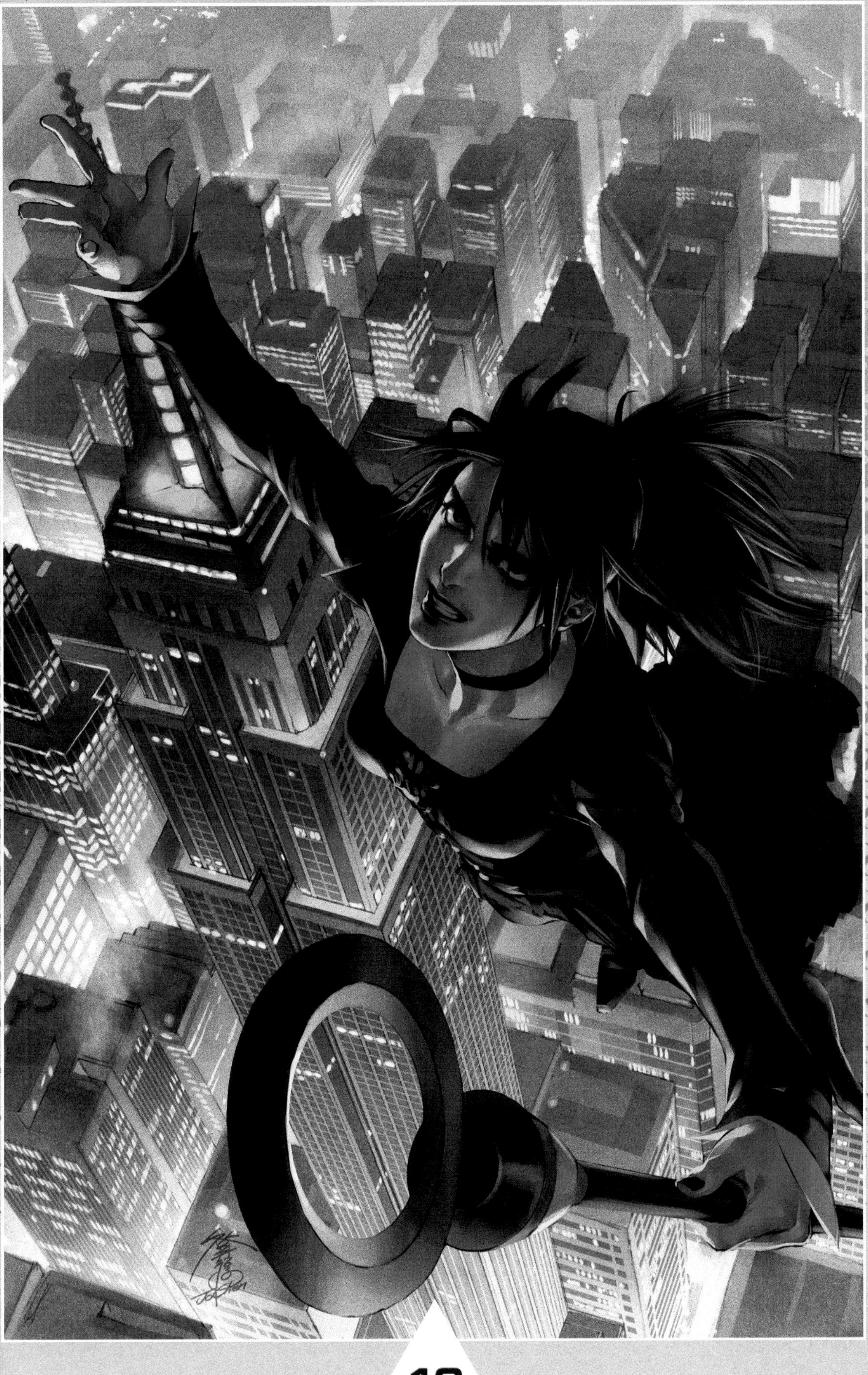

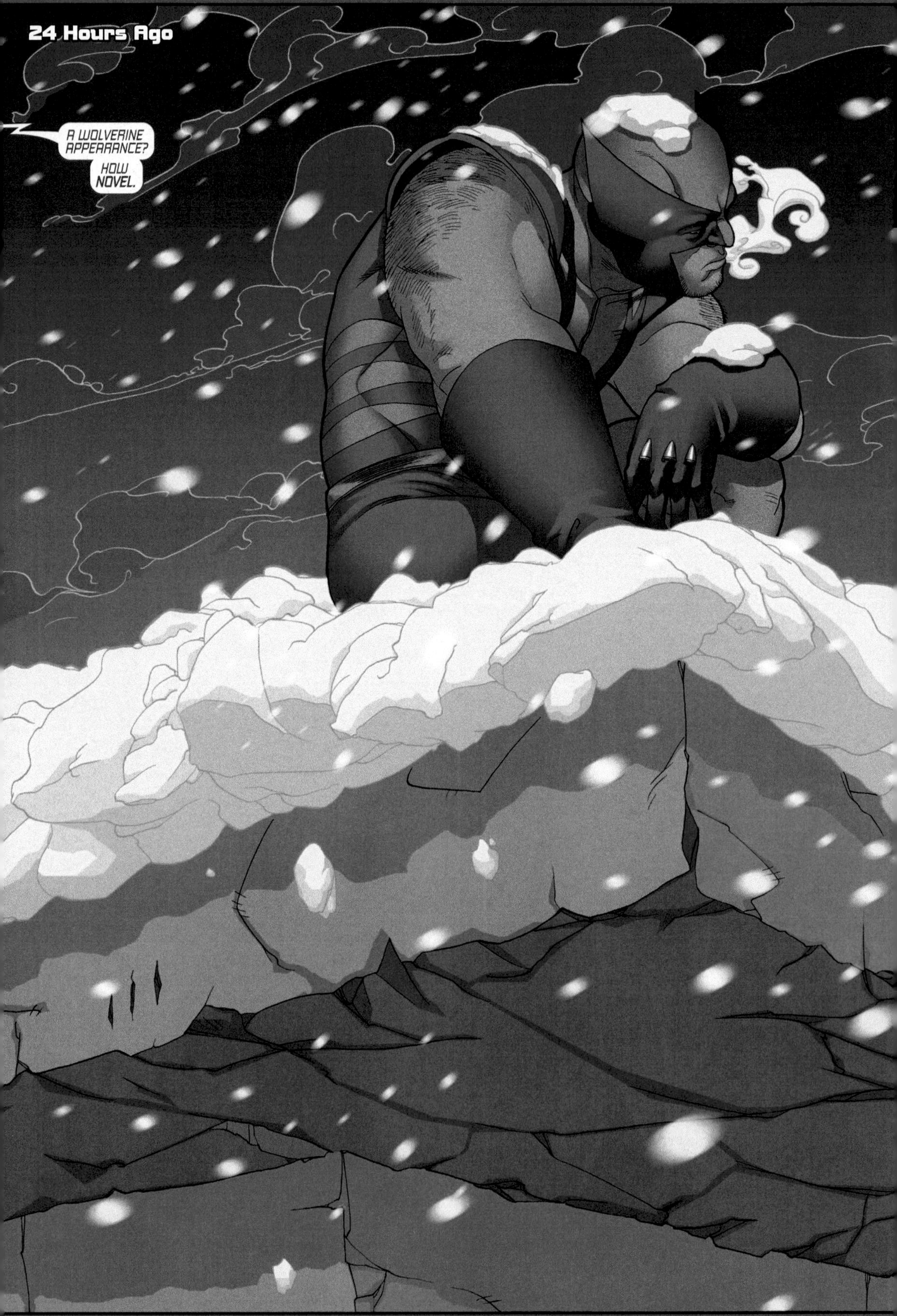

24 Hours Ago
A WOLVERINE APPEARANCE? HOW NOVEL.

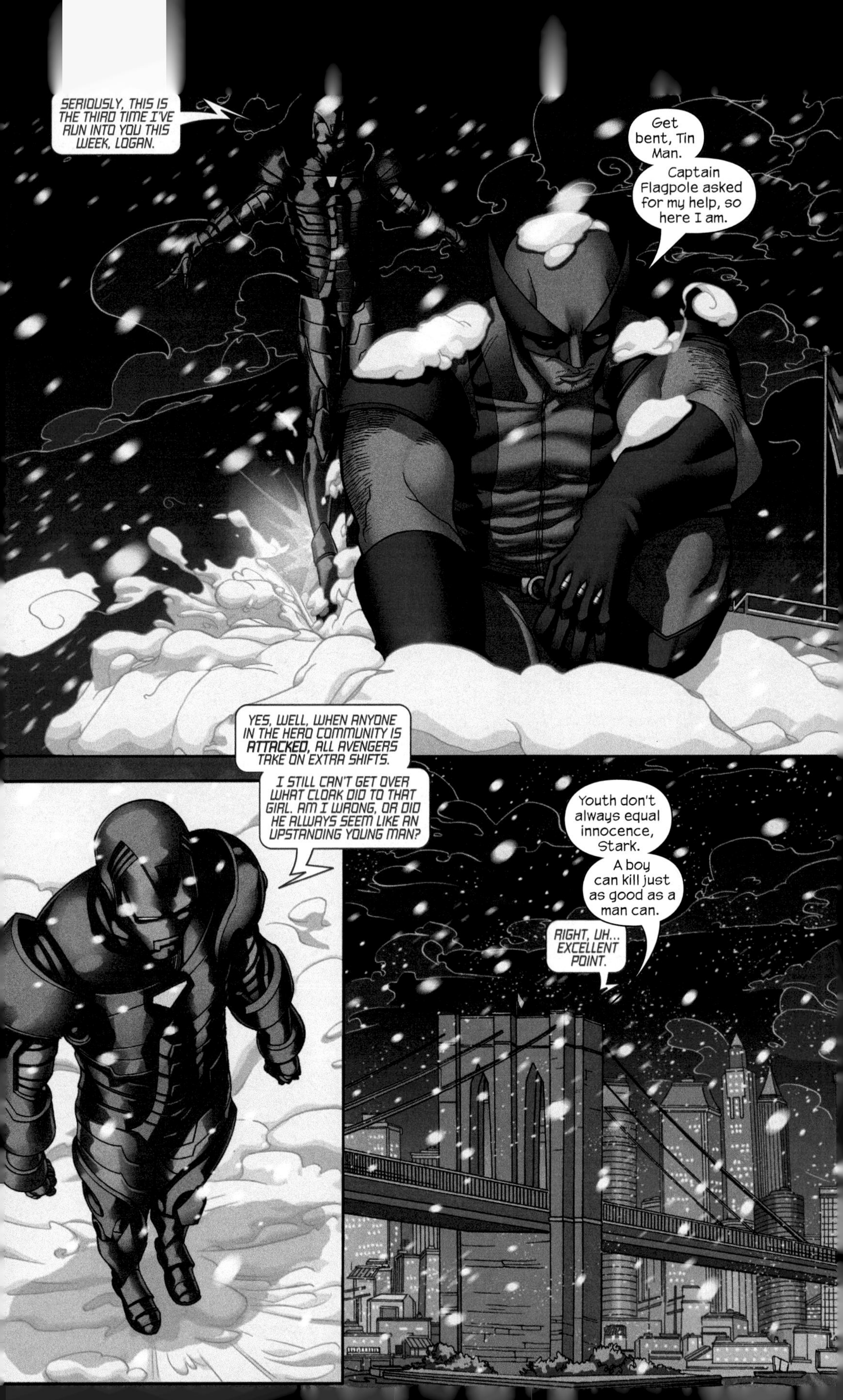
SERIOUSLY, THIS IS THE THIRD TIME I'VE RUN INTO YOU THIS WEEK, LOGAN.
Get bent, Tin Man.
Captain Flagpole asked for my help, so here I am.
YES, WELL, WHEN ANYONE IN THE HERO COMMUNITY IS ATTACKED, ALL AVENGERS TAKE ON EXTRA SHIFTS.
I STILL CAN'T GET OVER WHAT CLOAK DID TO THAT GIRL. AM I WRONG, OR DID HE ALWAYS SEEM LIKE AN UPSTANDING YOUNG MAN?
Youth don't always equal innocence, Stark.
A boy can kill just as good as a man can.
RIGHT, UH... EXCELLENT POINT.

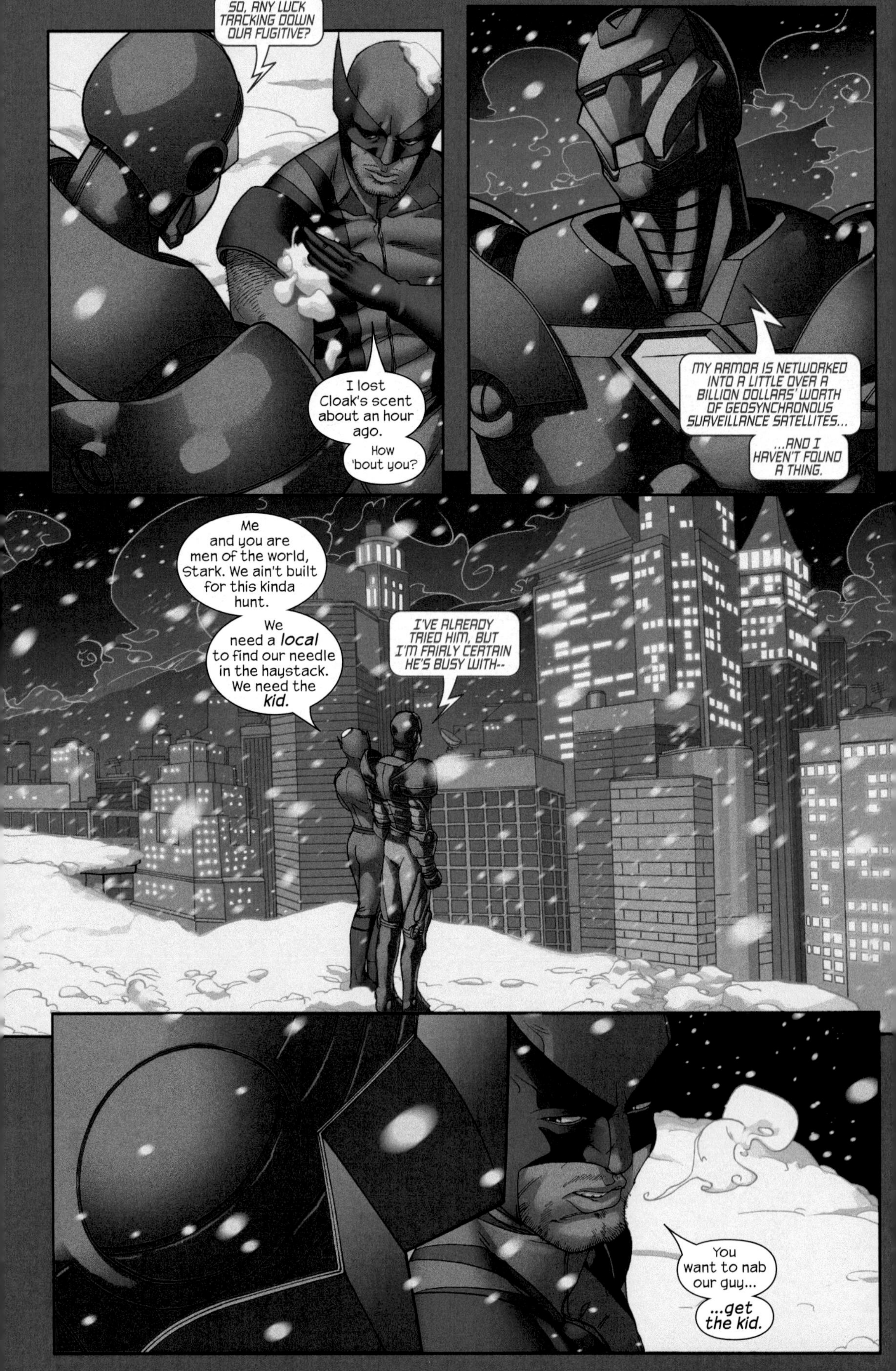

SO, ANY LUCK TRACKING DOWN OUR FUGITIVE?
I lost Cloak's scent about an hour ago.
How 'bout you?
MY ARMOR IS NETWORKED INTO A LITTLE OVER A BILLION DOLLARS' WORTH OF GEOSYNCHRONOUS SURVEILLANCE SATELLITES...
...AND I HAVEN'T FOUND A THING.
Me and you are men of the world, Stark. We ain't built for this kinda hunt.
We need a *local* to find our needle in the haystack. We need the *kid.*
I'VE ALREADY TRIED HIM, BUT I'M FAIRLY CERTAIN HE'S BUSY WITH--
You want to nab our guy...
...get the kid.

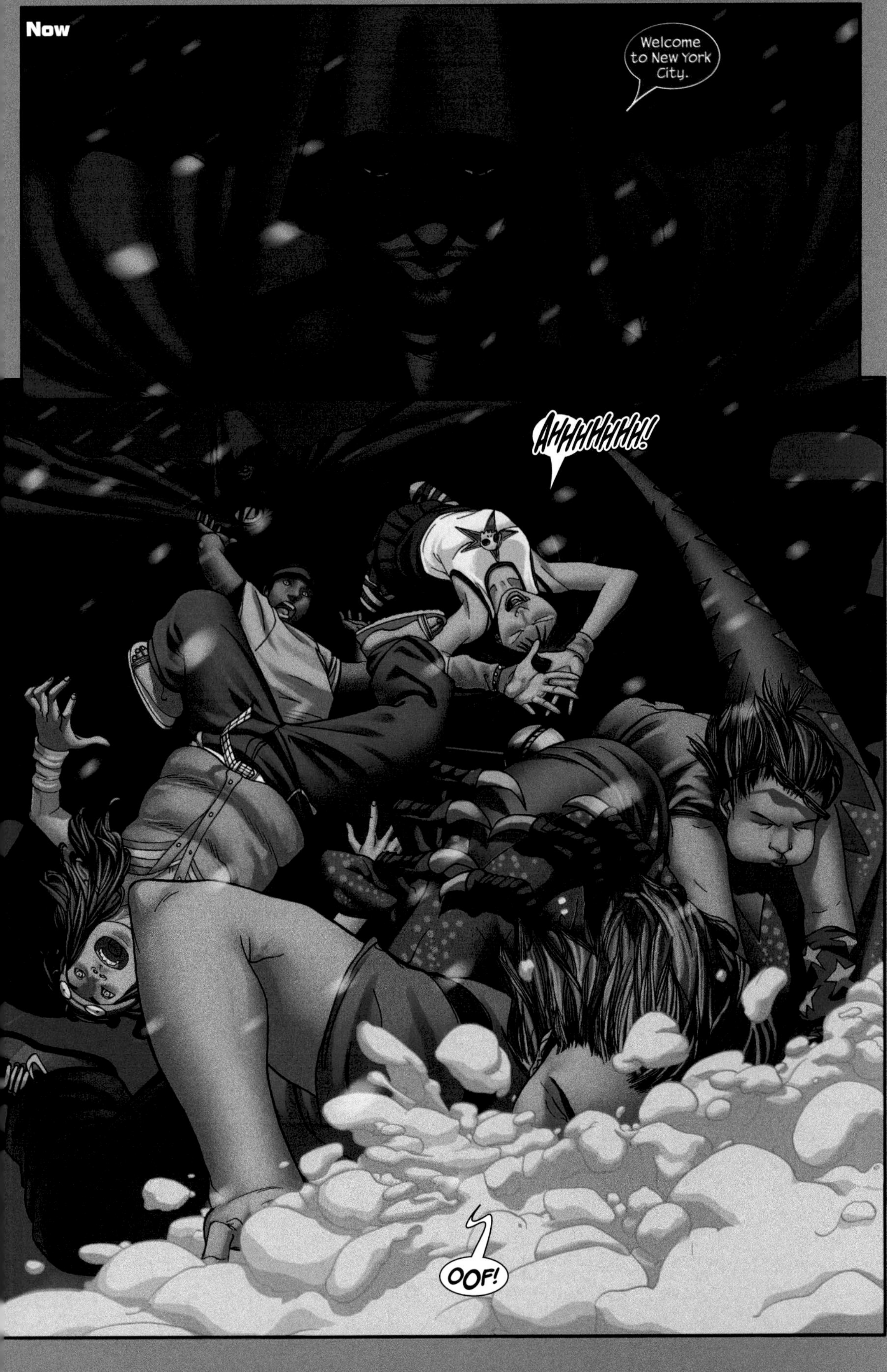
Now
Welcome to New York City.
AHHHHHHH!
OOF!

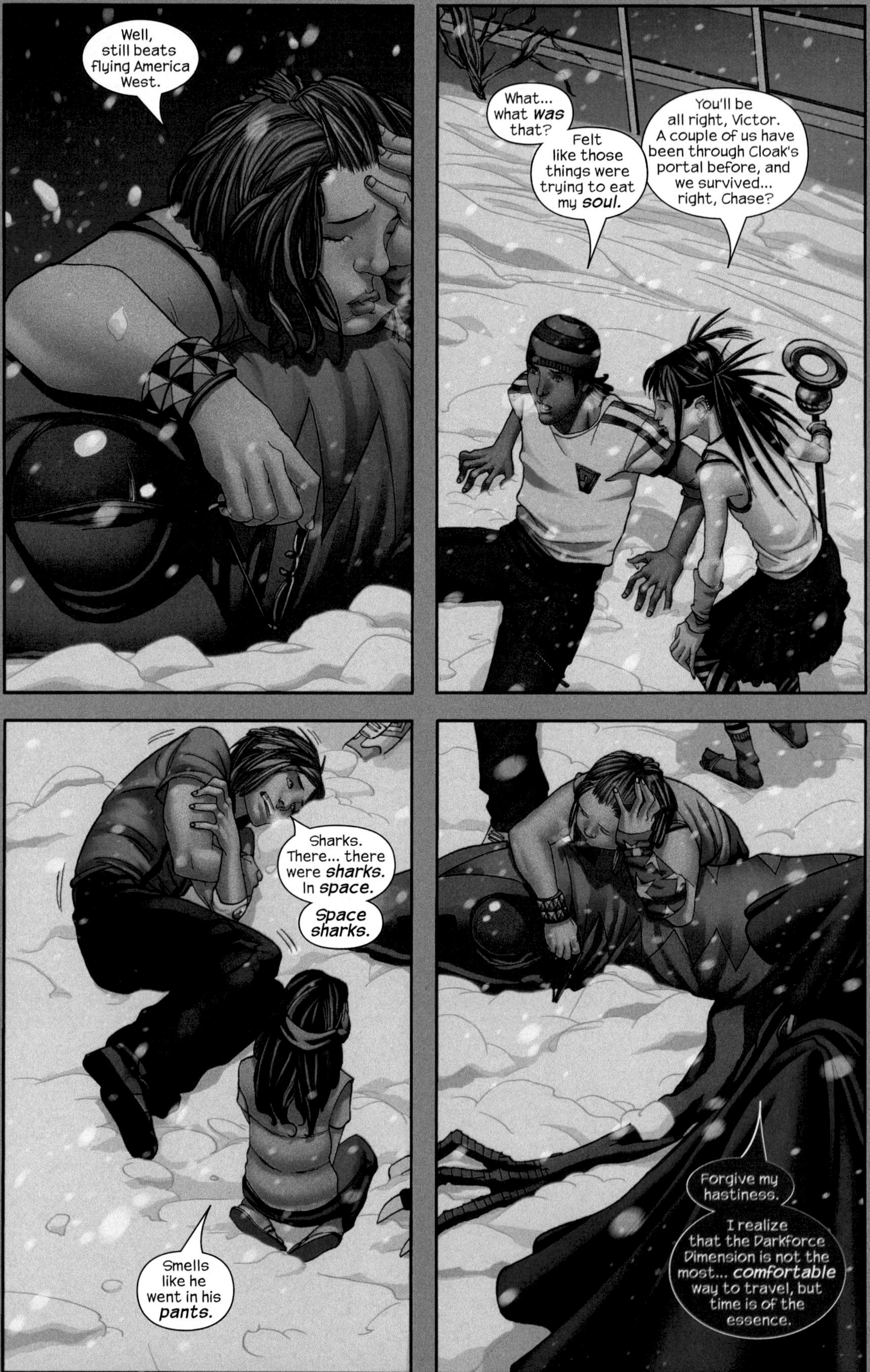
Well, still beats flying America West.
What... what *was* that?
Felt like those things were trying to eat my *soul.*
You'll be all right, Victor. A couple of us have been through Cloak's portal before, and we survived... right, Chase?
Sharks. There... there were *sharks.* In *space.*
Space sharks.
Smells like he went in his *pants.*
Forgive my hastiness.
I realize that the Darkforce Dimension is not the most... *comfortable* way to travel, but time is of the essence.

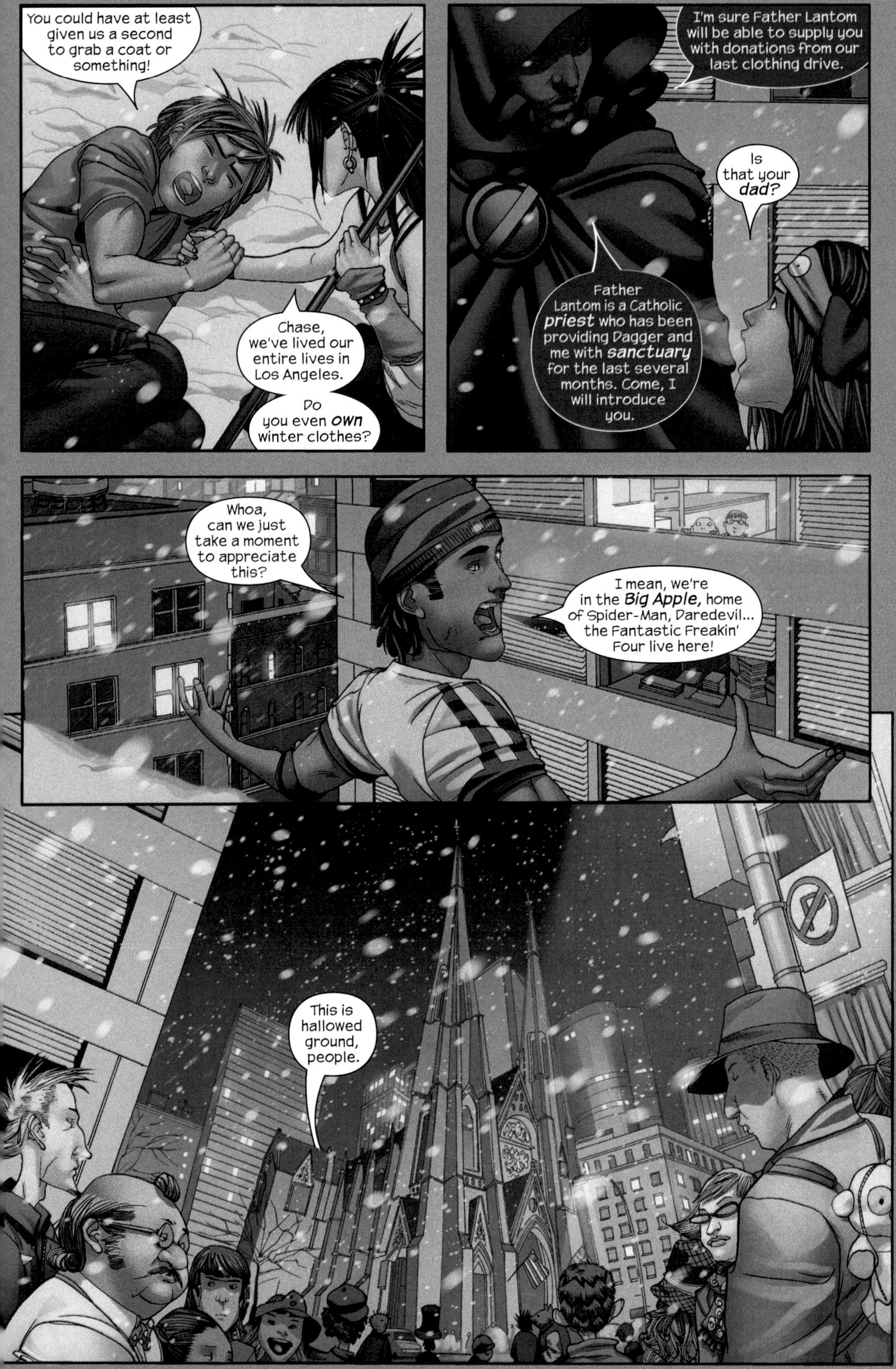

You could have at least given us a second to grab a coat or something!
Chase, we've lived our entire lives in Los Angeles.
Do you even *own* winter clothes?
I'm sure Father Lantom will be able to supply you with donations from our last clothing drive.
Is that your *dad?*
Father Lantom is a Catholic *priest* who has been providing Dagger and me with *sanctuary* for the last several months. Come, I will introduce you.
Whoa, can we just take a moment to appreciate this?
I mean, we're in the *Big Apple,* home of Spider-Man, Daredevil... the Fantastic Freakin' Four live here!
This is hallowed ground, people.

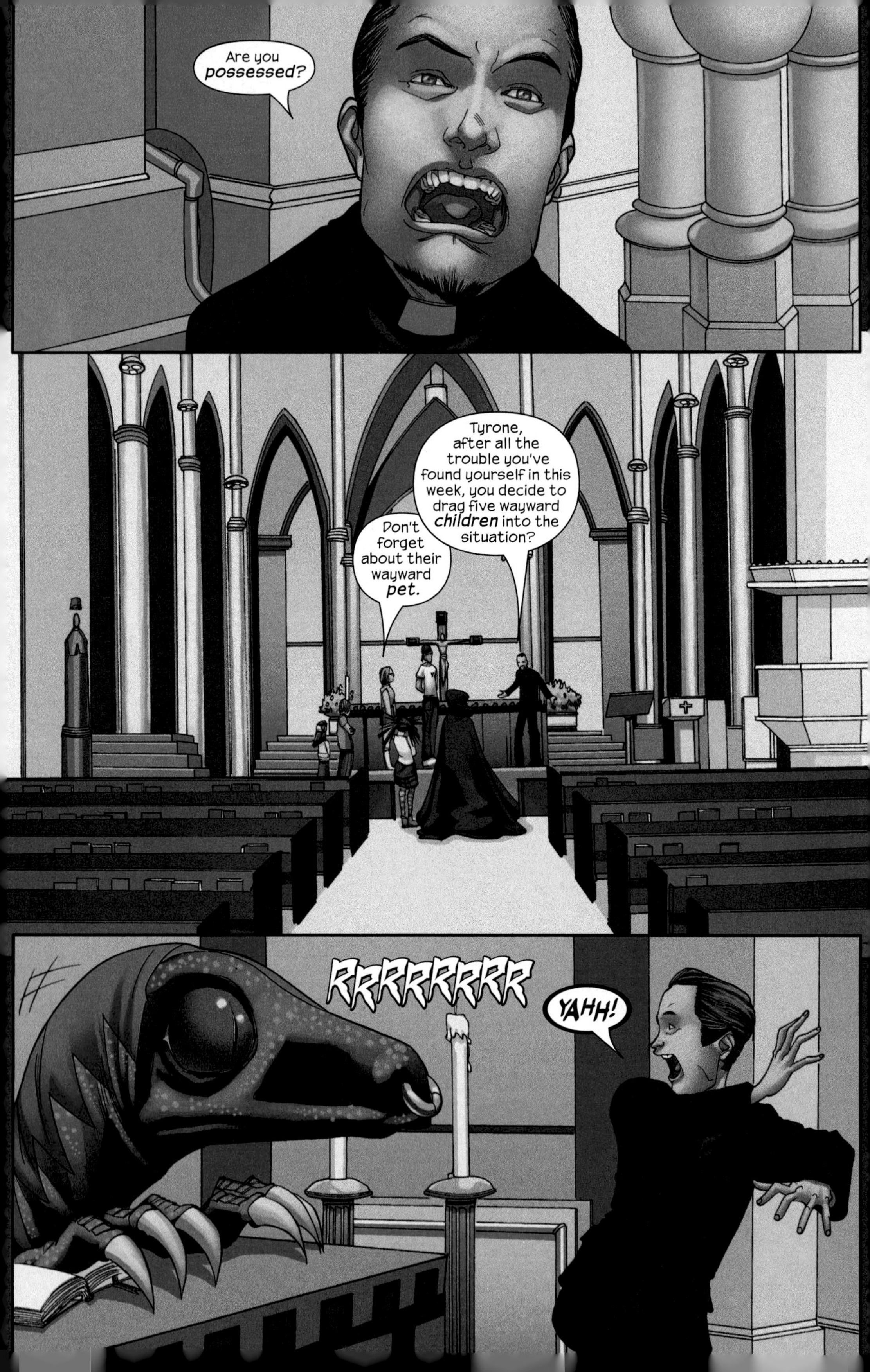
Are you possessed?
Tyrone, after all the trouble you've found yourself in this week, you decide to drag five wayward children into the situation?
Don't forget about their wayward pet.
RRRRRRRR
YAHH!

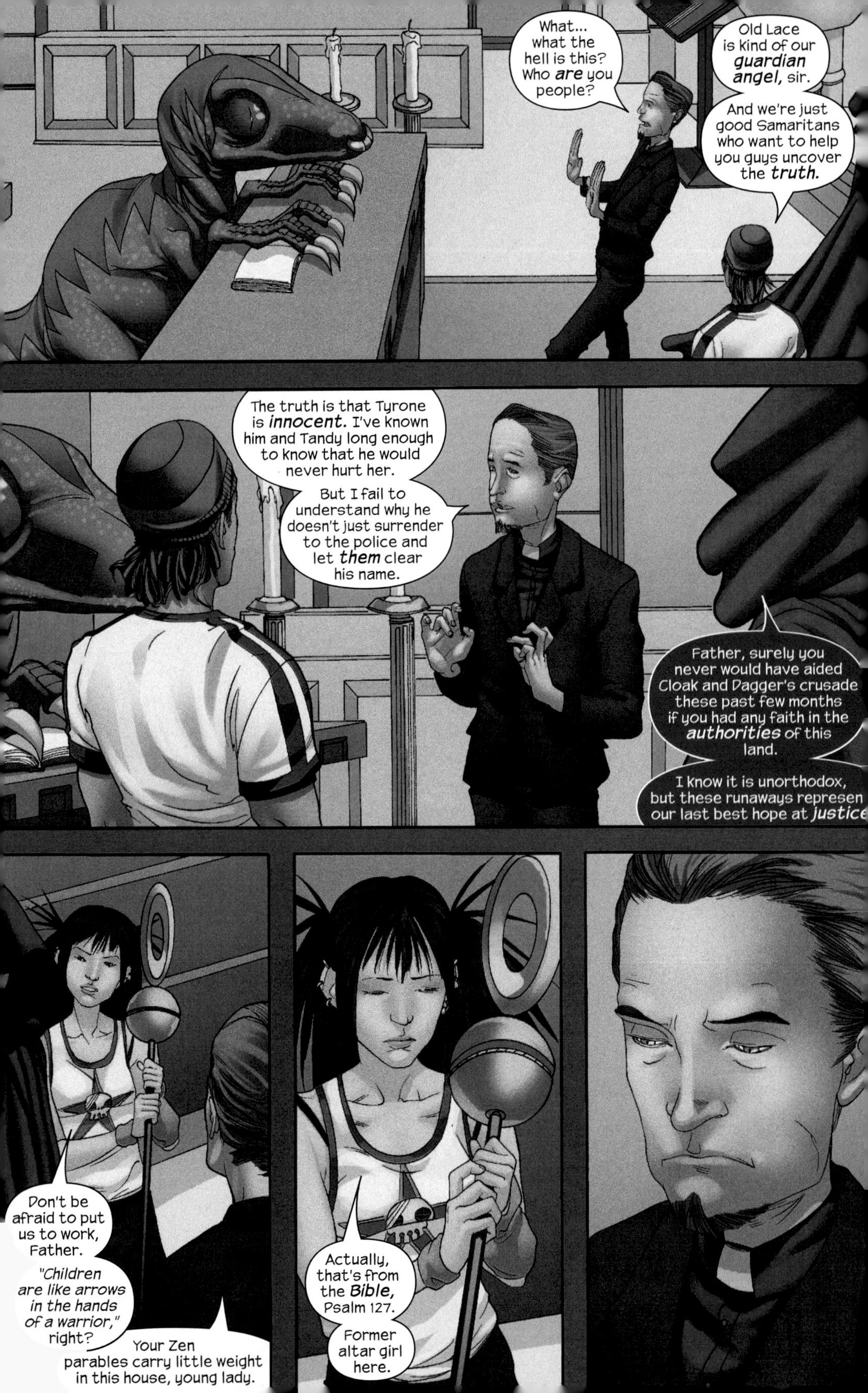

What... what the hell is this? Who are you people?
Old Lace is kind of our guardian angel, sir.
And we're just good Samaritans who want to help you guys uncover the truth.
The truth is that Tyrone is innocent. I've known him and Tandy long enough to know that he would never hurt her.
But I fail to understand why he doesn't just surrender to the police and let them clear his name.
Father, surely you never would have aided Cloak and Dagger's crusade these past few months if you had any faith in the authorities of this land.
I know it is unorthodox, but these runaways represen our last best hope at justice
Don't be afraid to put us to work, Father.
"Children are like arrows in the hands of a warrior," right?
Your Zen parables carry little weight in this house, young lady.
Actually, that's from the Bible, Psalm 127.
Former altar girl here.

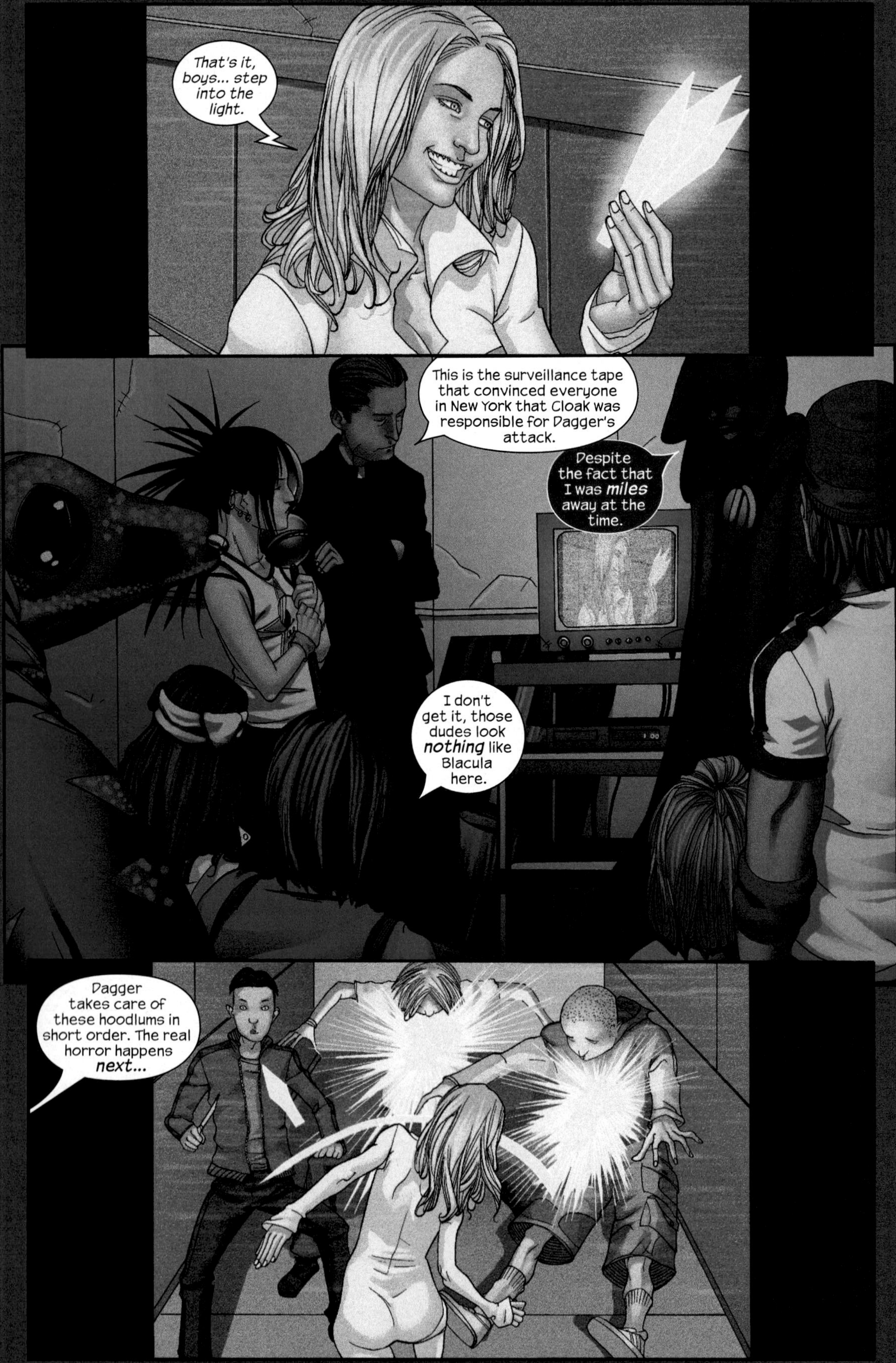
That's it, boys... step into the light.
This is the surveillance tape that convinced everyone in New York that Cloak was responsible for Dagger's attack.
Despite the fact that I was *miles* away at the time.
I don't get it, those dudes look *nothing* like Blacula here.
Dagger takes care of these hoodlums in short order. The real horror happens *next...*

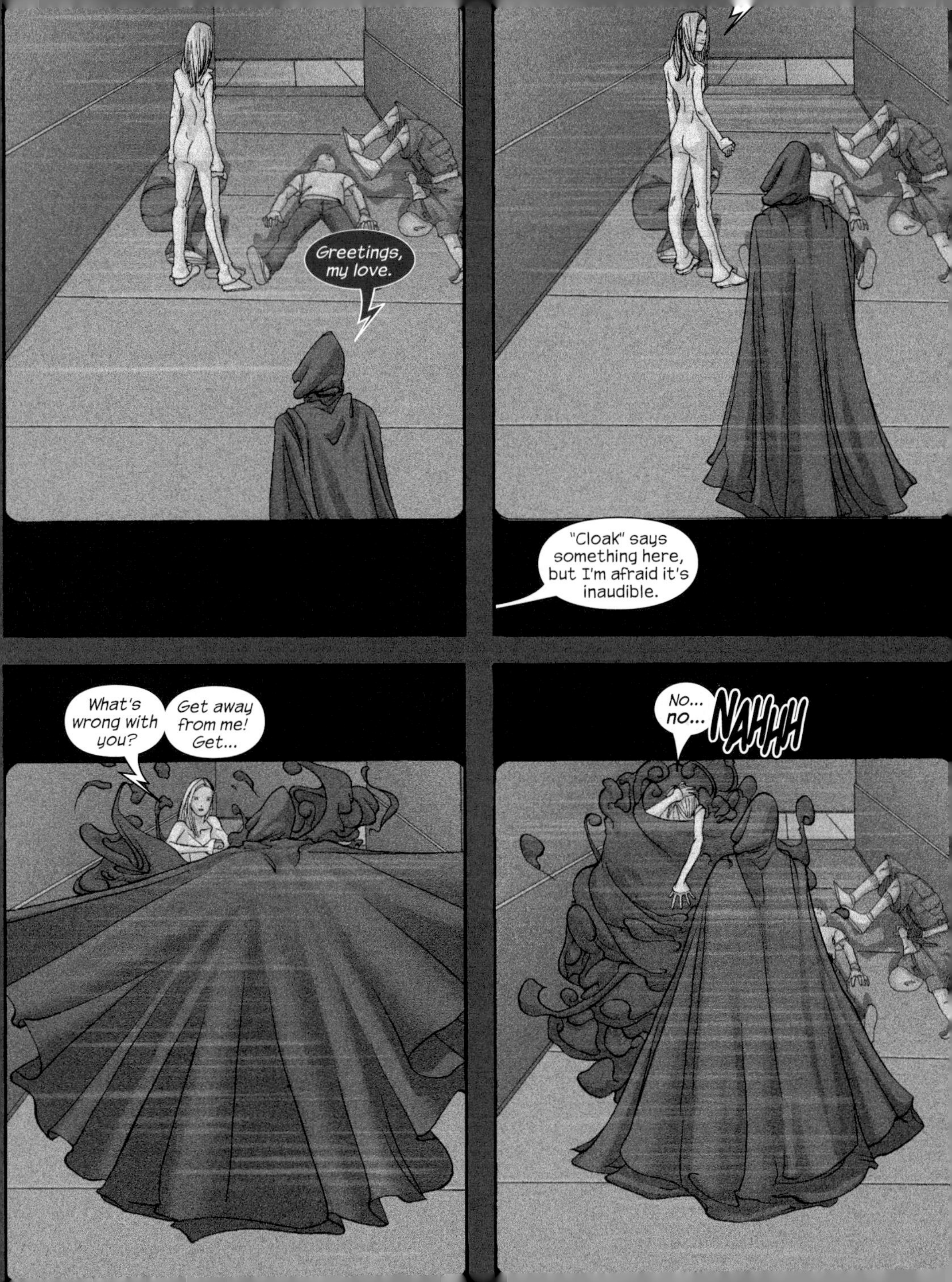

Greetings, my love.
"Cloak" says something here, but I'm afraid it's inaudible.
What's wrong with you?
Get away from me! Get...
No... no...
NAHHH

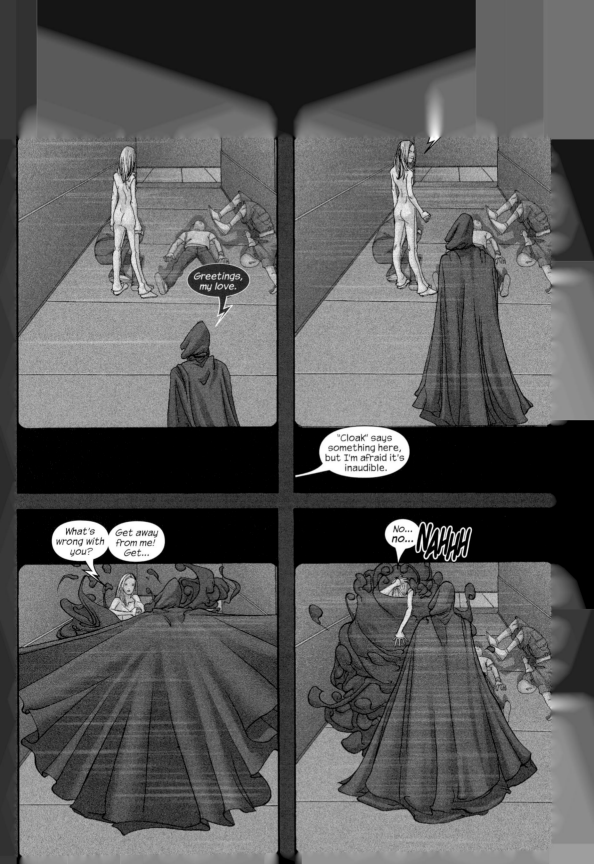

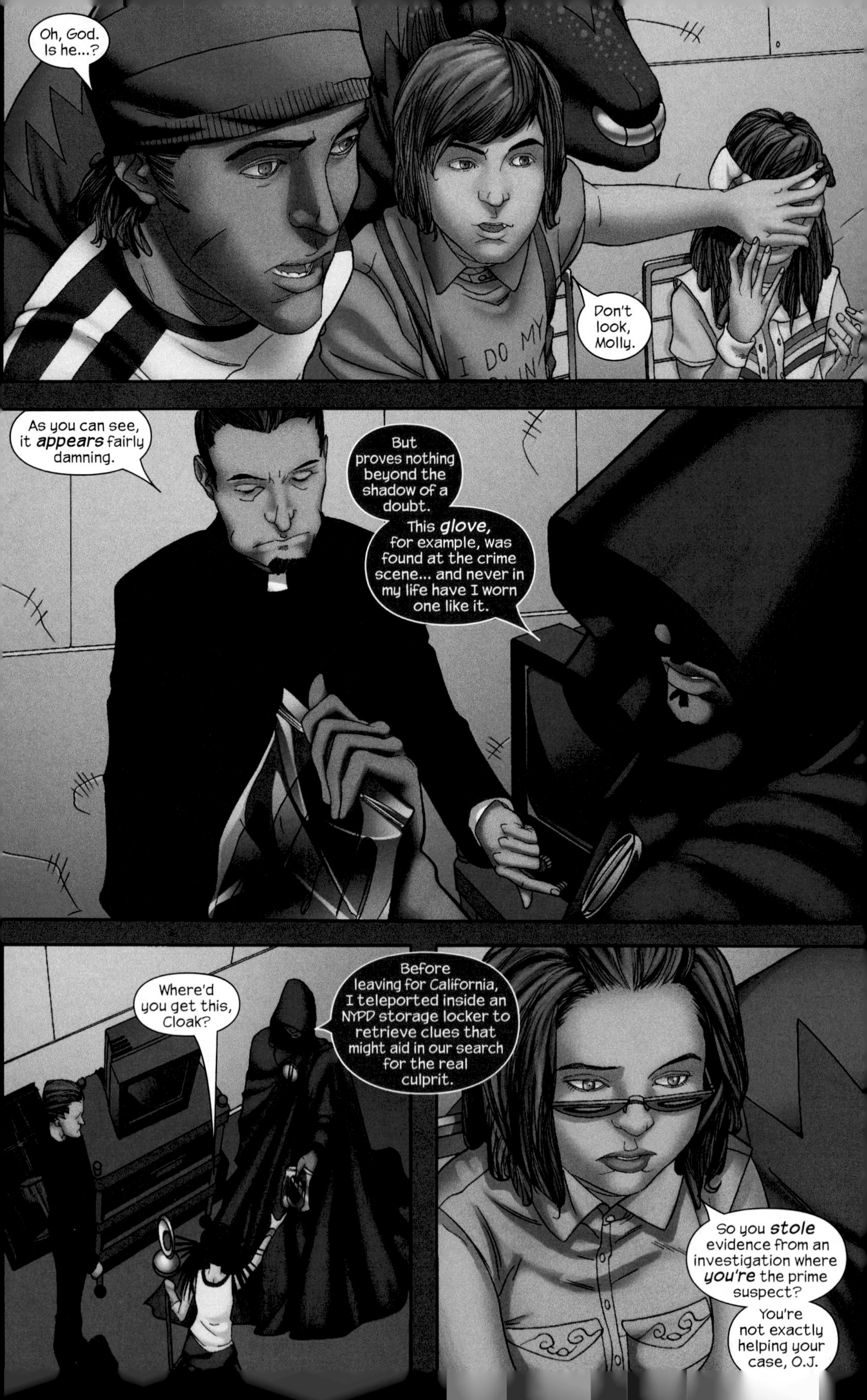
Oh, God. Is he...?
Don't look, Molly.
As you can see, it *appears* fairly damning.
But proves nothing beyond the shadow of a doubt.
This *glove,* for example, was found at the crime scene... and never in my life have I worn one like it.
Where'd you get this, Cloak?
Before leaving for California, I teleported inside an NYPD storage locker to retrieve clues that might aid in our search for the real culprit.
So you *stole* evidence from an investigation where *you're* the prime suspect?
You're not exactly helping your case, O.J.

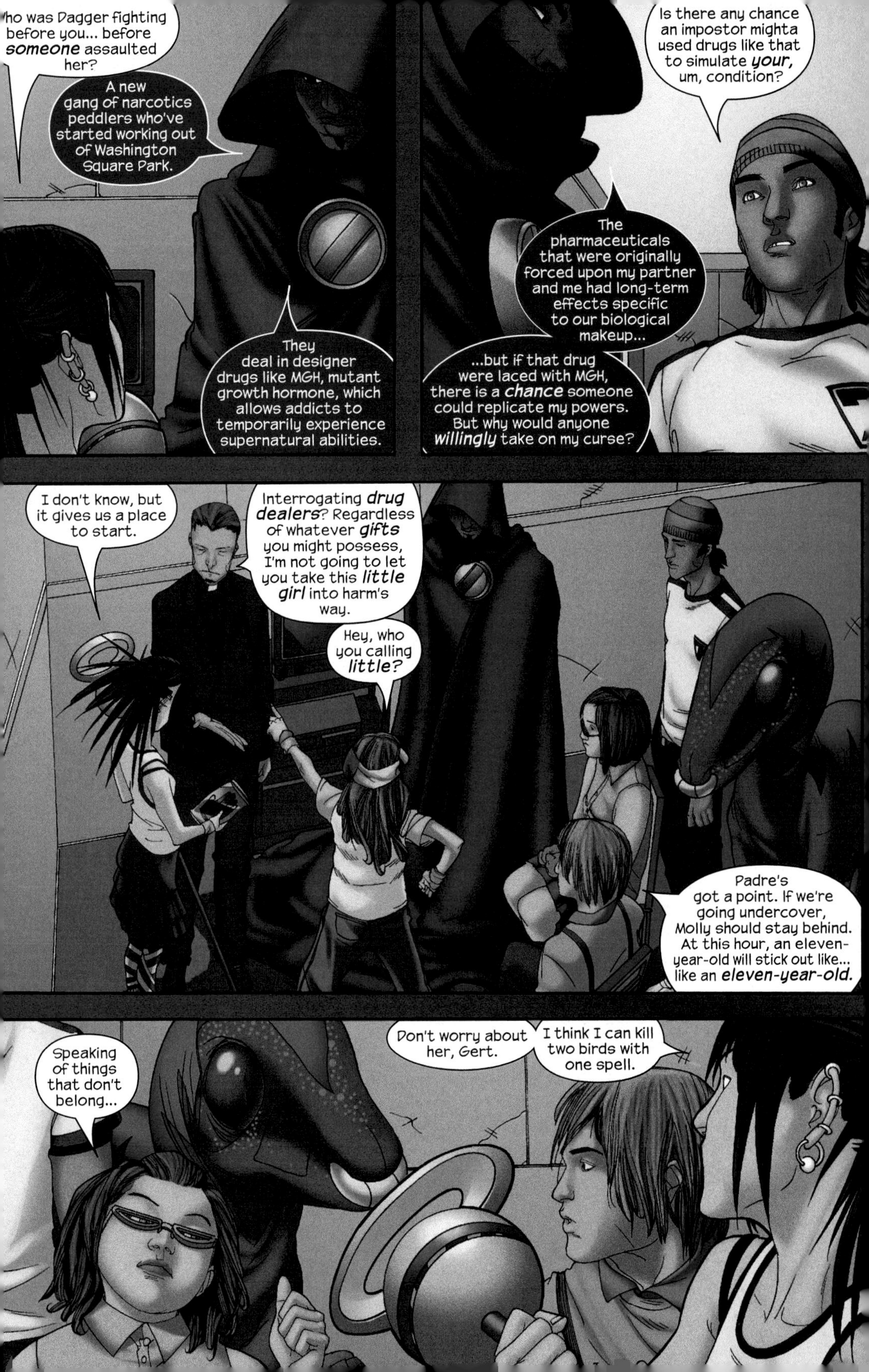

Who was Dagger fighting before you... before *someone* assaulted her?
A new gang of narcotics peddlers who've started working out of Washington Square Park.
They deal in designer drugs like MGH, mutant growth hormone, which allows addicts to temporarily experience supernatural abilities.
Is there any chance an impostor mighta used drugs like that to simulate *your,* um, condition?
The pharmaceuticals that were originally forced upon my partner and me had long-term effects specific to our biological makeup...
...but if that drug were laced with MGH, there is a *chance* someone could replicate my powers. But why would anyone *willingly* take on my curse?
I don't know, but it gives us a place to start.
Interrogating *drug dealers*? Regardless of whatever *gifts* you might possess, I'm not going to let you take this *little girl* into harm's way.
Hey, who you calling *little?*
Padre's got a point. If we're going undercover, Molly should stay behind. At this hour, an eleven-year-old will stick out like... like an *eleven-year-old.*
Speaking of things that don't belong...
Don't worry about her, Gert.
I think I can kill two birds with one spell.

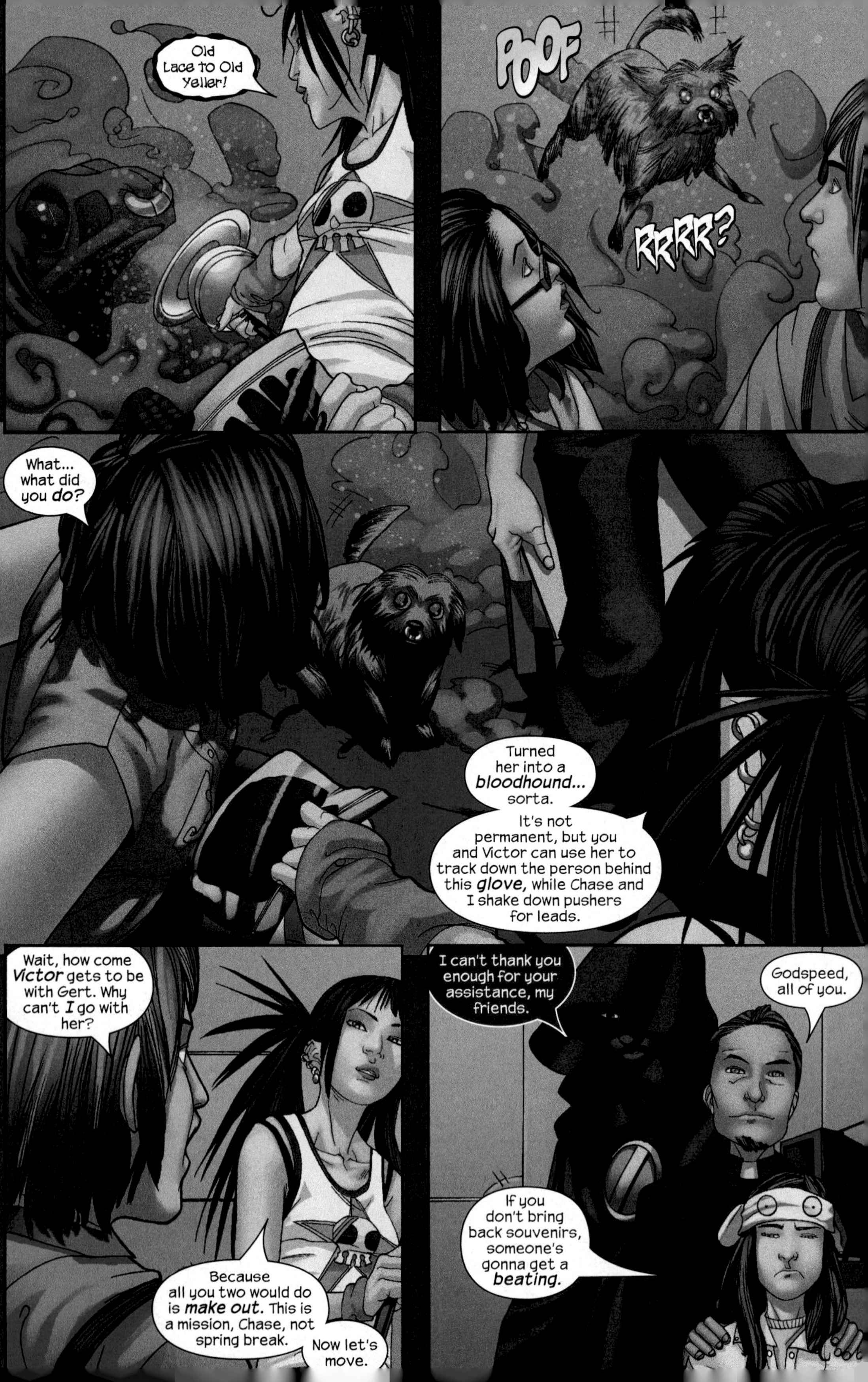
Old Lace to Old Yeller!
POOF
RRRR?
What... what did you do?
Turned her into a bloodhound... sorta.
It's not permanent, but you and Victor can use her to track down the person behind this glove, while Chase and I shake down pushers for leads.
Wait, how come Victor gets to be with Gert. Why can't I go with her?
Because all you two would do is make out. This is a mission, Chase, not spring break.
Now let's move.
I can't thank you enough for your assistance, my friends.
Godspeed, all of you.
If you don't bring back souvenirs, someone's gonna get a beating.

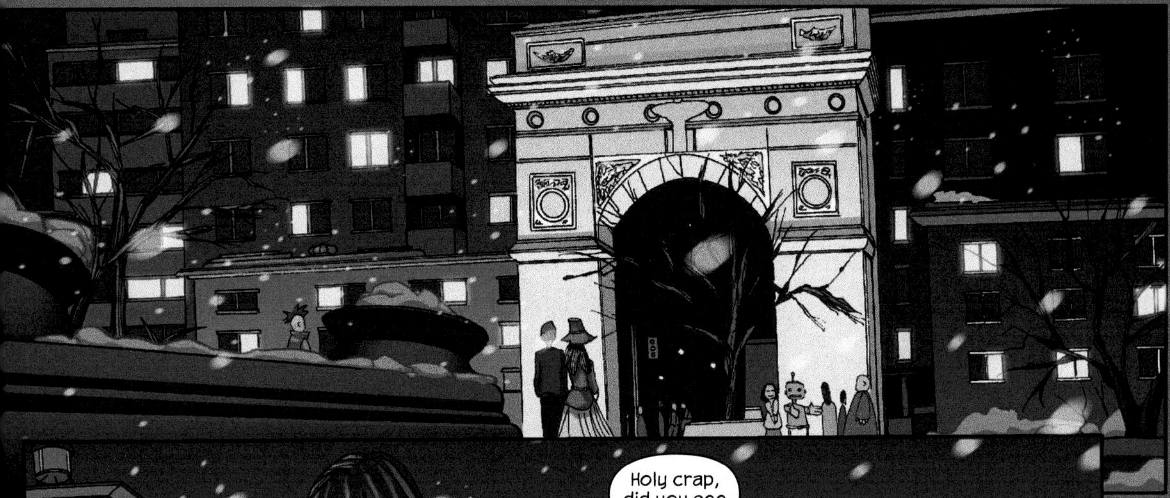

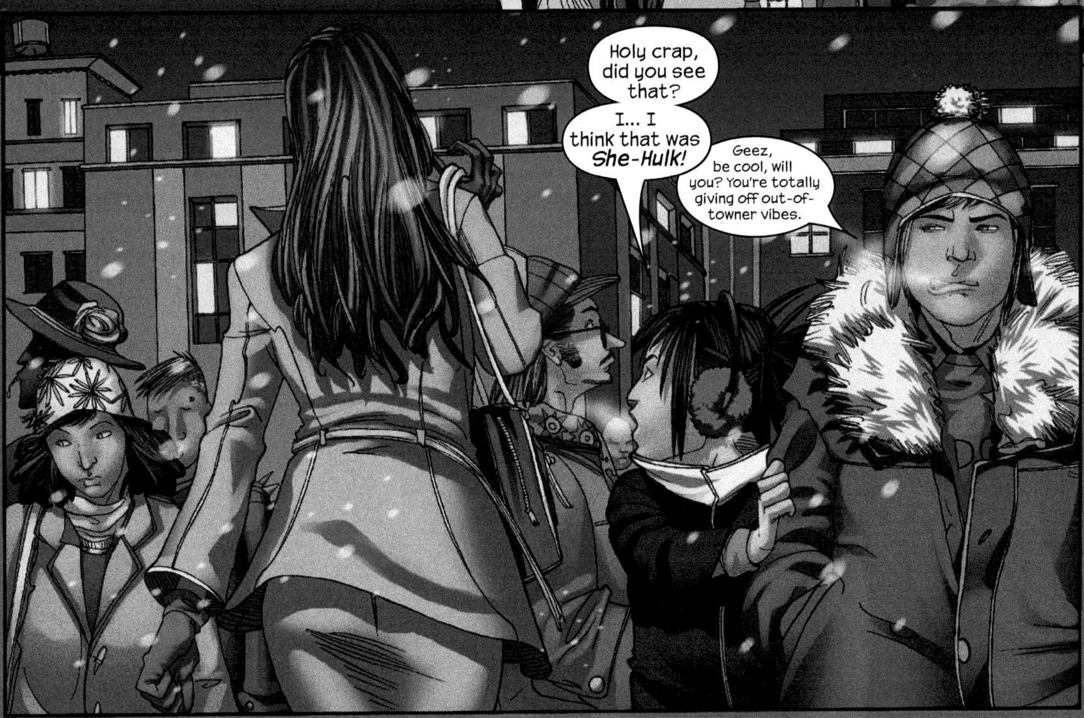
Holy crap, did you see that?
I... I think that was *She-Hulk!*
Geez, be cool, will you? You're totally giving off out-of-towner vibes.

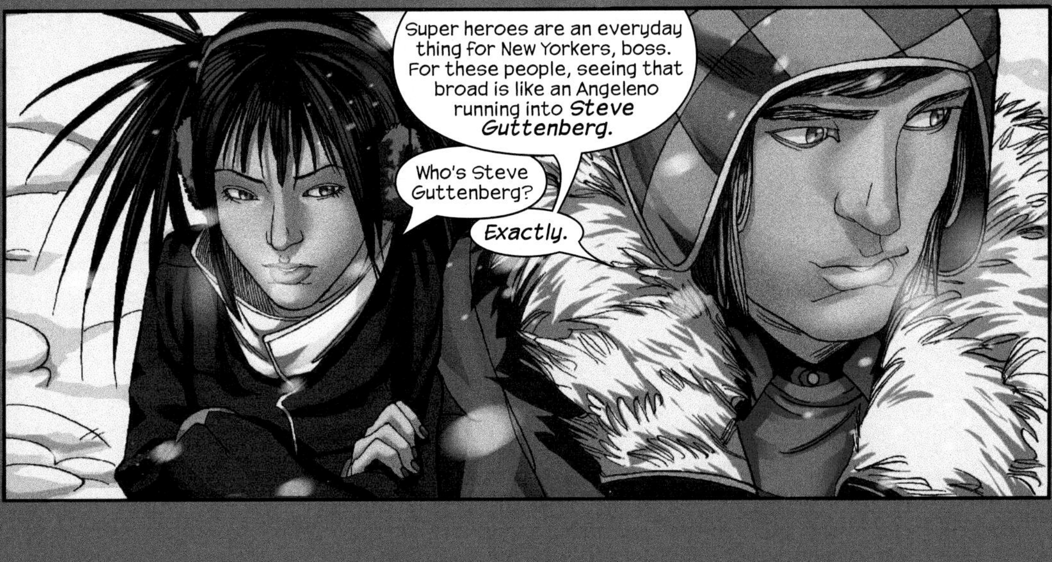
Super heroes are an everyday thing for New Yorkers, boss. For these people, seeing that broad is like an Angeleno running into **Steve Guttenberg.**
Who's Steve Guttenberg?
Exactly.

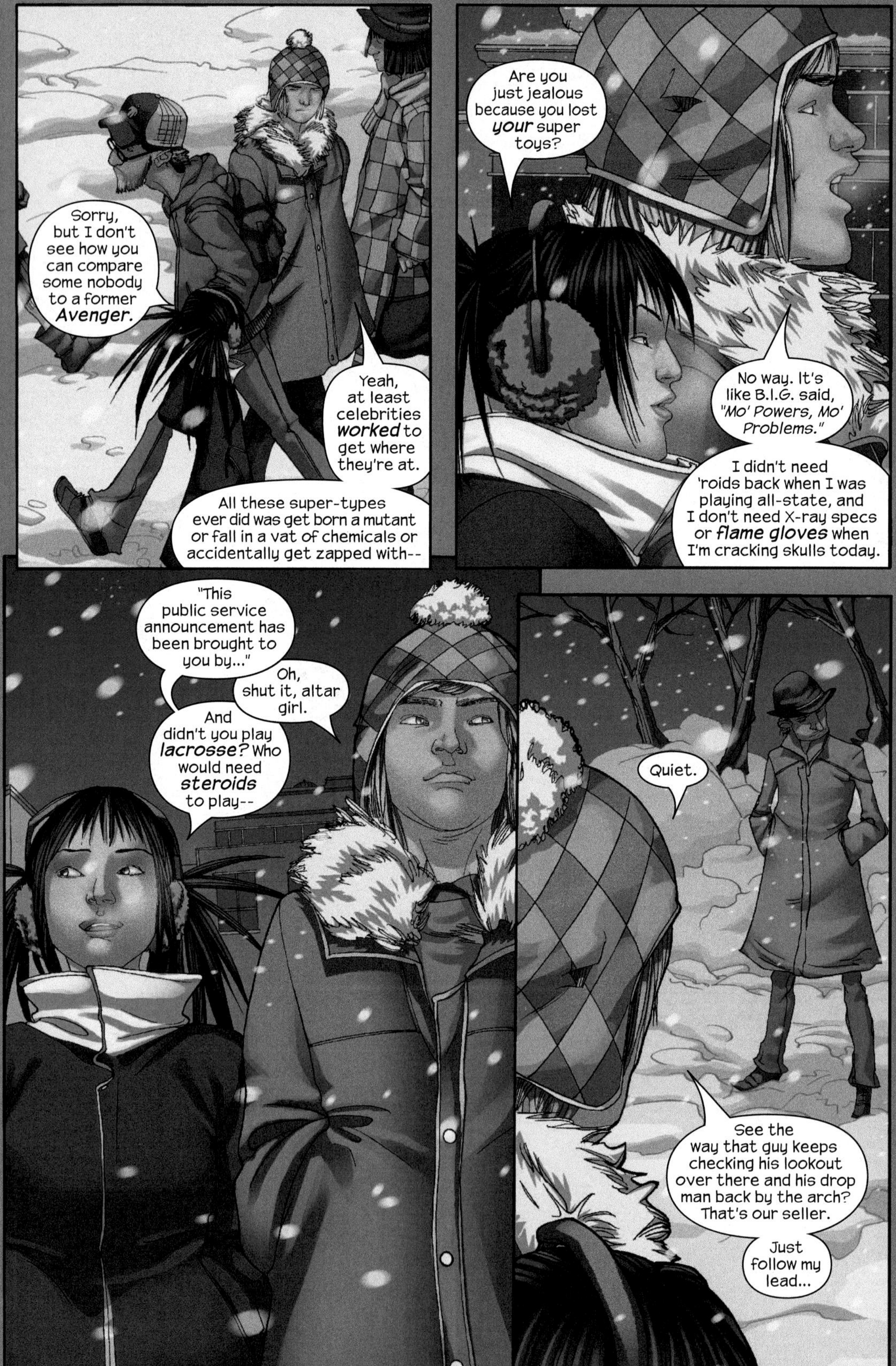

Sorry, but I don't see how you can compare some nobody to a former *Avenger.*
Yeah, at least celebrities *worked* to get where they're at.
All these super-types ever did was get born a mutant or fall in a vat of chemicals or accidentally get zapped with--
Are you just jealous because you lost *your* super toys?
No way. It's like B.I.G. said, *"Mo' Powers, Mo' Problems."*
I didn't need 'roids back when I was playing all-state, and I don't need X-ray specs or *flame gloves* when I'm cracking skulls today.
"This public service announcement has been brought to you by..."
Oh, shut it, altar girl.
And didn't you play *lacrosse?* Who would need *steroids* to play--
Quiet.
See the way that guy keeps checking his lookout over there and his drop man back by the arch? That's our seller.
Just follow my lead...

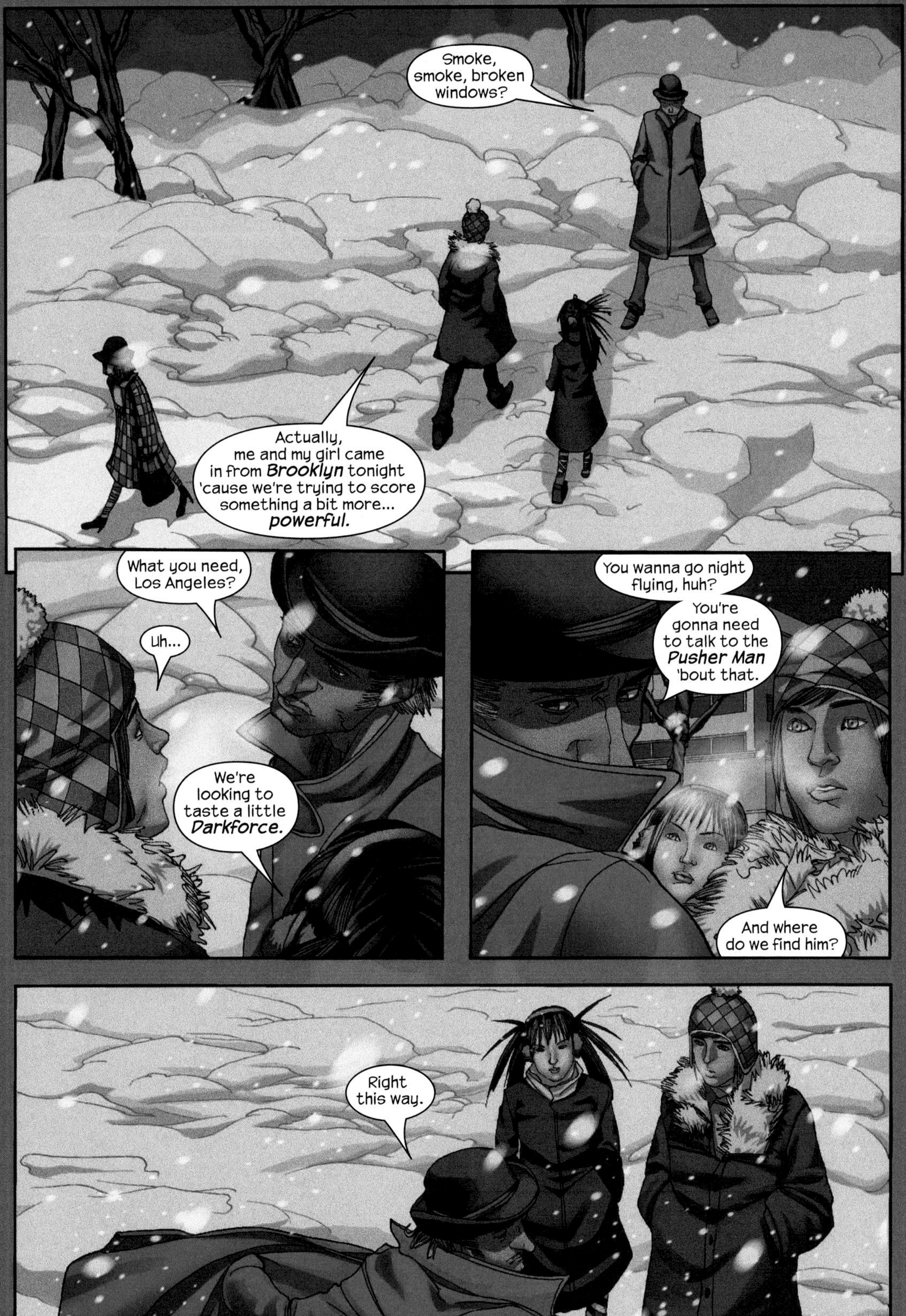

Smoke, smoke, broken windows?
Actually, me and my girl came in from *Brooklyn* tonight 'cause we're trying to score something a bit more... ***powerful.***
What you need, Los Angeles?
Uh...
We're looking to taste a little ***Darkforce.***
You wanna go night flying, huh?
You're gonna need to talk to the ***Pusher Man*** 'bout that.
And where do we find him?
Right this way.

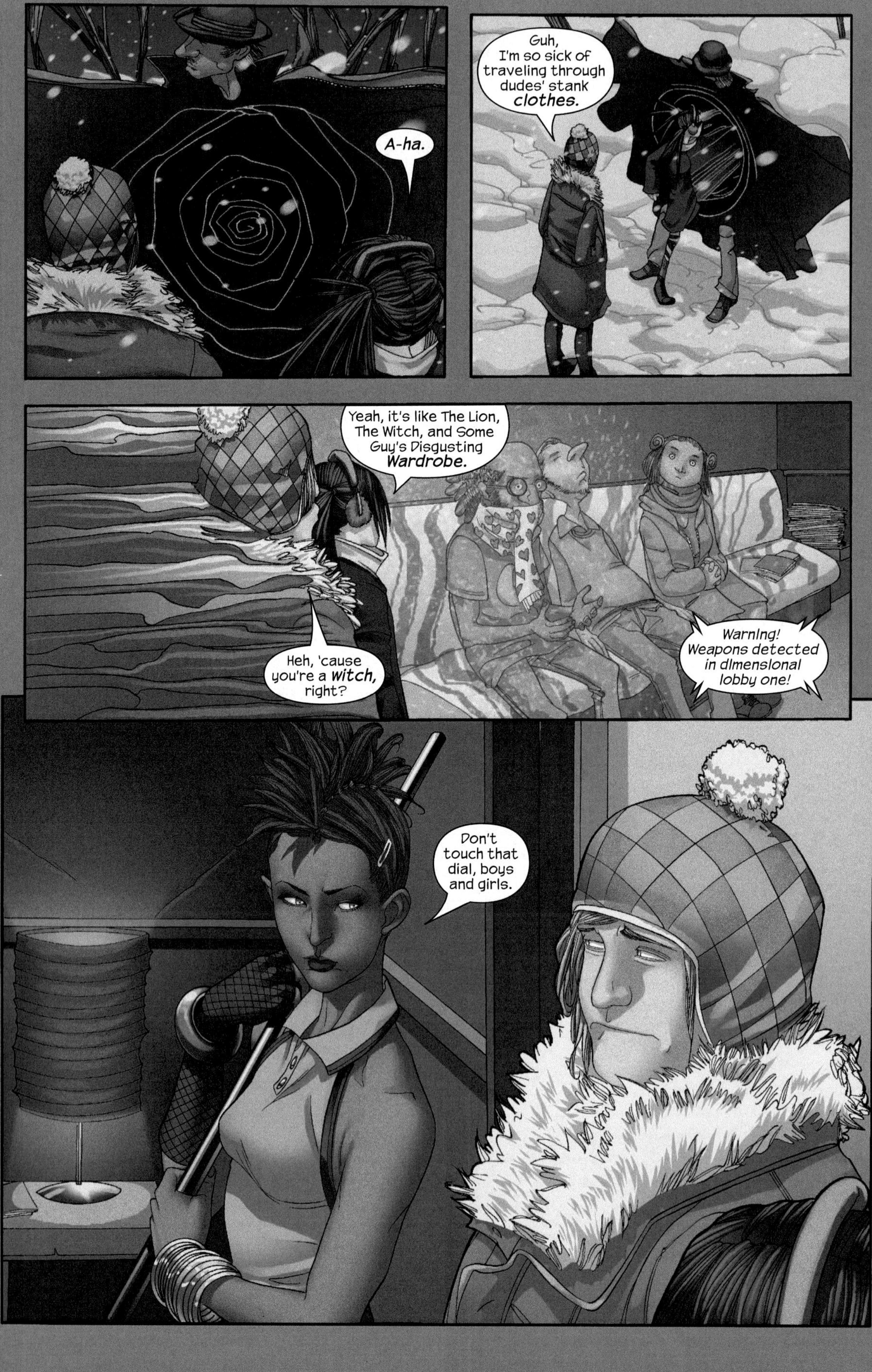
A-ha.
Guh, I'm so sick of traveling through dudes' stank clothes.
Yeah, it's like The Lion, The Witch, and Some Guy's Disgusting Wardrobe.
Heh, 'cause you're a witch, right?
Warning! Weapons detected in dimensional lobby one!
Don't touch that dial, boys and girls.

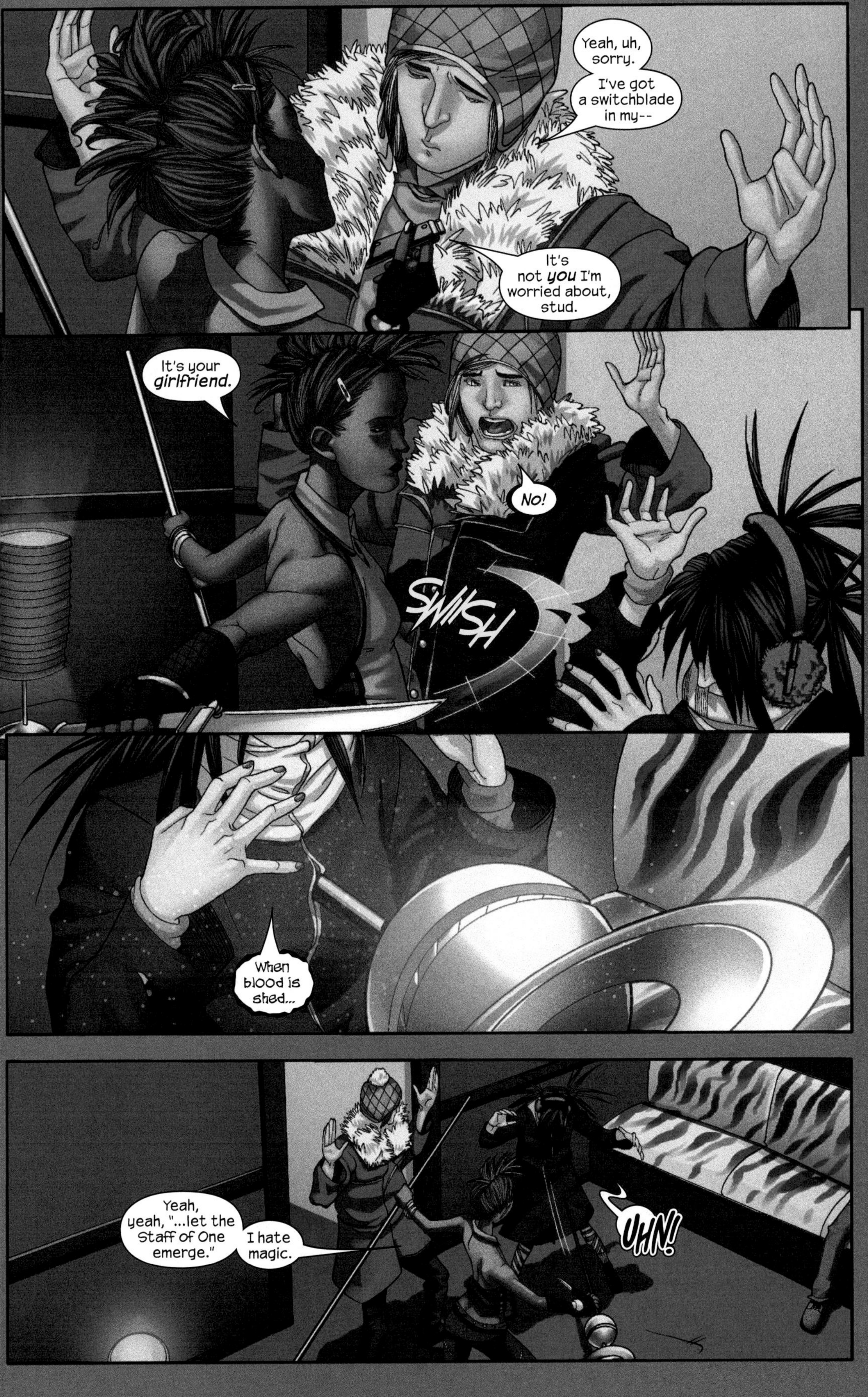
Yeah, uh, sorry.
I've got a switchblade in my--
It's not *you* I'm worried about, stud.
It's your *girlfriend*.
No!
SWISH
When blood is shed...
Yeah, yeah, "...let the Staff of One emerge."
I hate magic.
UHN!

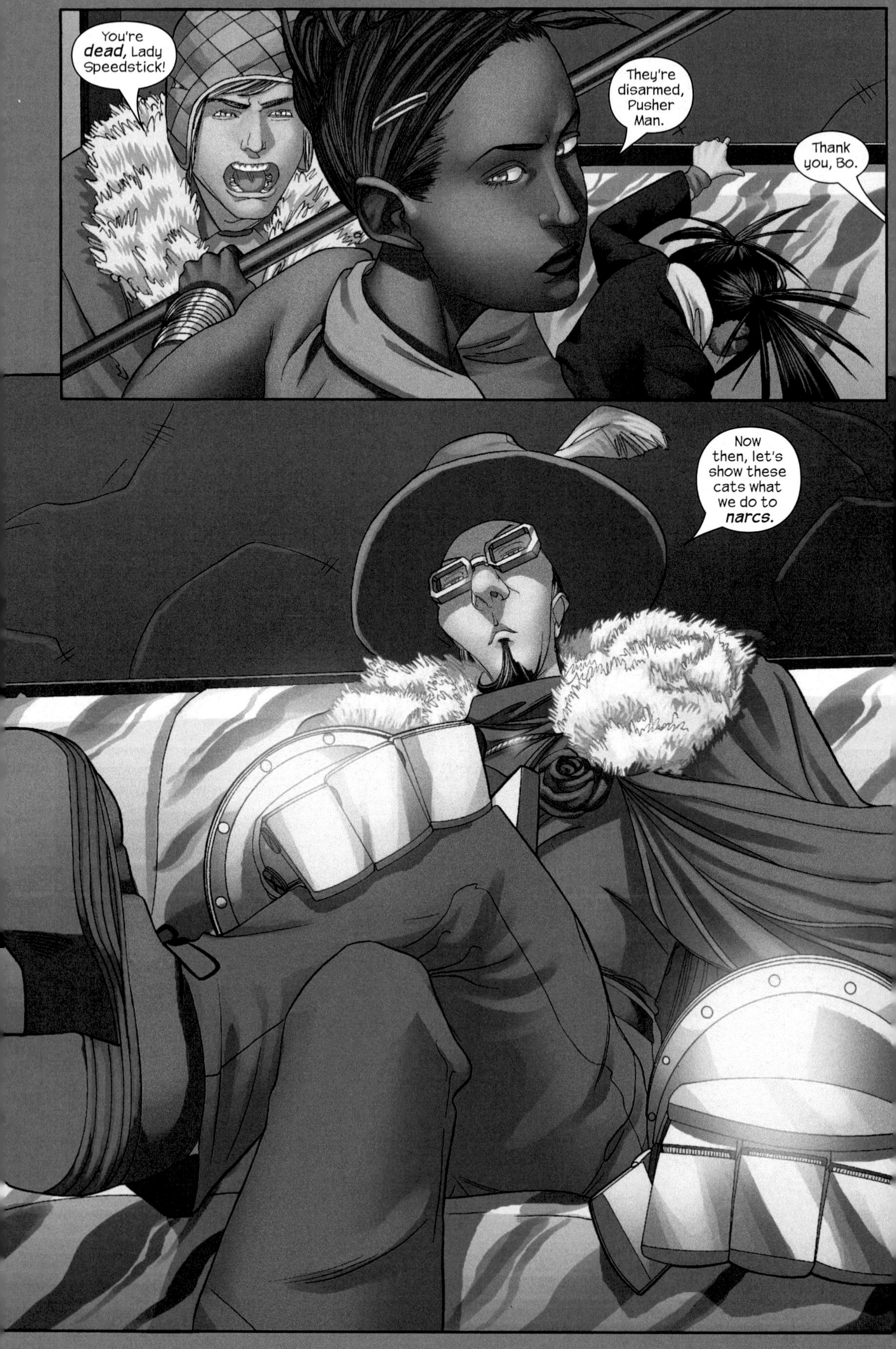
You're dead, Lady Speedstick!
They're disarmed, Pusher Man.
Thank you, Bo.
Now then, let's show these cats what we do to narcs.

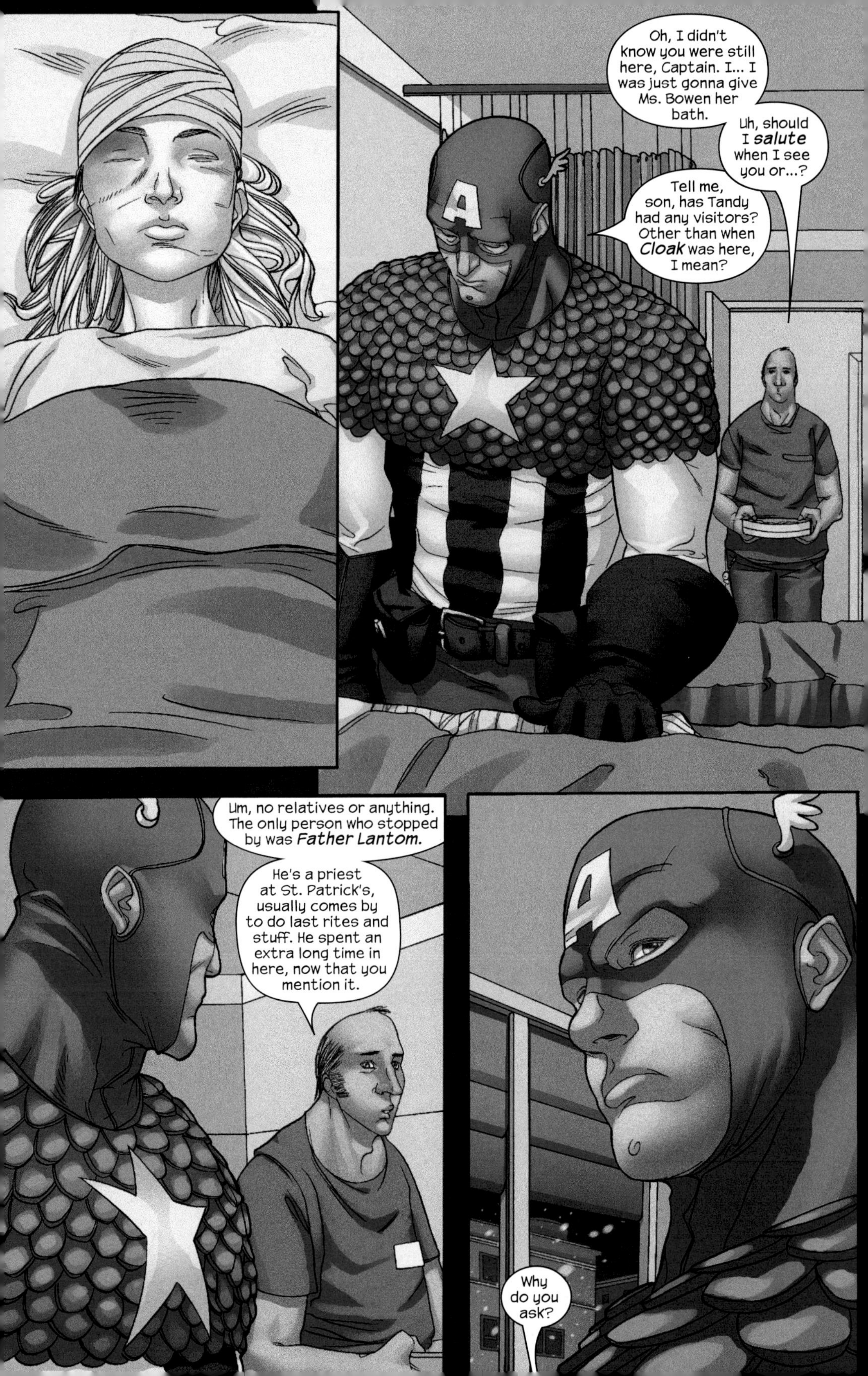
Oh, I didn't know you were still here, Captain. I... I was just gonna give Ms. Bowen her bath.
Uh, should I salute when I see you or...?
Tell me, son, has Tandy had any visitors? Other than when Cloak was here, I mean?
Um, no relatives or anything. The only person who stopped by was Father Lantom.
He's a priest at St. Patrick's, usually comes by to do last rites and stuff. He spent an extra long time in here, now that you mention it.
Why do you ask?

Man, this is *incredible.*

If you jaywalked like this back home, the cops would be all over you, but they don't even *care* out here. How *cool* is that?

If you think this is such a utopia, try my *burrito.*

For a town that supposedly has so many great restaurants, their Mexican food is a crime against humanity.

BUCKWH EATERY

CAPTAIN WOW COMICS

FOR EN'S OFFICE

113

UNCE TICE

Is... is that a *pickle* in there?

No offense, Vic, but I think you just love New York because your evil *"dad"* **taught** you to love it.

Yeah, well, no offense, but maybe you just hate New York because you're not so *special* out here.

AVERN

GARF GARF GARF

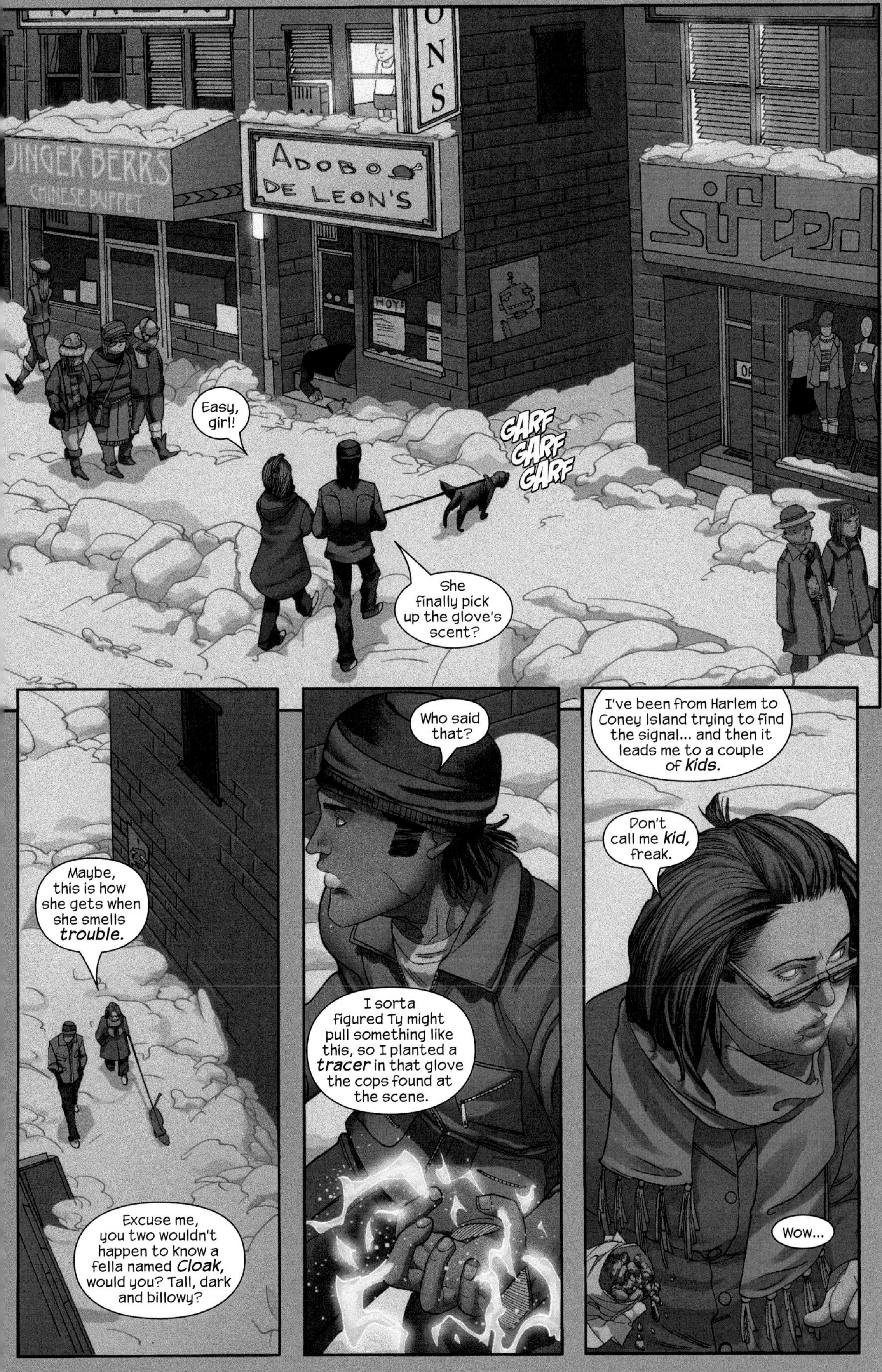
JINGER BERRS
CHINESE BUFFET
ADOBO
DE LEON'S
ONS
sifted
HOY!
Easy, girl!
GARF GARF GARF
She finally pick up the glove's scent?
Maybe, this is how she gets when she smells trouble.
Excuse me, you two wouldn't happen to know a fella named Cloak, would you? Tall, dark and billowy?
Who said that?
I sorta figured Ty might pull something like this, so I planted a tracer in that glove the cops found at the scene.
I've been from Harlem to Coney Island trying to find the signal... and then it leads me to a couple of kids.
Don't call me kid, freak.
Wow...

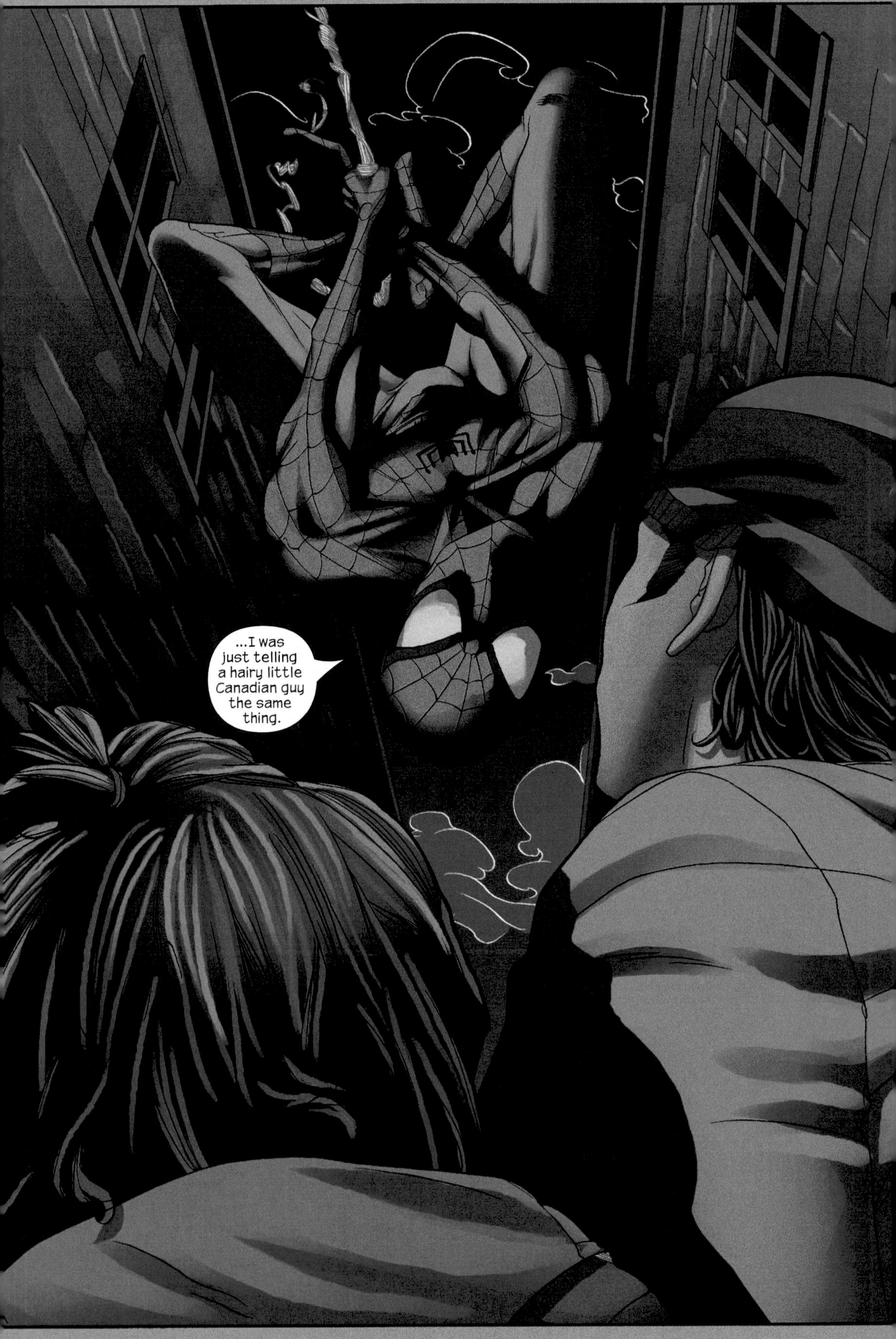
...I was just telling a hairy little Canadian guy the same thing.

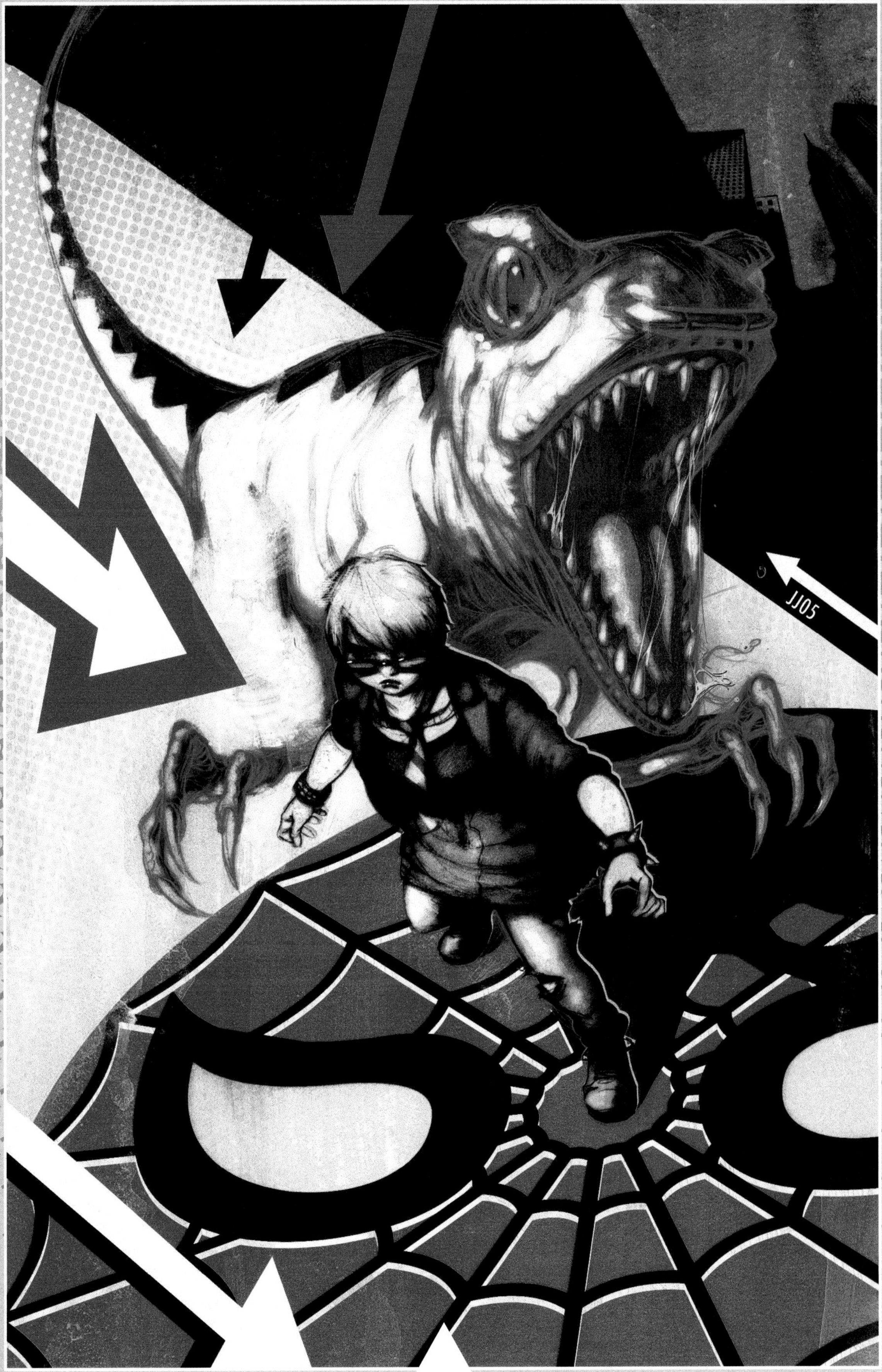
JJ05

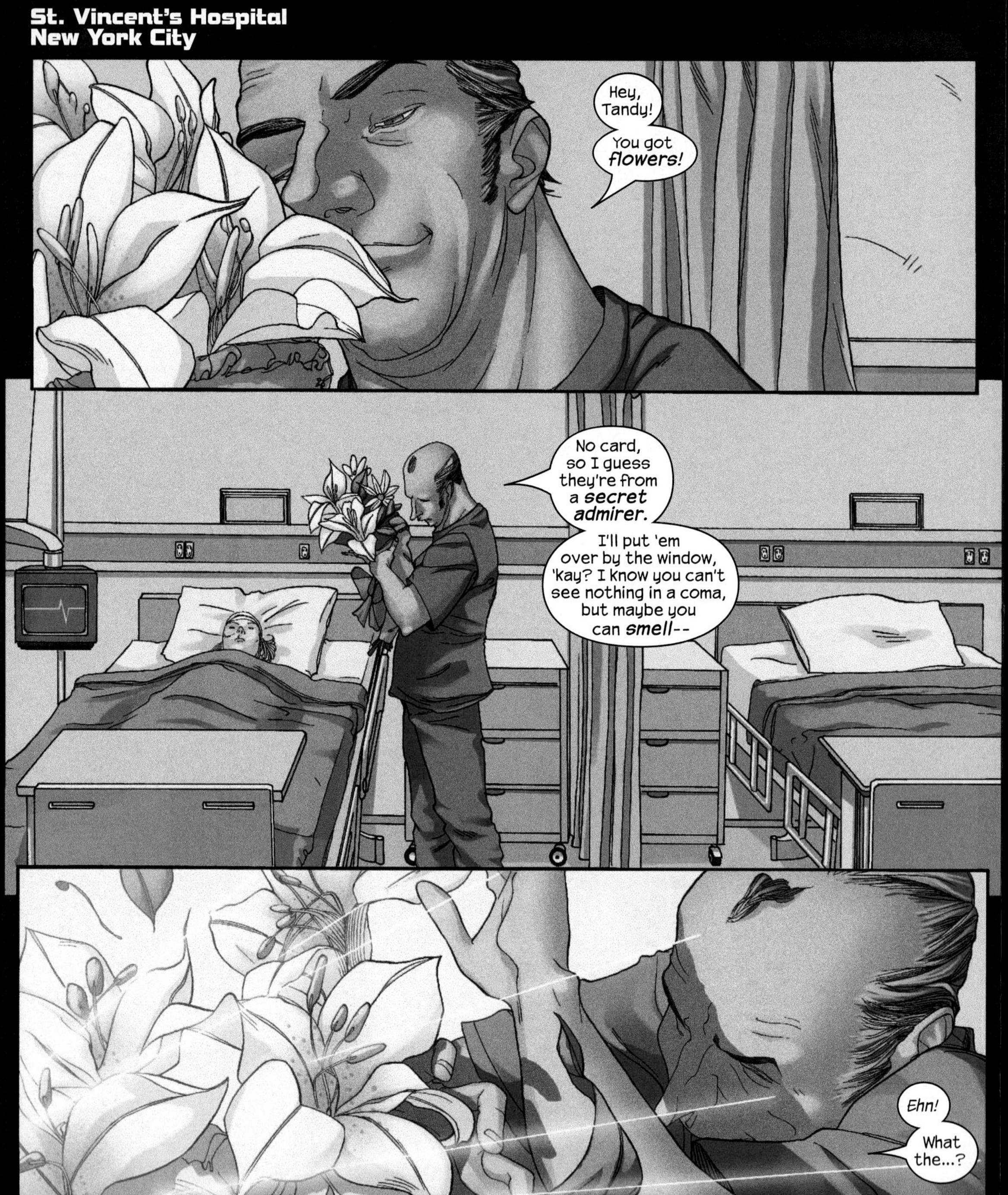
St. Vincent's Hospital
New York City
Hey, Tandy!
You got *flowers!*
No card, so I guess they're from a ***secret admirer.***
I'll put 'em over by the window, 'kay? I know you can't see nothing in a coma, but maybe you can ***smell***--
Ehn!
What the...?
Oh.
Oh, ***wow.***

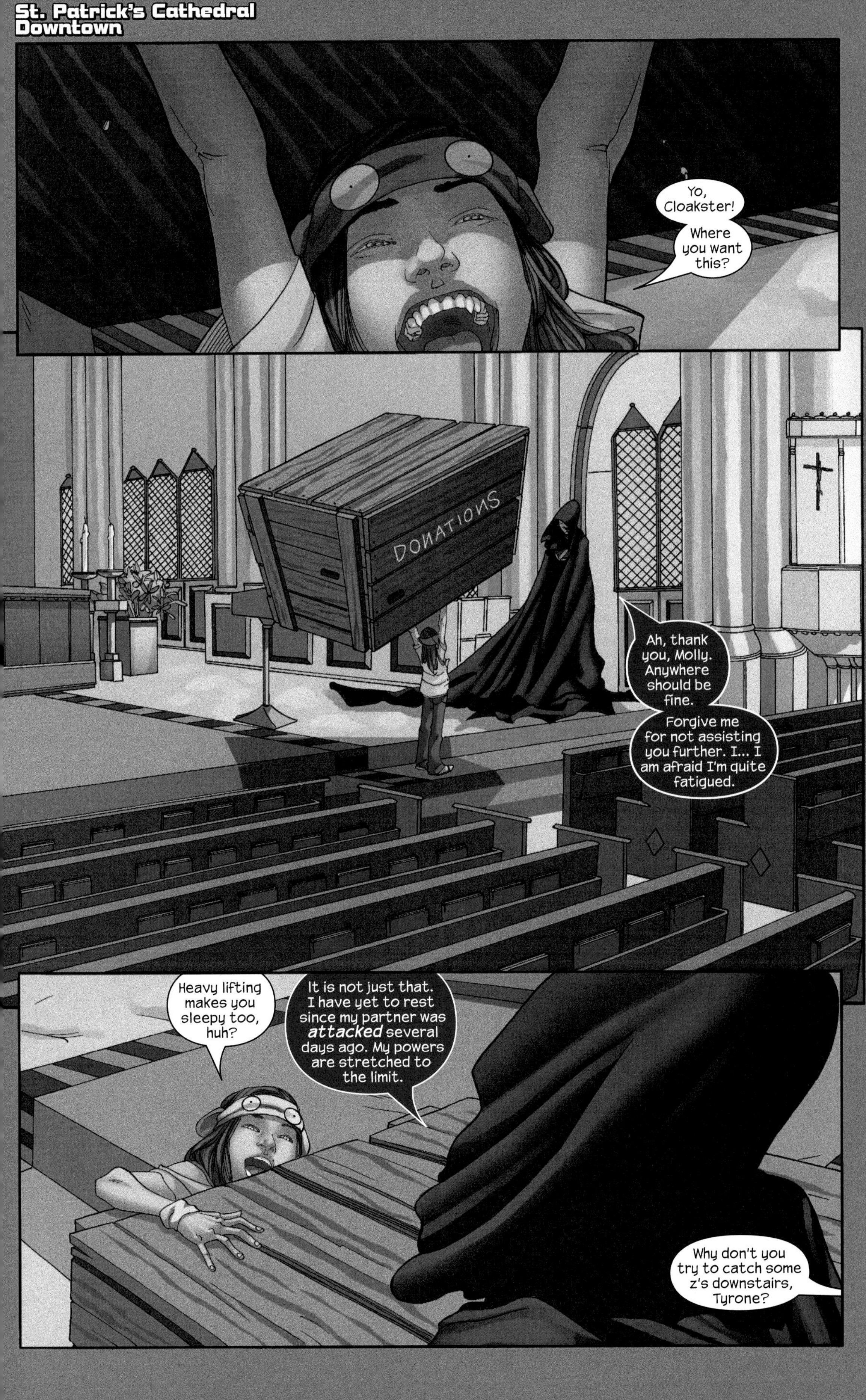

St. Patrick's Cathedral Downtown
Yo, Cloakster!
Where you want this?
DONATIONS
Ah, thank you, Molly. Anywhere should be fine.
Forgive me for not assisting you further. I... I am afraid I'm quite fatigued.
Heavy lifting makes you sleepy too, huh?
It is not just that. I have yet to rest since my partner was *attacked* several days ago. My powers are stretched to the limit.
Why don't you try to catch some z's downstairs, Tyrone?

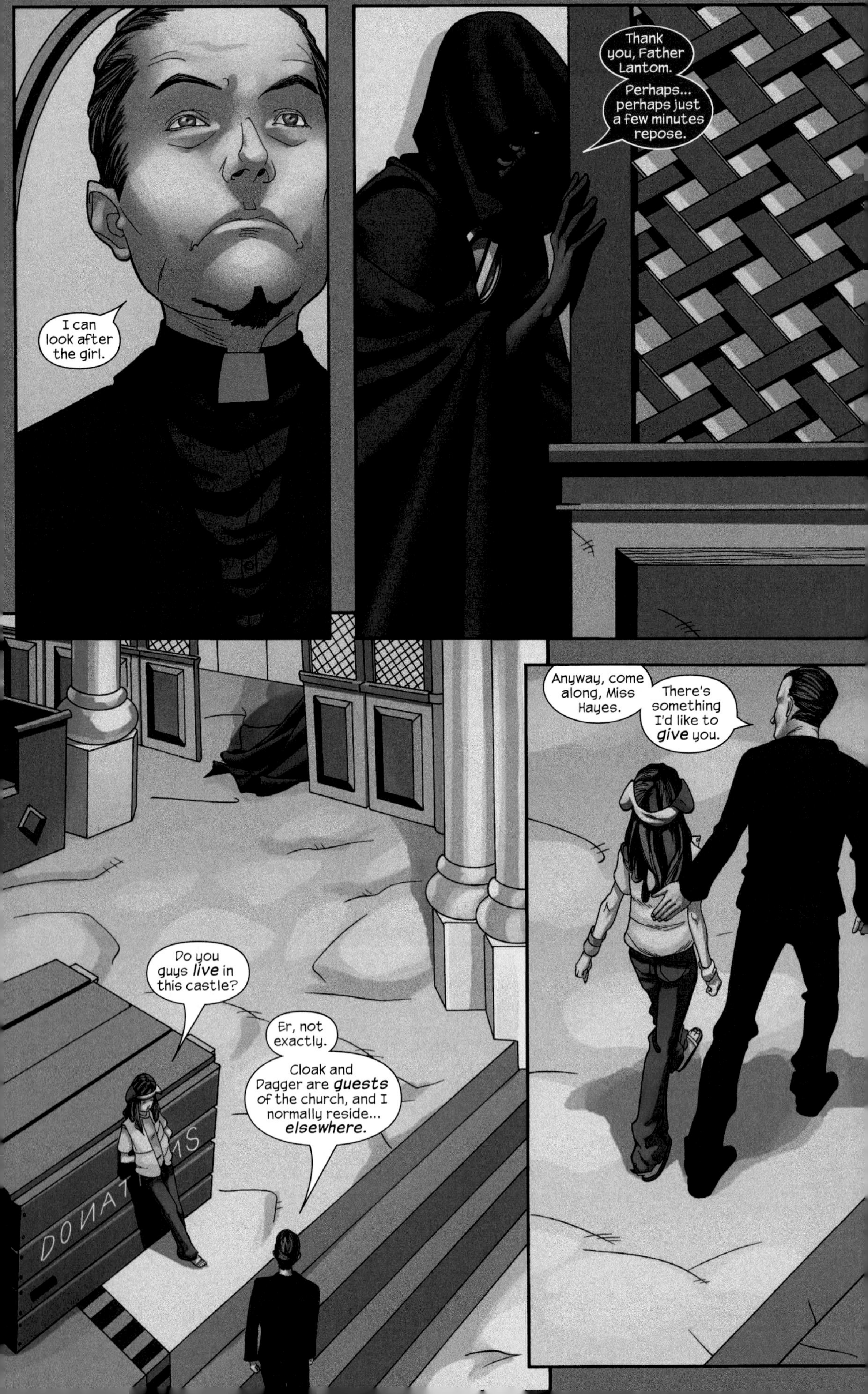
I can look after the girl.
Thank you, Father Lantom.
Perhaps... perhaps just a few minutes repose.
Do you guys *live* in this castle?
Er, not exactly.
Cloak and Dagger are *guests* of the church, and I normally reside... *elsewhere.*
Anyway, come along, Miss Hayes.
There's something I'd like to *give* you.

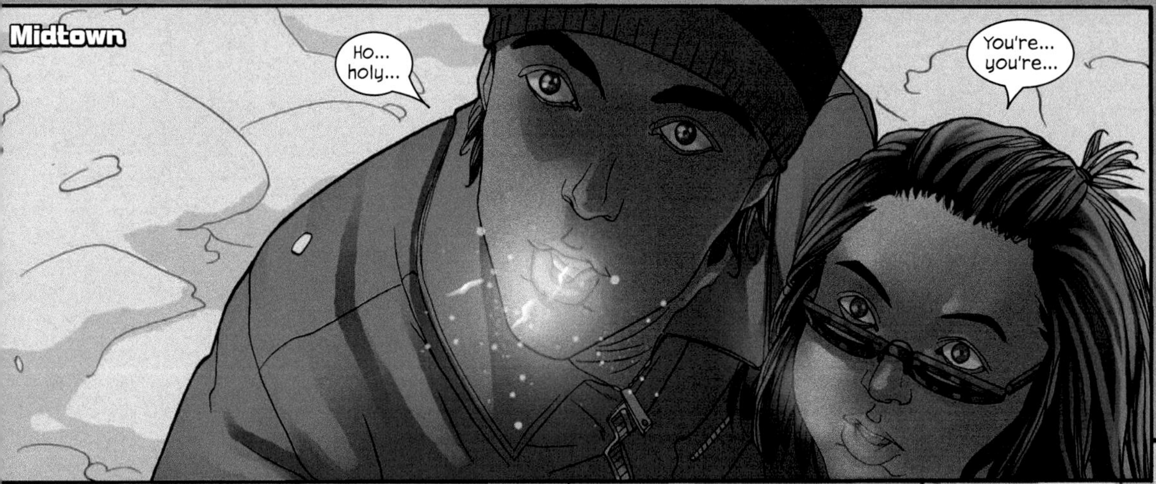
Midtown
Ho... holy...
You're... you're...

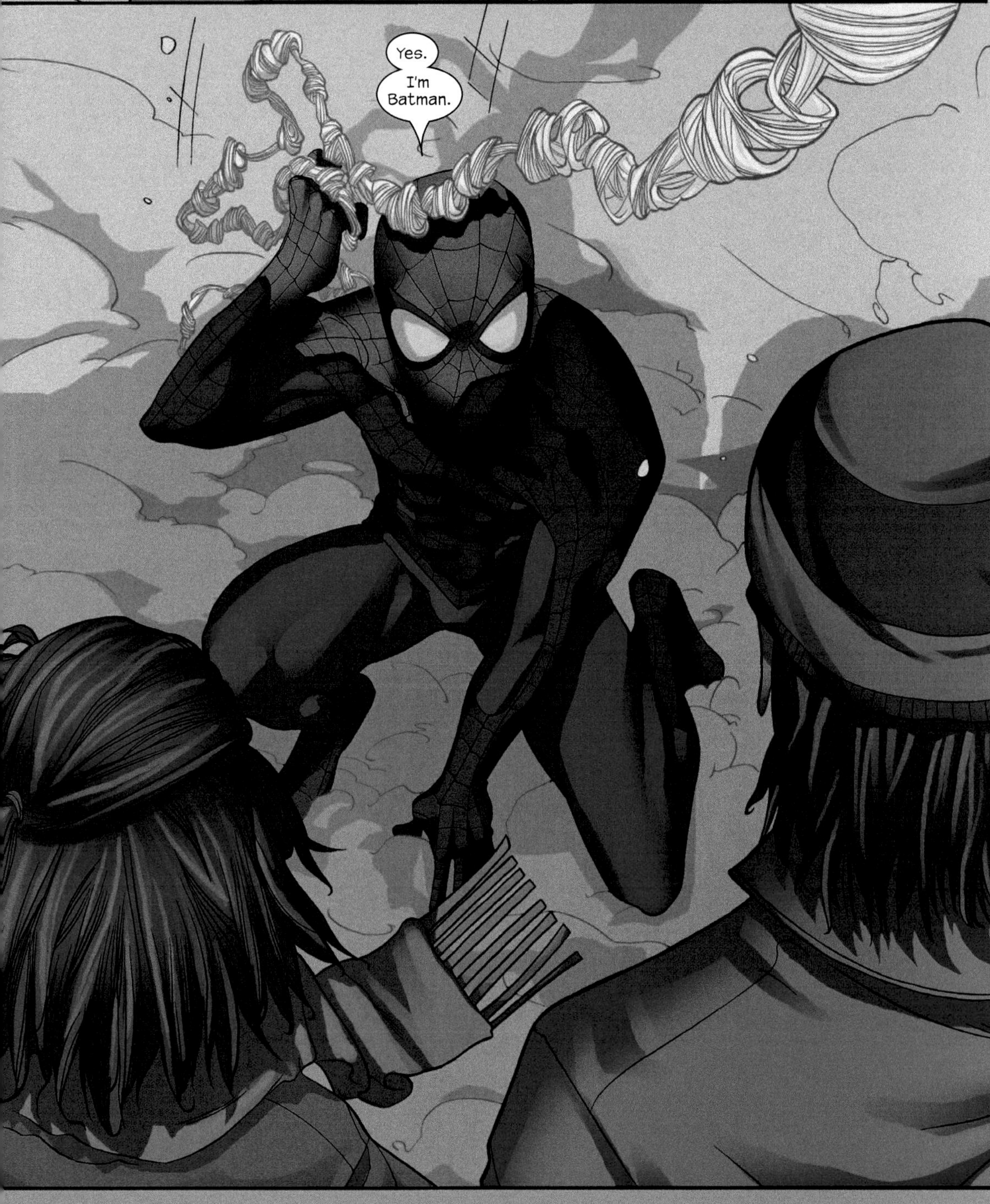
Yes. I'm Batman.

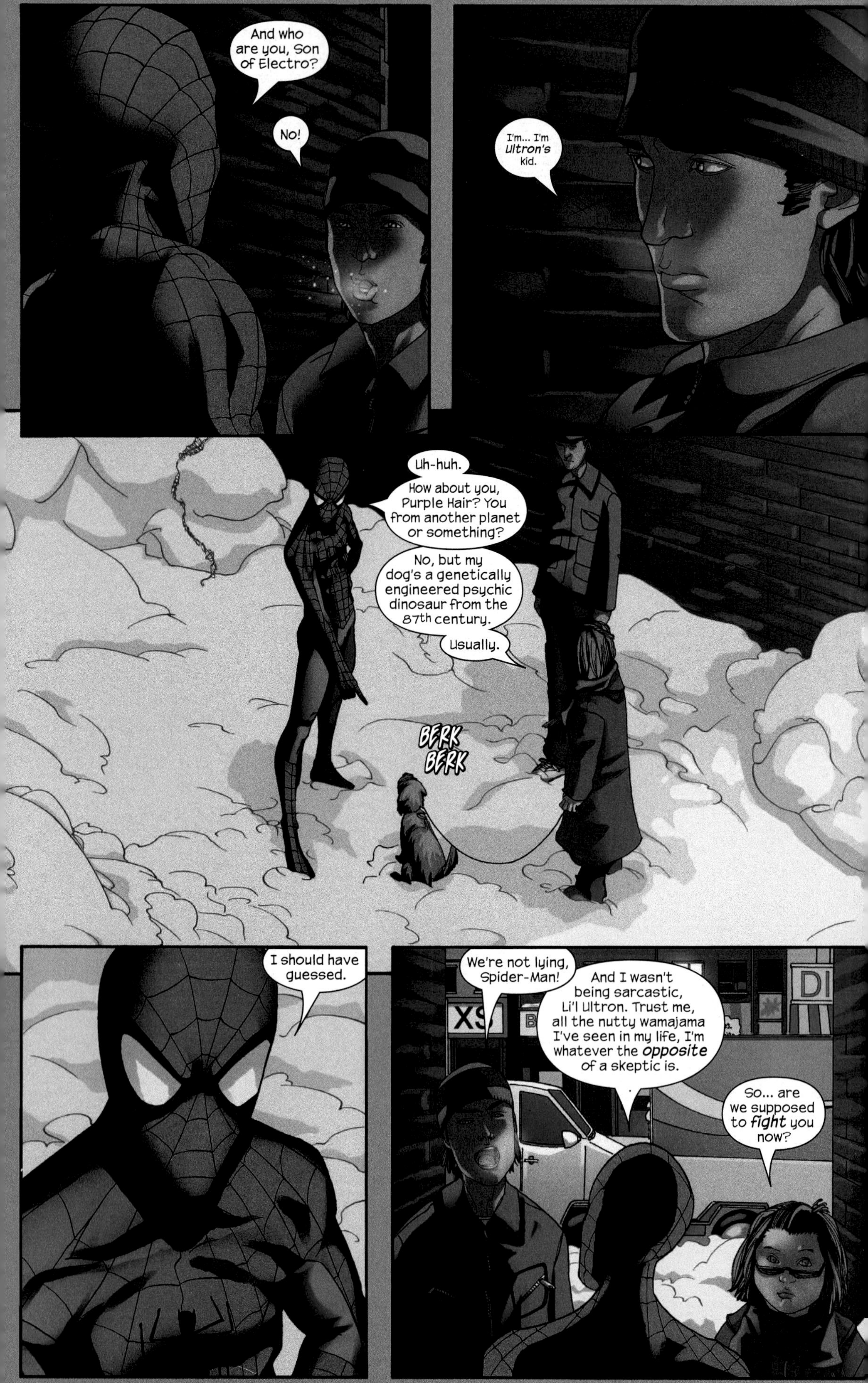
And who are you, Son of Electro?
No!
I'm... I'm *Ultron's* kid.
Uh-huh.
How about you, Purple Hair? You from another planet or something?
No, but my dog's a genetically engineered psychic dinosaur from the 87th century.
Usually.
BERK BERK
I should have guessed.
We're not lying, Spider-Man!
And I wasn't being sarcastic, Li'l Ultron. Trust me, all the nutty wamajama I've seen in my life, I'm whatever the *opposite* of a skeptic is.
So... are we supposed to *fight* you now?

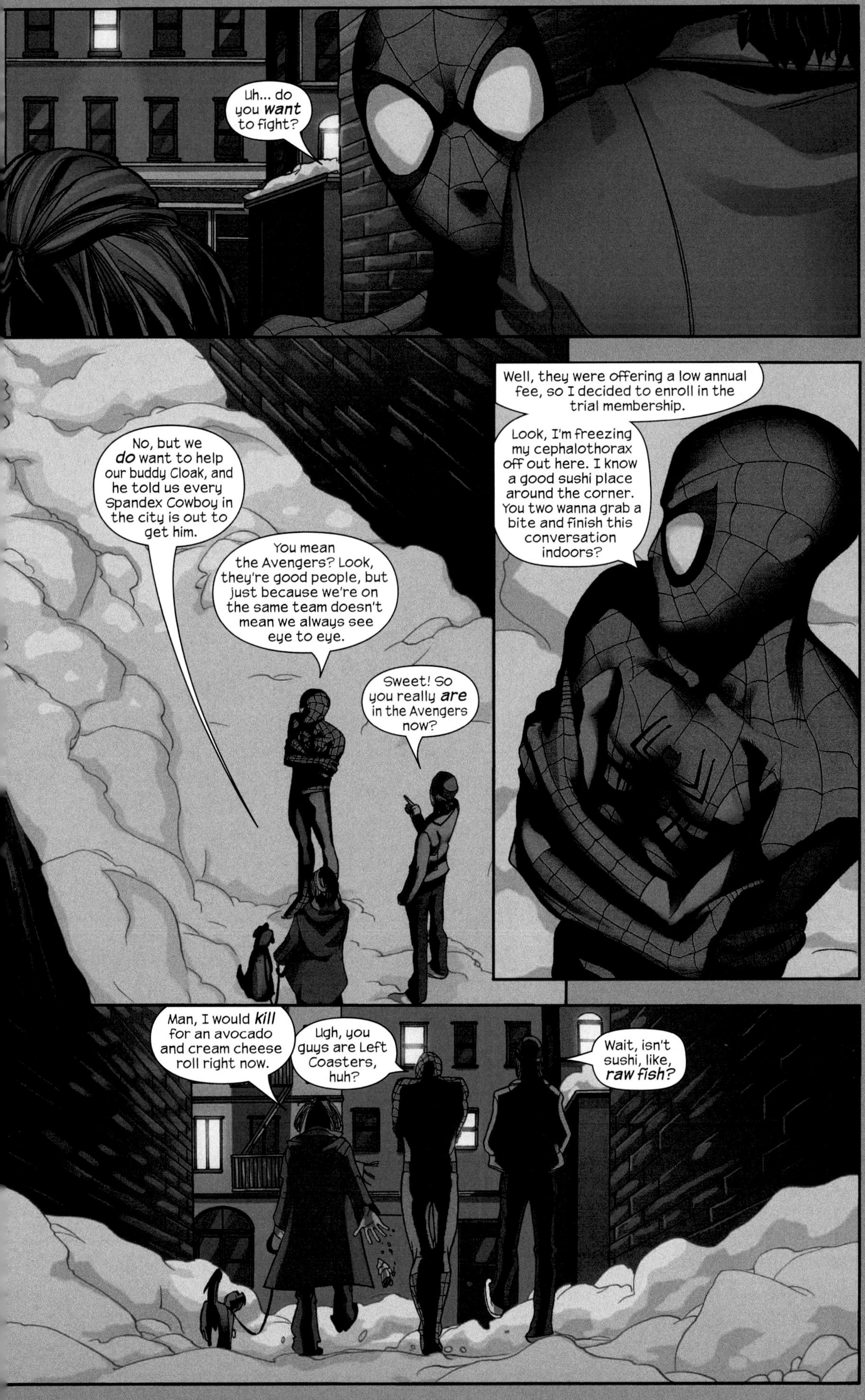
Uh... do you *want* to fight?
No, but we *do* want to help our buddy Cloak, and he told us every Spandex Cowboy in the city is out to get him.
You mean the Avengers? Look, they're good people, but just because we're on the same team doesn't mean we always see eye to eye.
Sweet! So you really *are* in the Avengers now?
Well, they were offering a low annual fee, so I decided to enroll in the trial membership.
Look, I'm freezing my cephalothorax off out here. I know a good sushi place around the corner. You two wanna grab a bite and finish this conversation indoors?
Man, I would *kill* for an avocado and cream cheese roll right now.
Ugh, you guys are Left Coasters, huh?
Wait, isn't sushi, like, *raw fish?*

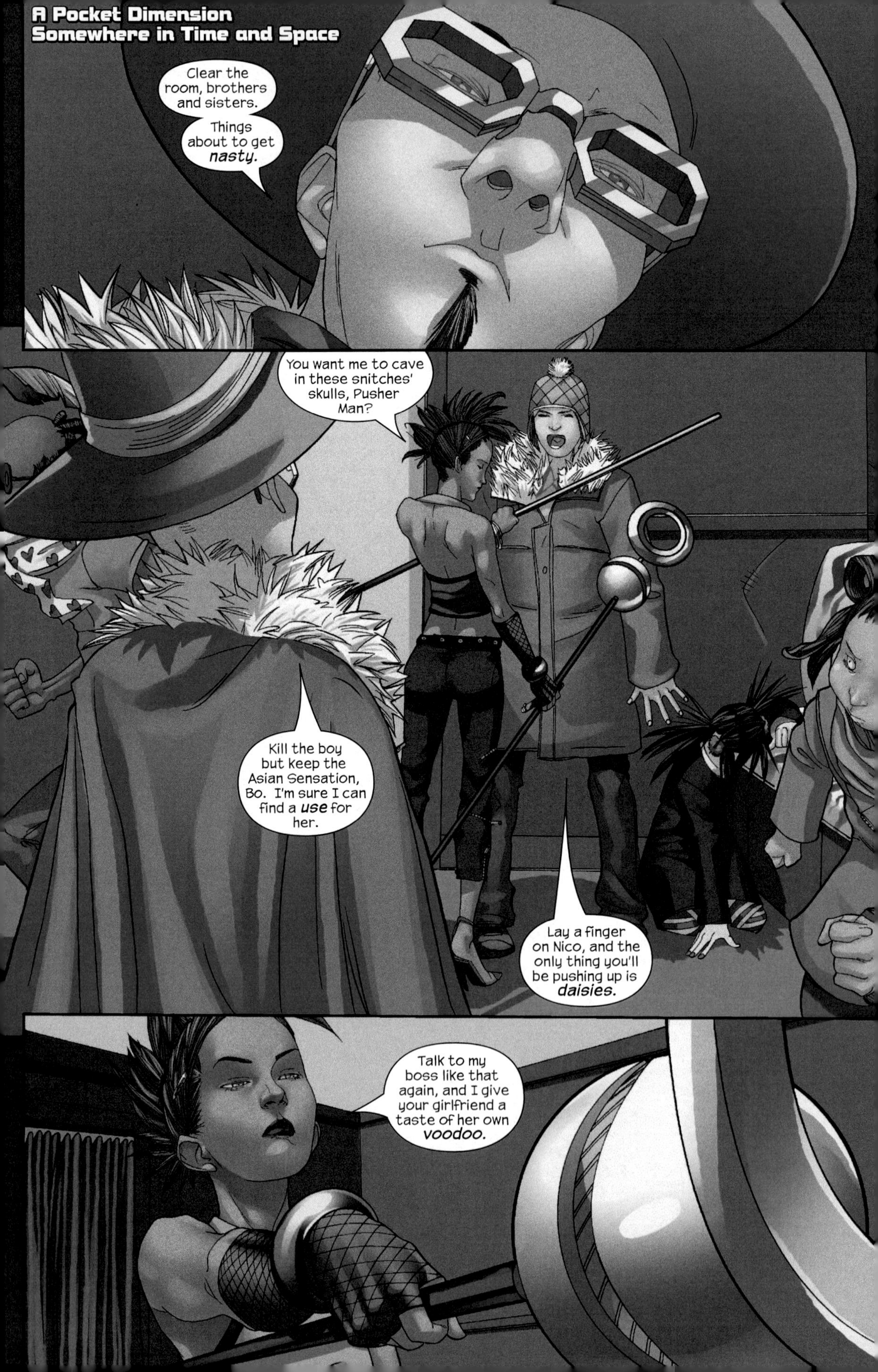
A Pocket Dimension Somewhere in Time and Space
Clear the room, brothers and sisters.
Things about to get nasty.
You want me to cave in these snitches' skulls, Pusher Man?
Kill the boy but keep the Asian Sensation, Bo. I'm sure I can find a use for her.
Lay a finger on Nico, and the only thing you'll be pushing up is daisies.
Talk to my boss like that again, and I give your girlfriend a taste of her own voodoo.

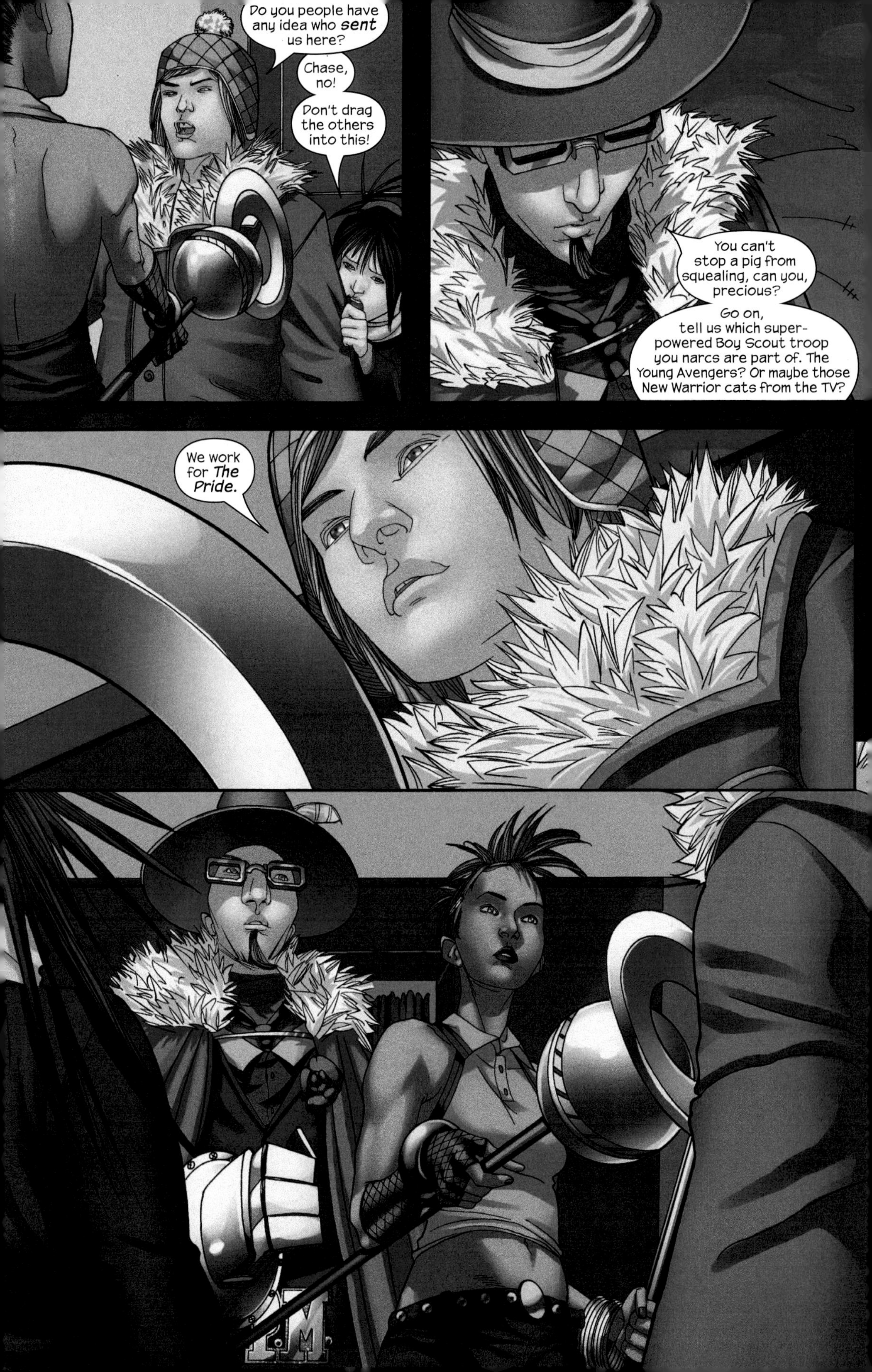
Do you people have any idea who *sent* us here?
Chase, no!
Don't drag the others into this!
You can't stop a pig from squealing, can you, precious?
Go on, tell us which super-powered Boy Scout troop you narcs are part of. The Young Avengers? Or maybe those New Warrior cats from the TV?
We work for *The Pride.*

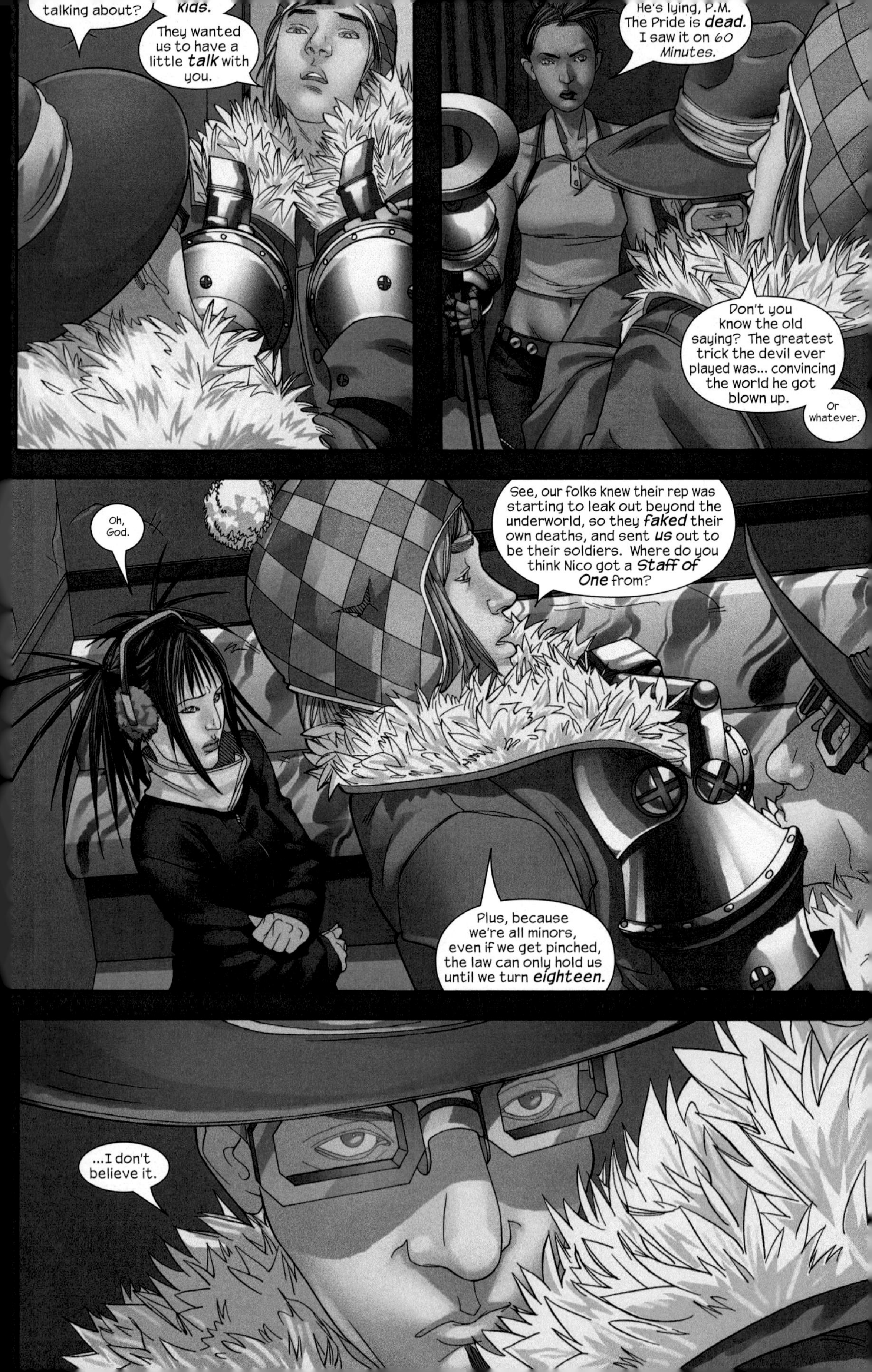
talking about?
kids.
They wanted us to have a little talk with you.
He's lying, P.M. The Pride is dead. I saw it on 60 Minutes.
Don't you know the old saying? The greatest trick the devil ever played was... convincing the world he got blown up.
Or whatever.
Oh, God.
See, our folks knew their rep was starting to leak out beyond the underworld, so they faked their own deaths, and sent us out to be their soldiers. Where do you think Nico got a Staff of One from?
Plus, because we're all minors, even if we get pinched, the law can only hold us until we turn eighteen.
...I don't believe it.

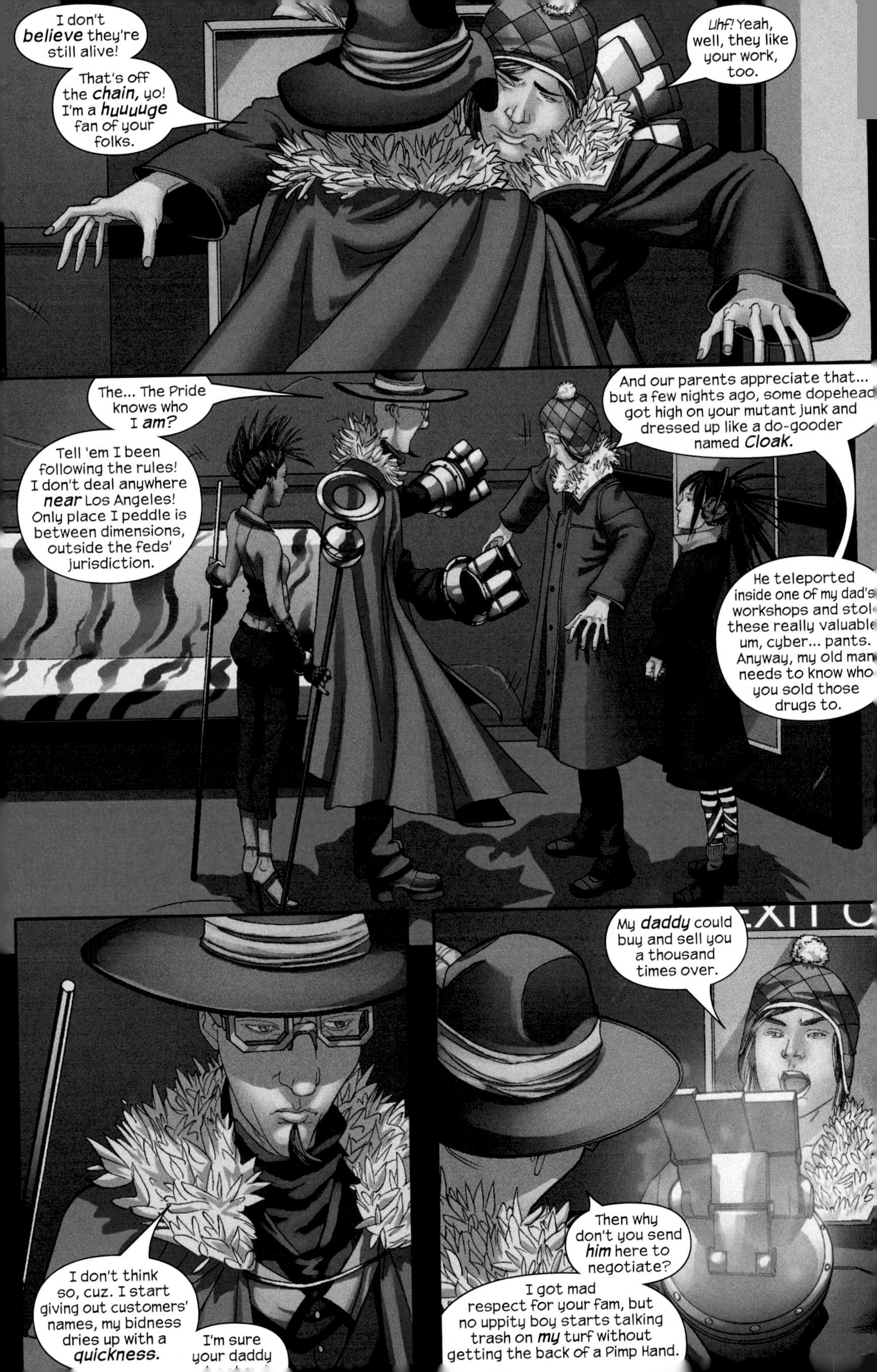
I don't believe they're still alive!
That's off the chain, yo! I'm a huuuuge fan of your folks.
Uhf! Yeah, well, they like your work, too.
The... The Pride knows who I am?
Tell 'em I been following the rules! I don't deal anywhere near Los Angeles! Only place I peddle is between dimensions, outside the feds' jurisdiction.
And our parents appreciate that... but a few nights ago, some dopehead got high on your mutant junk and dressed up like a do-gooder named Cloak.
He teleported inside one of my dad's workshops and stol these really valuable um, cyber... pants. Anyway, my old man needs to know who you sold those drugs to.
I don't think so, cuz. I start giving out customers' names, my bidness dries up with a quickness.
I'm sure your daddy
My daddy could buy and sell you a thousand times over.
Then why don't you send him here to negotiate?
I got mad respect for your fam, but no uppity boy starts talking trash on my turf without getting the back of a Pimp Hand.

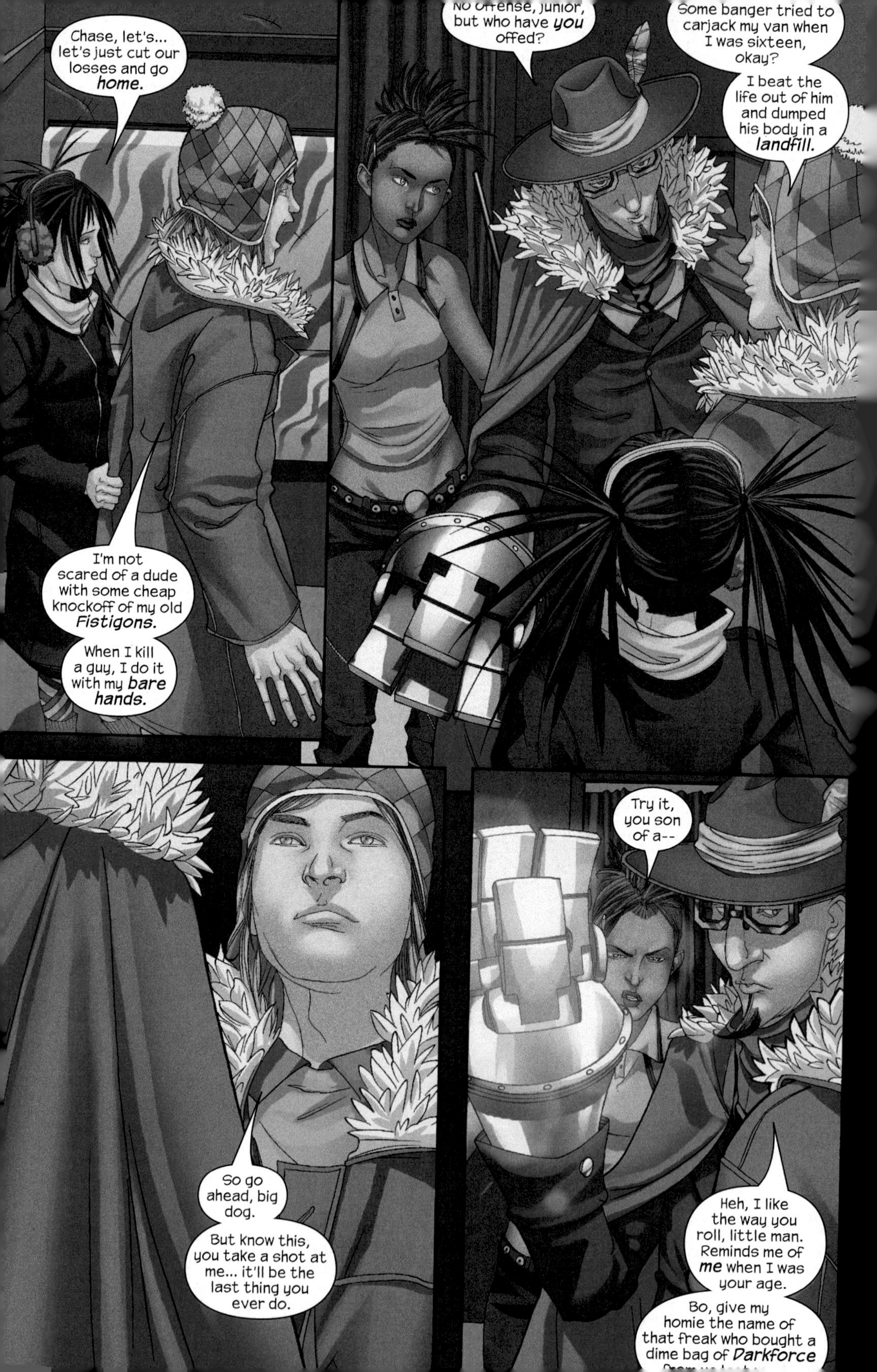
Chase, let's... let's just cut our losses and go *home.*
I'm not scared of a dude with some cheap knockoff of my old *Fistigons.*
When I kill a guy, I do it with my *bare hands.*
No offense, junior, but who have *you* offed?
Some banger tried to carjack my van when I was sixteen, okay?
I beat the life out of him and dumped his body in a *landfill.*
So go ahead, big dog.
But know this, you take a shot at me... it'll be the last thing you ever do.
Try it, you son of a--
Heh, I like the way you roll, little man. Reminds me of *me* when I was your age.
Bo, give my homie the name of that freak who bought a dime bag of *Darkforce*

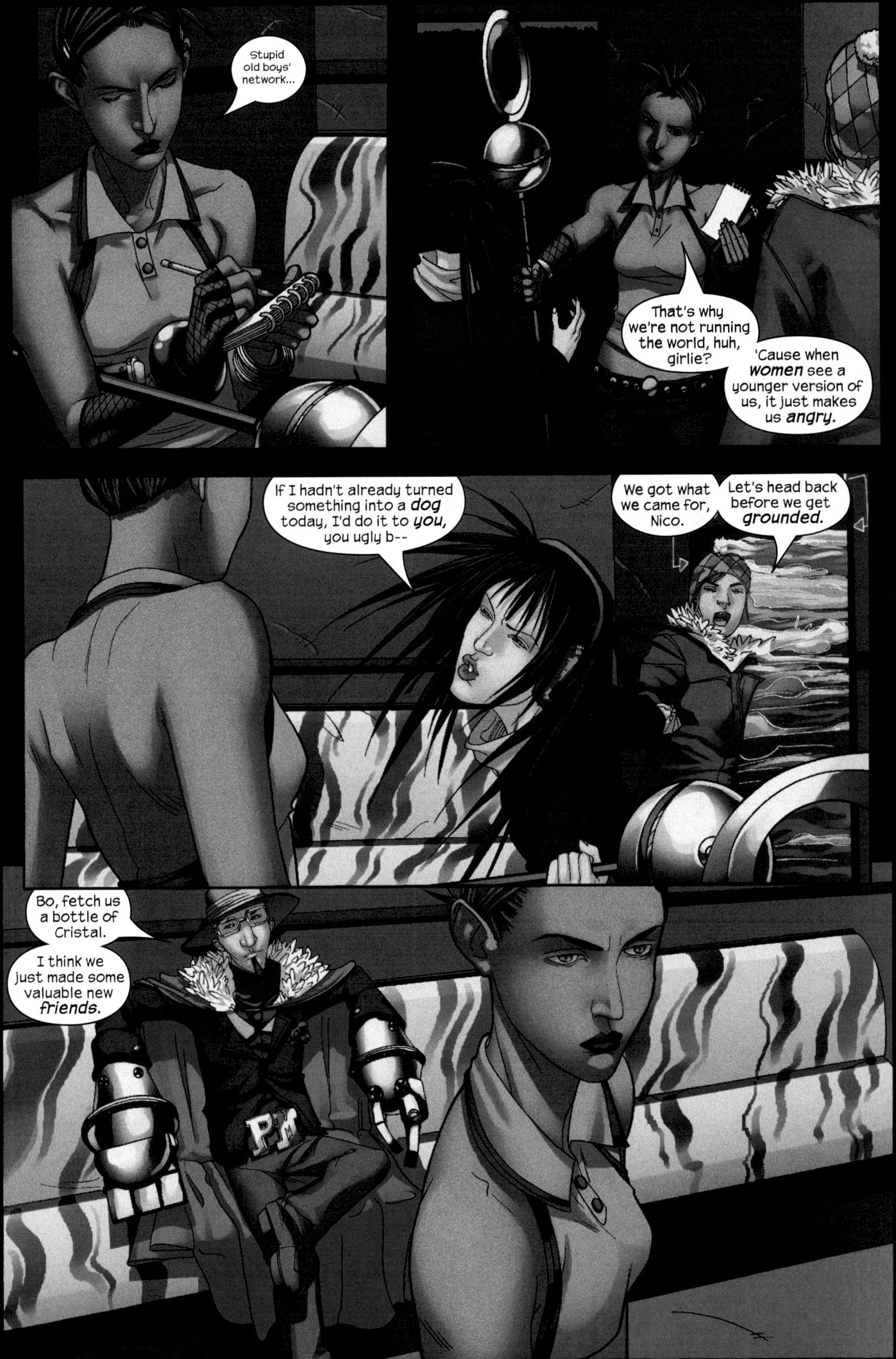
Stupid old boys' network...
That's why we're not running the world, huh, girlie?
'Cause when *women* see a younger version of us, it just makes us *angry.*
If I hadn't already turned something into a *dog* today, I'd do it to *you,* you ugly b--
We got what we came for, Nico.
Let's head back before we get *grounded.*
Bo, fetch us a bottle of Cristal.
I think we just made some valuable new *friends.*

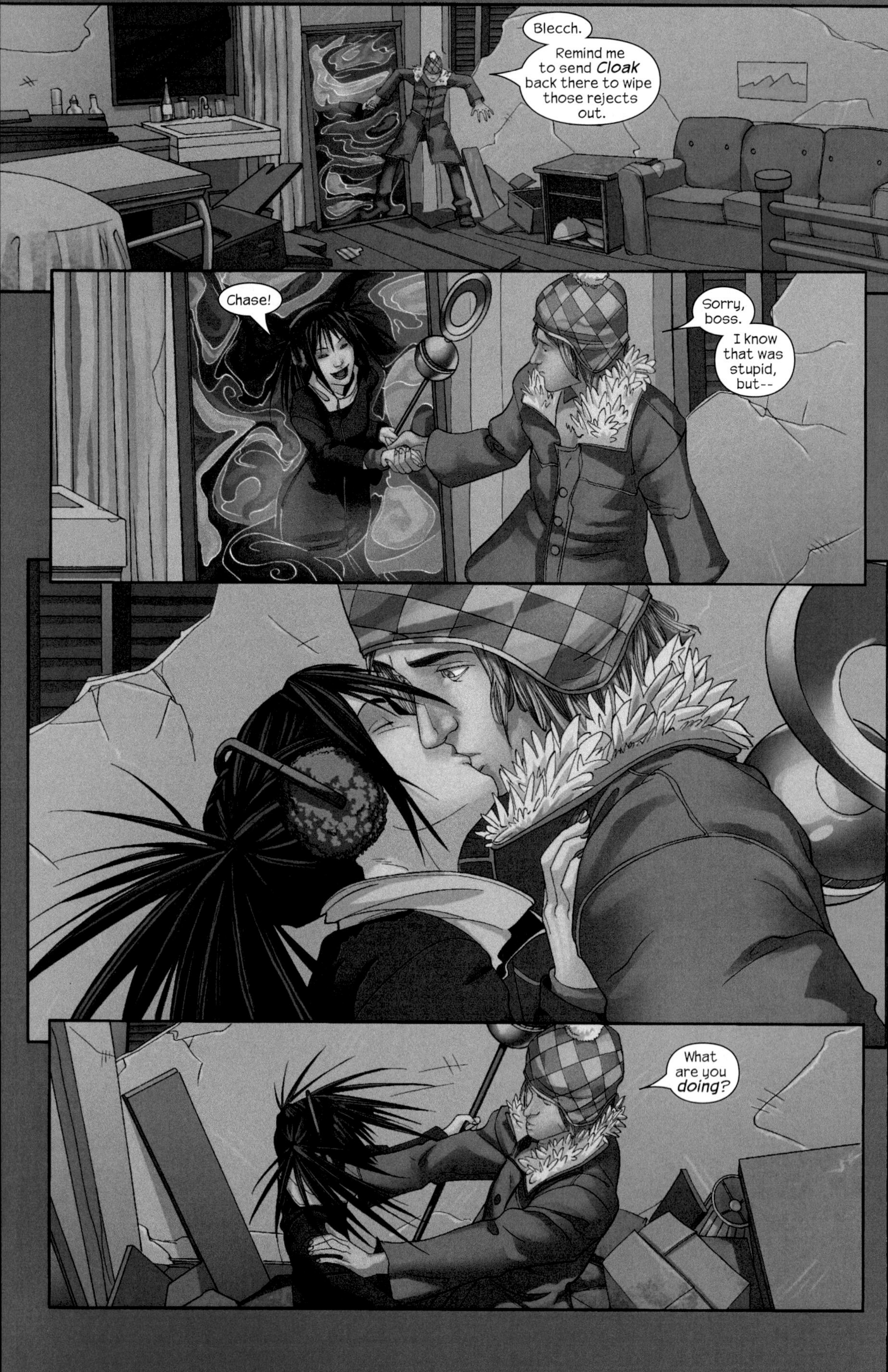

Blecch.
Remind me to send *Cloak* back there to wipe those rejects out.
Chase!
Sorry, boss.
I know that was stupid, but--
What are you *doing*?

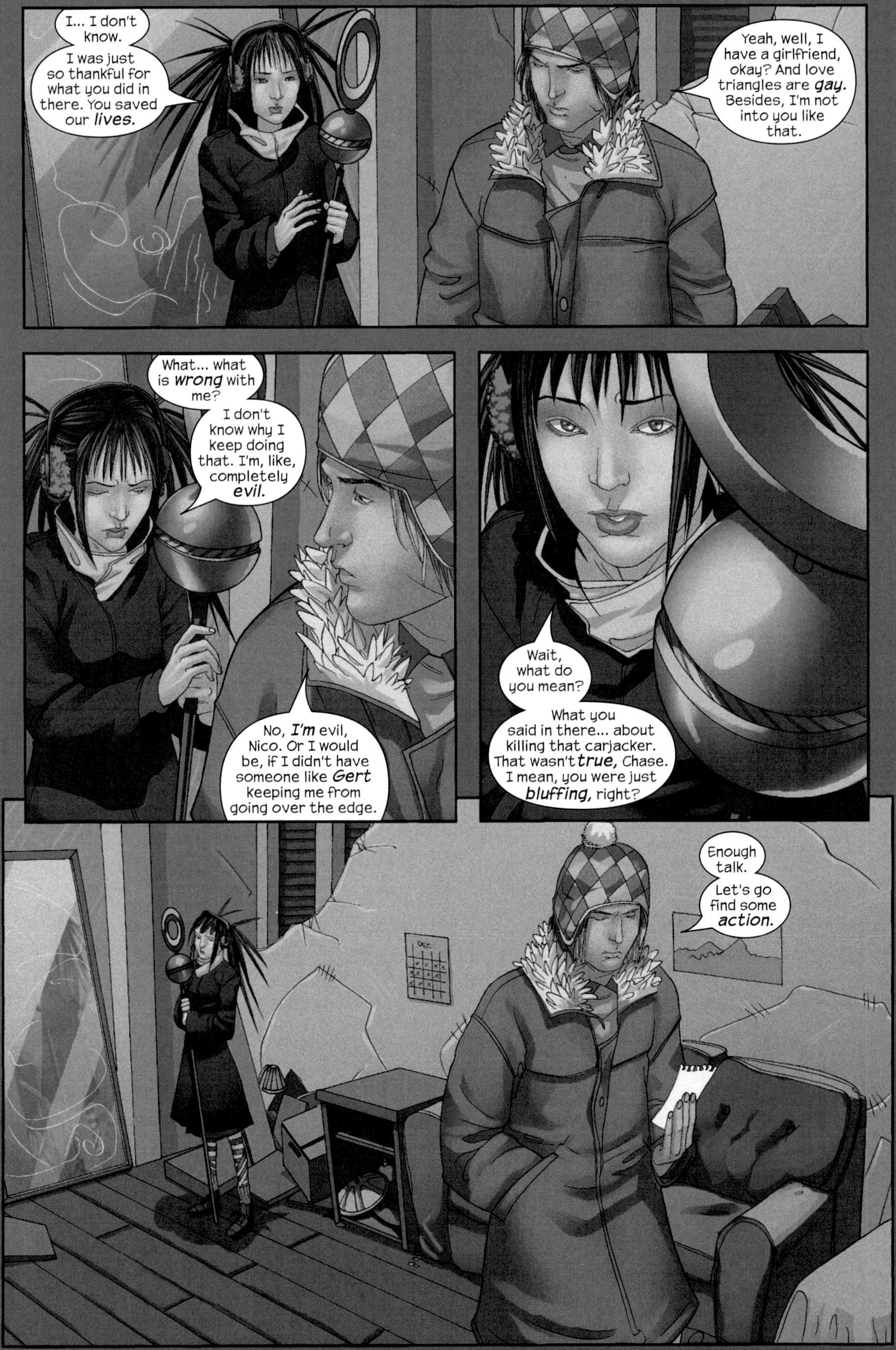

I... I don't know.
I was just so thankful for what you did in there. You saved our *lives.*
Yeah, well, I have a girlfriend, okay? And love triangles are *gay.* Besides, I'm not into you like that.
What... what is *wrong* with me?
I don't know why I keep doing that. I'm, like, completely *evil.*
No, *I'm* evil, Nico. Or I would be, if I didn't have someone like *Gert* keeping me from going over the edge.
Wait, what do you mean?
What you said in there... about killing that carjacker. That wasn't *true,* Chase. I mean, you were just *bluffing,* right?
Enough talk.
Let's go find some *action.*

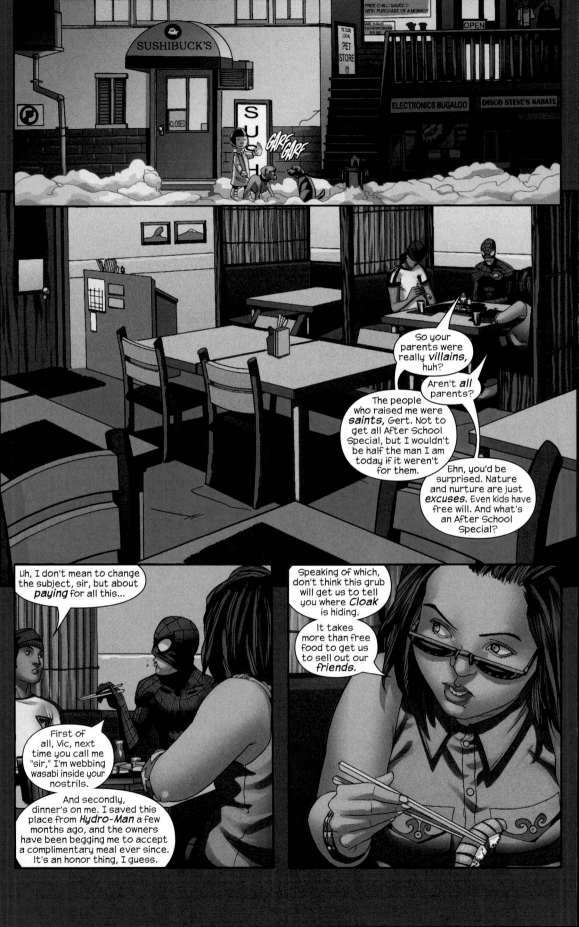

SUSHIBUCK'S

CLOSED

GARF GARF

YE OLDE
LOCAL
PET
STORE
!!!

WE HAVE
FREE CHILI SAUCE !!
WITH PURCHASE OF A MONKEY

OPEN

ELECTRONICS BUGALOO

DISCO STEVE'S KARATE

So your parents were really *villains*, huh?

Aren't *all* parents?

The people who raised me were *saints*, Gert. Not to get all After School Special, but I wouldn't be half the man I am today if it weren't for them.

Ehn, you'd be surprised. Nature and nurture are just *excuses*. Even kids have free will. And what's an After School Special?

Uh, I don't mean to change the subject, sir, but about *paying* for all this...

First of all, Vic, next time you call me "sir," I'm webbing wasabi inside your nostrils.

And secondly, dinner's on me. I saved this place from *Hydro-Man* a few months ago, and the owners have been begging me to accept a complimentary meal ever since. It's an honor thing, I guess.

Speaking of which, don't think this grub will get us to tell you where *Cloak* is hiding.

It takes more than free food to get us to sell out our *friends.*

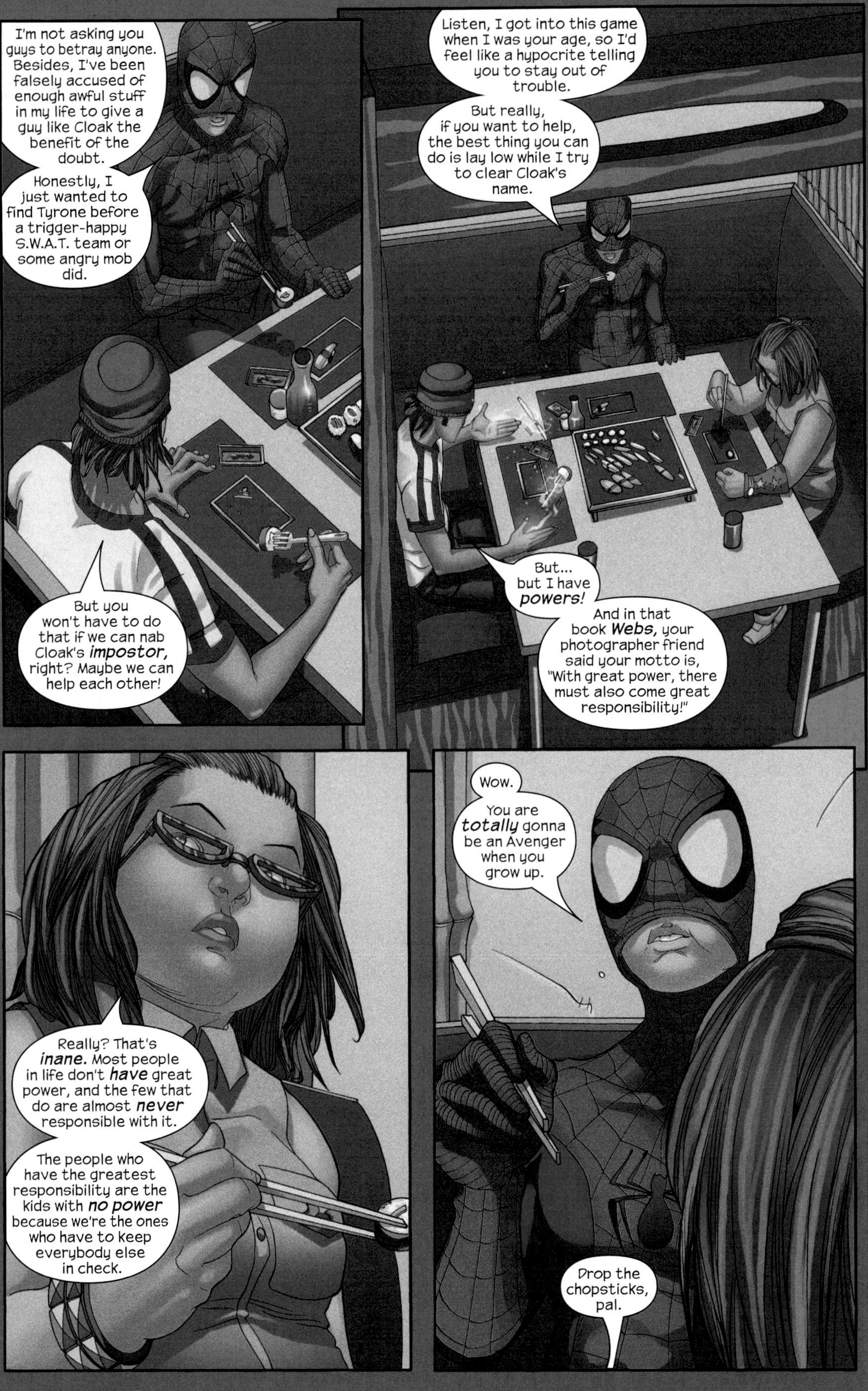
I'm not asking you guys to betray anyone. Besides, I've been falsely accused of enough awful stuff in my life to give a guy like Cloak the benefit of the doubt.
Honestly, I just wanted to find Tyrone before a trigger-happy S.W.A.T. team or some angry mob did.
But you won't have to do that if we can nab Cloak's *impostor,* right? Maybe we can help each other!
Listen, I got into this game when I was your age, so I'd feel like a hypocrite telling you to stay out of trouble.
But really, if you want to help, the best thing you can do is lay low while I try to clear Cloak's name.
But... but I have *powers!*
And in that book *Webs,* your photographer friend said your motto is, "With great power, there must also come great responsibility!"
Really? That's *inane.* Most people in life don't *have* great power, and the few that do are almost *never* responsible with it.
The people who have the greatest responsibility are the kids with *no power* because we're the ones who have to keep everybody else in check.
Wow.
You are *totally* gonna be an Avenger when you grow up.
Drop the chopsticks, pal.

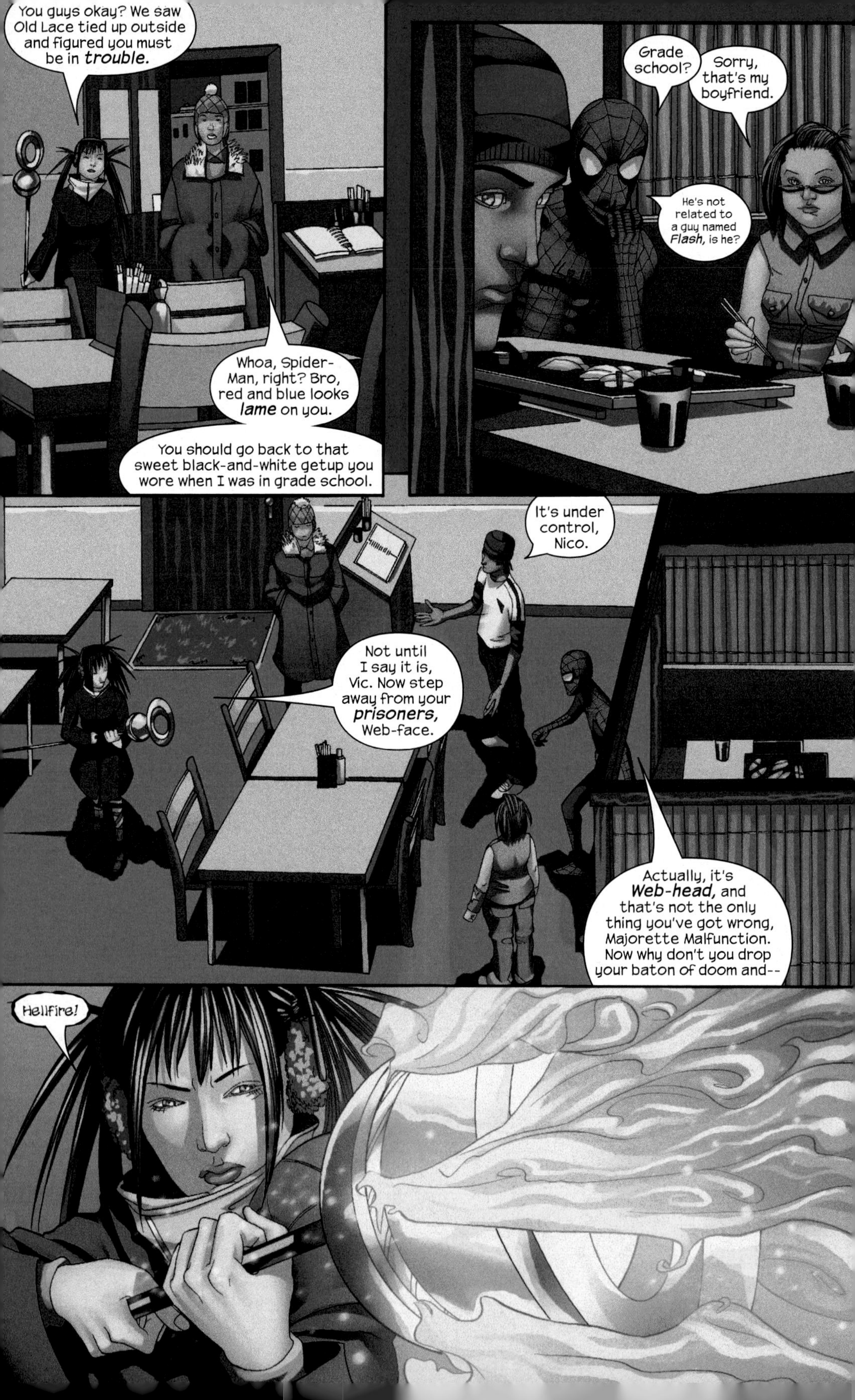
You guys okay? We saw Old Lace tied up outside and figured you must be in trouble.
Whoa, Spider-Man, right? Bro, red and blue looks lame on you.
You should go back to that sweet black-and-white getup you wore when I was in grade school.
Grade school?
Sorry, that's my boyfriend.
He's not related to a guy named Flash, is he?
It's under control, Nico.
Not until I say it is, Vic. Now step away from your prisoners, Web-face.
Actually, it's Web-head, and that's not the only thing you've got wrong, Majorette Malfunction. Now why don't you drop your baton of doom and--
Hellfire!

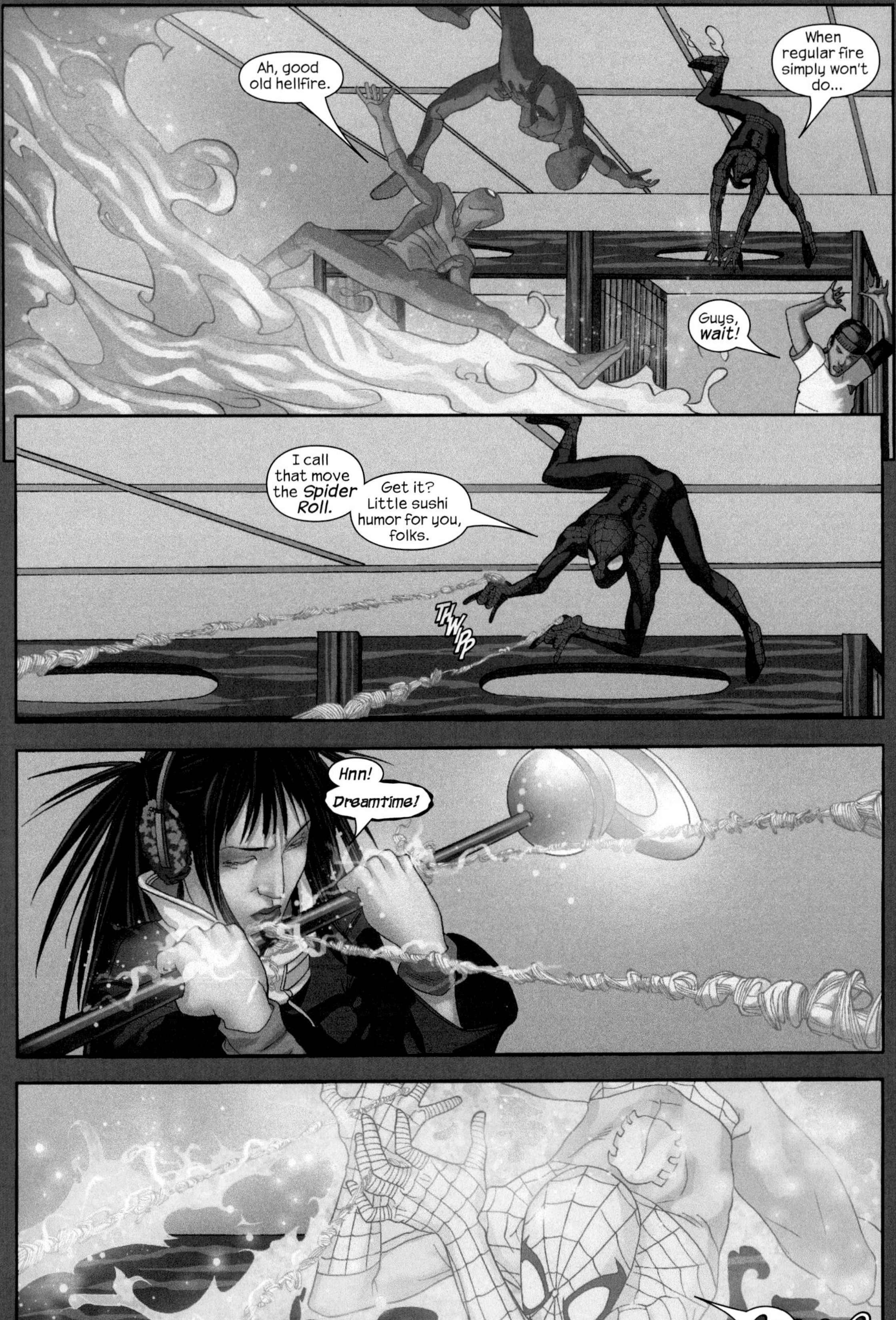
Ah, good old hellfire.
When regular fire simply won't do...
Guys, wait!
I call that move the Spider Roll.
Get it? Little sushi humor for you, folks.
THWIPP
Hnn!
Dreamtime!
GUZZAH!

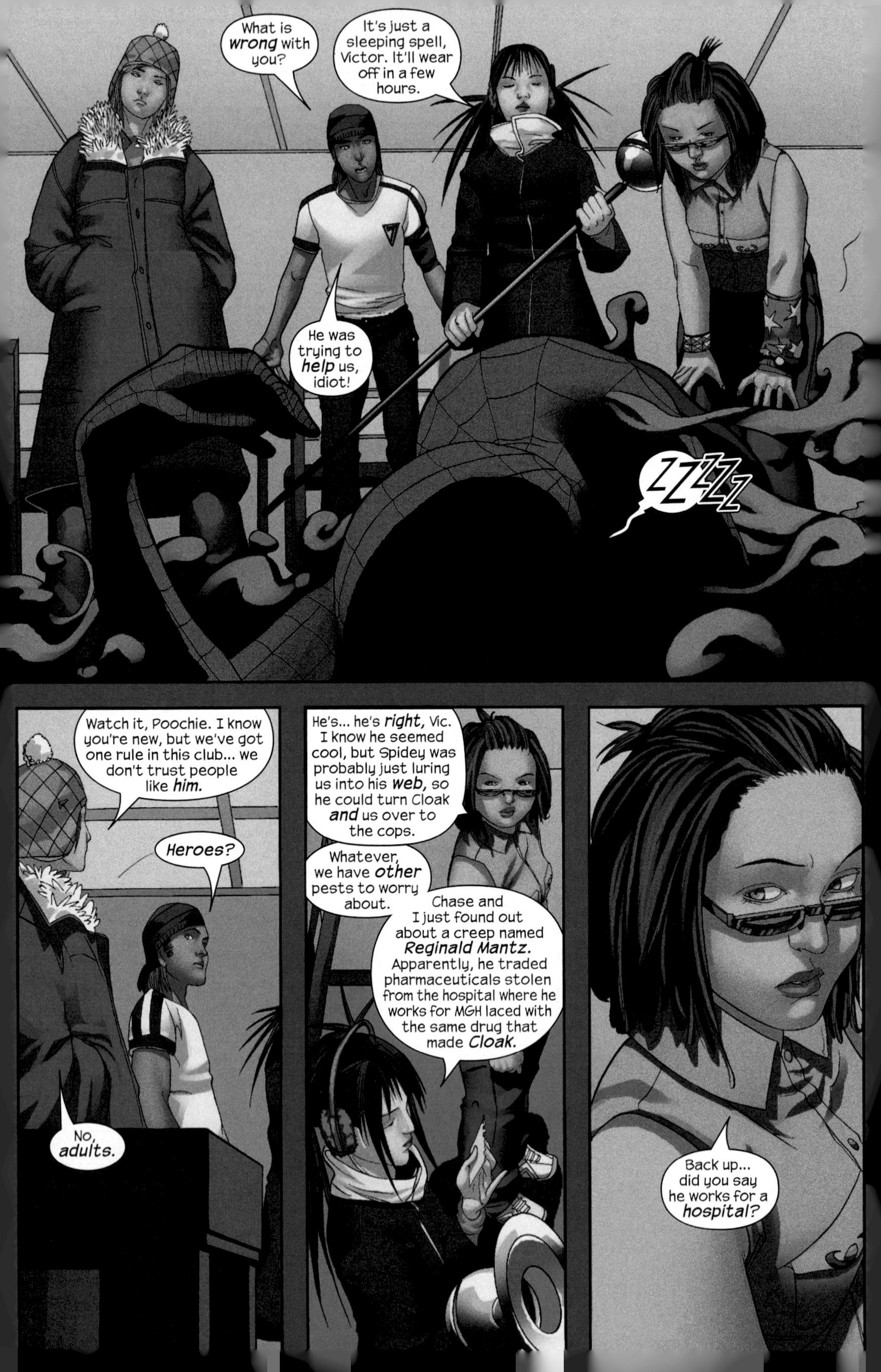

What is wrong with you?
It's just a sleeping spell, Victor. It'll wear off in a few hours.
He was trying to help us, idiot!
ZZZZZ
Watch it, Poochie. I know you're new, but we've got one rule in this club... we don't trust people like him.
Heroes?
No, adults.
He's... he's right, Vic. I know he seemed cool, but Spidey was probably just luring us into his web, so he could turn Cloak and us over to the cops.
Whatever, we have other pests to worry about.
Chase and I just found out about a creep named Reginald Mantz. Apparently, he traded pharmaceuticals stolen from the hospital where he works for MGH laced with the same drug that made Cloak.
Back up... did you say he works for a hospital?

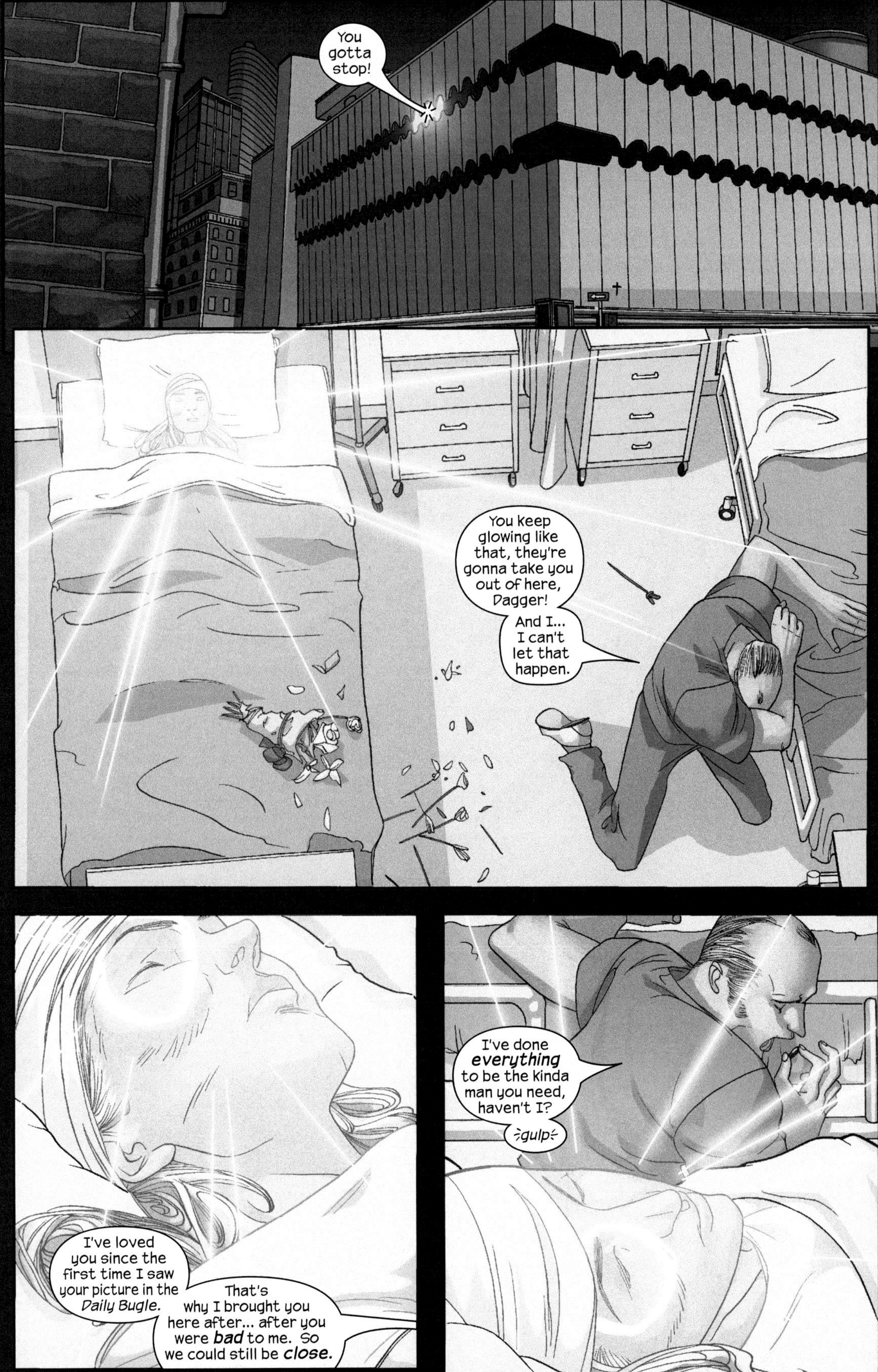

You gotta stop!
You keep glowing like that, they're gonna take you out of here, Dagger!
And I... I can't let that happen.
I've loved you since the first time I saw your picture in the *Daily Bugle*.
That's why I brought you here after... after you were ***bad*** to me. So we could still be ***close.***
I've done ***everything*** to be the kinda man you need, haven't I?
gulp

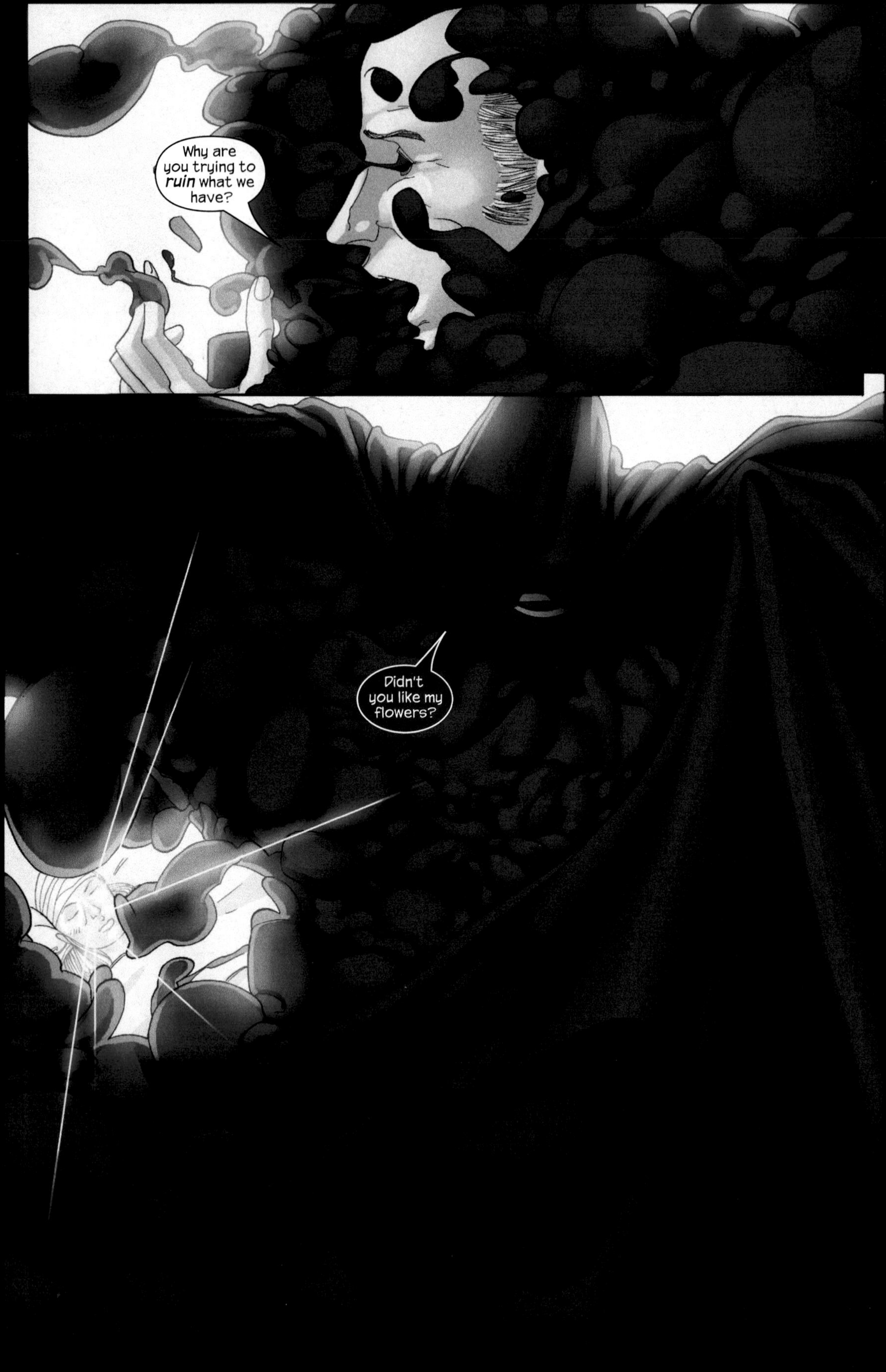
Why are you trying to *ruin* what we have?
Didn't you like my flowers?

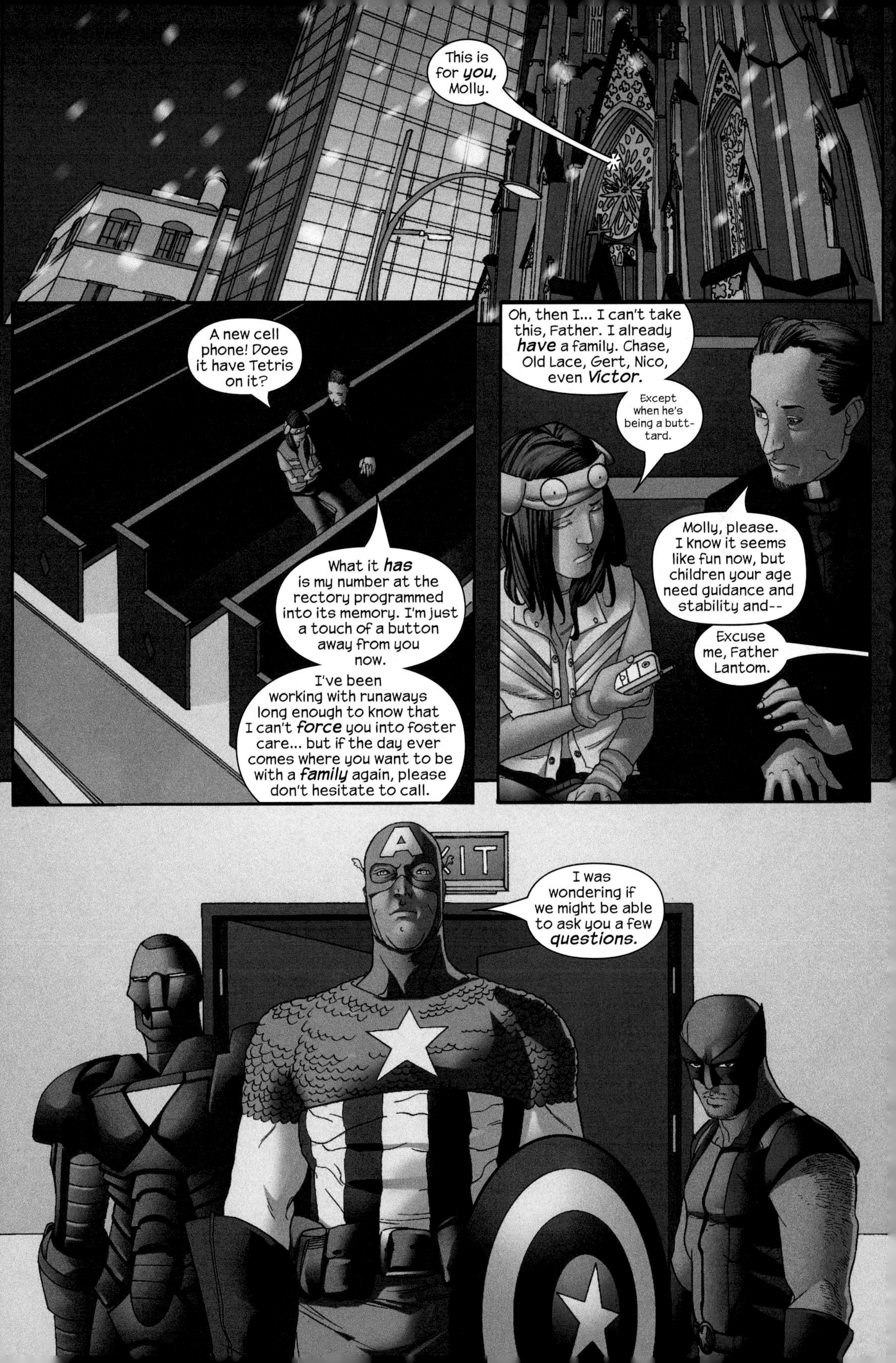
This is for *you,* Molly.
A new cell phone! Does it have Tetris on it?
What it ***has*** is my number at the rectory programmed into its memory. I'm just a touch of a button away from you now.
I've been working with runaways long enough to know that I can't ***force*** you into foster care... but if the day ever comes where you want to be with a ***family*** again, please don't hesitate to call.
Oh, then I... I can't take this, Father. I already ***have*** a family. Chase, Old Lace, Gert, Nico, even ***Victor.***
Except when he's being a butt-tard.
Molly, please. I know it seems like fun now, but children your age need guidance and stability and--
Excuse me, Father Lantom.
I was wondering if we might be able to ask you a few ***questions.***

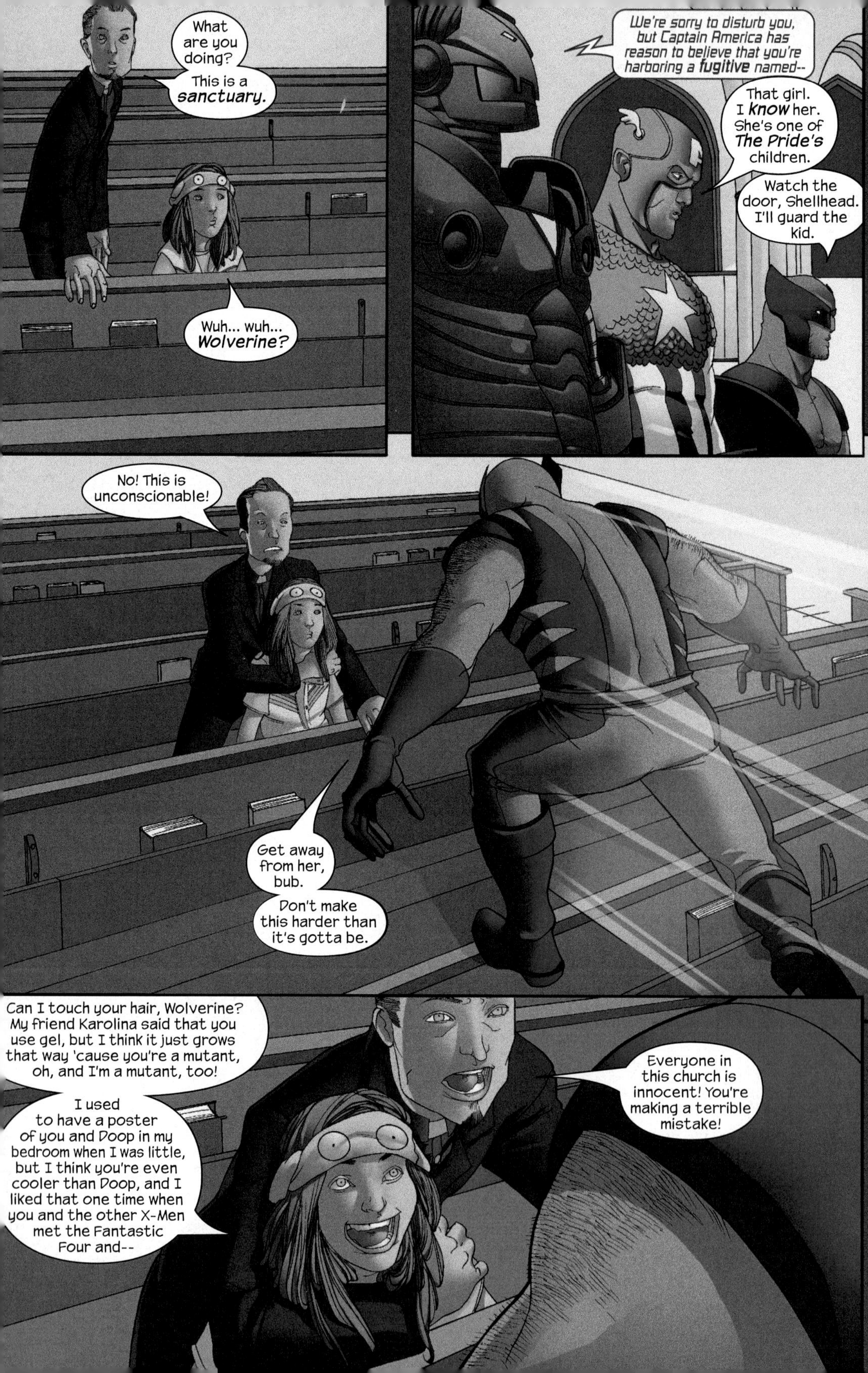
What are you doing?
This is a sanctuary.
Wuh... wuh... Wolverine?
We're sorry to disturb you, but Captain America has reason to believe that you're harboring a fugitive named--
That girl. I know her. She's one of The Pride's children.
Watch the door, Shellhead. I'll guard the kid.
No! This is unconscionable!
Get away from her, bub.
Don't make this harder than it's gotta be.
Can I touch your hair, Wolverine? My friend Karolina said that you use gel, but I think it just grows that way 'cause you're a mutant, oh, and I'm a mutant, too!
I used to have a poster of you and Doop in my bedroom when I was little, but I think you're even cooler than Doop, and I liked that one time when you and the other X-Men met the Fantastic Four and--
Everyone in this church is innocent! You're making a terrible mistake!

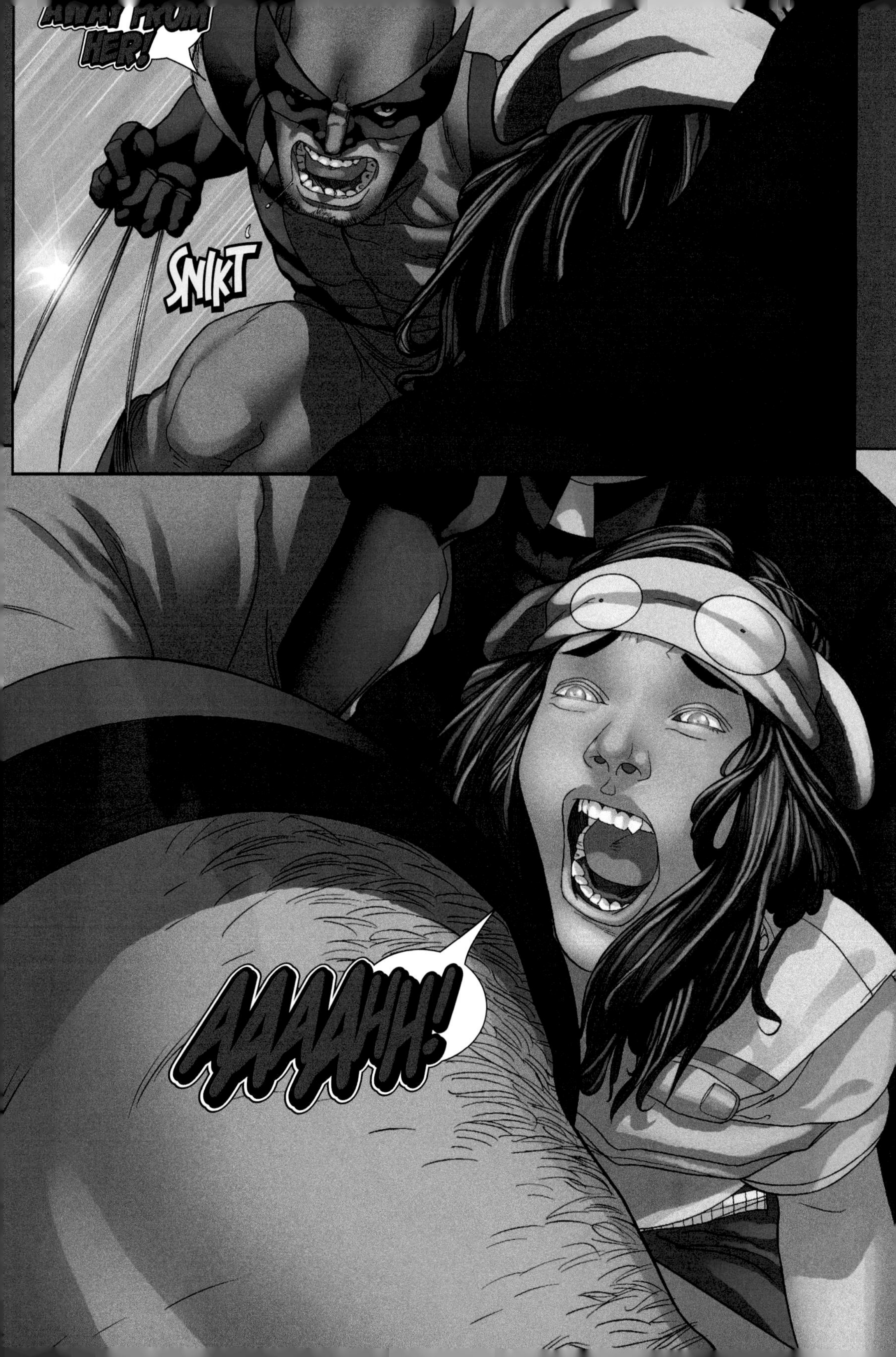
HER!
SNIKT
AAAAHH!

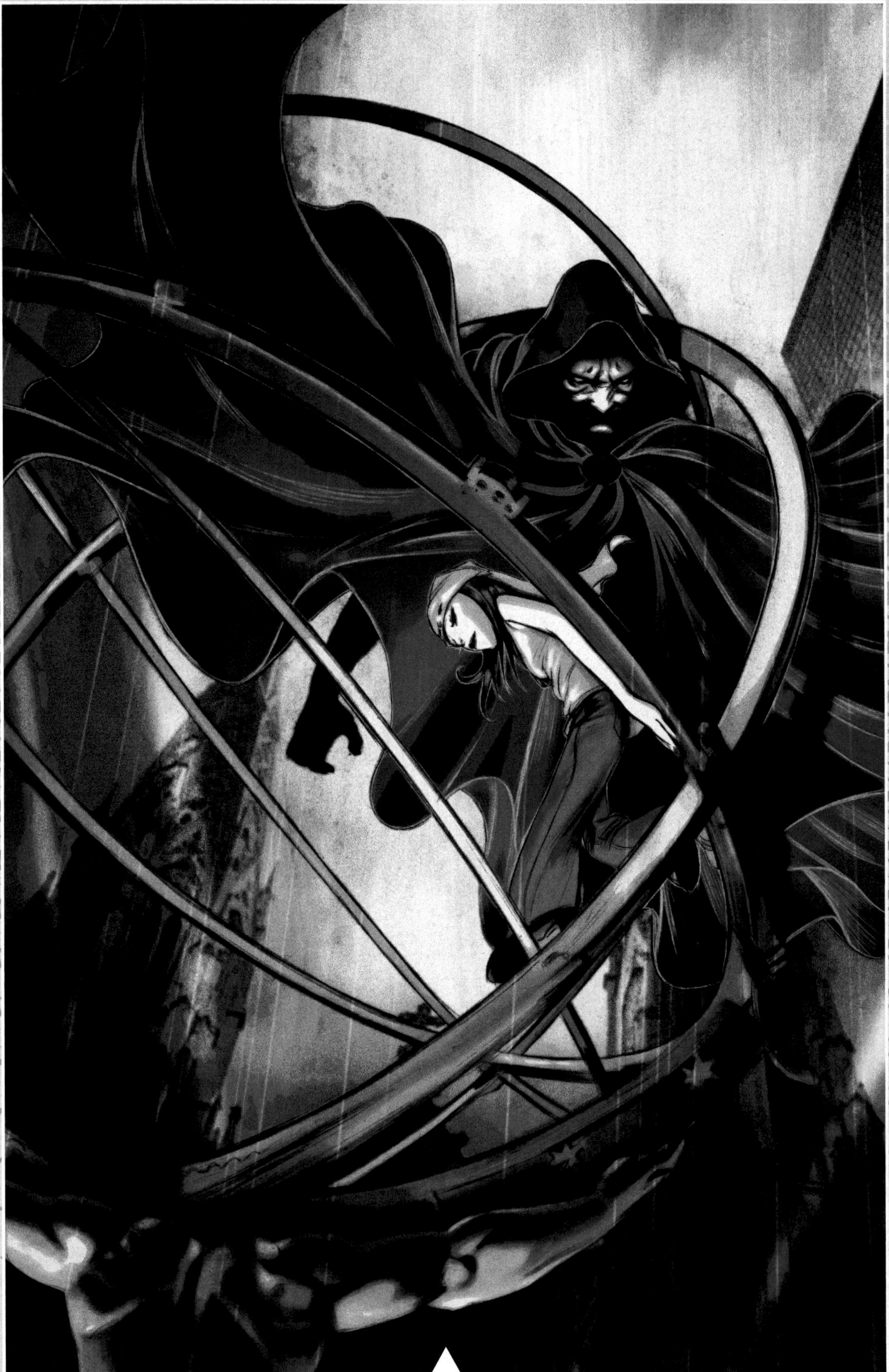

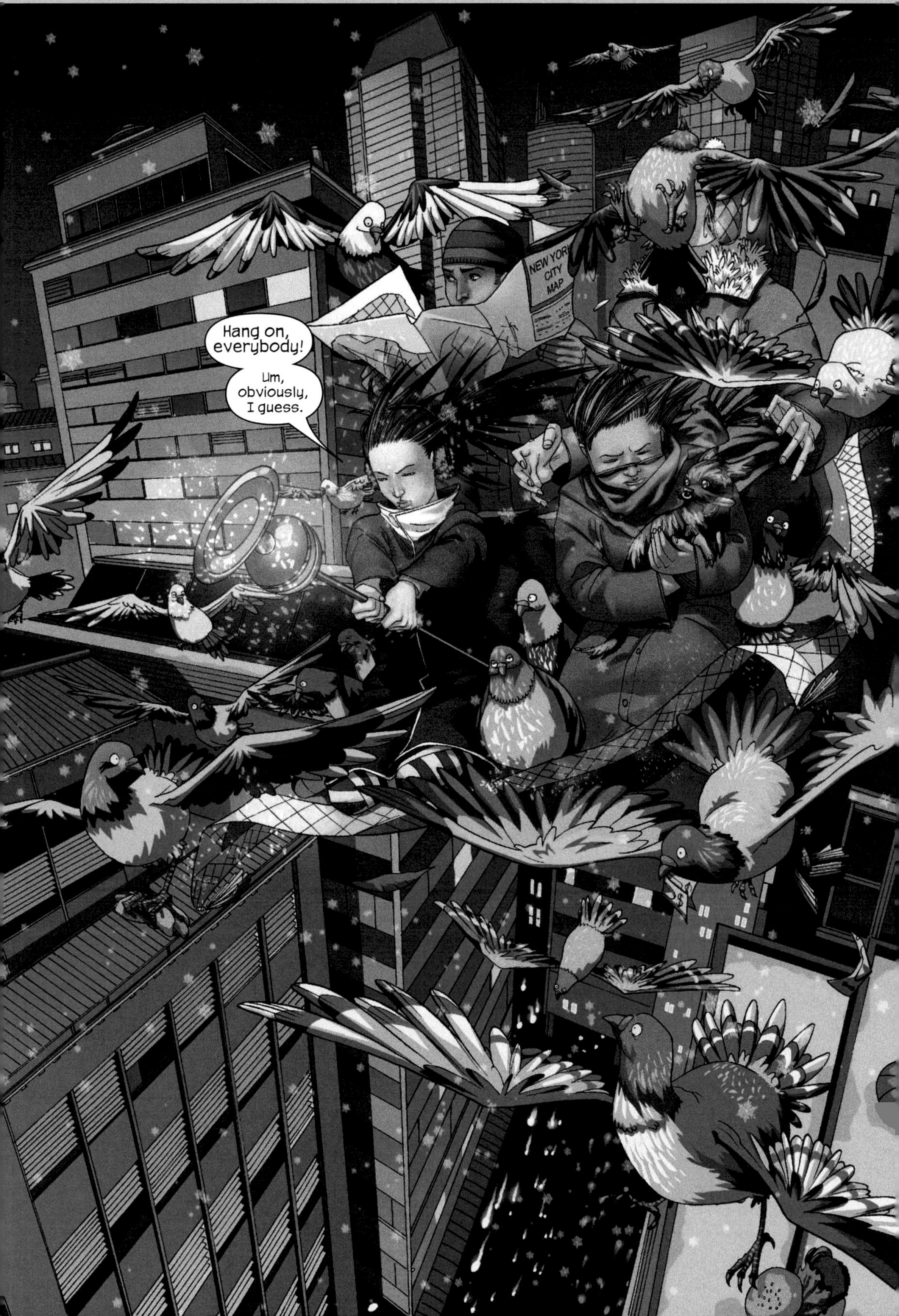
Hang on, everybody!
Um, obviously, I guess.
NEW YORK CITY MAP

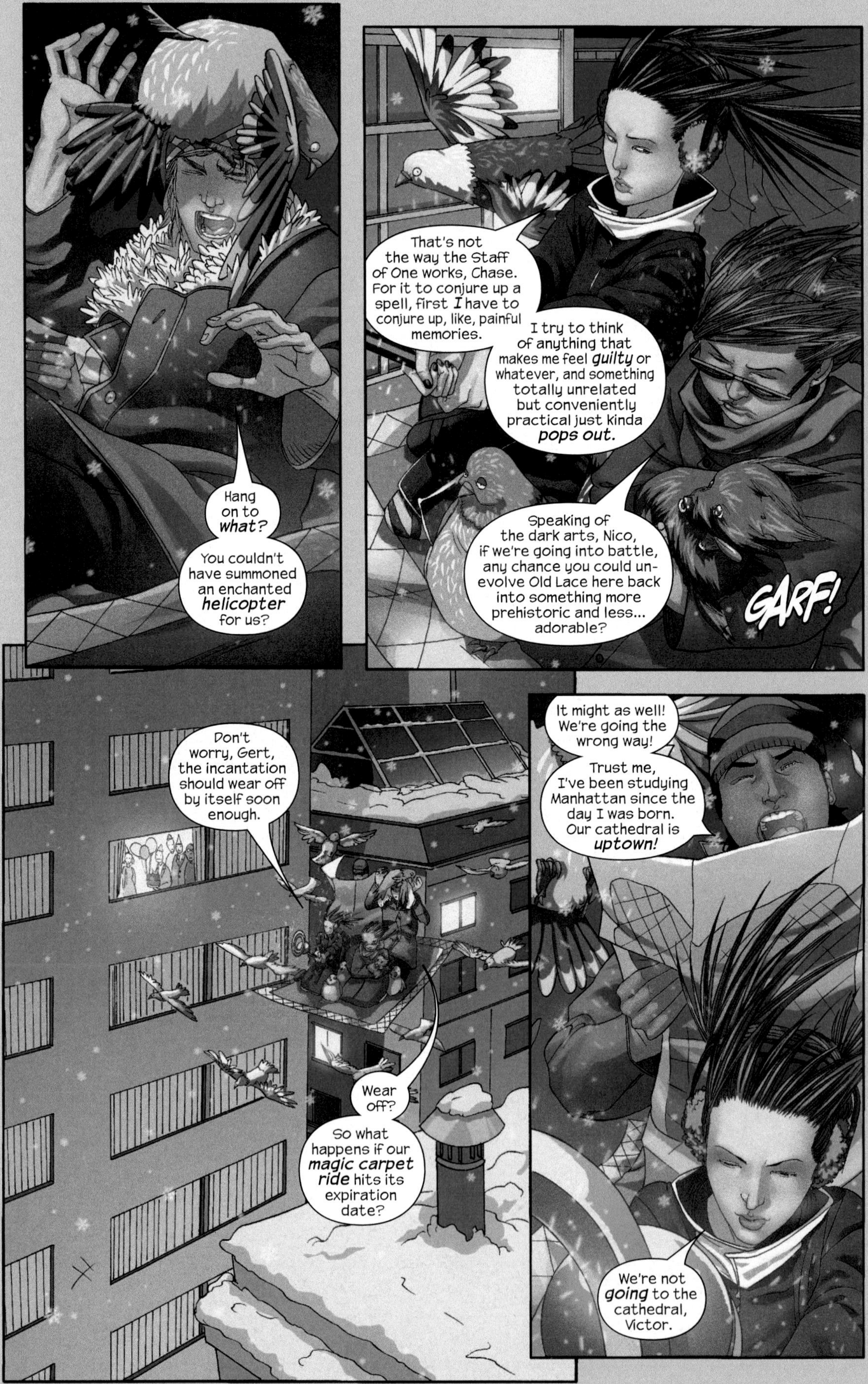
Hang on to *what?*
You couldn't have summoned an enchanted *helicopter* for us?
That's not the way the Staff of One works, Chase. For it to conjure up a spell, first *I* have to conjure up, like, painful memories.
I try to think of anything that makes me feel *guilty* or whatever, and something totally unrelated but conveniently practical just kinda *pops out.*
Speaking of the dark arts, Nico, if we're going into battle, any chance you could un-evolve Old Lace here back into something more prehistoric and less... adorable?
GARF!
Don't worry, Gert, the incantation should wear off by itself soon enough.
Wear off?
So what happens if our *magic carpet ride* hits its expiration date?
It might as well! We're going the wrong way!
Trust me, I've been studying Manhattan since the day I was born. Our cathedral is *uptown!*
We're not *going* to the cathedral, Victor.

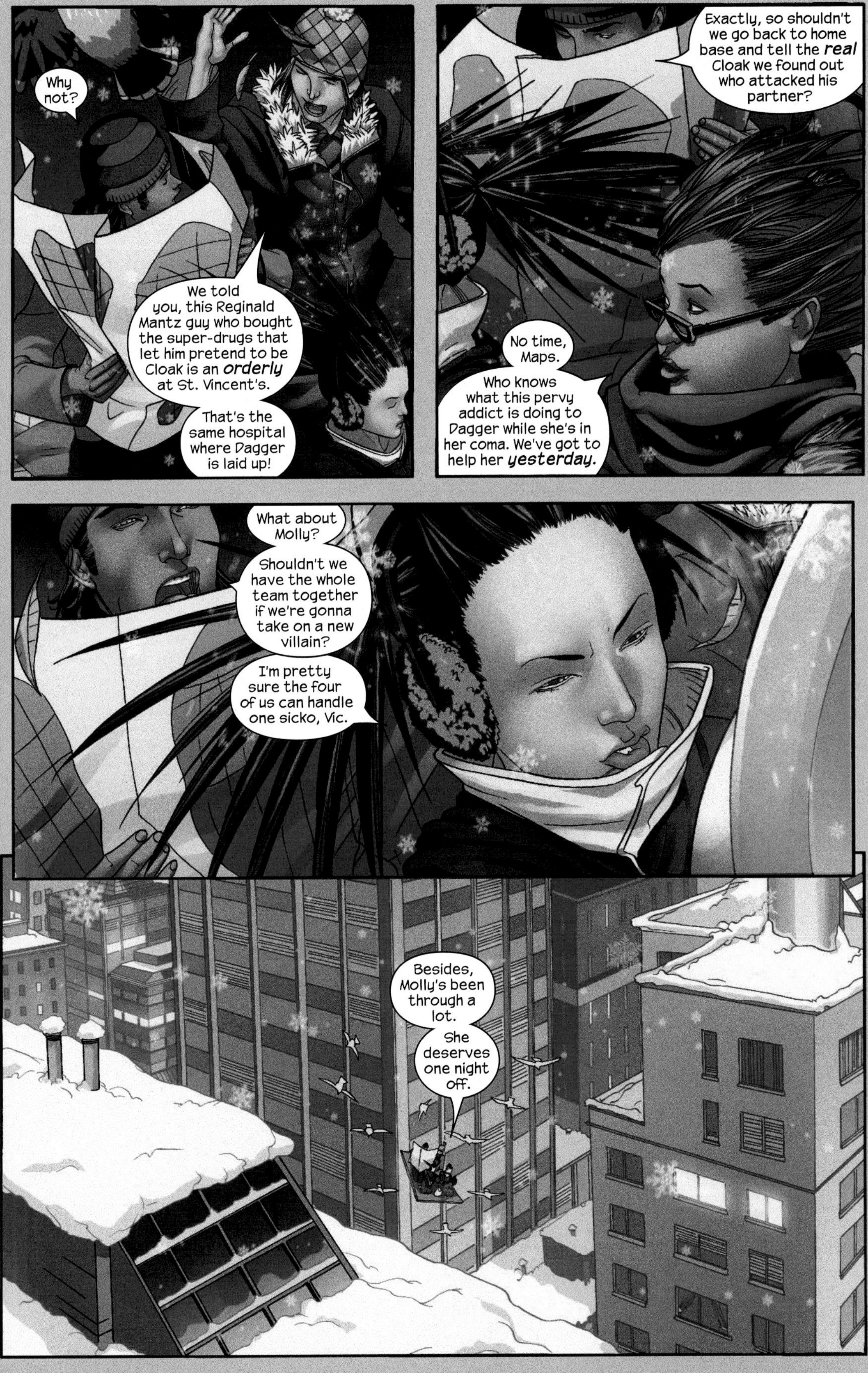

Why not?
We told you, this Reginald Mantz guy who bought the super-drugs that let him pretend to be Cloak is an *orderly* at St. Vincent's.
That's the same hospital where Dagger is laid up!
Exactly, so shouldn't we go back to home base and tell the *real* Cloak we found out who attacked his partner?
No time, Maps.
Who knows what this pervy addict is doing to Dagger while she's in her coma. We've got to help her *yesterday.*
What about Molly?
Shouldn't we have the whole team together if we're gonna take on a new villain?
I'm pretty sure the four of us can handle one sicko, Vic.
Besides, Molly's been through a lot.
She deserves one night off.

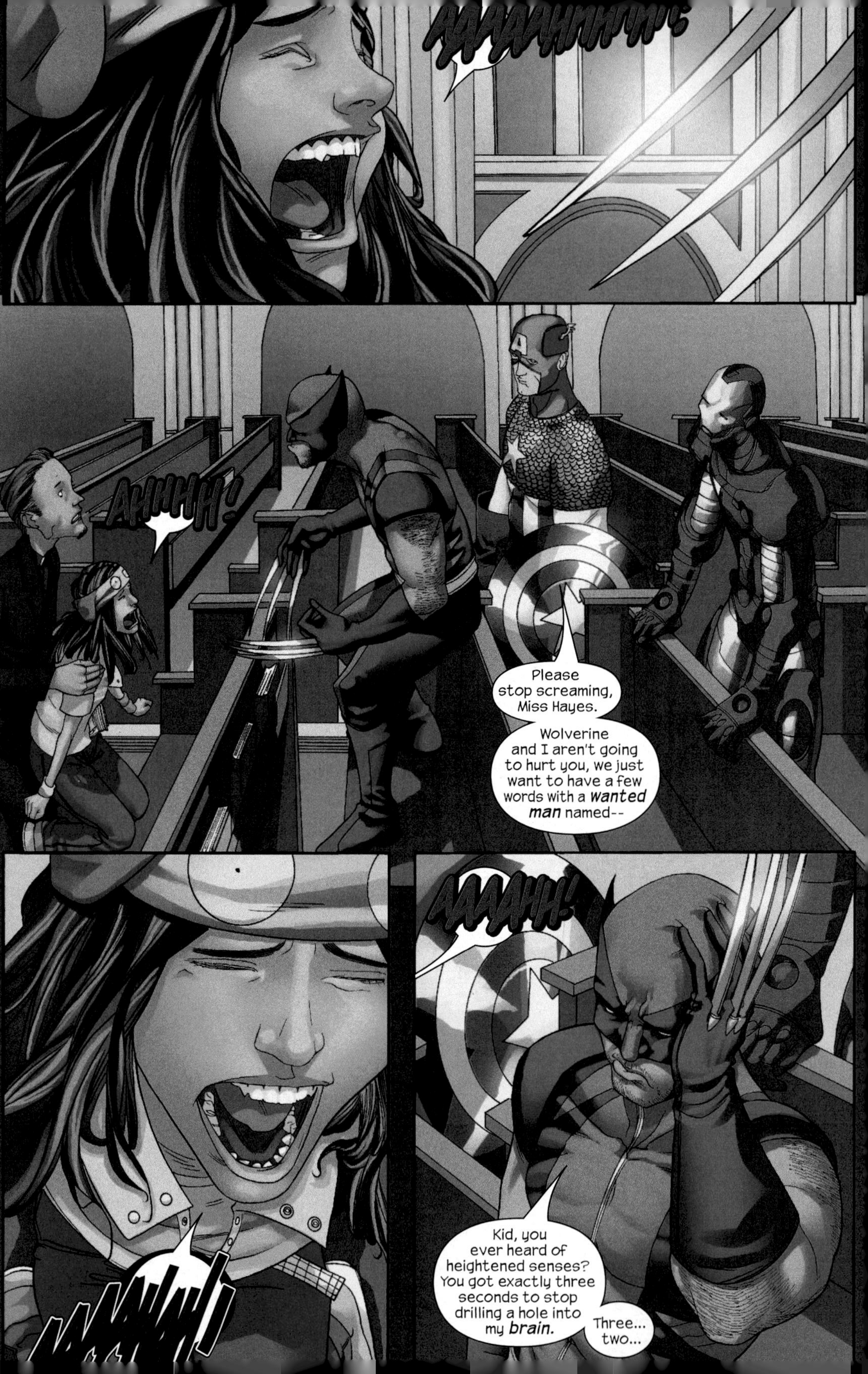
AAAAAHHHHH!
AHHHHH!
Please stop screaming, Miss Hayes.
Wolverine and I aren't going to hurt you, we just want to have a few words with a *wanted man* named--
AAAAHH!
AAAAHH!
Kid, you ever heard of heightened senses? You got exactly three seconds to stop drilling a hole into my *brain.*
Three... two...

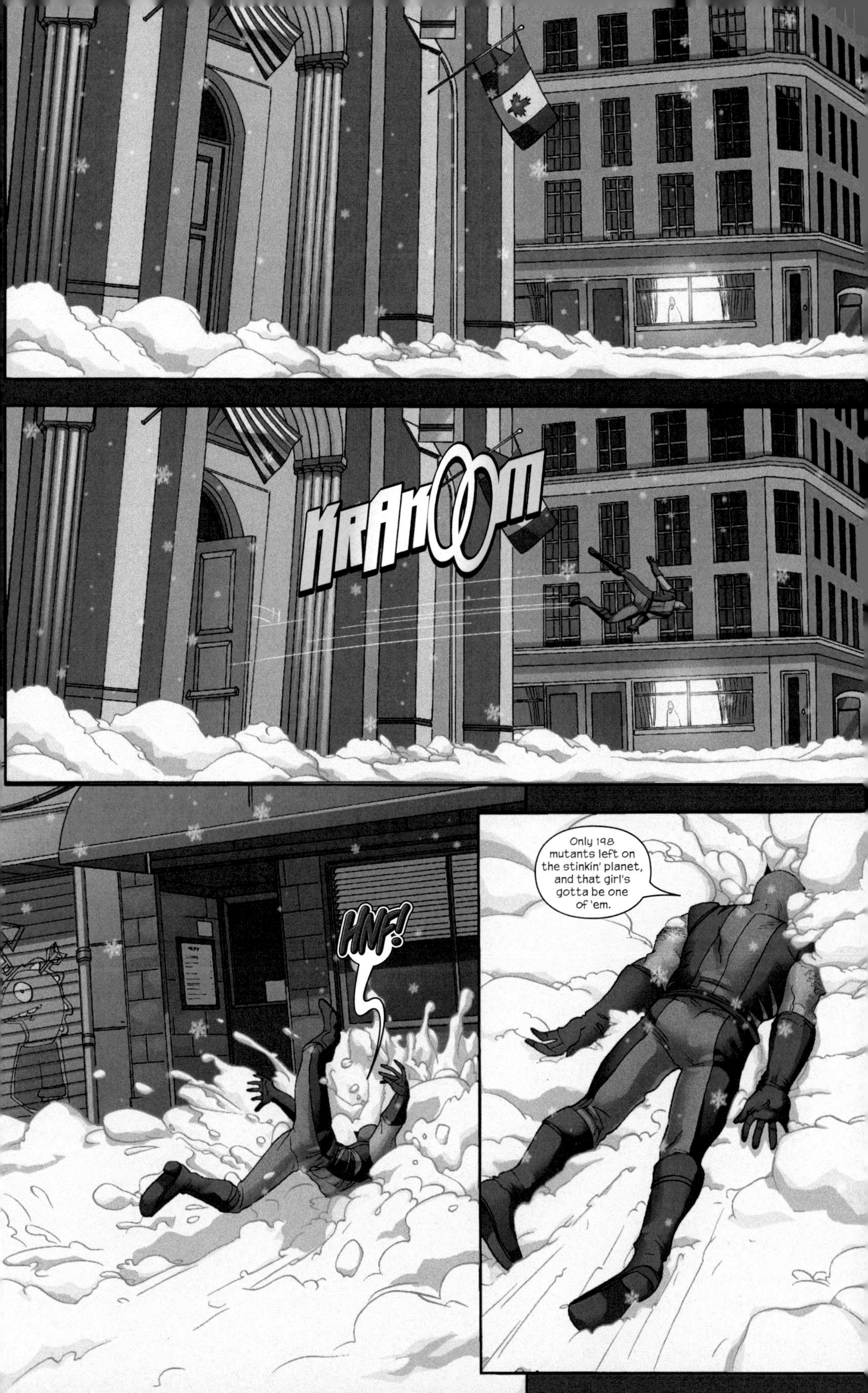
KRAKOOM
HNF!
Only 198 mutants left on the stinkin' planet, and that girl's gotta be one of 'em.

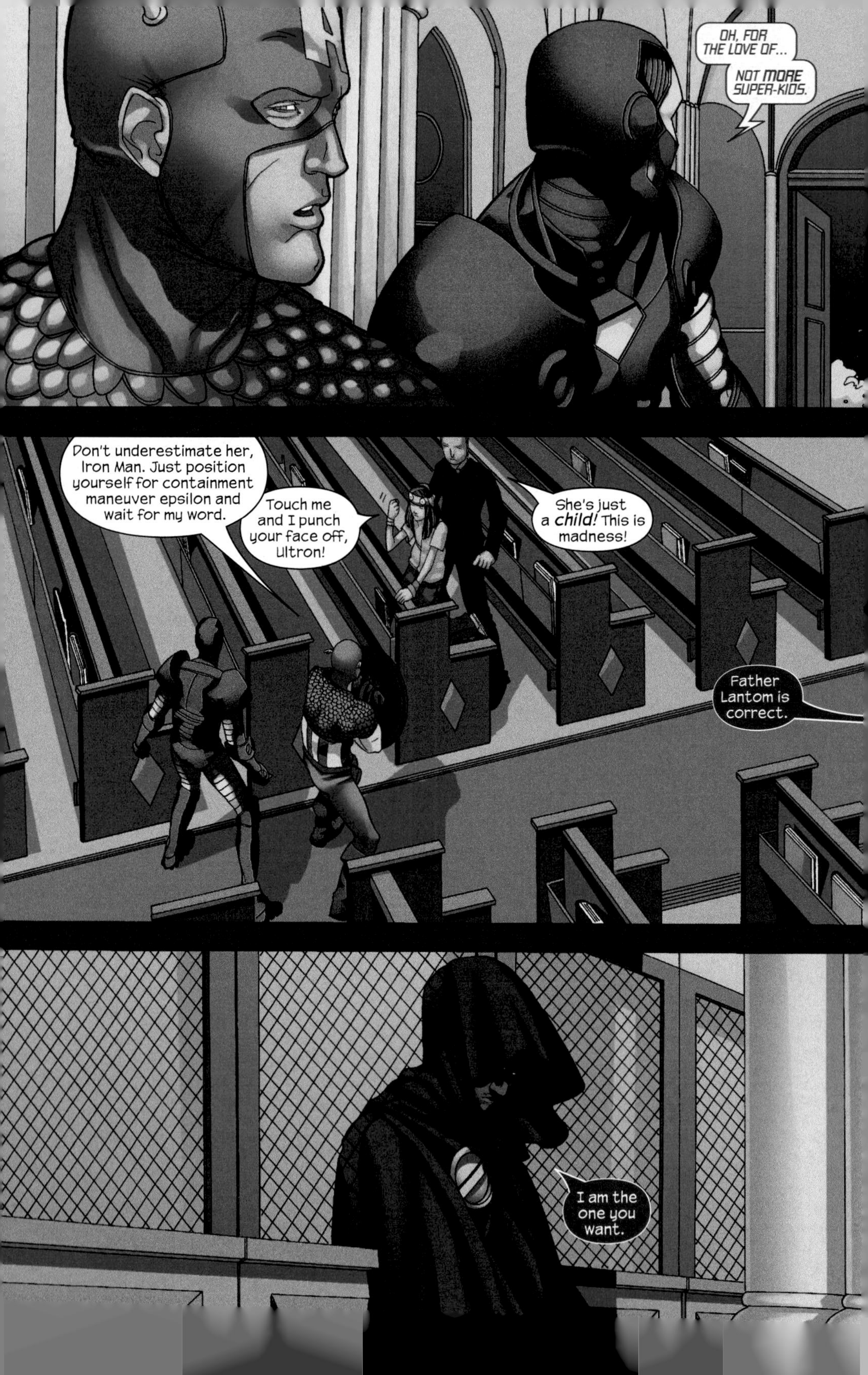
OH, FOR THE LOVE OF...
NOT MORE SUPER-KIDS.
Don't underestimate her, Iron Man. Just position yourself for containment maneuver epsilon and wait for my word.
Touch me and I punch your face off, Ultron!
She's just a child! This is madness!
Father Lantom is correct.
I am the one you want.

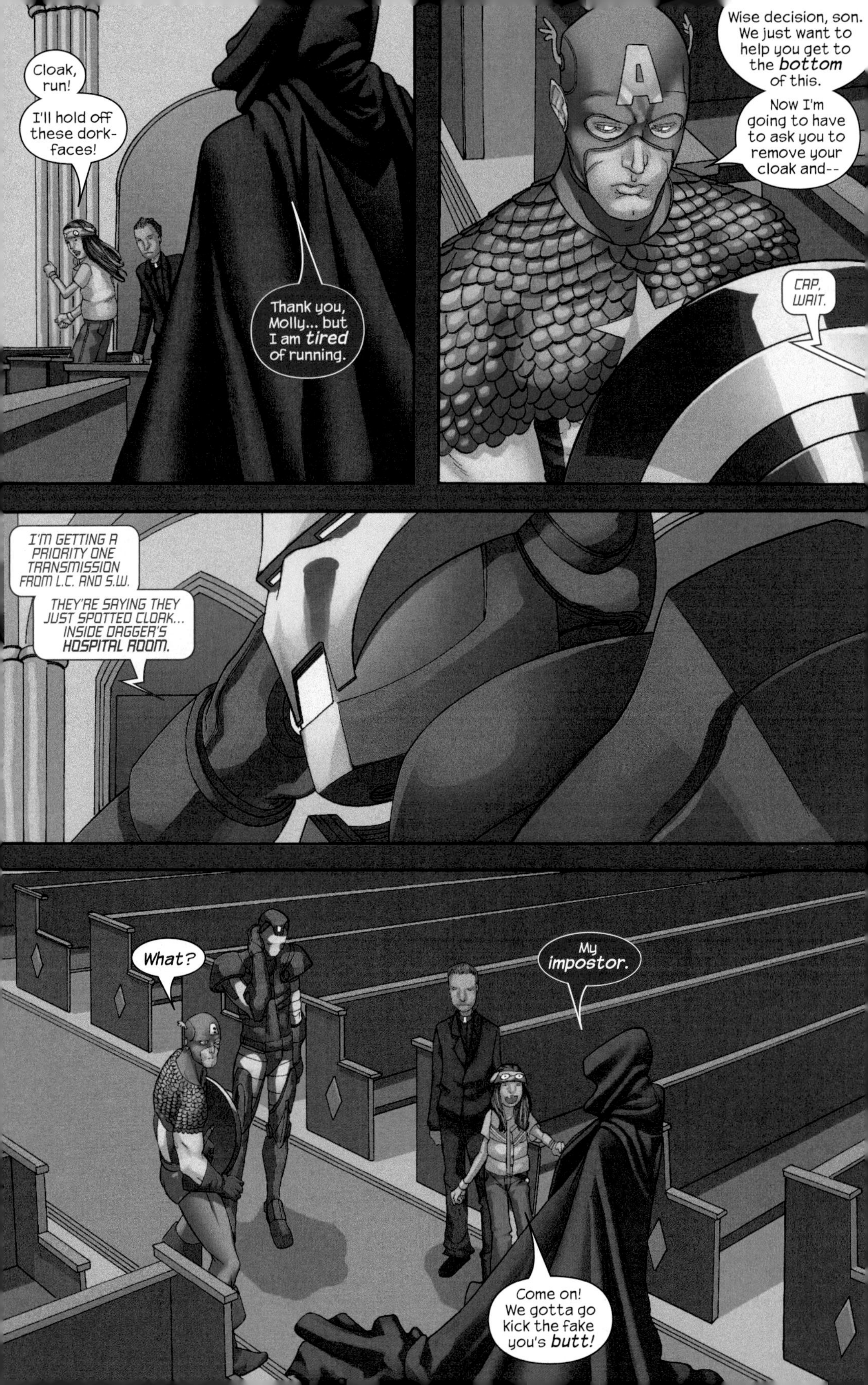
Cloak, run!
I'll hold off these dork-faces!
Thank you, Molly... but I am tired of running.
Wise decision, son. We just want to help you get to the bottom of this.
Now I'm going to have to ask you to remove your cloak and--
CAP, WAIT.
I'M GETTING A PRIORITY ONE TRANSMISSION FROM L.C. AND S.W.
THEY'RE SAYING THEY JUST SPOTTED CLOAK... INSIDE DAGGER'S HOSPITAL ROOM.
What?
My impostor.
Come on! We gotta go kick the fake you's butt!

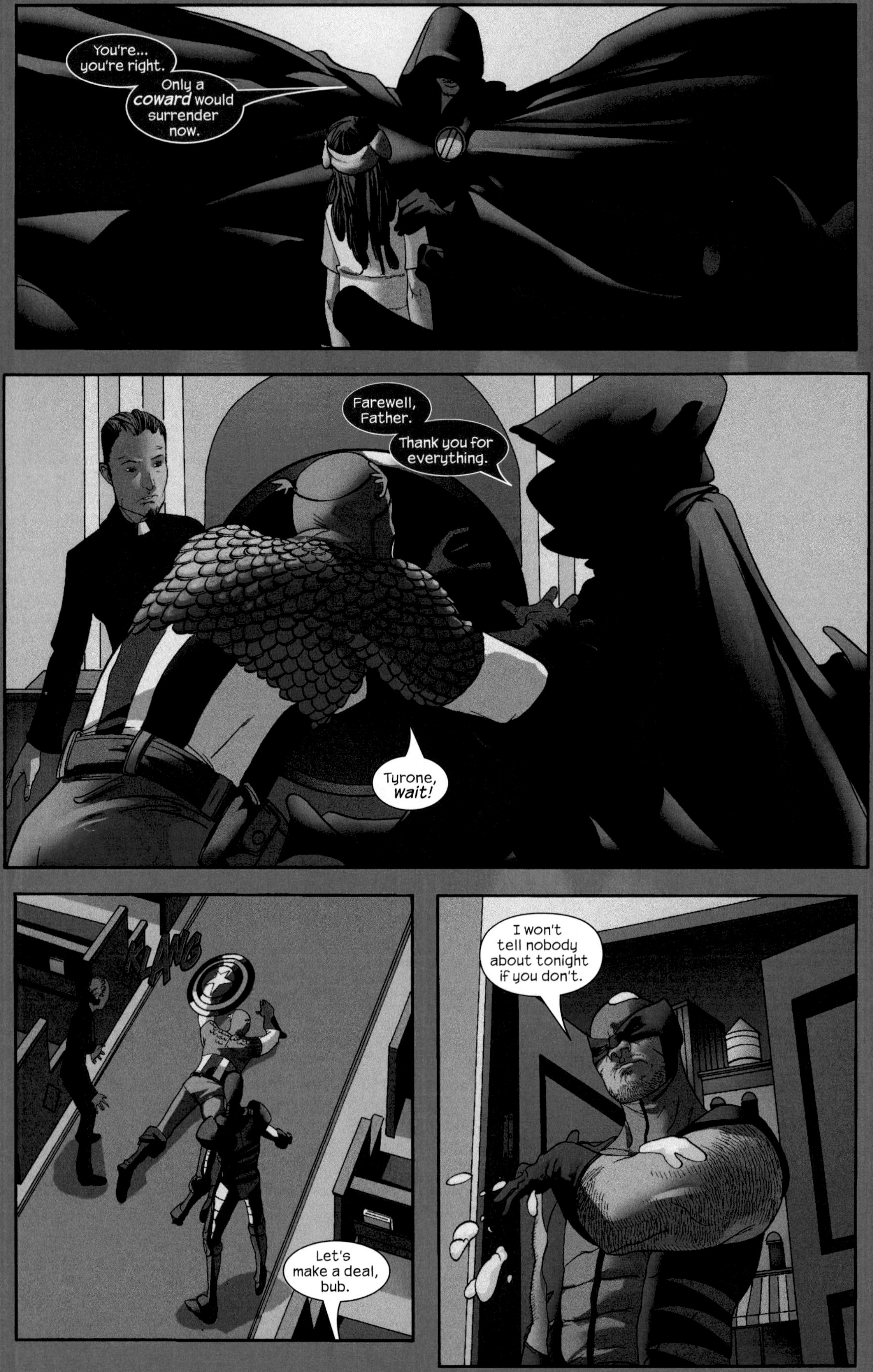
You're... you're right.
Only a *coward* would surrender now.
Farewell, Father.
Thank you for everything.
Tyrone, *wait!*
KLANG
Let's make a deal, bub.
I won't tell nobody about tonight if you don't.

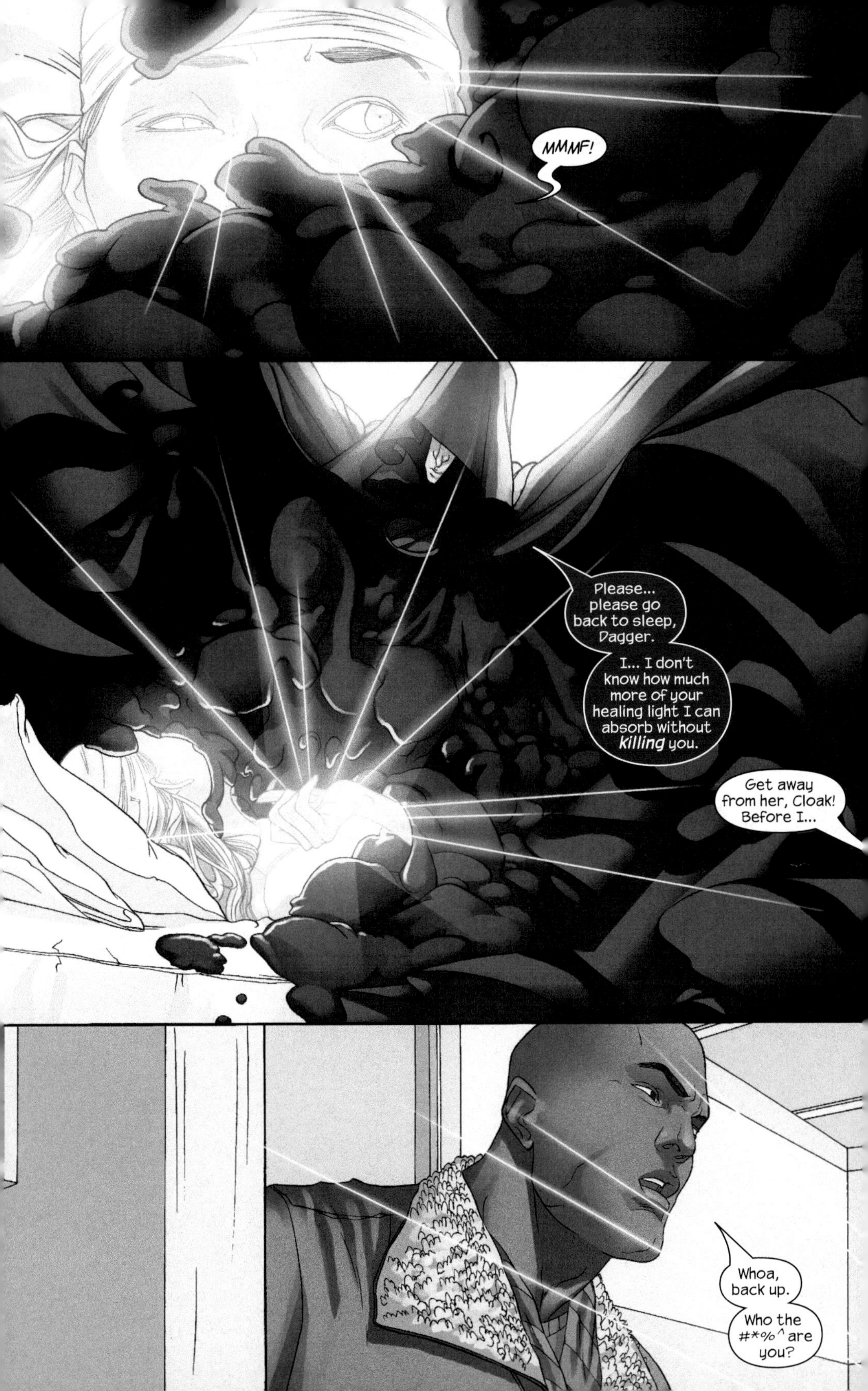
MMMF!
Please... please go back to sleep, Dagger.
I... I don't know how much more of your healing light I can absorb without *killing* you.
Get away from her, Cloak! Before I...
Whoa, back up.
Who the #*%^ are you?

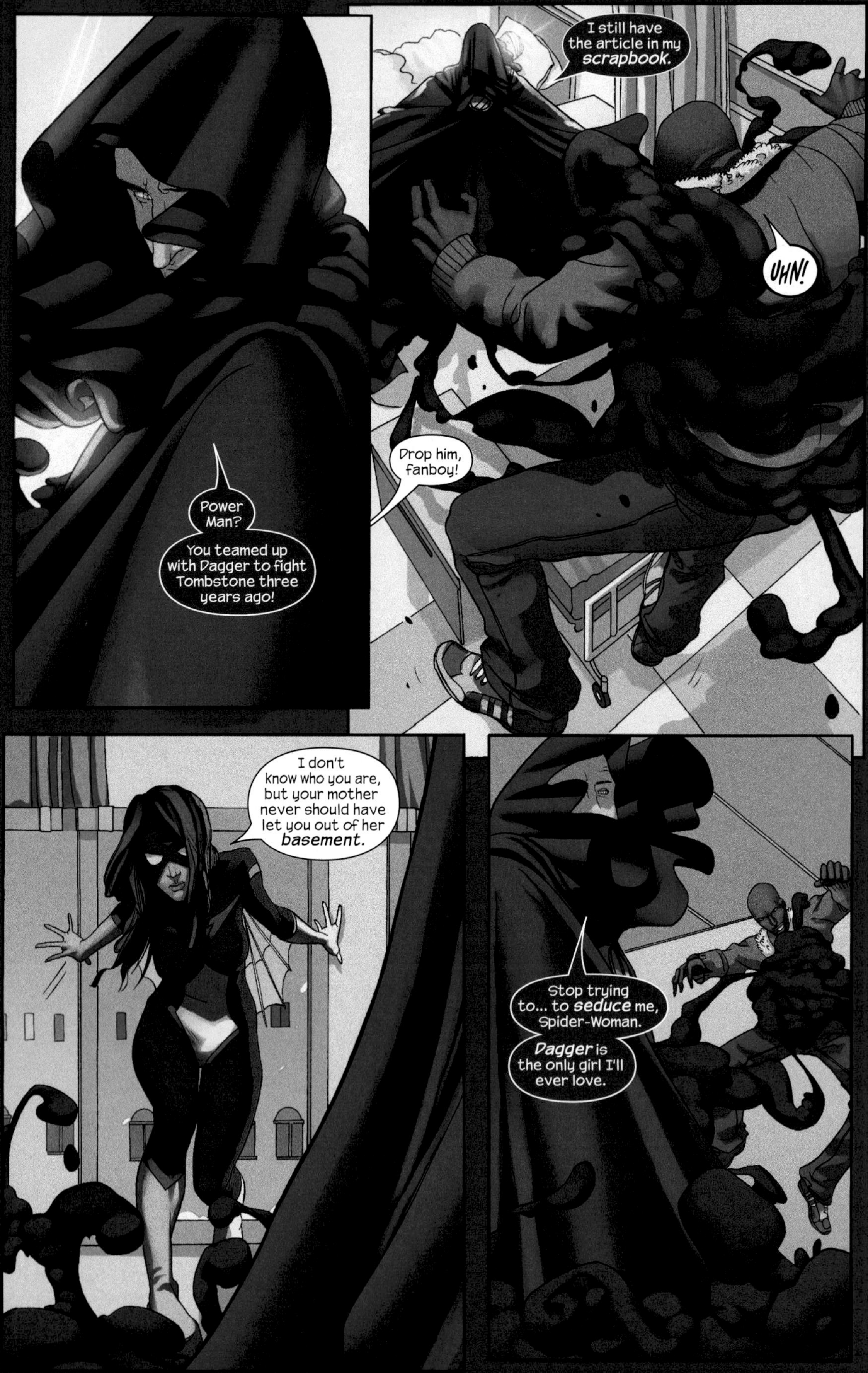
Power Man?
You teamed up with Dagger to fight Tombstone three years ago!
I still have the article in my scrapbook.
UHN!
Drop him, fanboy!
I don't know who you are, but your mother never should have let you out of her basement.
Stop trying to... to seduce me, Spider-Woman.
Dagger is the only girl I'll ever love.

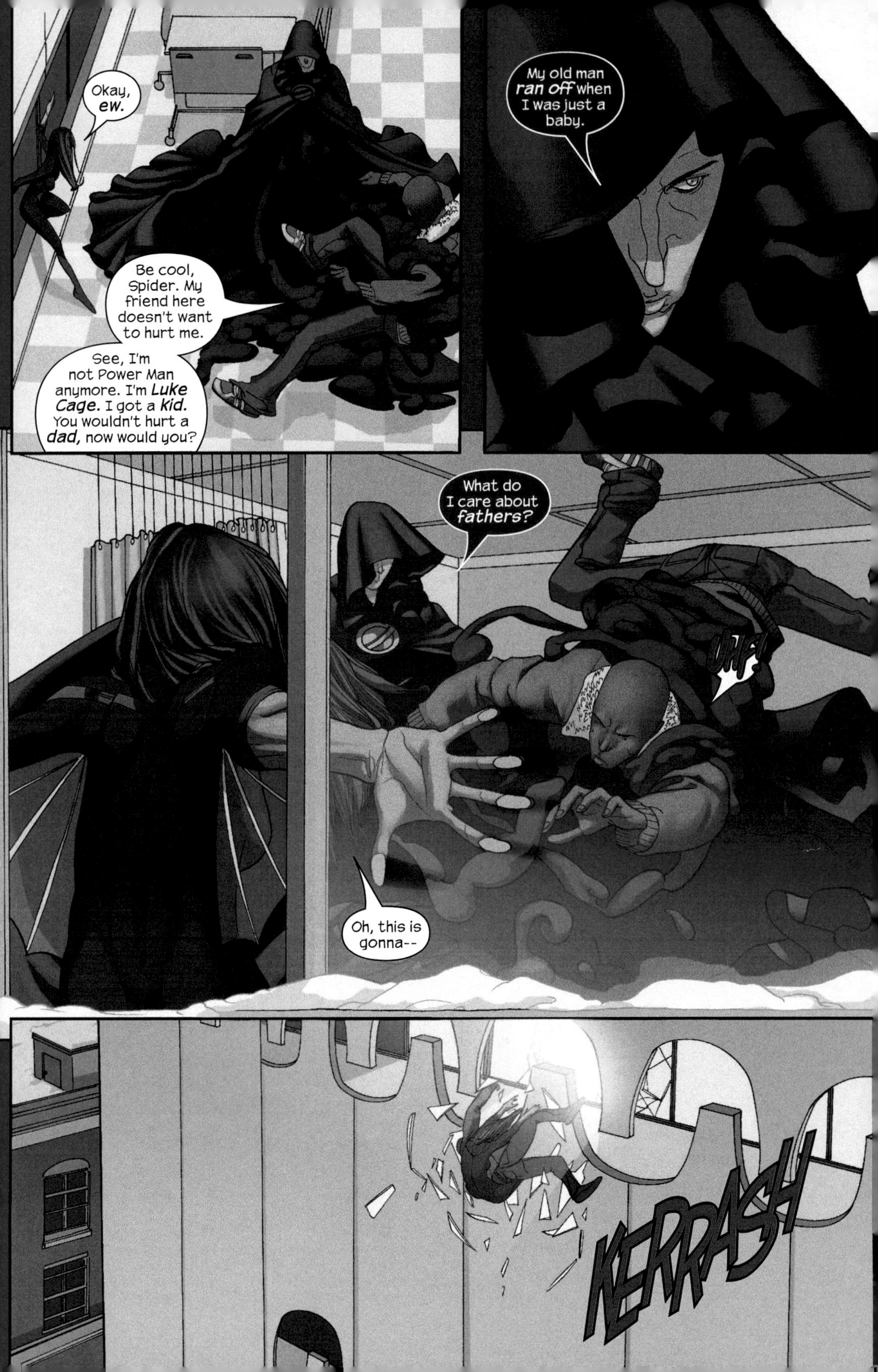
Okay, ew.
Be cool, Spider. My friend here doesn't want to hurt me.
See, I'm not Power Man anymore. I'm Luke Cage. I got a kid. You wouldn't hurt a dad, now would you?
My old man ran off when I was just a baby.
What do I care about fathers?
UHF!
Oh, this is gonna--
KERRASH

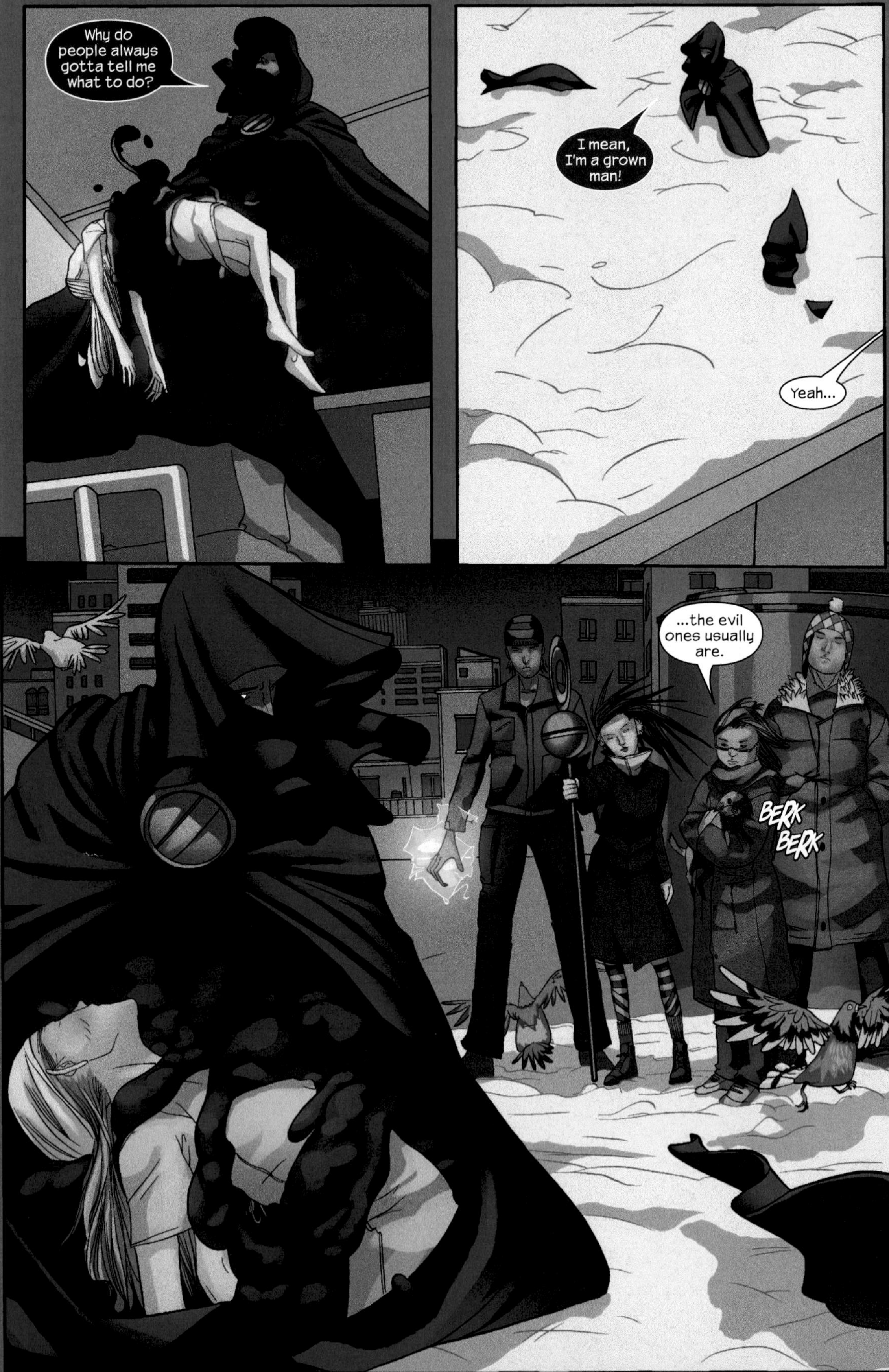
Why do people always gotta tell me what to do?
I mean, I'm a grown man!
Yeah...
...the evil ones usually are.
BERK
BERK

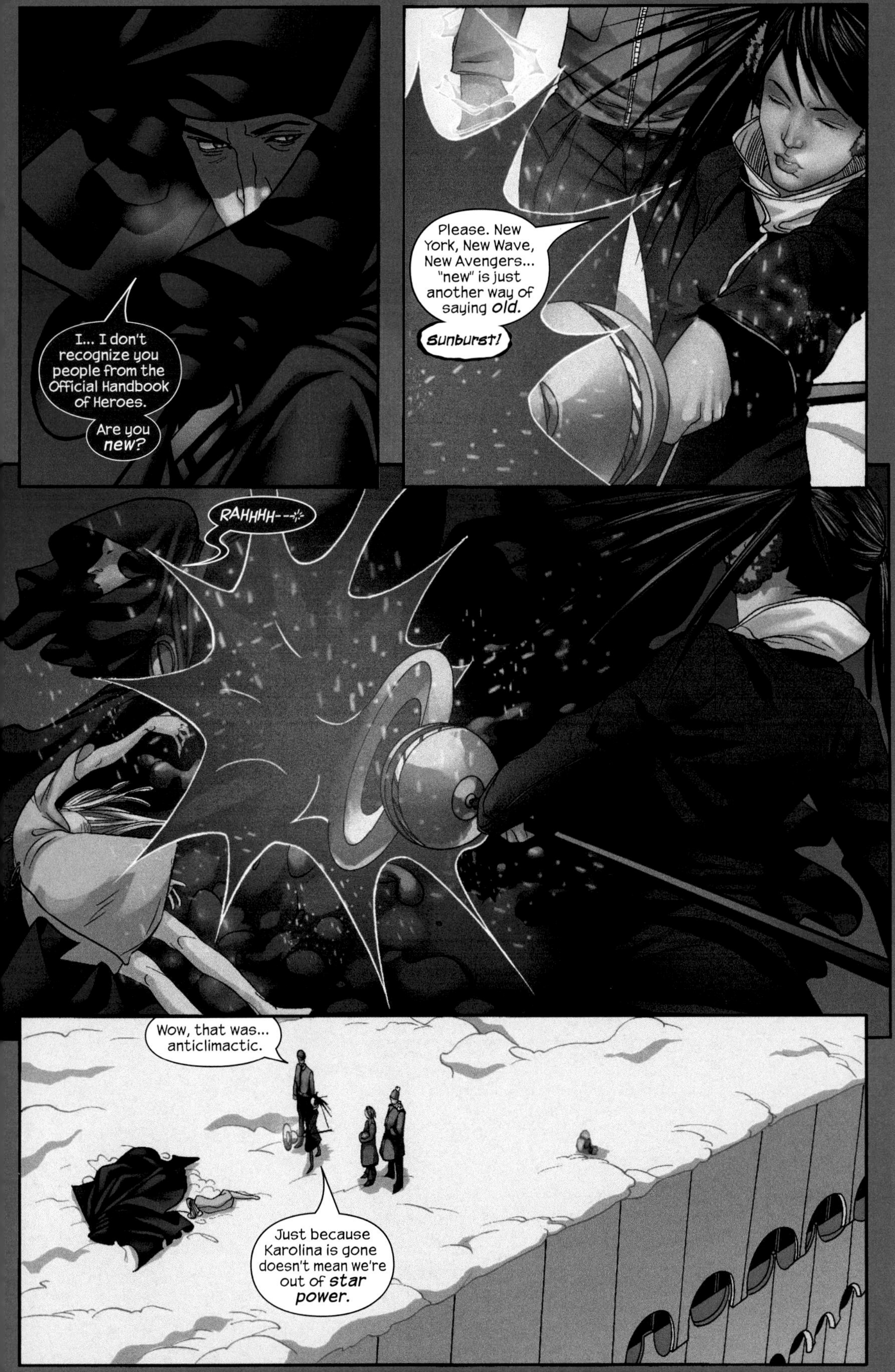
I... I don't recognize you people from the Official Handbook of Heroes.
Are you new?
Please. New York, New Wave, New Avengers... "new" is just another way of saying old.
Sunburst!
RAHHHH--
Wow, that was... anticlimactic.
Just because Karolina is gone doesn't mean we're out of star power.

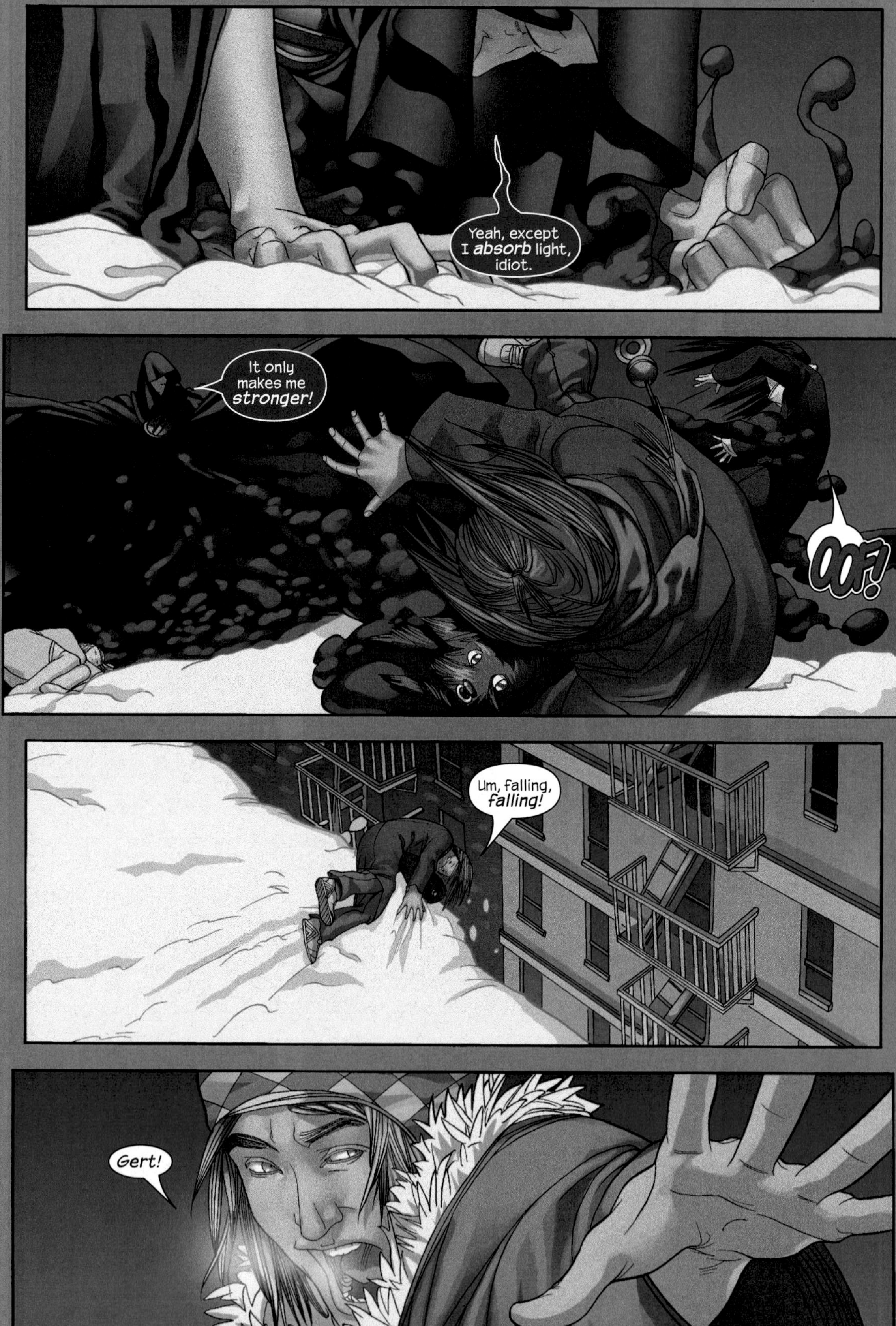

Yeah, except I *absorb* light, idiot.
It only makes me *stronger!*
OOF!
Um, falling, *falling!*
Gert!

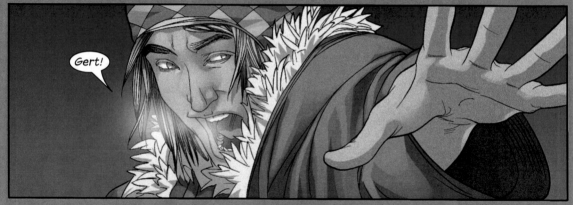

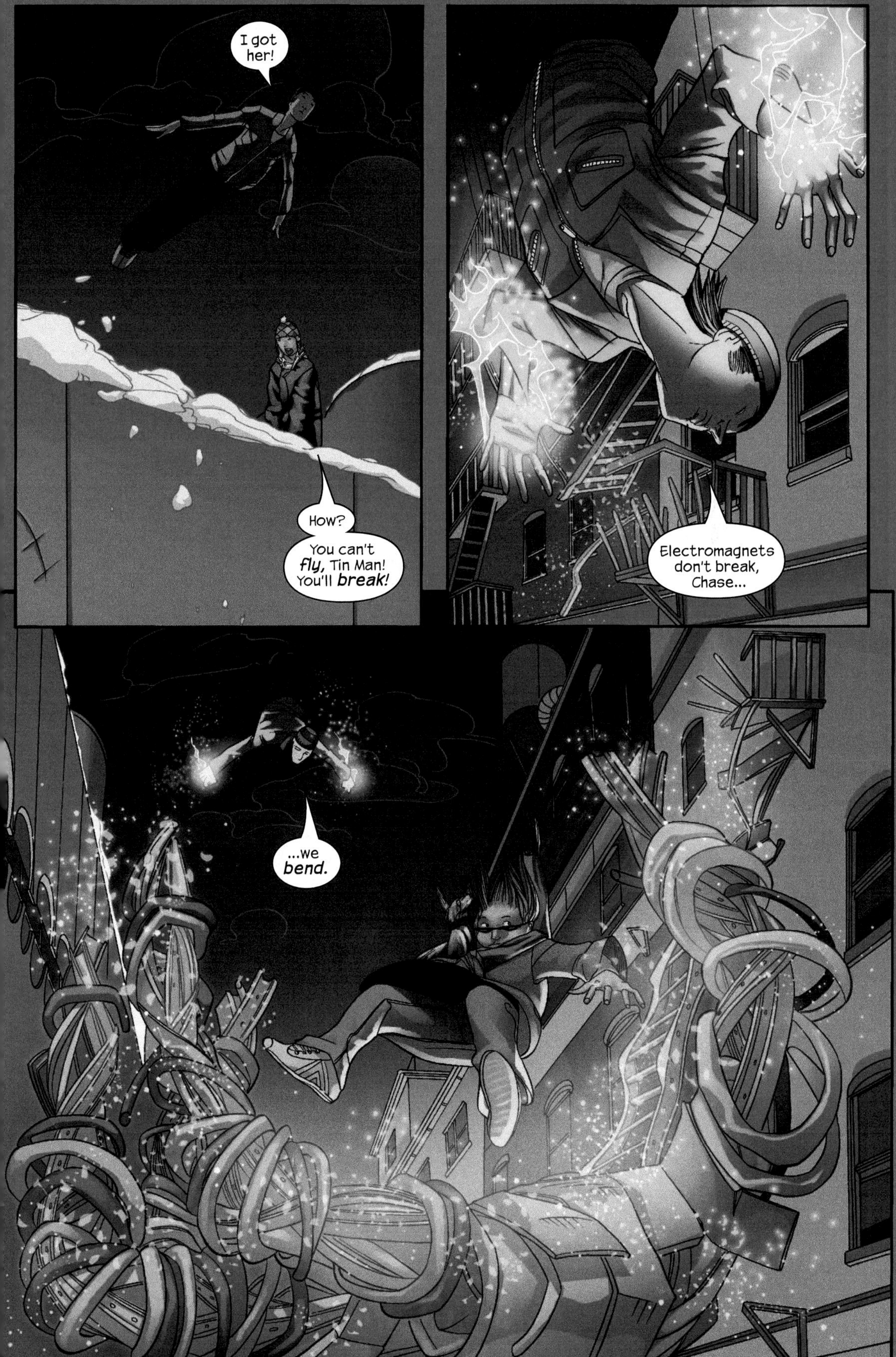
I got her!
How?
You can't *fly,* Tin Man! You'll *break!*
Electromagnets don't break, Chase...
...we *bend.*

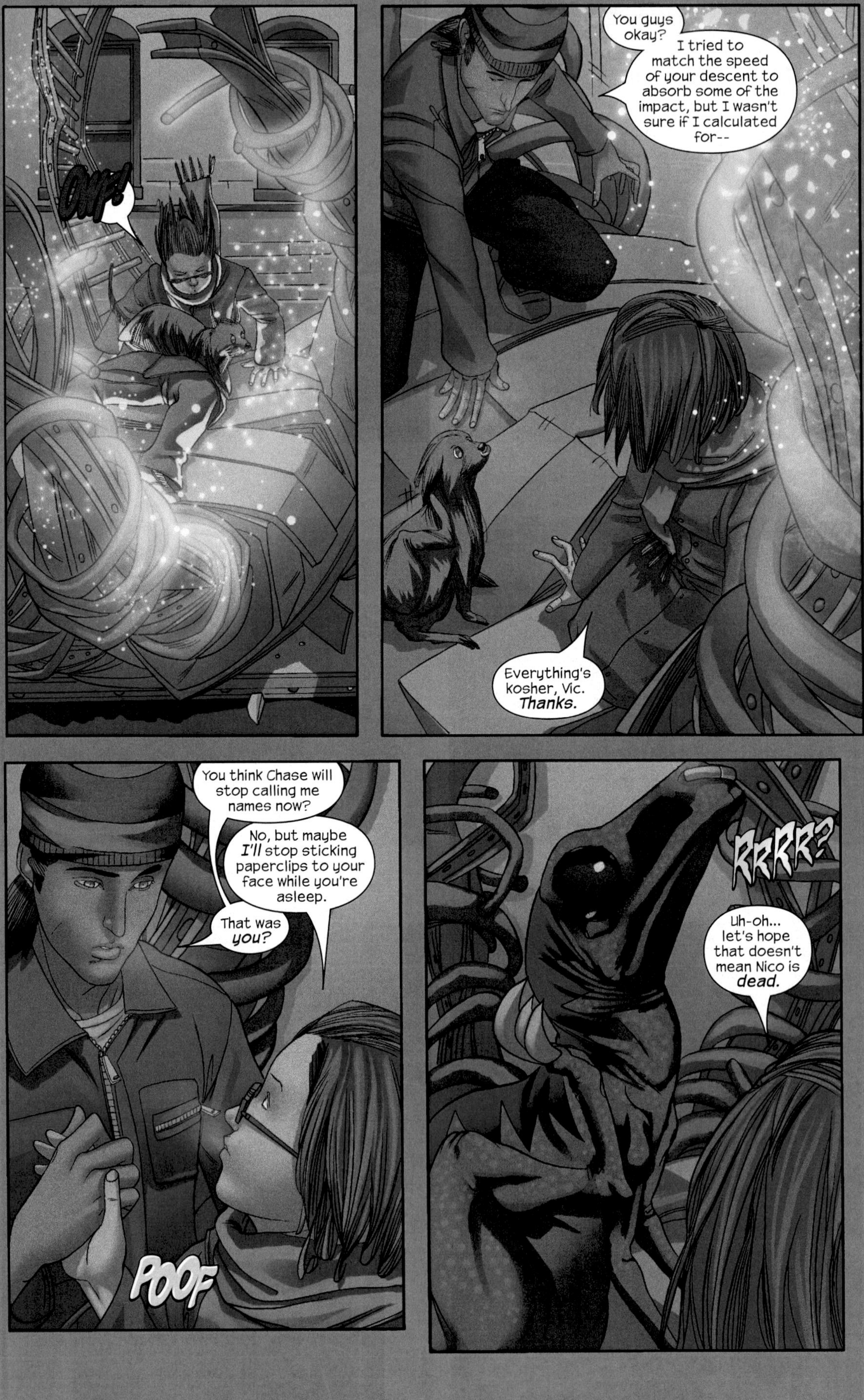
OMF!
You guys okay?
I tried to match the speed of your descent to absorb some of the impact, but I wasn't sure if I calculated for--
Everything's kosher, Vic. *Thanks.*
You think Chase will stop calling me names now?
No, but maybe *I'll* stop sticking paperclips to your face while you're asleep.
That was *you?*
POOF
RRRR?
Uh-oh... let's hope that doesn't mean Nico is *dead.*

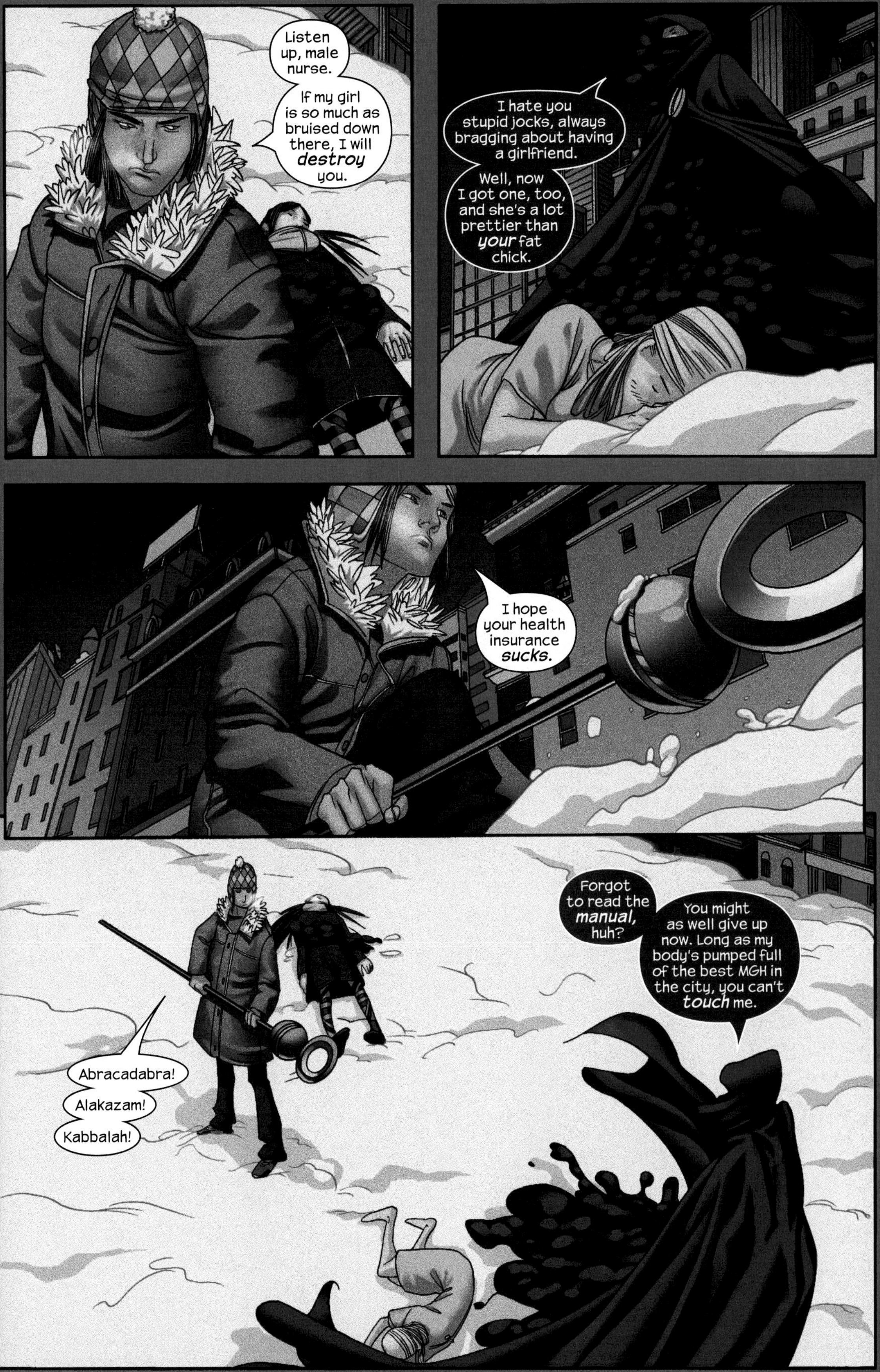
Listen up, male nurse.
If my girl is so much as bruised down there, I will destroy you.
I hate you stupid jocks, always bragging about having a girlfriend.
Well, now I got one, too, and she's a lot prettier than your fat chick.
I hope your health insurance sucks.
Forgot to read the manual, huh?
You might as well give up now. Long as my body's pumped full of the best MGH in the city, you can't touch me.
Abracadabra!
Alakazam!
Kabbalah!

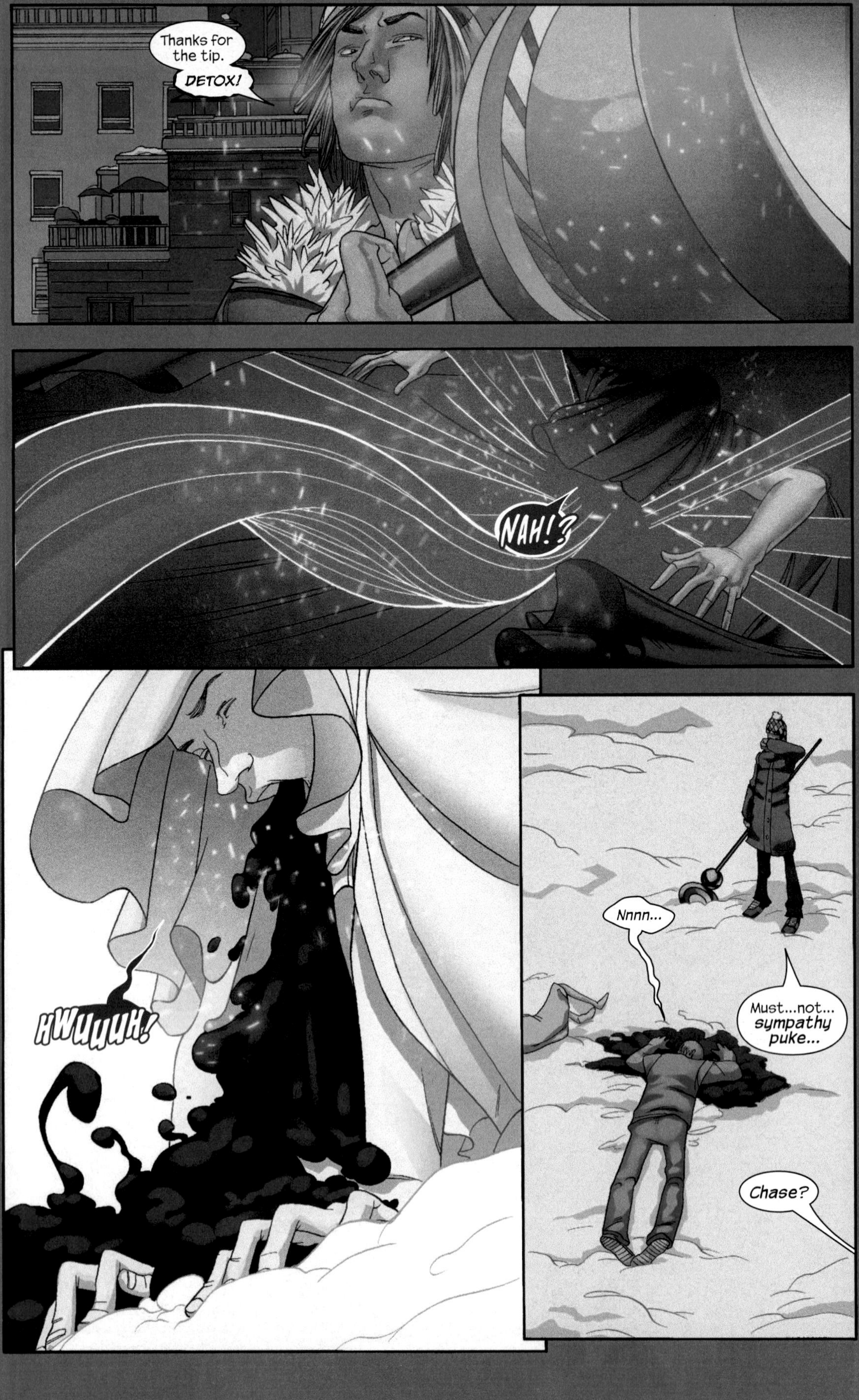
Thanks for the tip.
DETOX!
NAH!?
HWUUUH!
Nnnn...
Must...not... sympathy puke...
Chase?

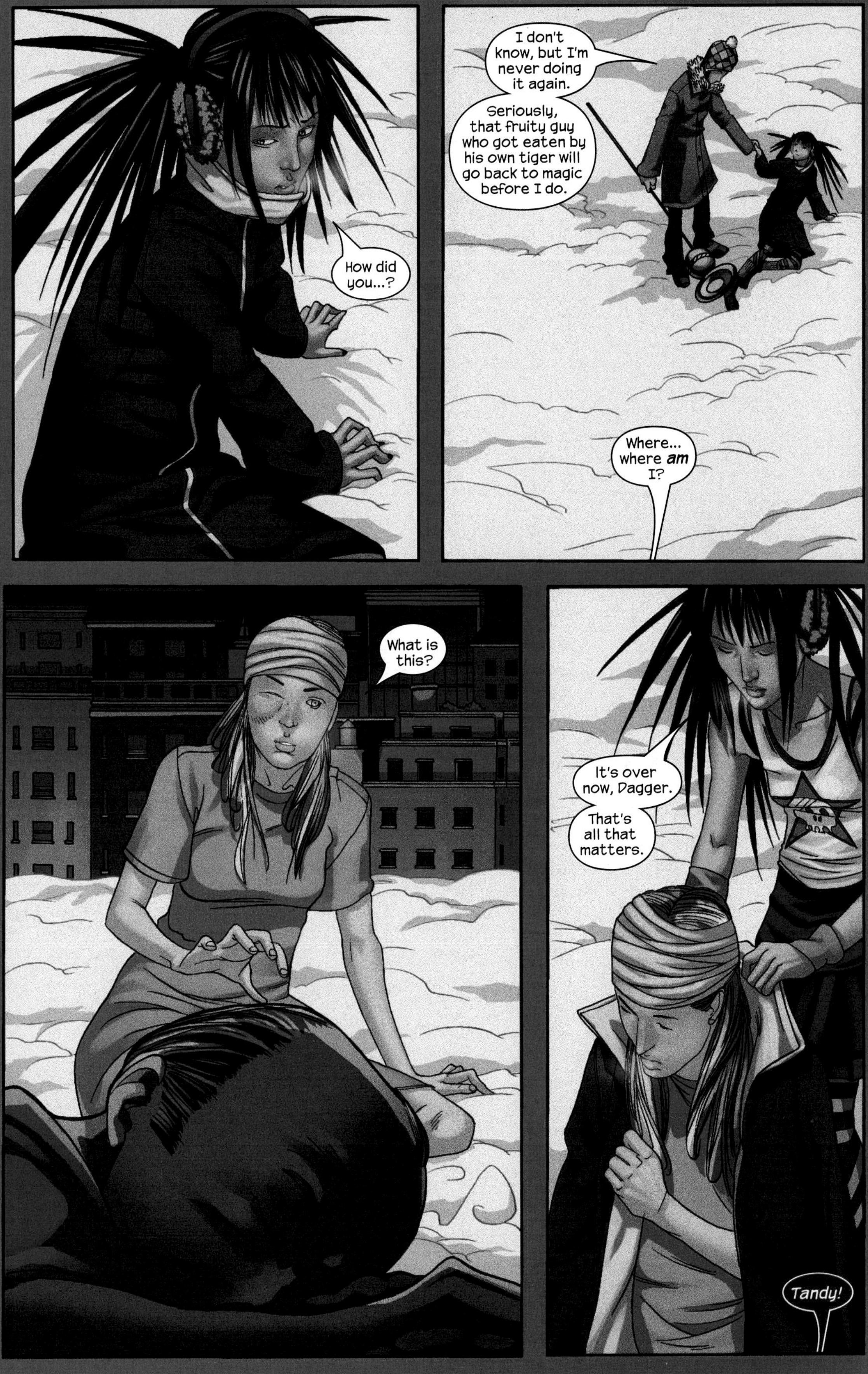
How did you...?
I don't know, but I'm never doing it again.
Seriously, that fruity guy who got eaten by his own tiger will go back to magic before I do.
Where... where *am* I?
What is this?
It's over now, Dagger.
That's all that matters.
Tandy!

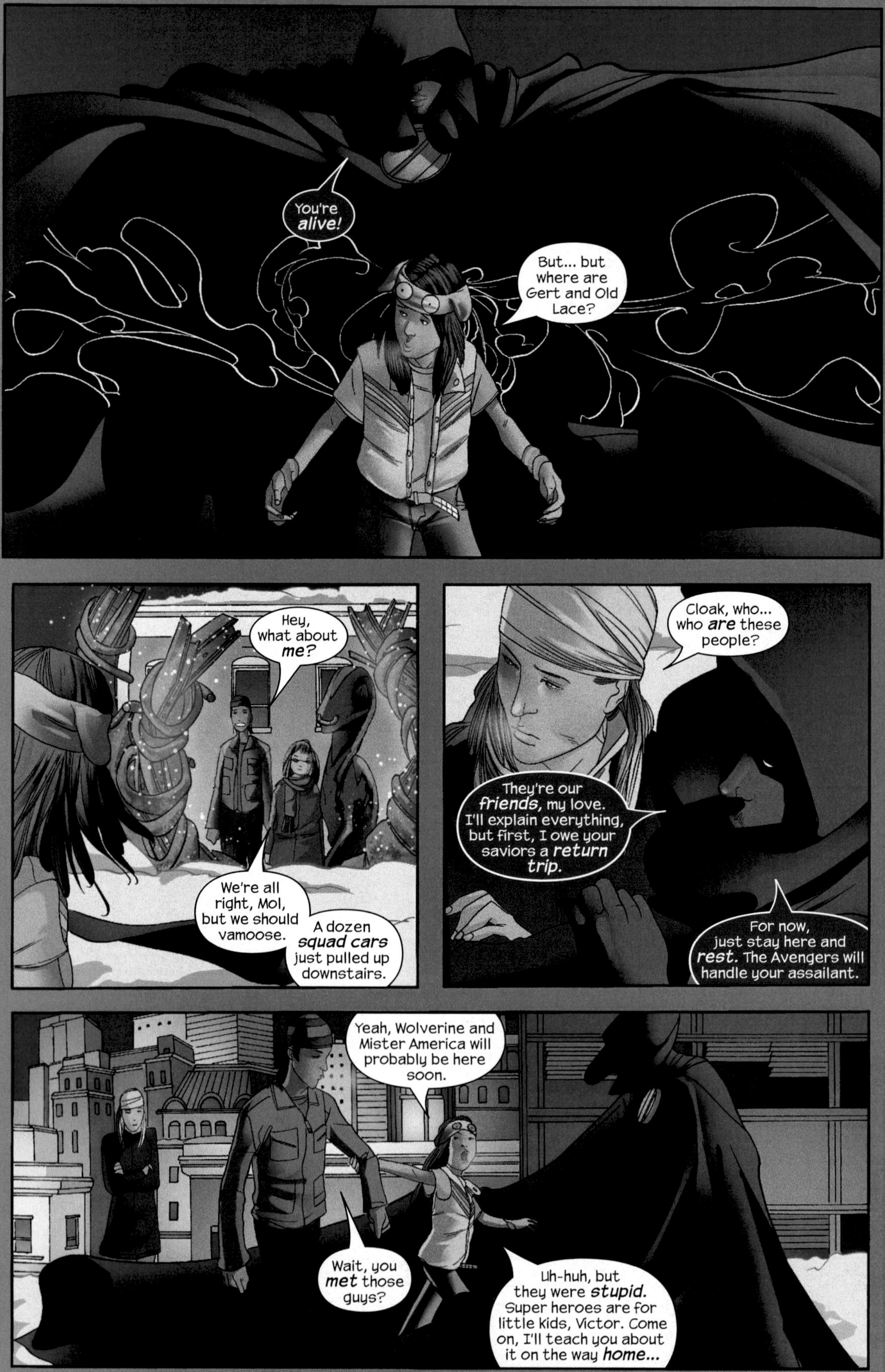

You're alive!
But... but where are Gert and Old Lace?
Hey, what about me?
We're all right, Mol, but we should vamoose.
A dozen squad cars just pulled up downstairs.
Cloak, who... who are these people?
They're our friends, my love. I'll explain everything, but first, I owe your saviors a return trip.
For now, just stay here and rest. The Avengers will handle your assailant.
Yeah, Wolverine and Mister America will probably be here soon.
Wait, you met those guys?
Uh-huh, but they were stupid. Super heroes are for little kids, Victor. Come on, I'll teach you about it on the way home...

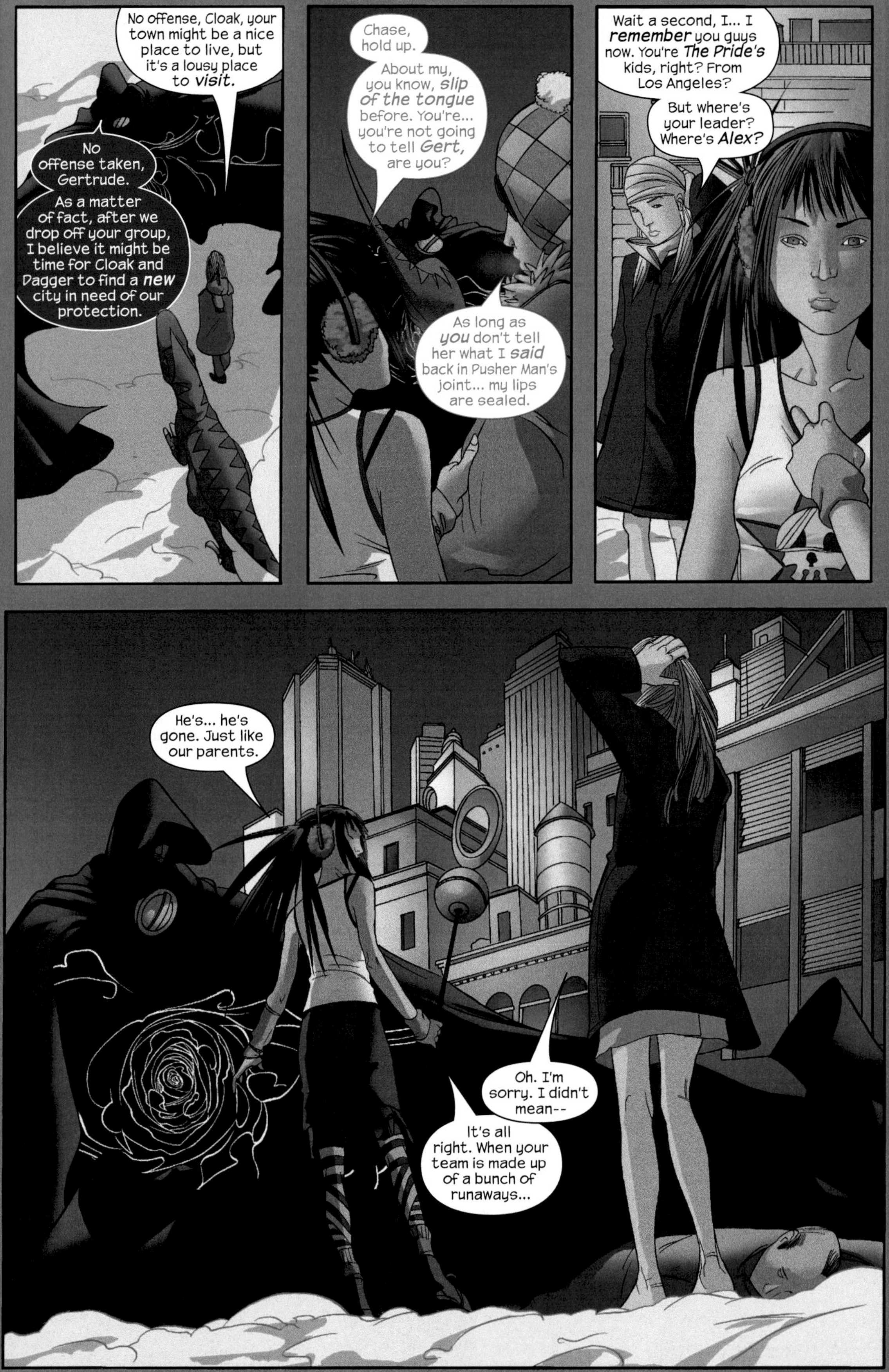
No offense, Cloak, your town might be a nice place to live, but it's a lousy place to visit.
No offense taken, Gertrude.
As a matter of fact, after we drop off your group, I believe it might be time for Cloak and Dagger to find a new city in need of our protection.
Chase, hold up.
About my, you know, slip of the tongue before. You're... you're not going to tell Gert, are you?
As long as you don't tell her what I said back in Pusher Man's joint... my lips are sealed.
Wait a second, I... I remember you guys now. You're The Pride's kids, right? From Los Angeles?
But where's your leader? Where's Alex?
He's... he's gone. Just like our parents.
Oh. I'm sorry. I didn't mean--
It's all right. When your team is made up of a bunch of runaways...

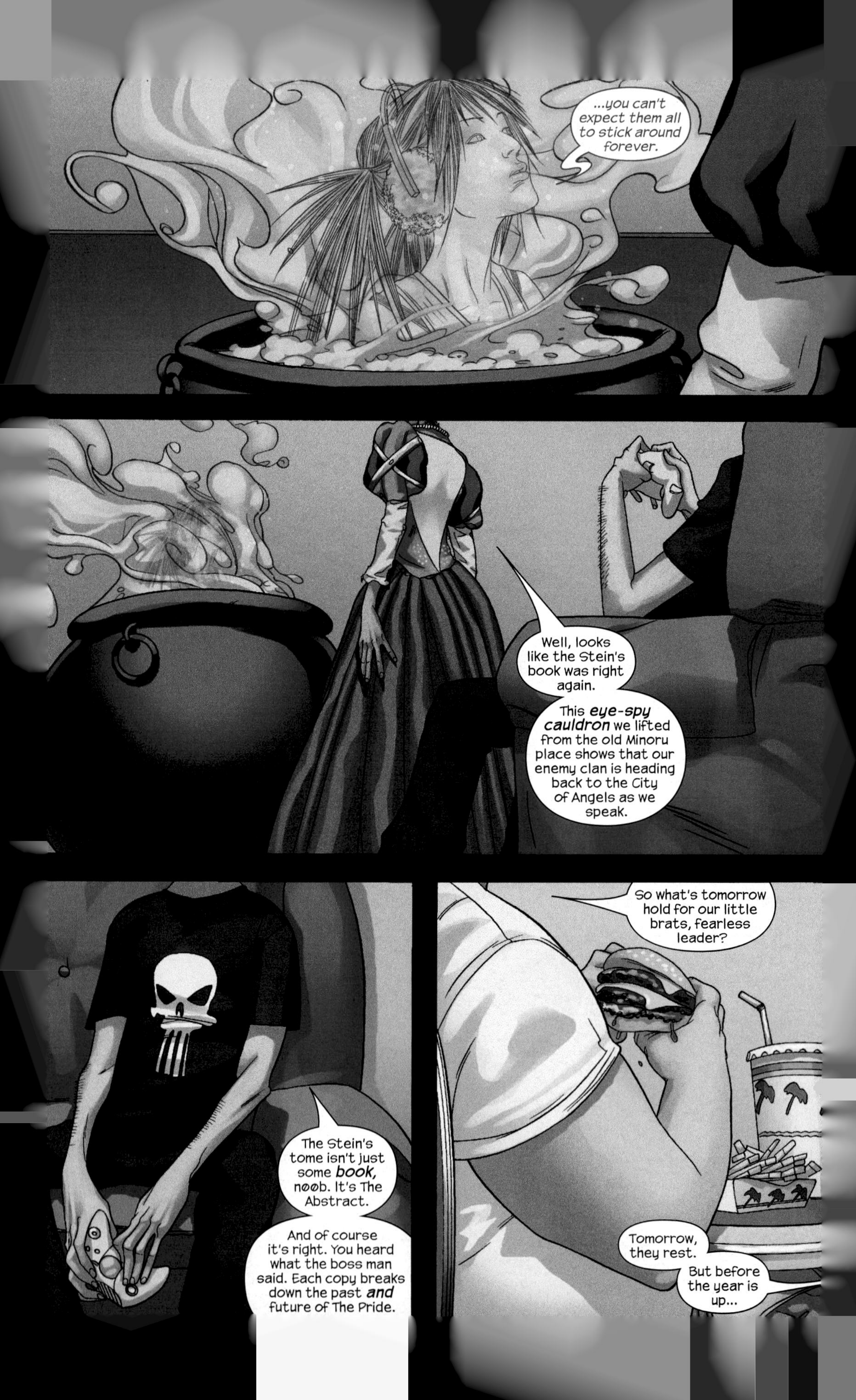
...you can't expect them all to stick around forever.
Well, looks like the Stein's book was right again.
This eye-spy cauldron we lifted from the old Minoru place shows that our enemy clan is heading back to the City of Angels as we speak.
The Stein's tome isn't just some book, nøøb. It's The Abstract.
And of course it's right. You heard what the boss man said. Each copy breaks down the past and future of The Pride.
So what's tomorrow hold for our little brats, fearless leader?
Tomorrow, they rest.
But before the year is up...

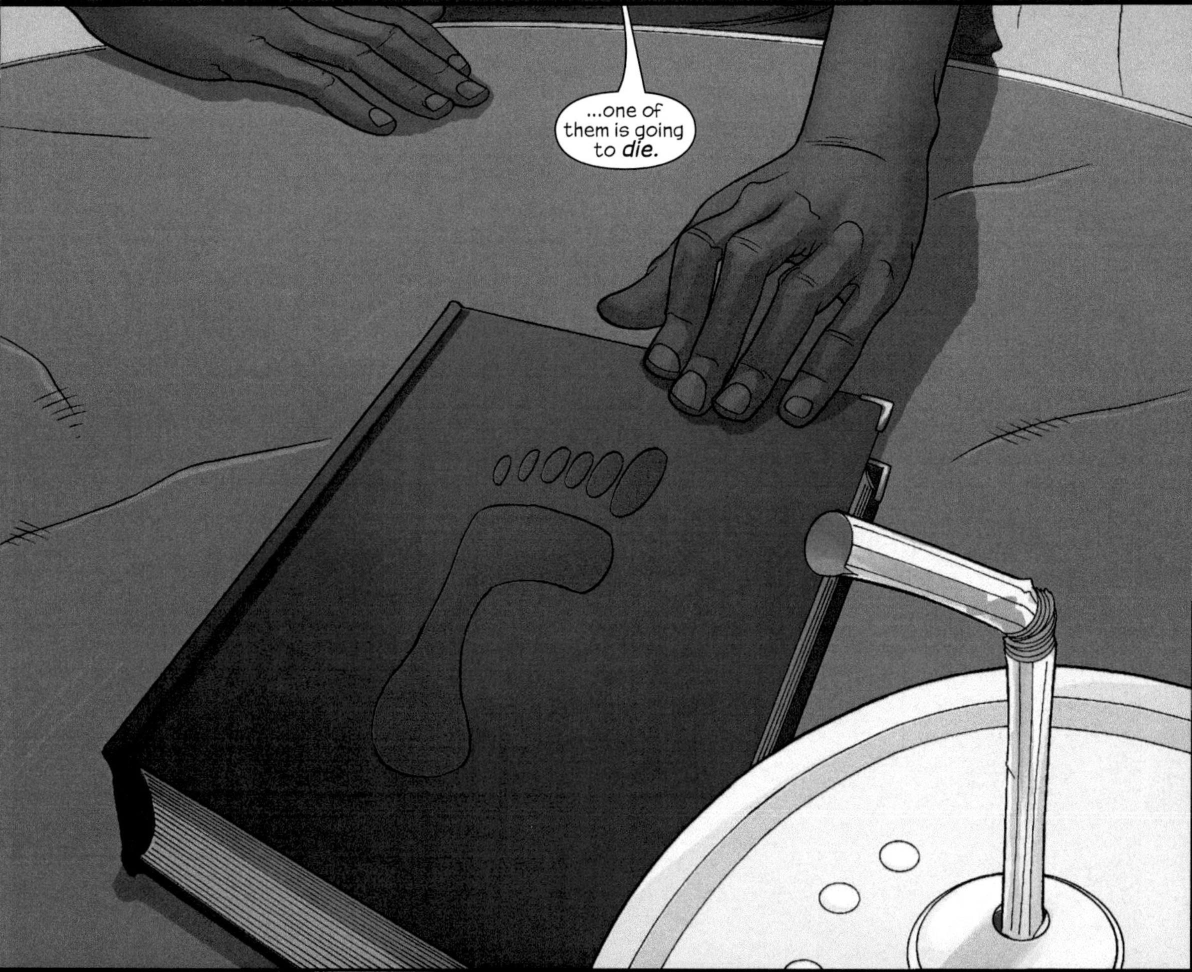
...one of them is going to die.

Next: Parental Guidance

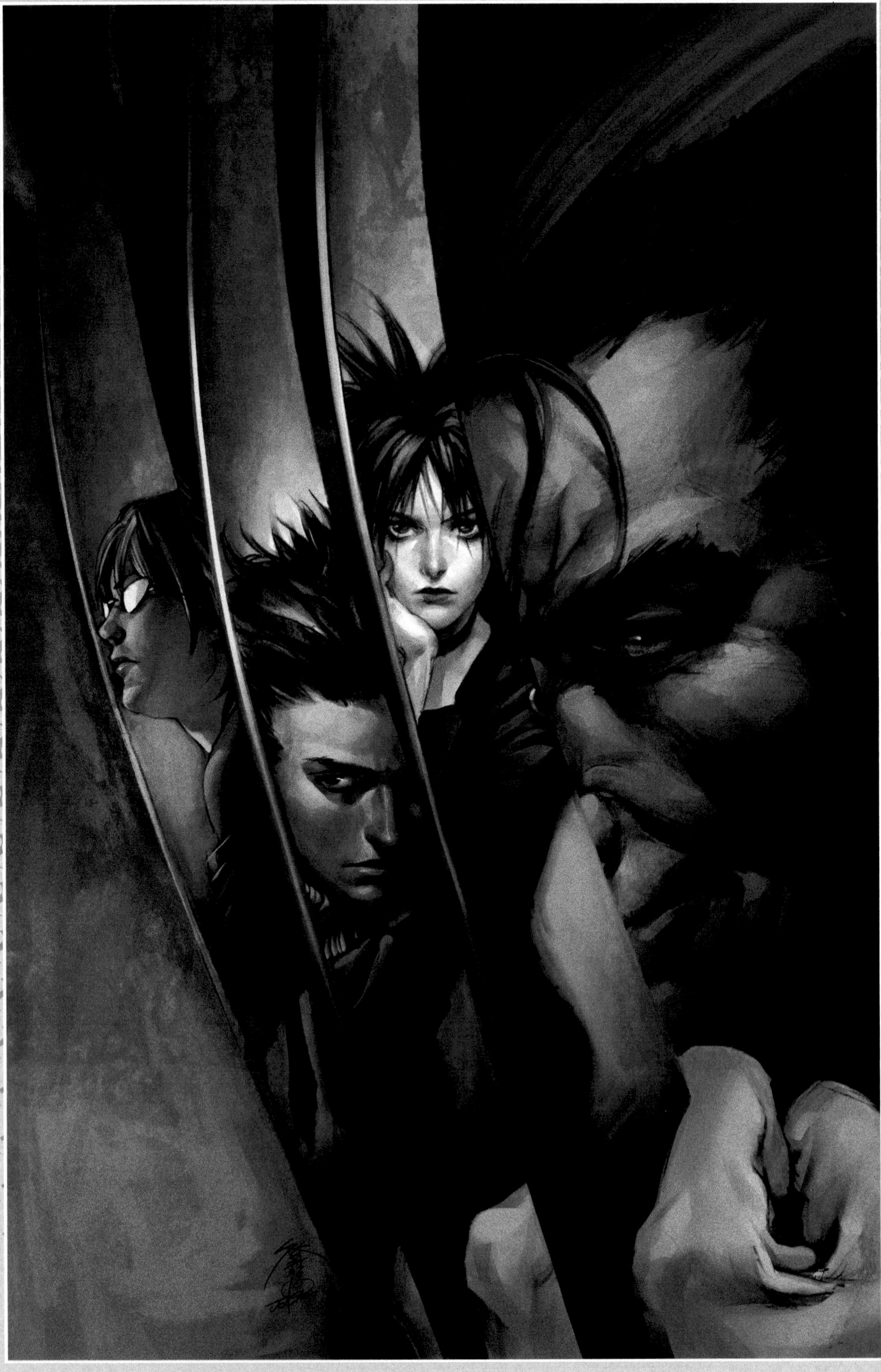

FREE COMIC BOOK DAY 2006

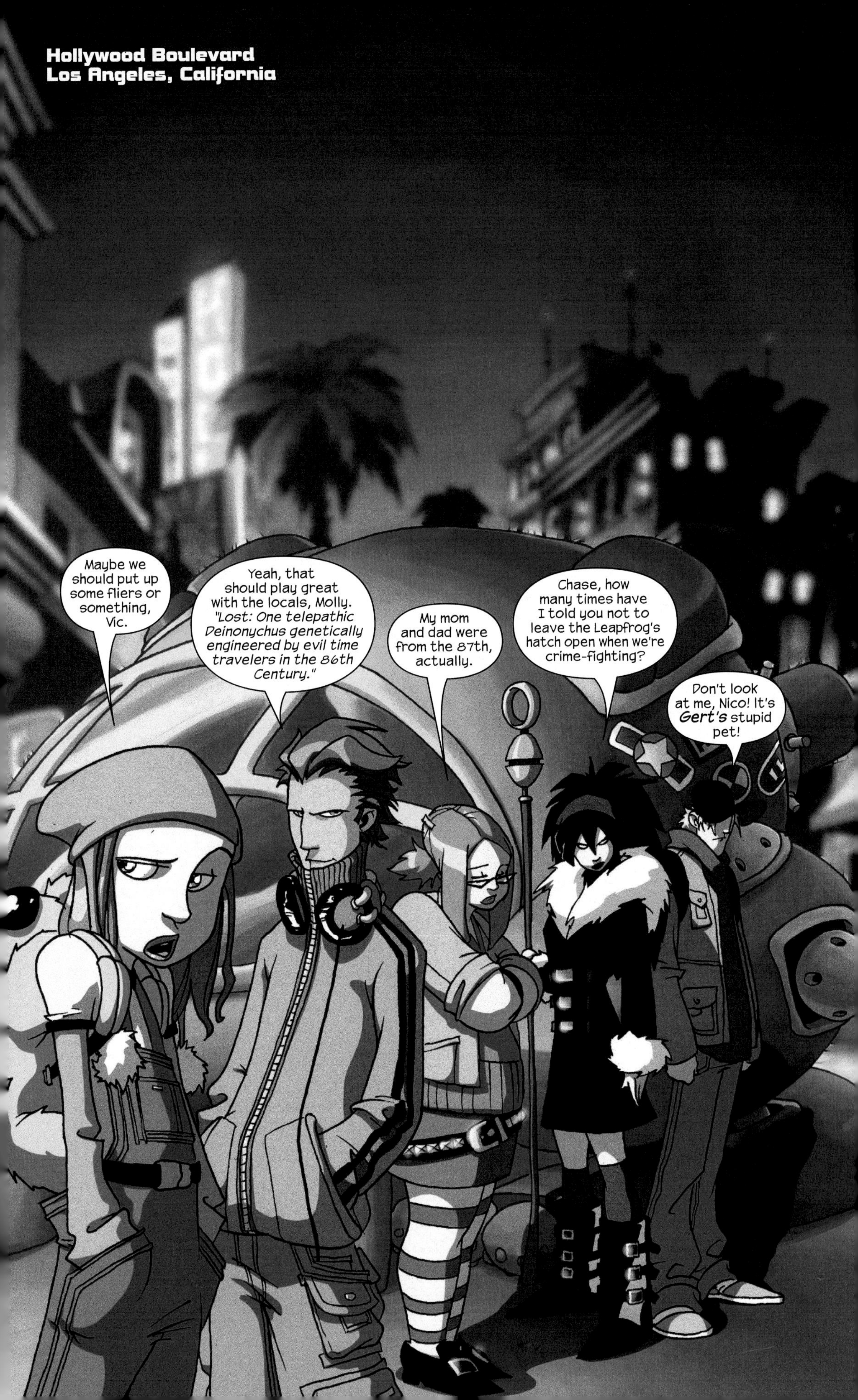
Hollywood Boulevard
Los Angeles, California
Maybe we should put up some fliers or something, Vic.
Yeah, that should play great with the locals, Molly. "Lost: One telepathic Deinonychus genetically engineered by evil time travelers in the 86th Century."
My mom and dad were from the 87th, actually.
Chase, how many times have I told you not to leave the Leapfrog's hatch open when we're crime-fighting?
Don't look at me, Nico! It's Gert's stupid pet!

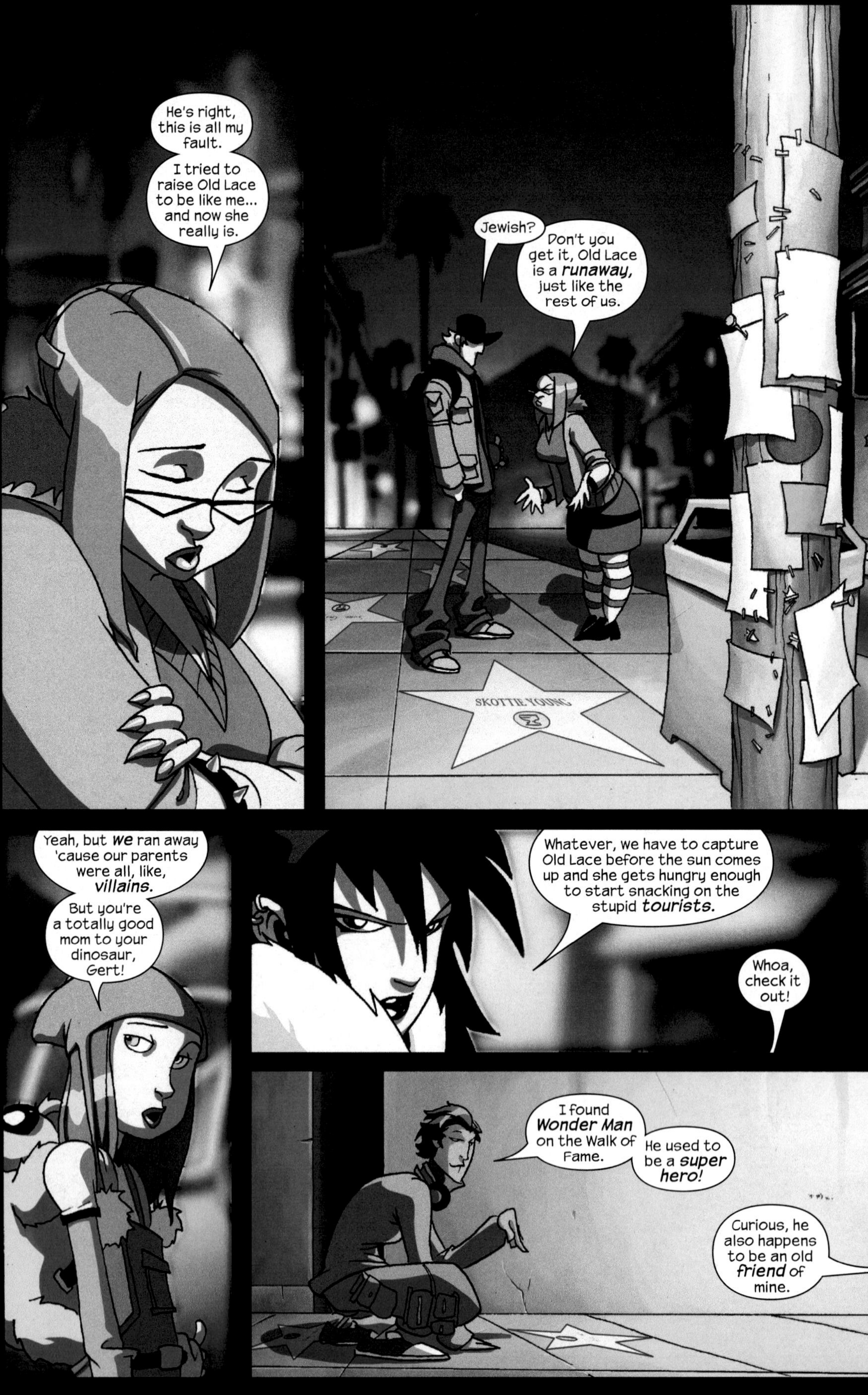
He's right, this is all my fault.
I tried to raise Old Lace to be like me... and now she really is.
Jewish?
Don't you get it, Old Lace is a *runaway*, just like the rest of us.
SKOTTIE YOUNG
Yeah, but *we* ran away 'cause our parents were all, like, *villains*.
But you're a totally good mom to your dinosaur, Gert!
Whatever, we have to capture Old Lace before the sun comes up and she gets hungry enough to start snacking on the stupid *tourists*.
Whoa, check it out!
I found *Wonder Man* on the Walk of Fame.
He used to be a *super hero*!
Curious, he also happens to be an old *friend* of mine.

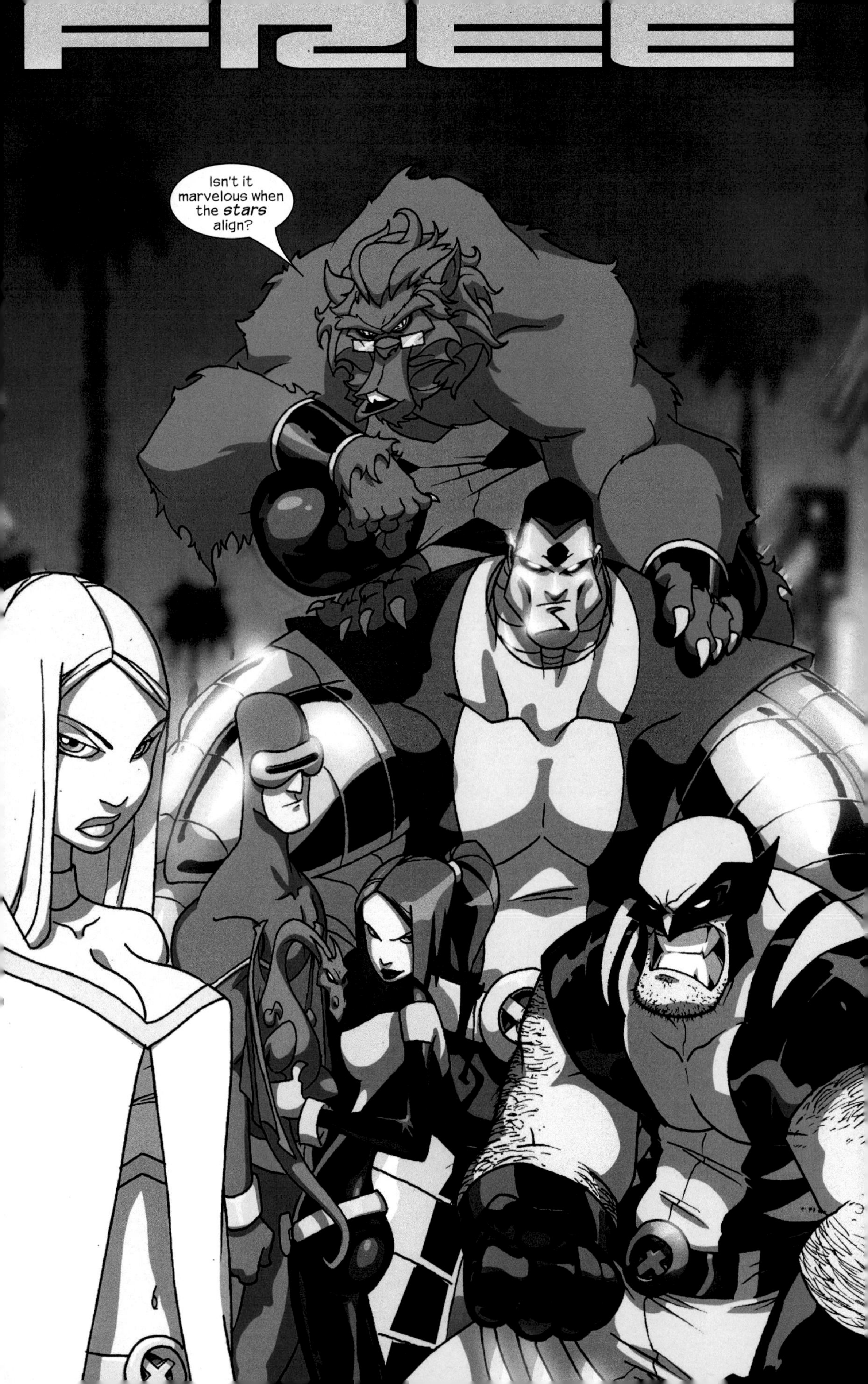
FREE
Isn't it marvelous when the *stars* align?

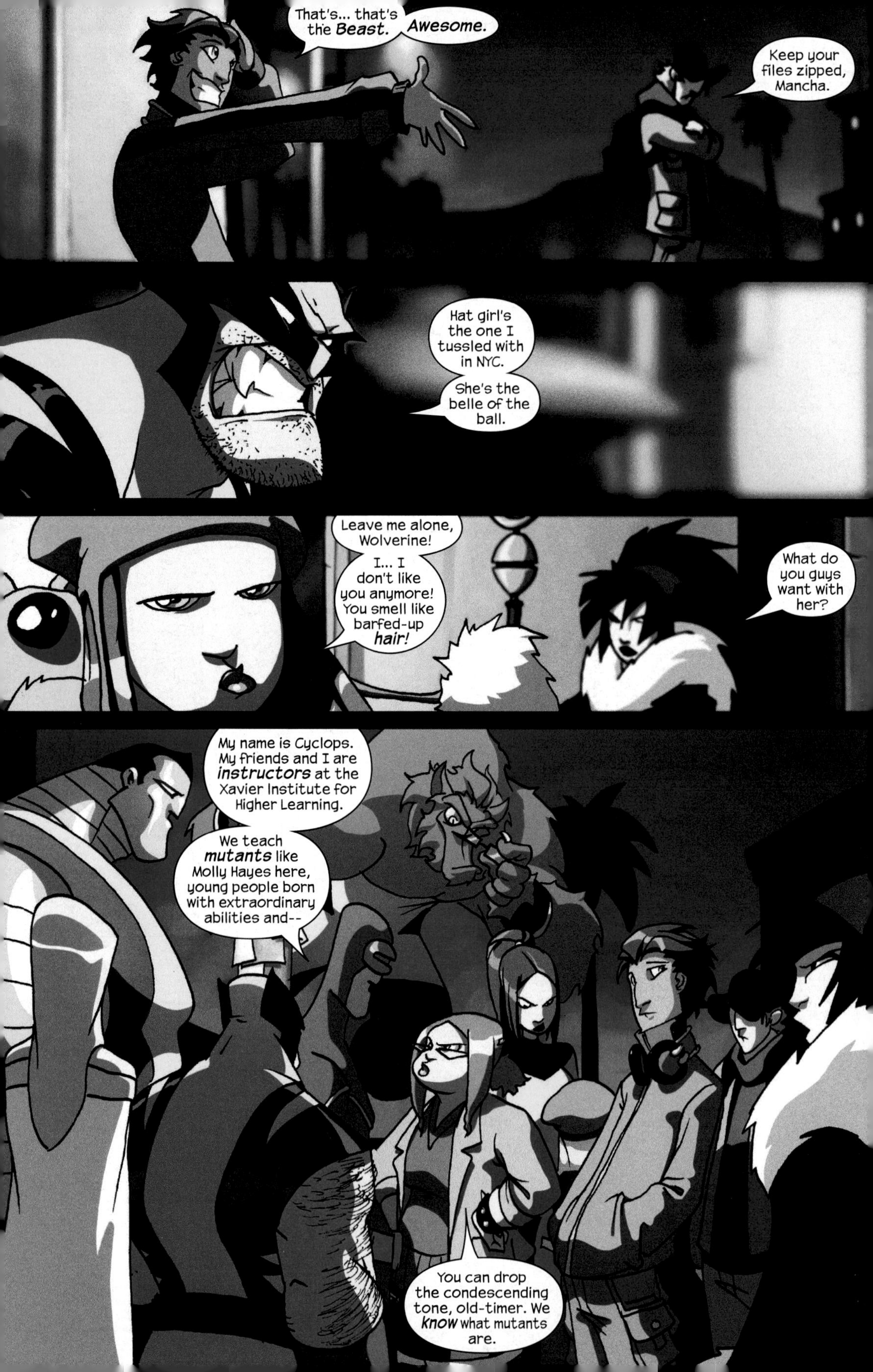

That's... that's the Beast.
Awesome.
Keep your files zipped, Mancha.
Hat girl's the one I tussled with in NYC.
She's the belle of the ball.
Leave me alone, Wolverine!
I... I don't like you anymore! You smell like barfed-up hair!
What do you guys want with her?
My name is Cyclops. My friends and I are instructors at the Xavier Institute for Higher Learning.
We teach mutants like Molly Hayes here, young people born with extraordinary abilities and--
You can drop the condescending tone, old-timer. We know what mutants are.

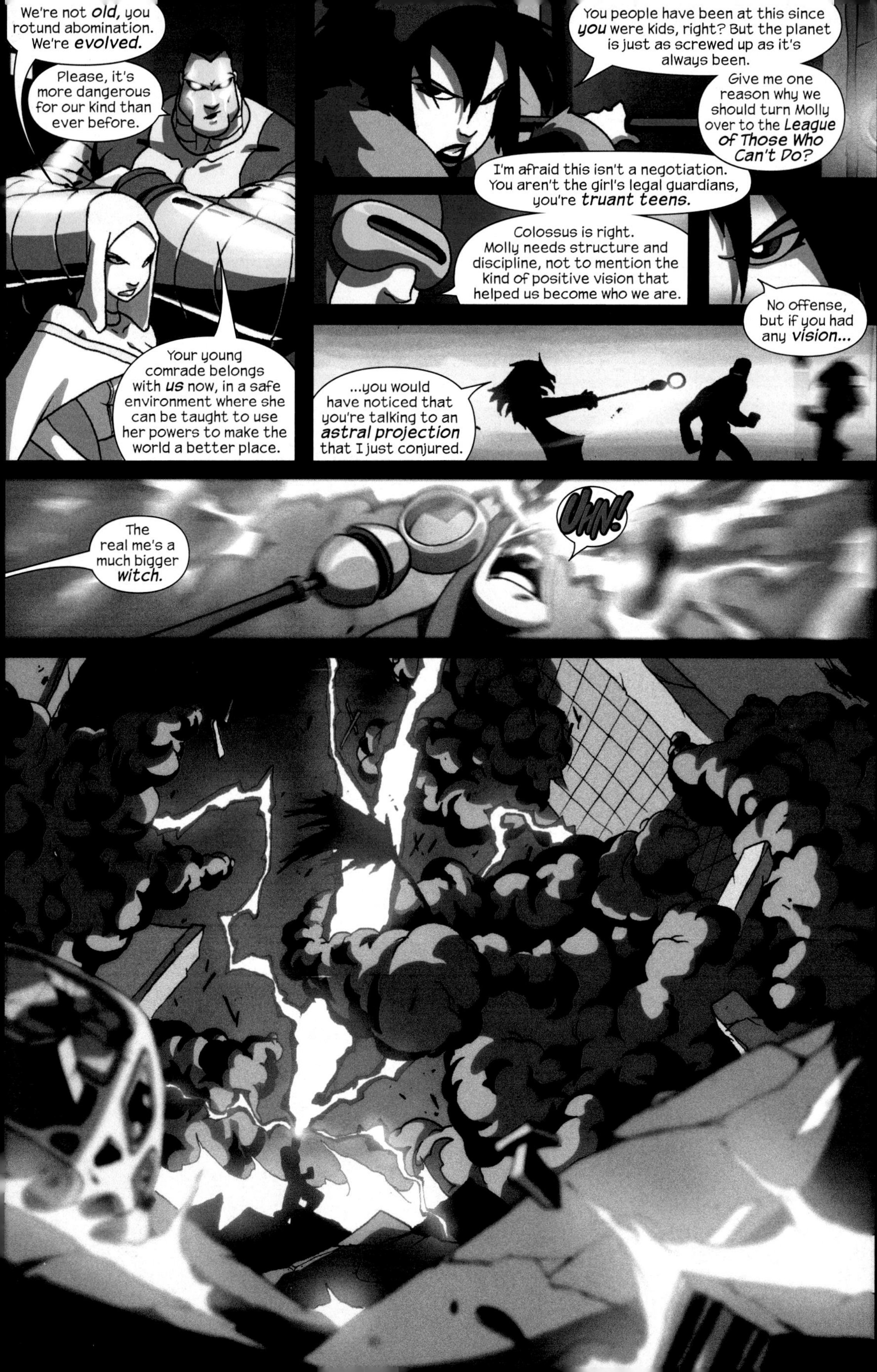
We're not *old,* you rotund abomination. We're *evolved.*
Please, it's more dangerous for our kind than ever before.
You people have been at this since *you* were kids, right? But the planet is just as screwed up as it's always been.
Give me one reason why we should turn Molly over to the *League of Those Who Can't Do?*
I'm afraid this isn't a negotiation. You aren't the girl's legal guardians, you're *truant teens.*
Colossus is right. Molly needs structure and discipline, not to mention the kind of positive vision that helped us become who we are.
Your young comrade belongs with *us* now, in a safe environment where she can be taught to use her powers to make the world a better place.
No offense, but if you had any *vision...*
...you would have noticed that you're talking to an *astral projection* that I just conjured.
The real me's a much bigger *witch.*
UHN!

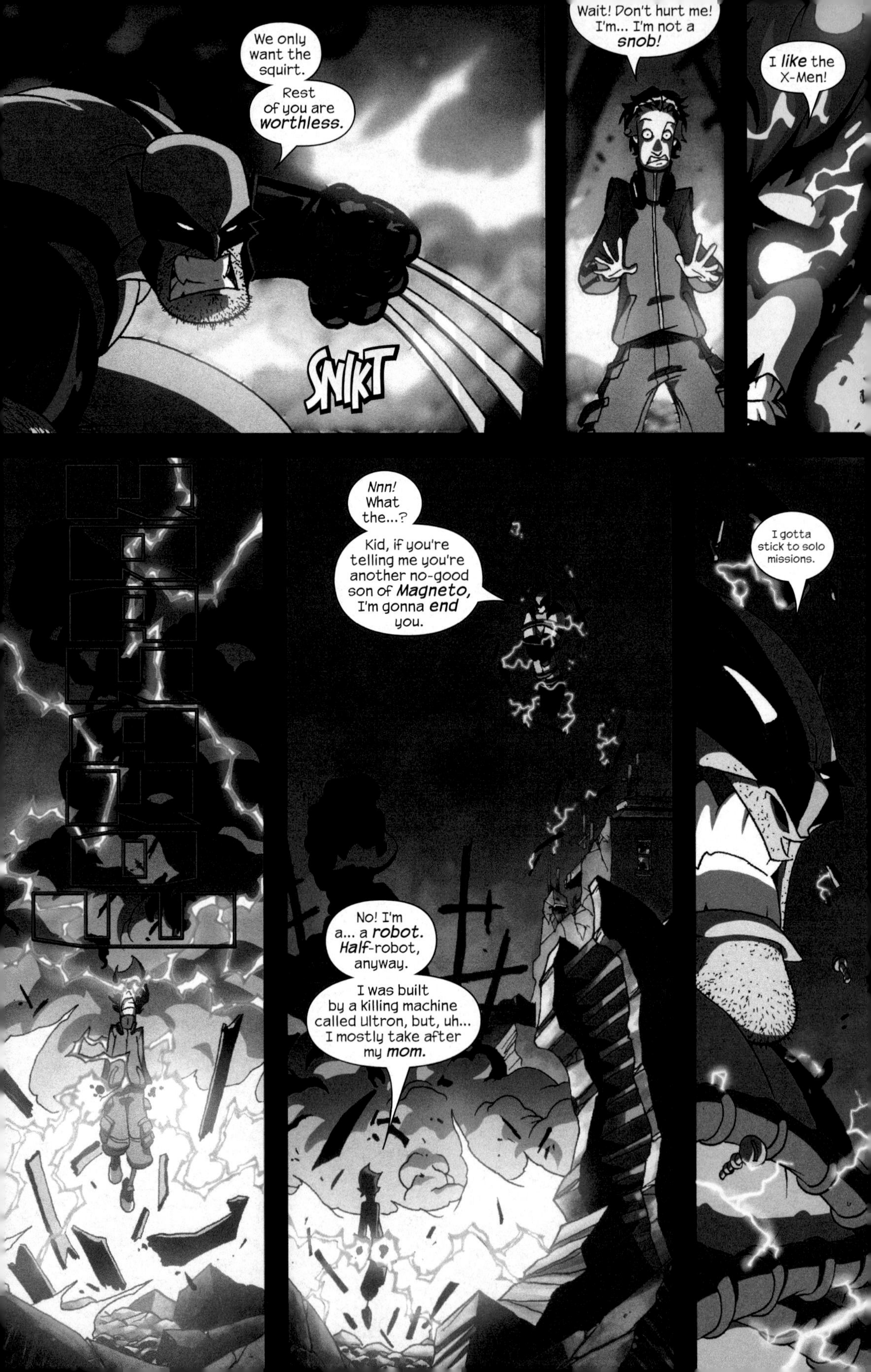
We only want the squirt.
Rest of you are worthless.
SNIKT
Wait! Don't hurt me! I'm... I'm not a snob!
I like the X-Men!
Nnn! What the...?
Kid, if you're telling me you're another no-good son of Magneto, I'm gonna end you.
No! I'm a... a robot. Half-robot, anyway.
I was built by a killing machine called Ultron, but, uh... I mostly take after my mom.
I gotta stick to solo missions.

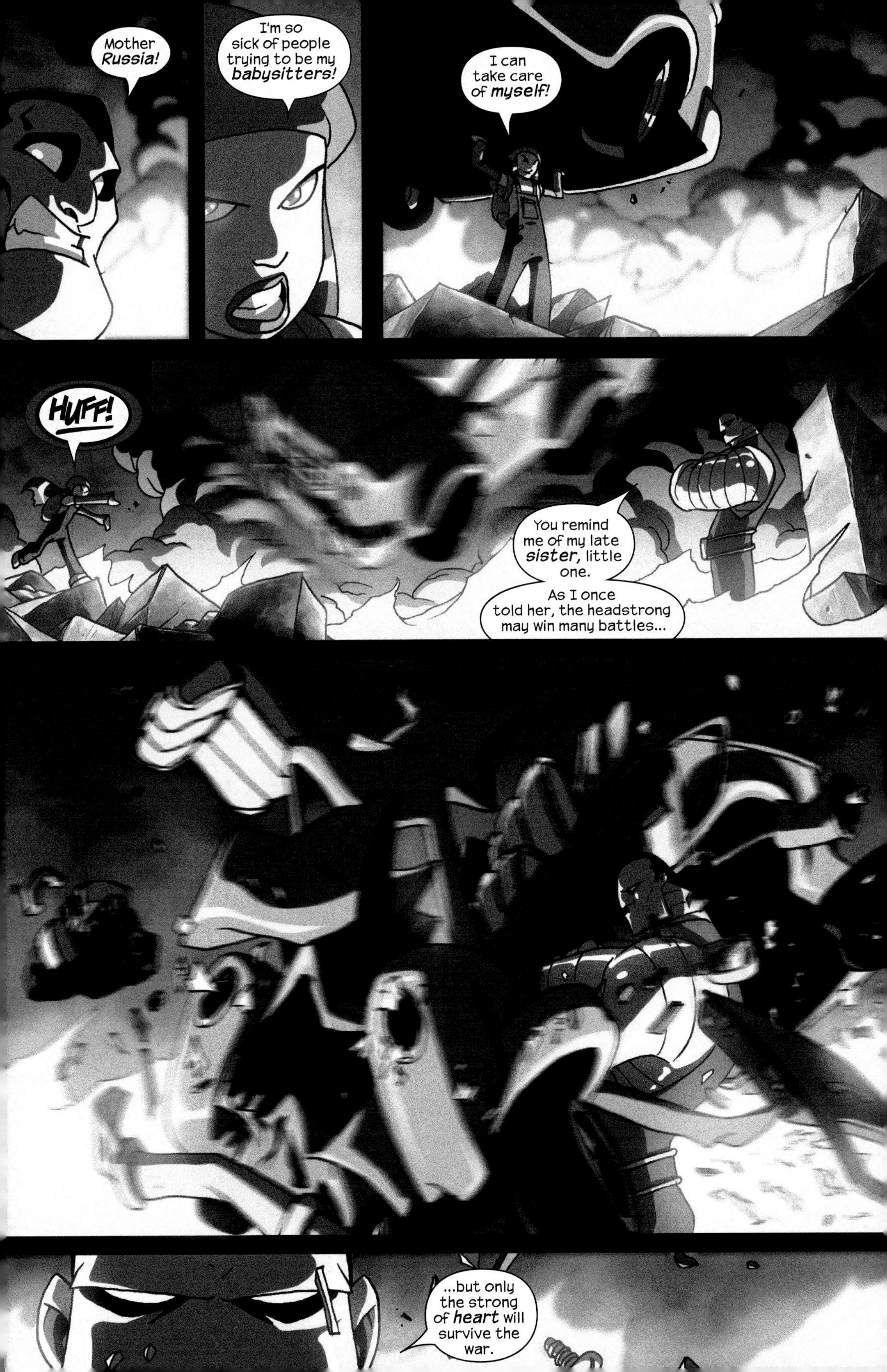
Mother Russia!
I'm so sick of people trying to be my babysitters!
I can take care of myself!
HUFF!
You remind me of my late sister, little one.
As I once told her, the headstrong may win many battles...
...but only the strong of heart will survive the war.

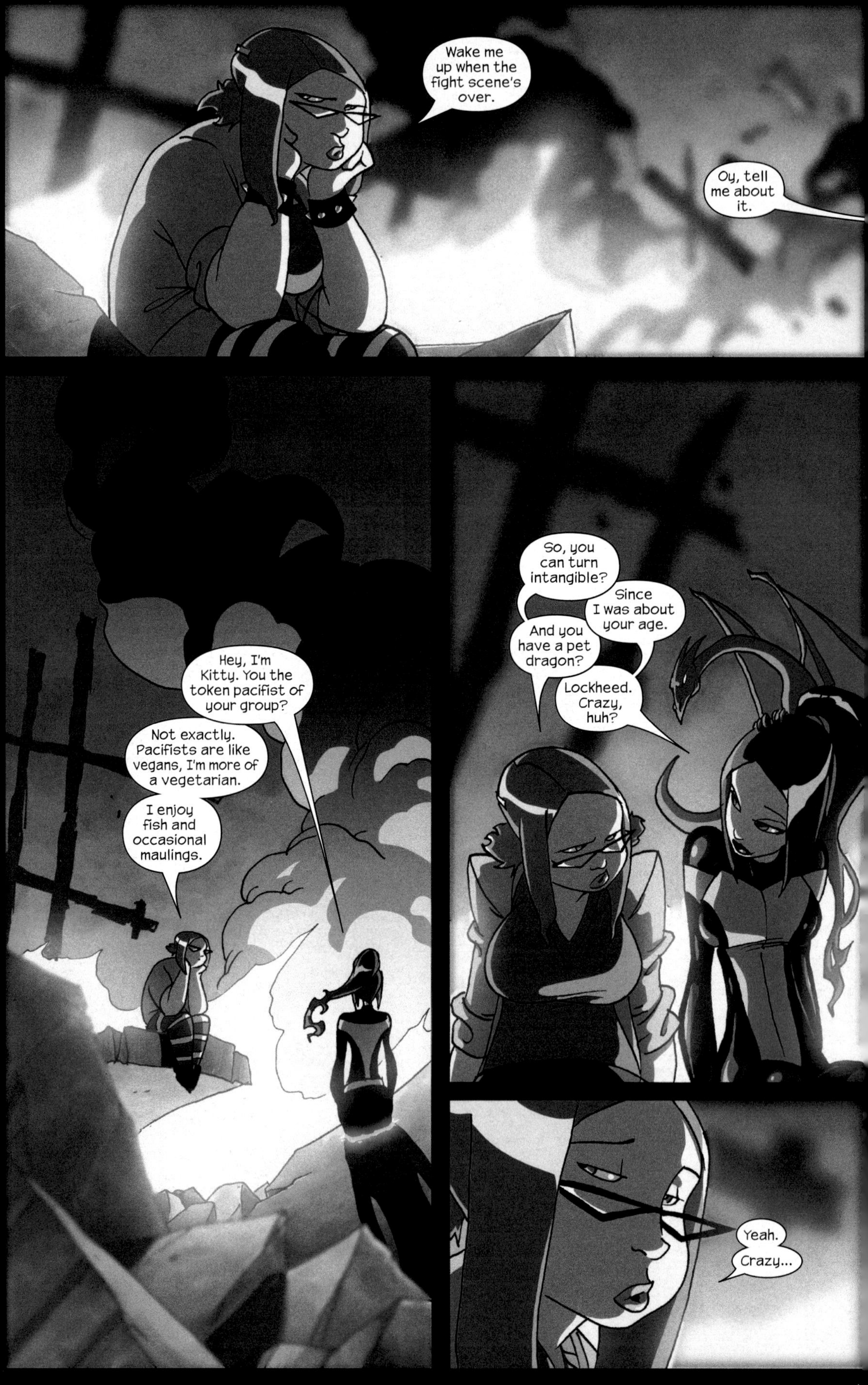
Wake me up when the fight scene's over.
Oy, tell me about it.
Hey, I'm Kitty. You the token pacifist of your group?
Not exactly. Pacifists are like vegans, I'm more of a vegetarian.
I enjoy fish and occasional maulings.
So, you can turn intangible?
Since I was about your age.
And you have a pet dragon?
Lockheed. Crazy, huh?
Yeah.
Crazy...

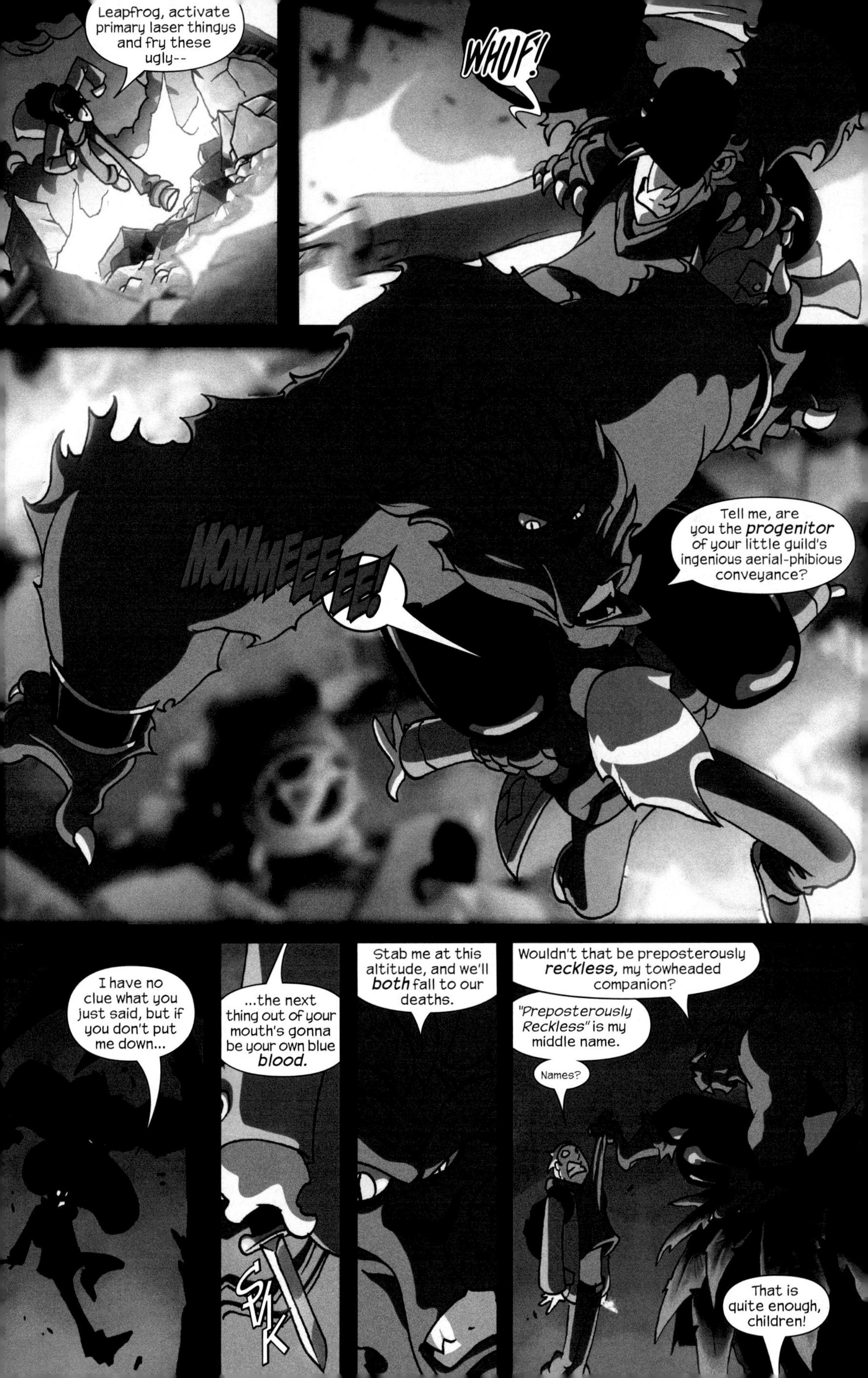
Leapfrog, activate primary laser thingys and fry these ugly--
WHUF!
MOMMEEEEEE!
Tell me, are you the progenitor of your little guild's ingenious aerial-phibious conveyance?
I have no clue what you just said, but if you don't put me down...
...the next thing out of your mouth's gonna be your own blue blood.
SHUK
Stab me at this altitude, and we'll both fall to our deaths.
Wouldn't that be preposterously reckless, my towheaded companion?
"Preposterously Reckless" is my middle name.
Names?
That is quite enough, children!

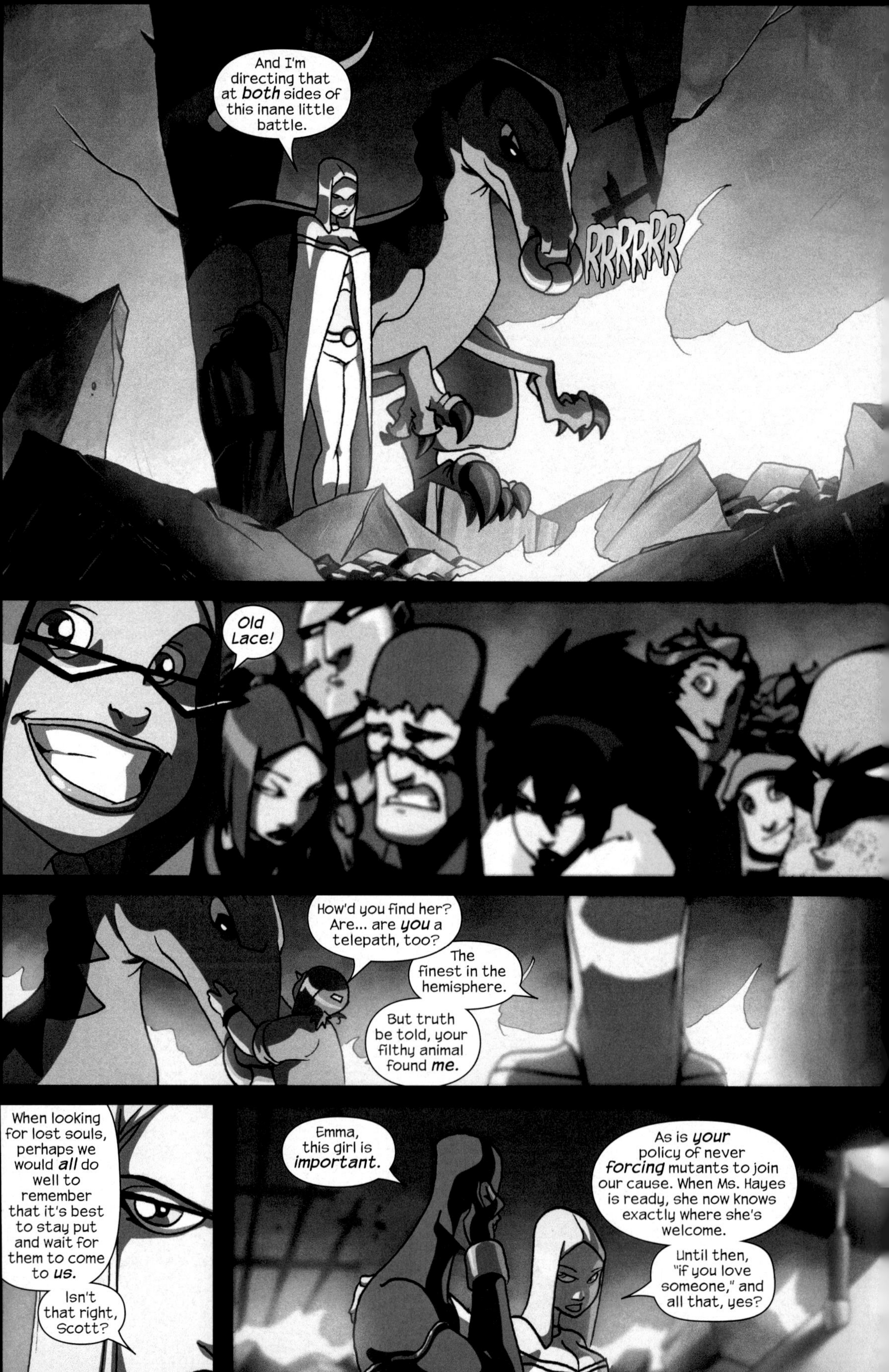

And I'm directing that at both sides of this inane little battle.
RRRRRR
Old Lace!
How'd you find her? Are... are you a telepath, too?
The finest in the hemisphere.
But truth be told, your filthy animal found me.
When looking for lost souls, perhaps we would all do well to remember that it's best to stay put and wait for them to come to us.
Isn't that right, Scott?
Emma, this girl is important.
As is your policy of never forcing mutants to join our cause. When Ms. Hayes is ready, she now knows exactly where she's welcome.
Until then, "if you love someone," and all that, yes?

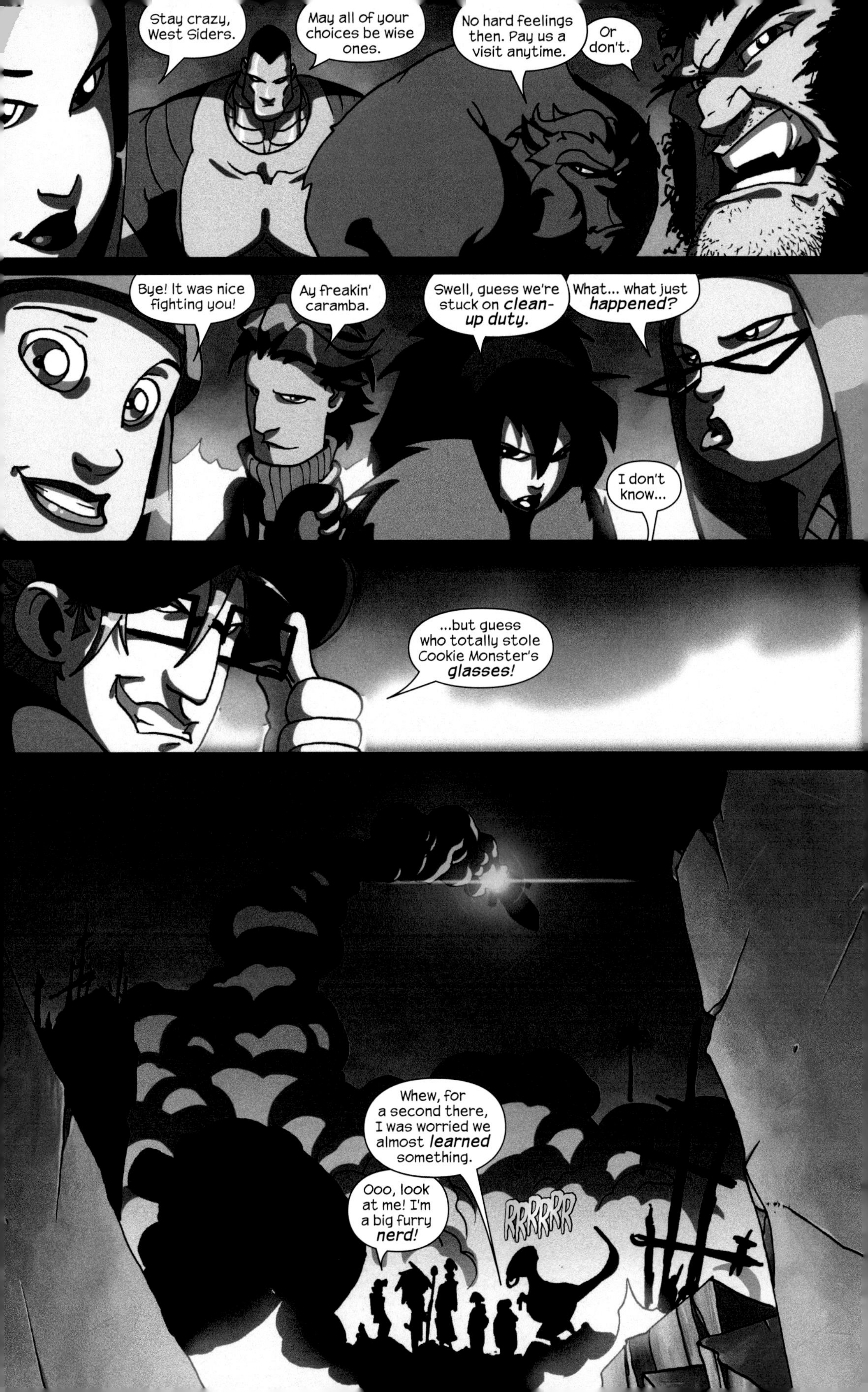
Stay crazy, West Siders.
May all of your choices be wise ones.
No hard feelings then. Pay us a visit anytime.
Or don't.
Bye! It was nice fighting you!
Ay freakin' caramba.
Swell, guess we're stuck on *clean-up duty.*
What... what just *happened?*
I don't know...
...but guess who totally stole Cookie Monster's *glasses!*
Whew, for a second there, I was worried we almost *learned* something.
Ooo, look at me! I'm a big furry *nerd!*
RRRRRR

ADRIAN ALPHONA SKETCHBOOK

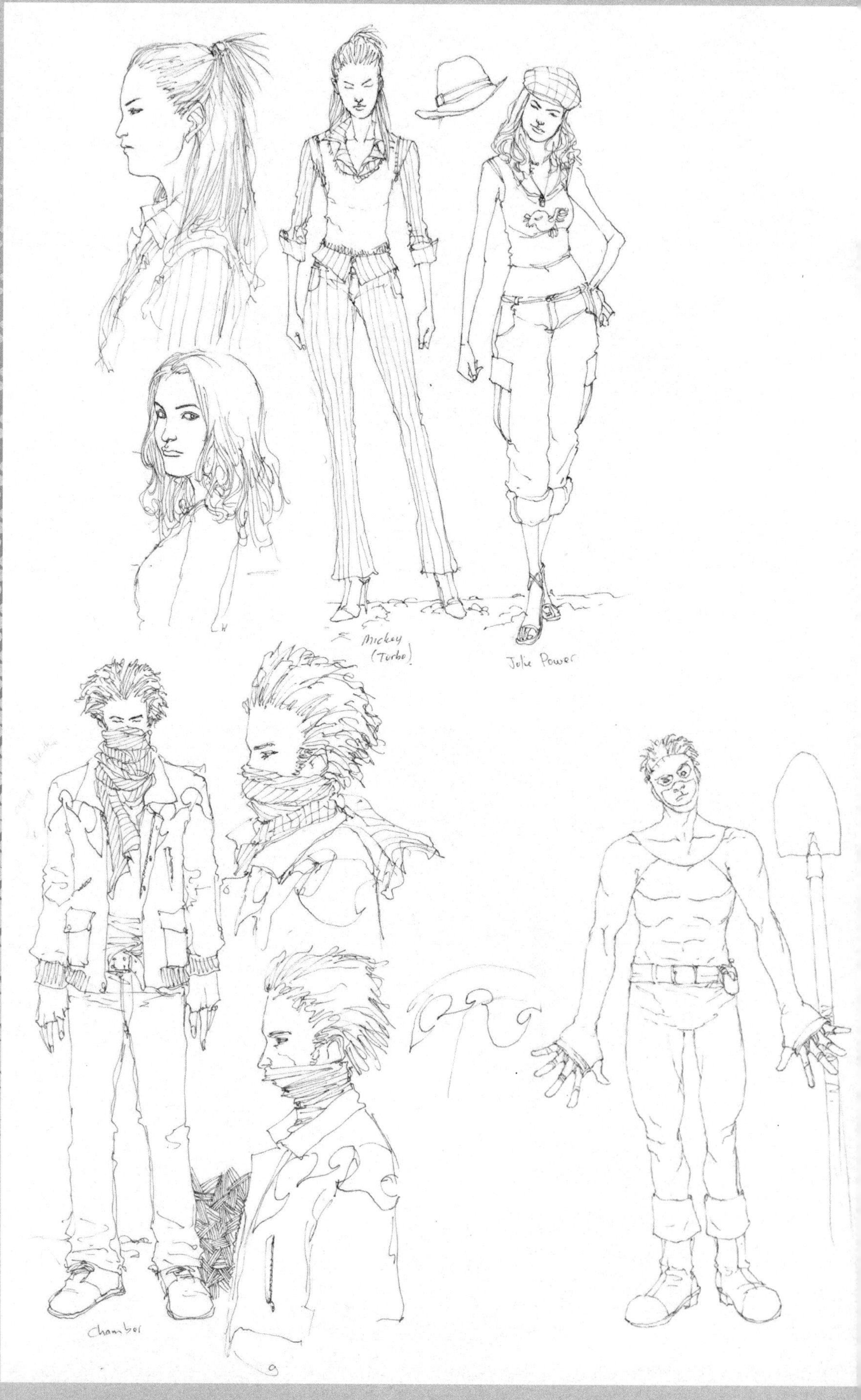
Mickey
(Turbo)
Julie Power
Chamber

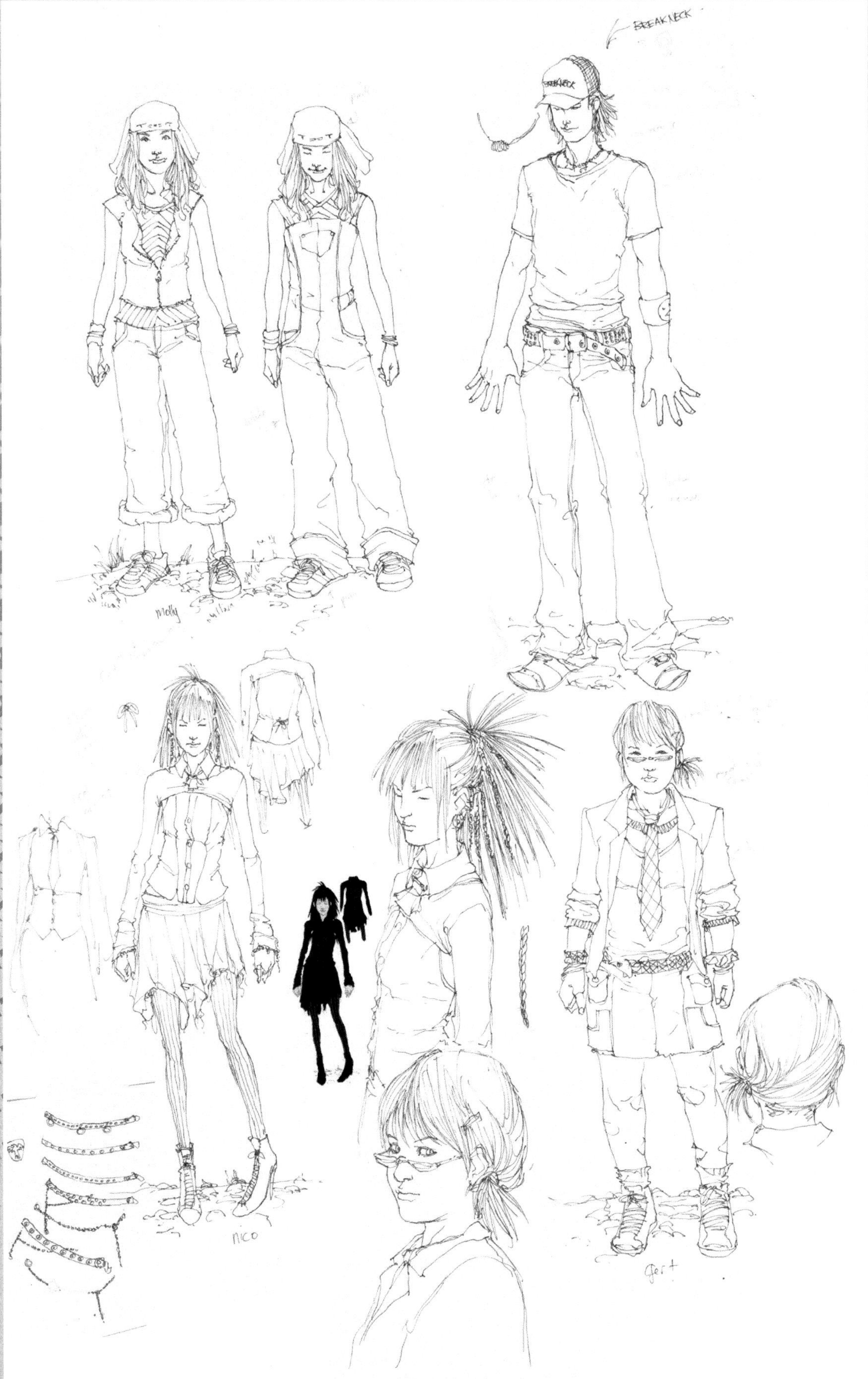
BREAKNECK
Molly
nico
gert

Runaways ish 10 AUG05

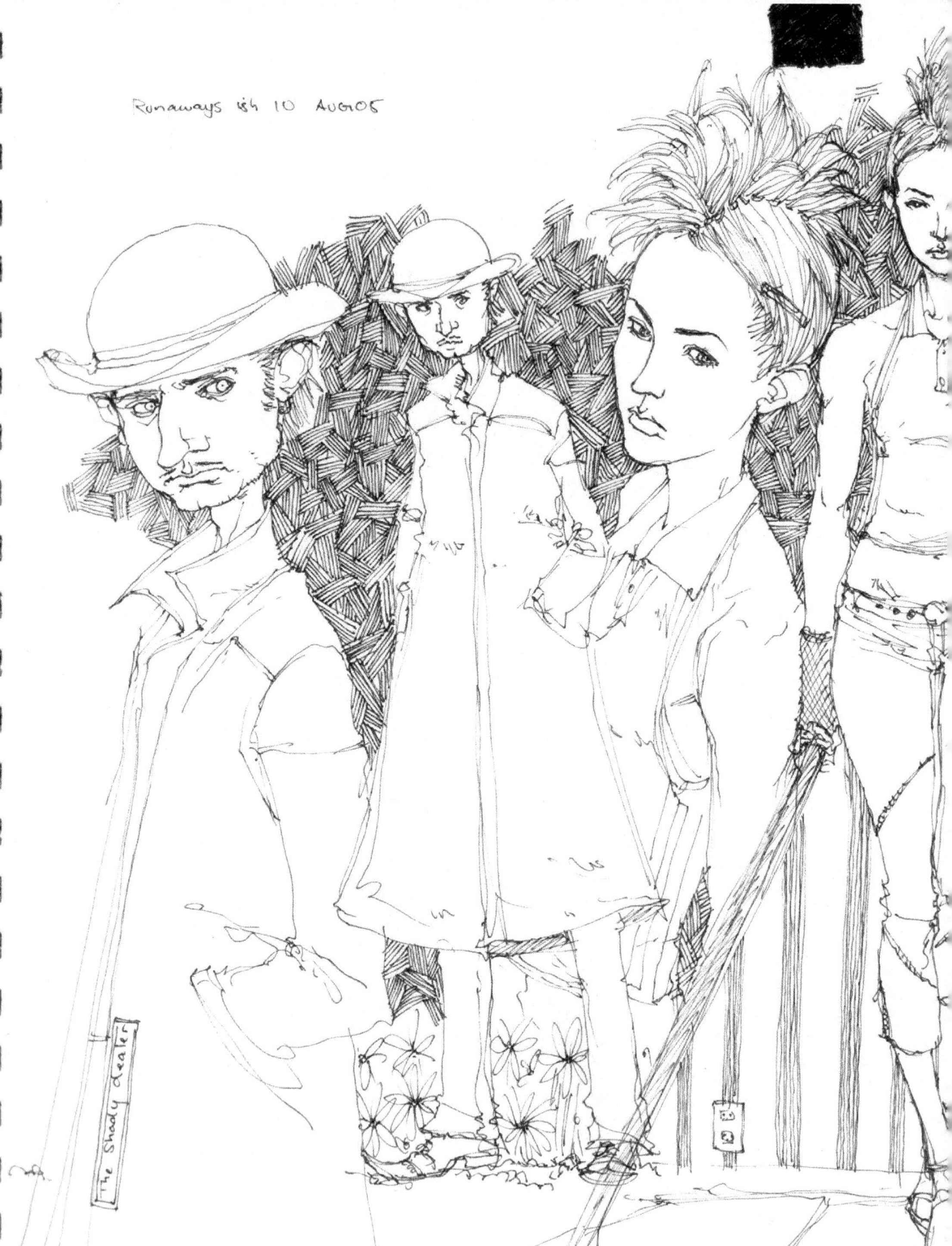
The shady dealer
Bo

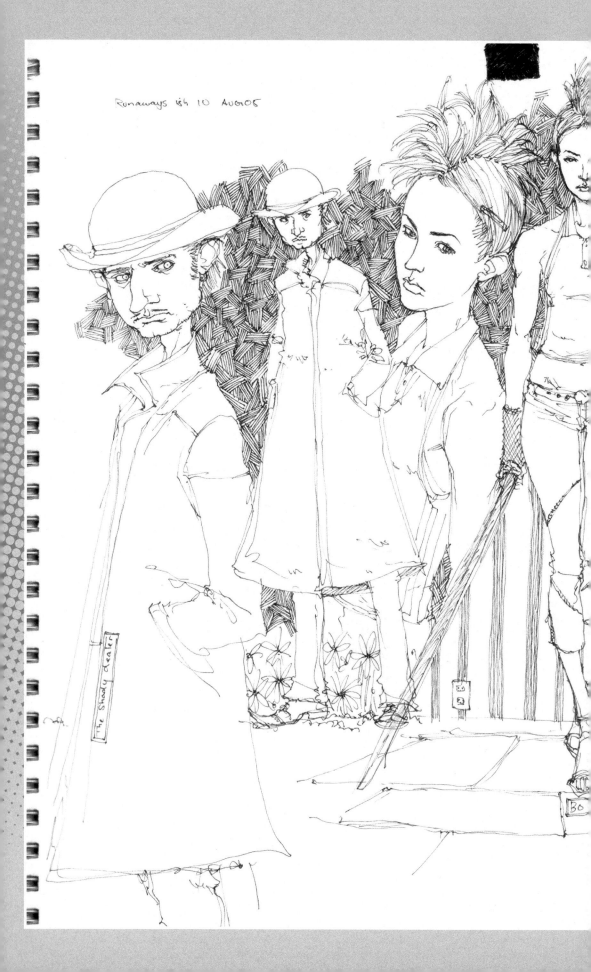

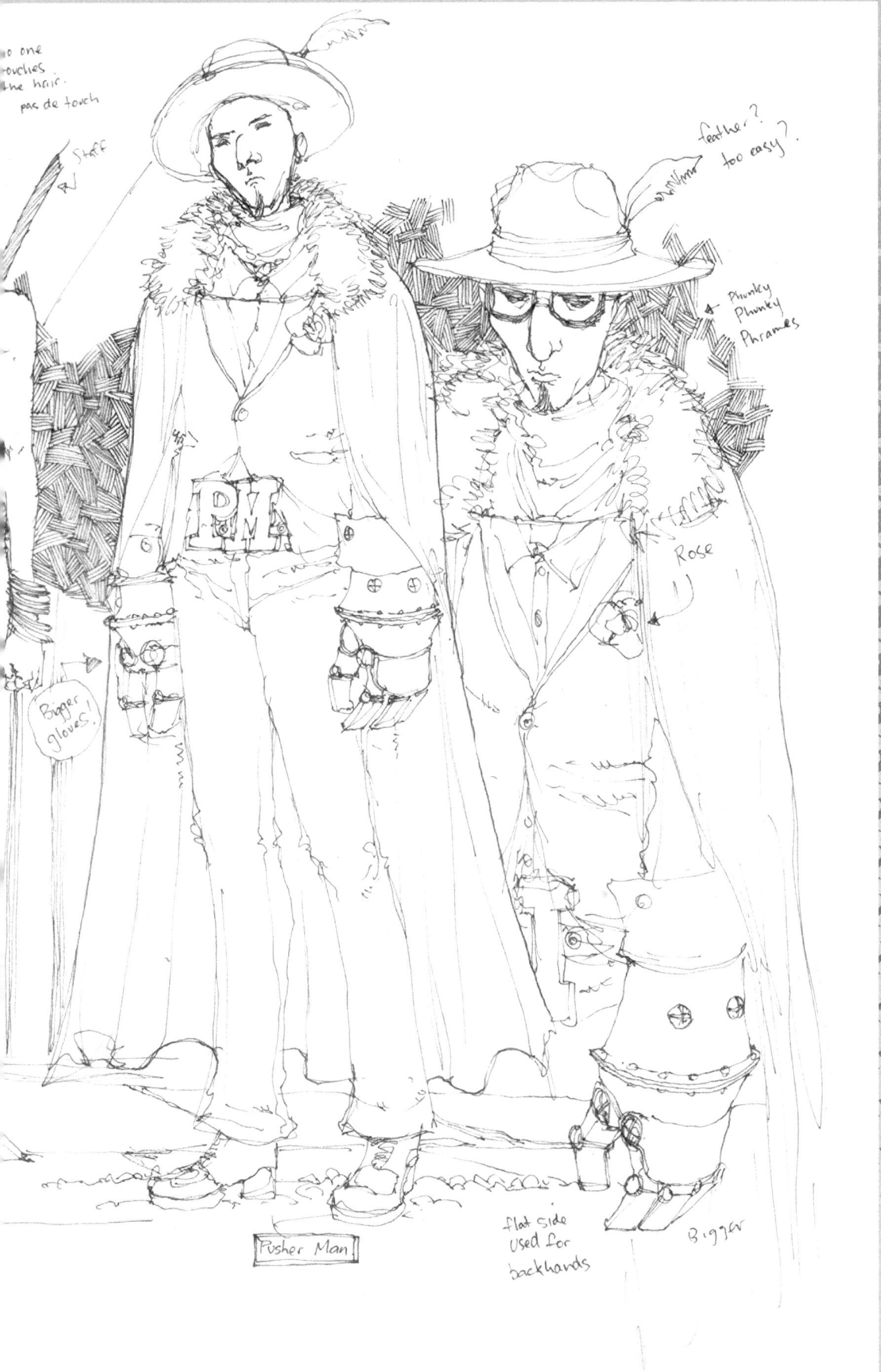

o one
ouches
the hair.
pas de touch
Staff
feather?
too easy?
Phunky
Phunky
Phrames
Rose
Bigger
gloves!
flat side
used for
backhands
Bigger
Pusher Man

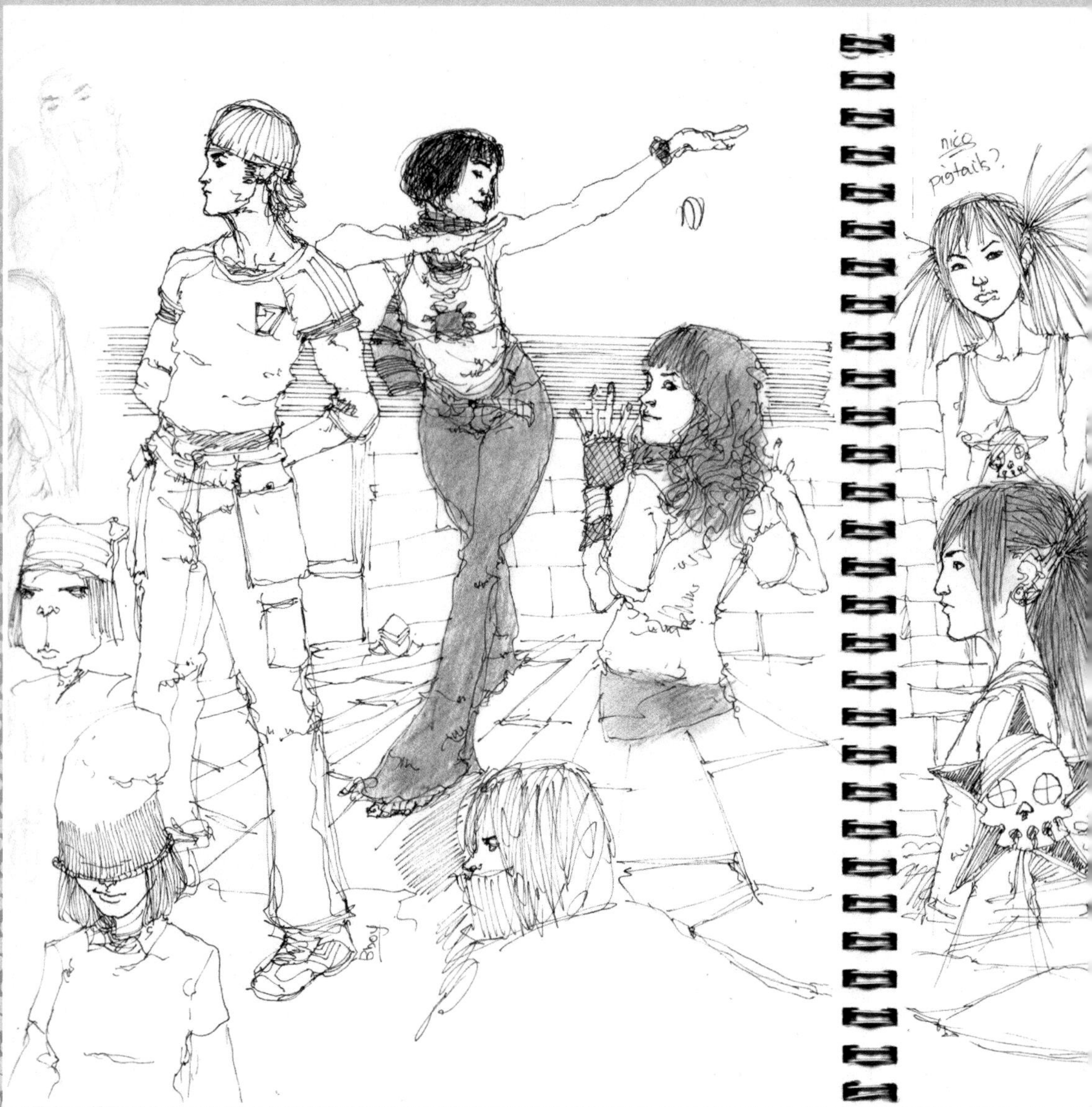
nico
pigtails?

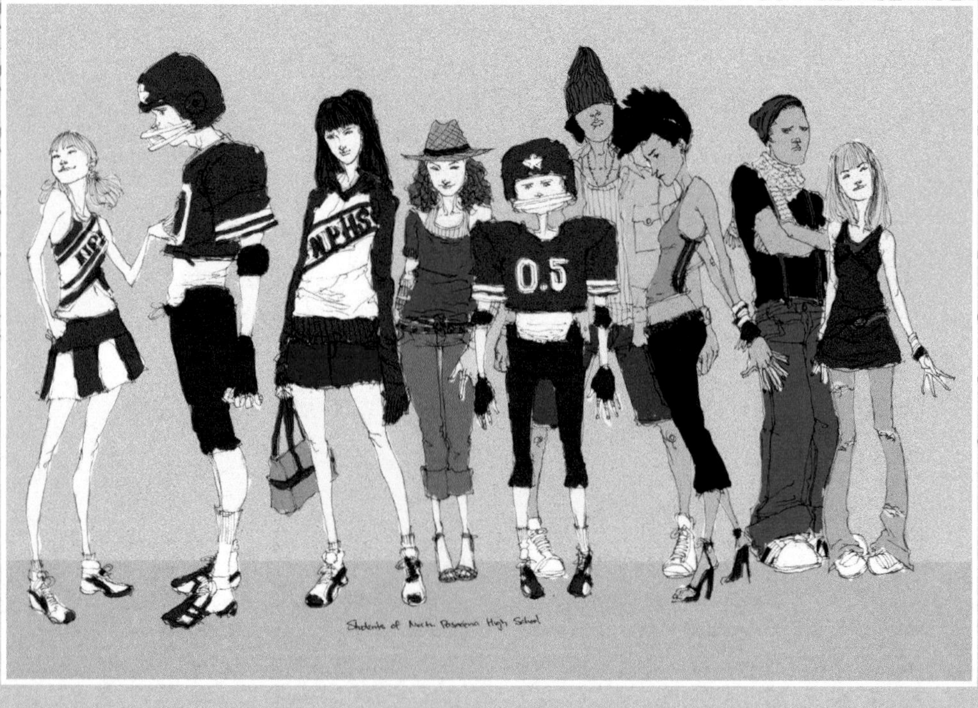
NPHS
0.5
Students of North Pasadena High School

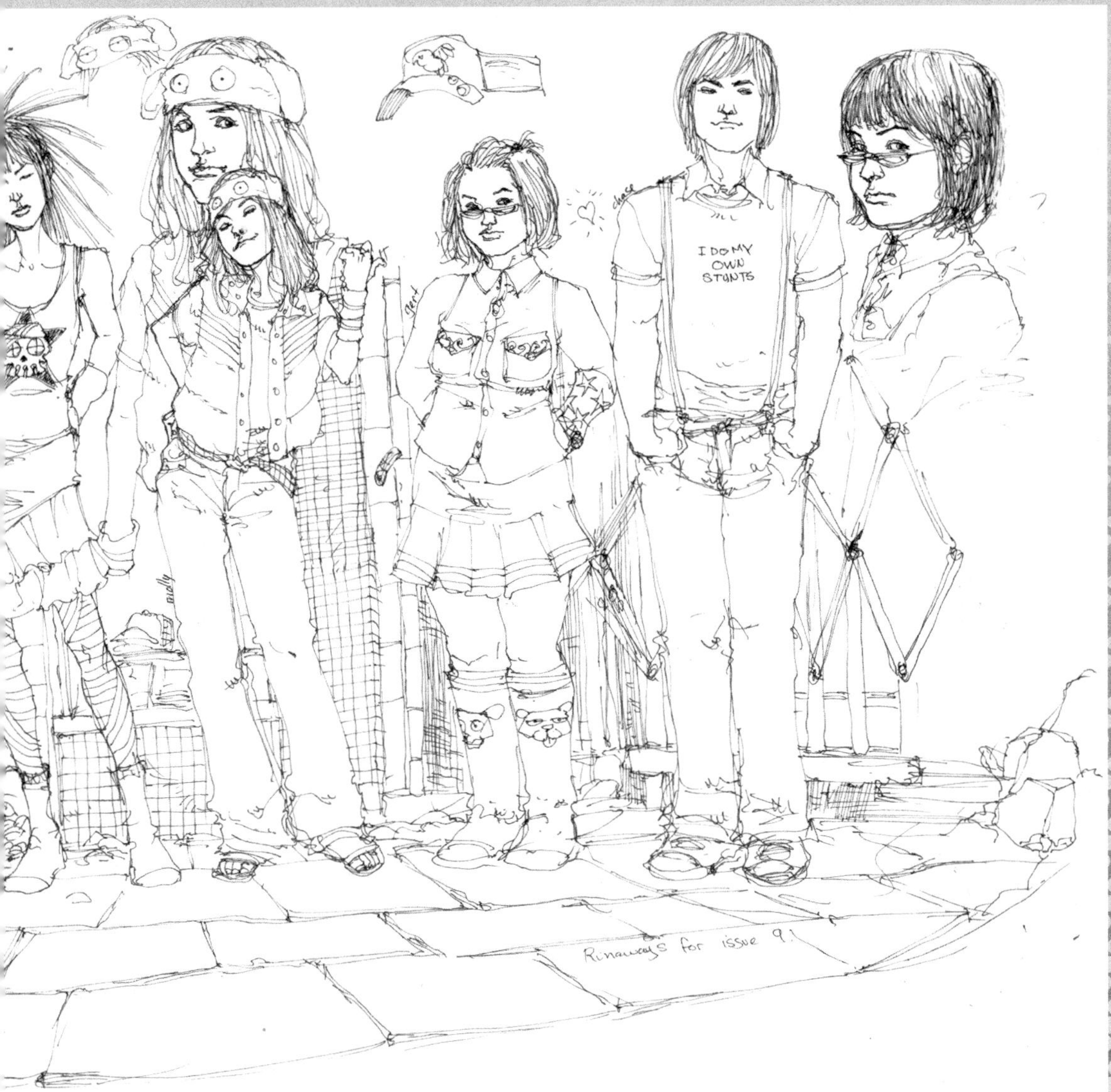
I DO MY OWN STUNTS
Runaways for issue 9!

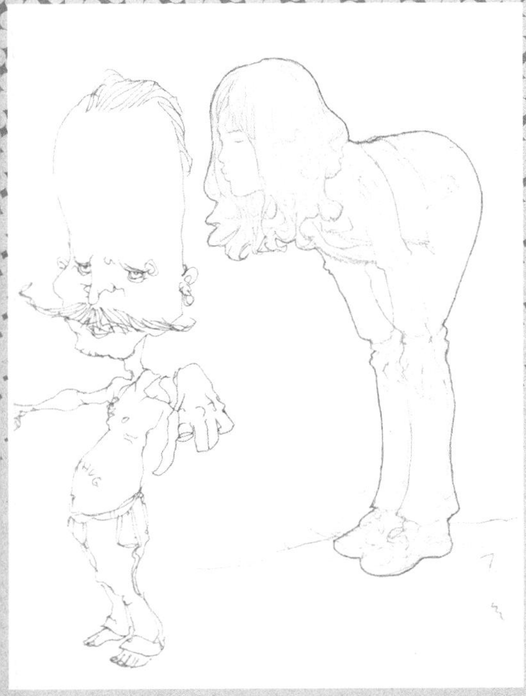

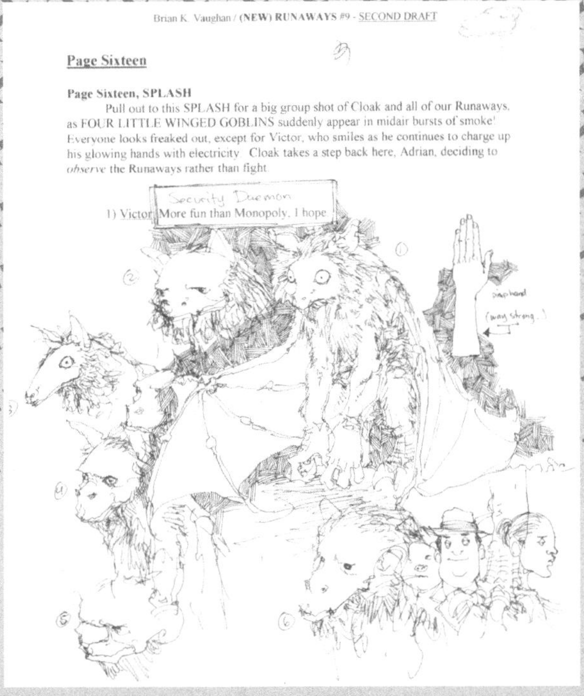
Brian K. Vaughan / **(NEW) RUNAWAYS** #9 - SECOND DRAFT

Page Sixteen

Page Sixteen, SPLASH

Pull out to this SPLASH for a big group shot of Cloak and all of our Runaways, as FOUR LITTLE WINGED GOBLINS suddenly appear in midair bursts of smoke! Everyone looks freaked out, except for Victor, who smiles as he continues to charge up his glowing hands with electricity. Cloak takes a step back here, Adrian, deciding to *observe* the Runaways rather than fight.

1) Victor: More fun than Monopoly, I hope.
Security Daemon

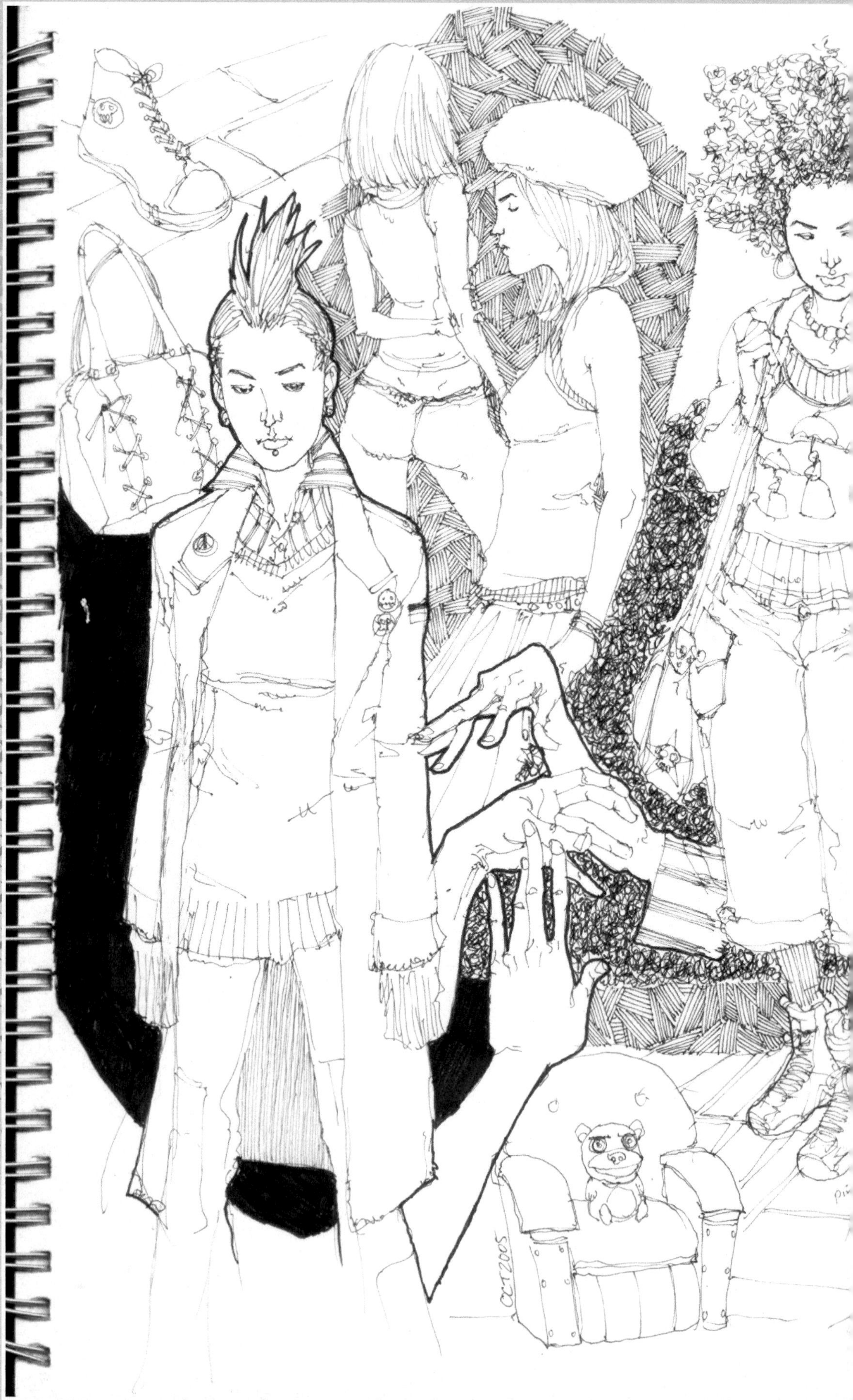
OCT 2005

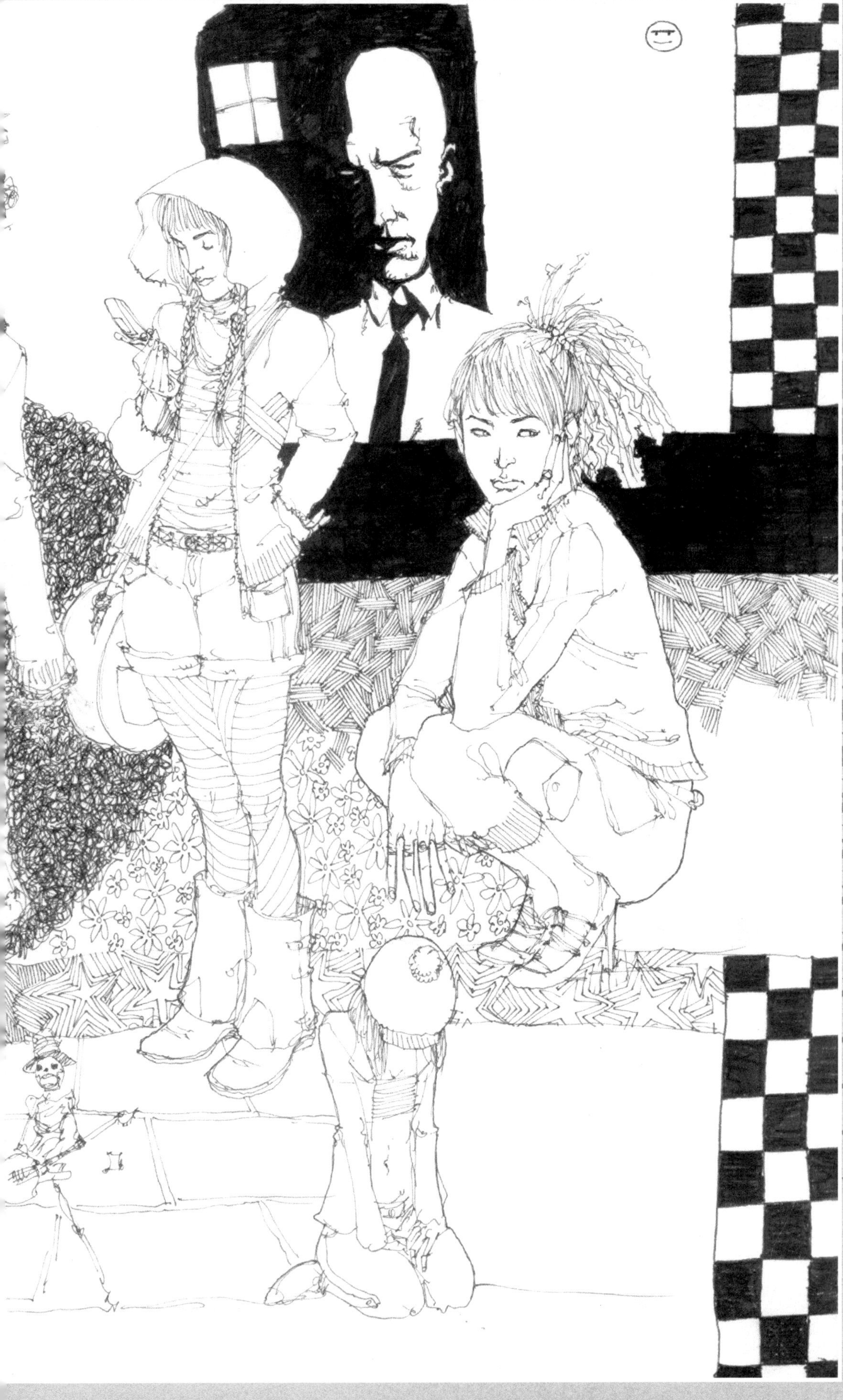

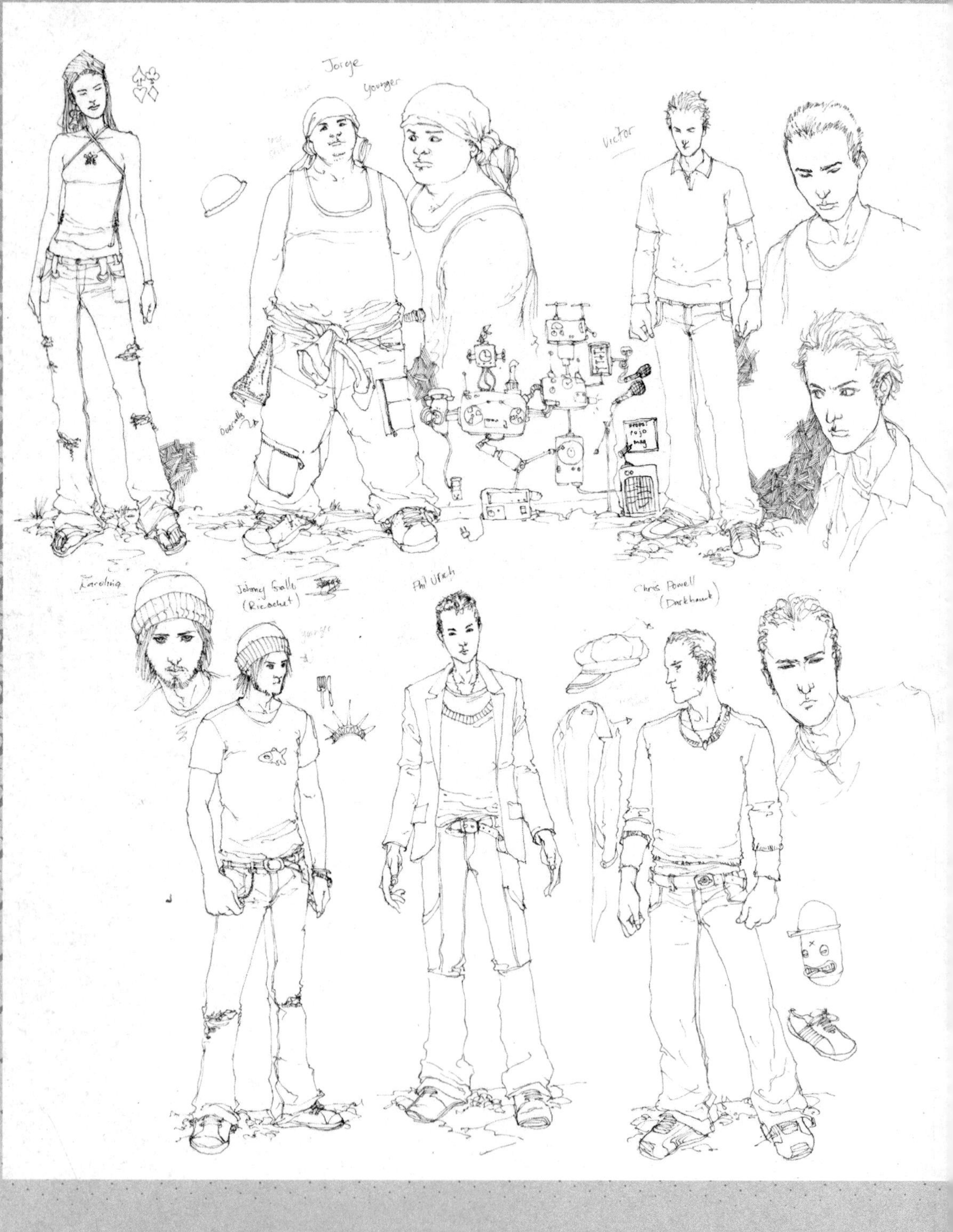
Jorge
younger
Victor
Karolina
Johnny Gallo
(Ricochet)
Phil Urich
Chris Powell
(Darkhawk)